A HISTORY
OF IRELAND,
1800–1922

Anthem Perspectives in History

Titles in the Anthem Perspectives in History series combine a thematic overview with analyses of key areas, topics or personalities in history. The series is targeted at high-achieving A Level, International Baccalaureate and Advanced Placement pupils, first-year undergraduates and an intellectually curious audience.

Series Editors

Helen Pike – Director of Studies at the Royal Grammar School, Guildford, UK
Suzanne Mackenzie – Teacher of History at St Paul's School, London, UK

Other Titles in the Series

Britain in India, 1858–1947
Lionel Knight

Disraeli and the Art of Victorian Politics
Ian St John

Gladstone and the Logic of Victorian Politics
Ian St John

King John: An Underrated King
Graham E. Seel

A HISTORY
OF IRELAND,
1800–1922

THEATRES OF DISORDER?

Hilary Larkin

ANTHEM PRESS
LONDON · NEW YORK · DELHI

Anthem Press
An imprint of Wimbledon Publishing Company
www.anthempress.com

This edition first published in UK and USA 2014
by ANTHEM PRESS
75–76 Blackfriars Road, London SE1 8HA, UK
or PO Box 9779, London SW19 7ZG, UK
and
244 Madison Ave #116, New York, NY 10016, USA

Cover image: *The Irish Girl* (1860) by Ford Madox Brown, courtesy of the Yale Center for British Art, Paul Mellon Fund

British Library Cataloguing-in-Publication Data
A catalogue record for this book is available from the British Library.

Library of Congress Cataloging-in-Publication Data
Larkin, Hilary.
A history of Ireland, 1800–1922 : theatres of disorder? / Hilary Larkin.
pages cm. – (Anthem perspectives in history)
Includes bibliographical references and index.
ISBN 978-1-78308-036-6 (pbk. : alk. paper)
1. Ireland–History–19th century. 2. Ireland–History–1901–1910. 3. Ireland–
History–1910–1921. I. Title.
DA950.L37 2013
941.708–dc23
2013044577

ISBN-13: 978 1 78308 036 6 (Pbk)
ISBN-10: 1 78308 036 1 (Pbk)

This title is also available as an ebook.

Out of Ireland have we come.
Great hatred, little room,
Maimed us at the start.
I carry from my mother's womb
A fanatic heart.
                    —William Butler Yeats,
                    Remorse for Intemperate Speech (1933)

CONTENTS

PREFACE

I approached writing about nineteenth- and early twentieth-century Irish history with more than a slight sense of trepidation. Previously, I had researched the rather more manageable and less emotive topic of European influences on Ireland during the Enlightenment. But there is nothing that is not compelling about the history of this period and a desultory interest, in due course, became a fascination. I should like to thank those who have encouraged the project: Suzanne Mackenzie, Thomas Bartlett, Alvin Jackson, Aisling Byrne and Anna-Rose O'Dwyer. A long-term debt of gratitude is overdue to all my former teachers in Irish history in University College Dublin: Ronan Fanning, Michael Laffan and Tadhg Ó hAnracháin, who communicated such a passion for the subject, a passion even earlier communicated by an inspirational teacher, Maura Farrell. My senior students at St Paul's School, London have been an excellent sounding board for my ideas about British and Irish interactions and their questions and interests have helped to clarify my own. Latterly, I should like to thank Paul Kelton, who provided me with a research position at the University of Kansas; this has enabled me to complete this project transatlantically, making use of their library, the National Library of Ireland and the British Library. The University of Kansas indeed has inherited the 25,000 item collection of Irish books which once belonged to no less a person than P. S. O'Hegarty, whose name will appear in these pages. This has been an invaluable resource. I should add also that Renata Rua at the Irish Cultural Center here in Kansas City Missouri has been a great support in helping me chase up final references. Great thanks are due to Tej Sood, Rob Reddick, Janka Romero, Meredith Ramey and the whole editorial team at Anthem Press. Family and friends have been good enough to express their interest and their support; they have put me up and put up with me on numerous research visits to England and Ireland. I dedicate this book to my parents, John and Patricia, whose only substantial disagreements were, happily enough, about Irish history and politics.

The subtitle comes from Thomas Bartlett's description of Irish history as a theatre of disorder. To what extent this is the best summation of this period will be the question behind this book. I have chosen Ford Madox Brown's *Irish Girl* for the cover. This hauntingly lovely picture depicting a young but worldly wise girl, complete with red paisley shawl, is currently housed in the Yale Centre for British Art. Completed in 1860, it reminds us that the feminine representation of Ireland not only had a long trajectory in Irish poetry and prose but that it was central to British conceptions about the Irish. The Celtic other was deemed to be feminine, wild, uncontrollable, beyond the reach of Anglicisation and alluringly romantic. Few pictures better hint at the troubled nature of being Irish and the role that perceptions would play in shaping interactions and conflicts.

LIST OF ABBREVIATIONS

CDB	Congested Districts Board
DORA	Defence of the Realm Acts
DMT	Dublin Mean Time
GAA	Gaelic Athletic Association
GPO	General Post Office
IAOS	Irish Agricultural Organisation Society
ICA	Irish Citizen Army
IPP	Irish Parliamentary Party
IRA	Irish Republican Army
IRB	Irish Republican Brotherhood
ISRP	Irish Socialist Republican Party
ITGWU	Irish Transport and General Workers' Union
IVF	Irish Volunteer Force
RDS	Royal Dublin Society
RIC	Royal Irish Constabulary
TD	Teachta Dála (member of the Irish parliament)
TUC	British Trade Union Congress
UVF	Ulster Volunteer Force

INTRODUCTION

History or Politics?

The decade that is now upon us – 2012 to 2022 – is a historically significant one for Ireland. It ushers in a host of centenaries: the Home Rule bill of 1912, the foundation of civilian armies in 1913, the experience of World War I, the 1916 Rising, the spiritual birth, as it were, of the republic, the meeting of the Irish Dáil for the first time in 1919, the Government of Ireland Act in 1920, the Anglo–Irish Treaty in 1921 and the outbreak of the Civil War in 1922. Two centuries ago, such possibilities were unimagined. It is thus a particularly good time to take stock. Perhaps the most outstanding feature of the period 1800–1922 is what could well be called its outright sensationalism. The magnitude of the Great Famine alone and the exodus of millions in subsequent decades would be enough in itself to substantiate such a claim. Furthermore, there was an endemic level of violence in society which ran the gamut from spontaneous rural outburst to organised insurrection.[1] Not only did large dramas play themselves out in small places but international crises also bore down at key moments and complicated matters – in the 1790s when Britain feared that revolutionary France would use Ireland as a base from which to launch an attack on the mainland, for example, and much later in World War I when British intelligence monitored Irish radicals who were flirting with the Germans in the hope of building some sort of anti-British alliance.

The sensationalism of Irish history and Anglo–Irish relations comes with its own forcefulness. It is not the kind of history about which it is easy to be dispassionate. Zealousness has often been the norm in Irish and Anglo–Irish relations and this has often coloured both history and historians. Even if partisanship is kept at bay, one has at least to be sensitive to the high emotions attending all political and social issues. There are great hatreds and little intellectual room in which to manoeuvre. Alvin Jackson wryly observes that the divided communities of north and south are both alike in their consistent 'abuse of the past'.[2] The history of the period is also of some dramatic interest for the simple reason that it is not yet merely history, neatly archived. It is still, at root, political. 'The Irish have no history, only politics' runs the old cliché and it is true that history is nearer to the surface in public life than in some other countries. The question of Union with which this book begins is still with us albeit in a different form. Conflicts in Northern Ireland run close beneath the surface and sometimes not beneath the surface at all. In 2010, MI5 heightened the security alert surrounding dissident Irish Republican Army (IRA) groups to 'substantial'. This very sensationalism and the live political nature of some of the issues bring particular challenges for the historian.

Historiographical Strands

Four main strands in the historiography may be distinguished, in broad terms. Winston Churchill, as a cabinet minister in Lloyd George's ministry, said that 'nothing would annoy the Irish more than the conviction that they were not absorbing the minds of the people of Great Britain' and, traditionally, the attitude of British historians has been something along those lines. They have insisted that Irish affairs did not loom large in the British political mind, that its affairs were simply not absorbing over long periods and that there was much resort to crisis management. Examples of this sort of view are too found in the work of A. B. Cooke, John Vincent and Patricia Jalland.[3] Among the many useful aspects of their work is the insistence that the Irish Question was always enmeshed in larger contexts, not least the party political and the imperial. This is a useful corrective to the view that Irish history can be read 'on its own'. Not all British historians adopt a minimalist view of the subject, however; notable examples are the very fine studies of Charles Townshend and David Miller.[4]

Irish nationalist historiography, prominent in the first few decades after the achievement of a free state, sought to depict Irish history as a linear story from oppression and political slavery to freedom and independence. This is the history of the Irish *sonderweg* or special path and in it, events have already been assigned a meaning. Dorothy MacArdle and P. S. O'Hegarty were notable practitioners.[5] One of their central theses will be gleaned from the latter's description of the 'real Irish People' (i.e. Gaels and Catholics) who through 'indomitable tenacity' preserved a memory of their nation down through centuries of persecution.[6] The purpose of such history was pedagogic, celebratory, commemorative and explanatory. In a sense this was always more public than academic history, with a rhetorical emphasis on the 'Spirit of Ireland', and the narrative was predictably grandiose and politicised.

Its history had clearly defined heroes and villains as well as moments of regression and progression. Much was omitted that did not quite fit into the tight straitjacket of the nationalist canon. Social, economic and cultural histories were made subservient to the main political narrative.

Launched by R. Dudley Edwards and T. W. Moody, the editors of *Irish Historical Studies*, revisionists began to chip away at this story from the 1930s on, but it was really from the 1960s onwards that the full onslaught came.[7] These 'new' historians eschewed the political assumptions and commitments of an earlier generation and sought to inject a great deal of scepticism into traditional accounts, which they saw as overly simplistic or downright false. Their preferred conceptualisation of their role has been one of 'de-mythicisation'. In the words of F. S. L. Lyons, they wished to deliver scholarship (and indeed the sadly misinformed public) 'from the false history that has for too long masqueraded as the real thing'.[8] One of their main claims is that there is no genuine evidence for a unitary nationalist story. They decry the fact that the past has been 'continually and ritually sacrificed to a caricature of the present'.[9] They have claimed that the nationalist account is often no more than a moral fable. Some have offered an apologia for the British government of Ireland. Many have also sought to open up the closed domains of social, economic and cultural history which tended to be downplayed previously and made subordinate to the overarching republican narrative. Historians like Lyons, himself, Ronan Fanning and Michael Laffan are all prominent in this regard. A classic presentation of the revisionist case is made by Roy Foster in his *Modern Ireland 1600–1972*.[10]

A post-revisionist case has also been made of more recent years with implications in multiple fields of research. As passions ebb, the very self-confident iconoclasm of the revisionists becomes suspect. Their new orthodoxies need shading, modification and even rebuttal. In a post-modern intellectual environment, it is remarkably easy to take issue with the inflated claims to produce a value-free history and to argue that the vaunted neutrality cannot be absolute. The attempt to do so looks naive to a later generation of historians. On a populist level, Desmond Fennell has made the criticism that revisionism is not a history which sustains and energises a nation but rather undercuts it.[11] But that criticism is a rather weak one, at least as far as professional historians are concerned. With more justice, Brendan Bradshaw, the most distinguished of the post-revisionists, claims that revisionists have been too dismissive of the genuinely 'catastrophic' dimension of Irish history, of the lived experience of oppression and hardship which did so much to define a collective sense of self.[12] Ciaran Brady sums this up with '[t]he fashionably sardonic tone, the narrow, calculating mode of argument and the cynical mode of assessment which the university history schools had encouraged, had served to desensitise modern historical writing to the sufferings and injustices of Ireland's past'.[13] In conjunction with more general sociological and intellectual analyses, much more work has now been done on the politics of (official) violence and the systemic flaws of various policy choices which exacerbated Irish problems.[14] So the battle rages on, inside and outside the academy, as seems very fitting for a country whose past has been defined so very obviously by conflict.[15]

Setting the Scene

A study of the inhabitants of Ireland in the 1700s gives us an idea about how conflict was inherent in social, political and cultural relations. At the apex of the sociopolitical pyramid were the Ascendancy, a name given to elite Irish Protestants in 1782. English settlers had been given large shares of land at the time of the Protestant Reformation and thereafter; their shares became larger and more permanent after legislation in 1689 heavily penalised Catholics. In its eighteenth-century heyday, this small elite (15 per cent of the population) dominated land, politics and society. Although there was much variation within Protestant society, as T. C. Barnard has shown in detail,[16] there were certain common threads. Their strongholds were in the Pale region of Ireland, that is to say, around Leinster. Their cultural weight was felt through publications, education and the professions. Their dominance was expressed in stone – the 1700s witnessed an extraordinary building programme, Georgian in style, in Dublin and Limerick. The English architect, James Gandon, came over at the behest of the *ton* and built the Custom House, Four Courts and King's Inns – reflections of their sense of their country's civic stature and their own privileges within it. The Ascendancy clearly saw themselves and their capital city very much in the grand style. It was a Protestant century. Yet, for all those pretensions to greatness, they were in an ambiguous and vulnerable position. What were they but a small, unrepresentative elite, dependent on Britain despite all their fierce protestations of liberty?

But such feelings did not draw them closer to the native Irish. Their patriotism did not, in most instances, take an inclusive turn – 'we Irish', as George Berkeley, the celebrated Anglo-Irish philosopher designated his kind, were content to exclude the Catholic masses, content with their elegant monopolies of politics, law and society. It was thus a deeply problematic identity partly because they knew their position was one of 'conscious but resented dependence' on Britain, as Foster says, and partly also because their claims to speak on behalf of the whole country were so seriously undermined by the realities.[17]

Numerically, the largest (75 per cent) and proportionately the most underprivileged group in Ireland were the Catholics.[18] Suffering under a range of legal disabilities (which affected everything from horse ownership to bearing arms and education), their position in Europe was quite unique. They were a religious majority suffering as if they were a minority. Enlightenment thinkers, in general so much in favour of oppressed groups, ignored their plight – most famously, Voltaire. Considered in popular stereotypes to be poor, feckless, ignorant and superstitious, Catholics were not exactly a chic *cause célèbre* of the day and, despite gradual emancipatory measures, prejudice against them remained strong. The conditions of life for Catholic peasantry were often extremely basic, especially in the west of the country where the majority lived in little more than mud cabins. Yet, the monolithic picture of poor, persecuted Catholics has been shown to be exaggerated.[19] A certain strand within the community was growing increasingly assertive and gaining in wealth and social status. A residual Catholic gentry had remained even after Cromwellian times and it was now joined by a growing middle class, educated, publishing and increasingly involved in trade and business. They were able to resist the worst effects of the penal laws and from the 1750s onwards they began to organise themselves and lobby for reform. It is true that only one-third of Dublin merchants were Catholic in the 1780s but this was a significant advance in itself. In the last two decades of the century, they achieved the right to purchase and bequeath land (except in parliamentary boroughs), the right to practice at the bar and finally the franchise for those financially in a position to qualify. In short, the picture that emerges is not all bleak and their consciousness of being a community on the rise undoubtedly enabled them to prosper further.

The other major community on the island was largely to be found in the northern province. Ulster was a land apart, in many ways. It is commonplace in some histories to talk in terms of two nations: the Catholic nation and the Protestant nation.[20] While the 'two nation' school of historiography may risk too emphatic a divide, the central points it makes are valid. Geographically, Ulster's proximity to Scotland – a mere 25 km at the nearest point – fostered a particular orientation east. This was compounded by a significant proportion of people with Scottish ancestry. Indeed its differentiation can, in part, be explained by this particular form of migration. Religiously, Presbyterians were in the majority, although in the island as a whole they counted for a mere 10 per cent. It is important to realise that Presbyterians started off in this period very much on the social periphery 'being neither part of a historic elite nor able to make common cause with the other outsiders, Catholics'.[21] Such difference as there was already increased with a distinct pattern of economic development, in particular as regards the linen industry and the growth of Belfast as a hub of the nascent industrial revolution. Economic and religious identity meshed. The Catholics of Ulster, Foster notes, were very much on the 'periphery' and not to be found so much in the 'thriving commercial centres'.[22] The Presbyterians were not merely the manufacturers and traders, they were also increasingly politically aware. A distinctive kind of politicisation occurred in the north which owed much to its Protestant character, its urban and industrial development and also to the influence of the Ulstermen who had moved to North America in the past century and a half, the last generation of whom had witnessed the successful War of Independence against the imperial power.[23]

As well as the particular groups inhabiting Ireland, the relationship between Britain and Ireland is a fundamental point of entry into the subject. It could be said that from 1169 to 1922, 'Irish history is really a history of Anglo–Irish relations'.[24] How did Britain govern Ireland? It was an old problem. In contrast to Scotland which had been united with England in 1707, Ireland had remained a separate dependency under the Crown since Henry VIII's time. The royal representative was known as the Lord Lieutenant or viceroy. He was one of their own, most often a peer and a member of the cabinet. Ministers and officials conducted the business of executive government from Dublin Castle in the centre of the city. The most important man-on-the-spot was the chief secretary who was charged with getting government business through the Irish parliament. He was at the centre of a network of patronage and influence, which were necessary to oil the wheels of eighteenth-century politics. The Irish parliament, for its part, was a medieval institution but it was severely circumscribed in its capacity to act by Poynings' Law (1494) and the Declaratory Act (1719).[25]

In the course of the 1700s, a belief in independence grew among the Ascendancy elite. These were Protestant nationalists – patriots, as they styled themselves – very much in the style of the American colonists. Brought to prominence by Henry Grattan, a talented orator in parliament, inspired by the War of Independence and given muscle by a Volunteer movement, the patriots wrung concessions out of a reforming Whig government and, in 1782, a constitution was granted whereby Ireland was given due measure of legislative independence. They had, in effect, forced the British government to repeal Poynings' Law, thus giving the Irish parliament, for the first time in its history, legislative initiative. 'Ireland is now a nation', Grattan had announced satisfactorily to the new Commons. It seemed to herald a new dawn in Irish history but change was rather more superficial than it seemed. The Crown still had the possibility of vetoing legislation and Dublin Castle, with the viceroy acting as the king's representative, remained in control of government. The executive was thus still very firmly in British hands and they had no intention of letting real control slip away.

It was in this context that international catastrophe bore down upon the heads of the Irish patriots. The French Revolution broke out in 1789 and subsequently the revolutionary wars which engulfed continental Europe and, from 1793 onwards, Britain.[26] Suddenly all was called into question: arbitrary privileges, Protestant exclusiveness, religion itself, and the cherished political shibboleths of a 'respectable' generation. France was America gone mad. Ireland, as R. B. McDowell makes clear, was awash with books and prints of contemporary French radical texts.[27] New forces with novel ideas began to emerge and threaten the very fabric of British rule in Ireland. Most notable was the Society of United Irishmen of 1791, a movement which originated in Ulster and became steadily more radical in its agenda, from the relatively mild demands for parliamentary reform and Catholic emancipation to out-and-out republican separatism.[28] This in turn bred a reaction, not so much among Anglicans, some of whom were leaders in the movement, but among doughty Ulster Presbyterians who set up the Orange Order in 1795 to mount a defence of Protestantism and the connection with the British Crown. A grand lodge ran the movement from 1797 onwards.[29] Violence on both sides began to be institutionalised. The neurotic response of William Pitt's government – overly repressive, according to some – only served to radicalise the rebels still further and, with plotting a revolution the most chic activity of the 1790s, plotting is accordingly what the society did, with a vengeance.

But the government was already one step ahead and, having infiltrated society networks by means of an elaborate spy system (one of the most fascinating developments of Pitt's time), the rebellion that did eventually occur in 1798 was doomed for lack of coherent leadership as well as a lack of coordination, the absence of a general enthusiasm for armed conflict and, of course, the inevitable *soupçon* of bad luck, the last owing to a botched French attempt to lend aid. When they did arrive, with 1,000 men from the Grande Armée, it was pretty much already over. A later expedition was captured and the leader of the society, Wolfe Tone, condemned to death.[30] The episode was a paroxysm of naive enthusiasm and misplaced belief in the revolutionary impulse of the masses and as such a very complete failure. Yet, it was a failure with important consequences. First it set up a basic divide that would be perpetuated to this day. The society adopted green as their colour; the order identified itself by Protestant hero William of Orange's colour. Significant identities in history are often captured by symbols which seem relatively superficial but quickly acquire an importance all their own. From now on, identities would be colour coded. Secondly, the myths of noble resistance and heroic gestures were once more renewed in 1798 – the belief that it was better to resist and die rather than to tolerate the intolerable. A political culture of violence had re-emerged and, via song and story, was engrained ever more deeply in the annals of national consciousness. Most importantly, for our purposes just now, was the response the rebellion called for from Britain – the Act of Union, the first modern legislative 'solution' to Ireland's manifest problems.

Chapter 1

FORGING THE UNION

The Act of 1801

The Act of Union, which came into force on 1 January 1801, may well be seen as the fulcrum of modern Irish history. The 'United Kingdom of Great Britain and Ireland' was born and a new flag, incorporating the cross of St Patrick, was raised over government buildings in both countries. The act established the framework in which all but the most revolutionary of political and social discourses must thereafter take place. The great Irish leaders of the nineteenth century, Daniel O'Connell and Charles Stuart Parnell, recognised it as a given and, however much they would have wished to see it revoked, worked within its possibilities and constraints. Their very presence in Westminster was testament to the power of this one piece of legislation. The Union had abolished the legislature at College Green in Dublin so that, from then on, all Irish representatives would sit with their British counterparts in Westminster. Since medieval times, Ireland had always had some kind of parliament; since 1782, it had achieved more status. In a dramatic policy reversal at the turn of the century, it was utterly abolished.

It was an act, said its architect, First Minister William Pitt, that was based upon 'fair, just and equitable principles'. However, the Union meant very different things to different people. Some saw it as the fulfilment of Ireland's destiny – it was now a properly constituent part in the great civilising mission of the British Empire. The Union was, for King George III, the 'happiest event' of his reign.[1] As this covered a period of 60 years (1760–1820), this was quite a claim. However, it was not to have such pacifying effects on the Irish or, at least, not universally so. It was, in time, to become the great fault line in opinion, dividing communities and cultures. It was the great evil, the 'infamous act'[2] of subsequent nationalist rhetoric. For them, it was the annihilation of all that Ireland was; its repeal would be necessary for any progress. For those differently minded, the Union became the institutional hope and the promise of security. Increasingly, Ulster Presbyterians would cling to it with dogged determination, more dogged indeed than any Briton anticipated in 1801. To those of Unionist tendencies, the act soon acquired – and indeed still has, in its modified form affecting only Northern Ireland – an immemorial nature.[3]

Historiography

Despite the fact that the Union is generally perceived as a turning point or, in Oliver MacDonagh's words, the 'most important single factor in shaping Ireland as a nation in the modern world',[4] it was for many years an understudied piece of legislation. In part this was owing to its timing. Occurring at the cusp of a new century (and the so-called late modern period), it fell into 'a no-man's land between the interest of the early modern and the modern historians'.[5] This has been substantially rectified and the act interrogated on many levels. In the macro-imperial narrative traced by J. G. A. Pocock in his classic essay, 'The Union in British History', the Union is to be seen as the last stage in a process – begun with the incorporation of Wales in 1535 and continued in the 1707 Scottish Union – of amalgamating an Anglocentric British polity. The Act of Union of 1801 was thus the last piece of the British jigsaw, or, as it were, the completion of a set of power relationships defined and framed by England. The year 1801 is thus interpreted as the pivotal date between the 'First Age of Union' (1707–1801) and the 'Second Age of Union' (1801–1921).[6] Pocock's perspective as a historian who insists on reading British history as plural and archipelagic – rather than singular and insular – is a valuable one. It is a corrective to an overly narrow reading focused on Ireland alone. But, it would be inadequate to regard the event solely in an imperial-colonial frame. In the traditional nationalist narrative, the Union was regarded as a violation, only achieved through means of corruption and bribery.[7] Recent decades have revised this account substantially. The first major revisionist study devoted to the subject was G. C. Bolton's *The Passing of the Irish Act of Union* (1966), which examined in scrupulous depth the way in which the British government turned early defeat into success; he reduced the story of corruption to an 'exaggeration' which did not explain the phenomenon satisfactorily.[8] More recently, Patrick Geoghegan entered the field with *The Irish Act of Union: A Study in High Politics, 1798–1801* (1999) and, in doing so, focused the debate on the main actors, especially Pitt, the complex play between cabinet, castle and court and the hardnosed use of secret service funds to get the measure passed.[9] He, however, did not take into account popular feelings to any great extent – his high politics excluded a complementary perspective on 'low' politics, which is crucial in any understanding of the nineteenth-century Irish scene. The historiography of Union has now become a much more various and contested field, especially since the scholarly activity of the bicentenary in 2001. Dáire Keogh and Kevin Whelan's edited volume *Acts of Union: The Causes, Contexts and Consequences of the Act of Union*, contains essays which consider the matter from a variety of different perspectives, including that of public opinion, the position of Catholics, literature, rhetoric, cartoons and political caricature as well as the formation of national identities.[10] It will be, therefore, necessary to position the Act of Union in multiple contexts and to seek to do justice to all angles upon the issue.

The Imperial Context

There are many reasons why Union became a political agenda in the late 1790s. The fundamental reason which underlies them all is imperial. The Union, as a measure, stemmed from the particular needs, aspirations and fears of the British state. Irish historians writing general histories have been somewhat slow to recognise the centrality of this dimension – it is not convincingly presented, for example, in either Roy Foster's or D. G. Boyce's classic studies. It is possible also to see Hibernocentricism in Dáire Keogh and Kevin Whelan's volume.[11] But 1801 was – in its genesis, its timing and its framing – an imperial measure. P. M. Geoghegan's monograph gives this dimension due importance in maintaining that '[f]or Pitt, union was grounded in imperial, not Irish, considerations'.[12] It is as much a part of British history as it is of Irish. To study the passage of the Act of Union is to find oneself caught up in the vortex of contemporary British debates surrounding such fundamental issues as constitutionalism, liberty, civilisation and security. It is also to find the articulation of a question which, in various forms, continued to preoccupy the British establishment throughout the nineteenth century. What was the basis upon which an imperial project such as theirs might be best grounded? How could they hope to consolidate a core territory and put in the safeguards deemed necessary without, in the process, antagonising its inhabitants or becoming too heavily embroiled?

The British Empire was entering a new phase of its development, a phase which would be characterised by massive expanse, greater coordination and more global outreach than ever before.[13] The story is familiar to us in its later outlines: by 1900 Britain would preside over a quarter of the world's land mass and about the same amount of its population. In 1800, it had neither that status nor that confidence. Ireland was, of course, far from being a new accretion. It was part of the core, was the earliest and still the most problematic of inheritances. Since 1169, England had always had some measure of control over its affairs but its control was never absolute. In the centralising Tudor period, Wales had been quietly integrated. Much later, in 1707, Scotland had been integrated and its parliament abolished. A new Britain, dominated by England, was taking shape. Ireland was very much next on the list of consolidations and circumstances in the late 1790s greatly favoured it. The French Revolutionary and Napoleonic Wars had given Britain both a new sense of drive and a new sense of fear.[14] The new drive was towards consolidating their existing empire (by concessions to French Québécois and Irish Catholics, for example) and seeking to pick up new territories from their old enemy, France. It is not hard to see their logic in this. France's difficulty was Britain's opportunity. When France defeated Holland, for example, one of Britain's main trading rivals since the 1600s, the British acted to secure control of the Dutch colonies of Ceylon and the Cape of Good Hope. So Pitt was not merely the pilot weathering the storm as depicted in contemporary propaganda, he was managing to come to port in strategic locations across the globe.[15] But not everything was so rosy. Their new sense of fear came from the reflection that their system of constitutional monarchy was being fiercely called into question by a republican regime intent on destroying monarchy everywhere. Ireland had made this fear more immediate. Not only was there generalised discontent (*that* was evident in mainland Britain, too) but there were radically separatist movements, notably the United Irishmen who believed in revolution and who passionately wanted to secure French aid for their endeavours.[16]

The resulting rebellion of 1798, as described previously, gave the British government the ideal opportunity to reverse their whole policy towards Ireland. For several decades past, the trend of policy had been towards devolution.[17] The Patriot Party in the 1760s, led by Henry Flood, and an Irish-Protestant militia, the Volunteers led by Henry Grattan, had put pressure on Britain to grant more independence. The parliament of 1782 had been established largely as a result. British legislators were not all happy with this settlement. The new first minister from 1784 onwards, William Pitt, certainly was not, but he had had no convincing pretext to claw back just yet. After 1798, he could say (and did) that the experiment of legislative independence had not worked. The Irish parliament had clearly failed in their primary job of maintaining the country in peace. Instead, it had 'plunged not only Ireland but the whole British Isles into a major political and strategic crisis'.[18] Pitt did not mince words on this one. He quite simply saw that the system as it stood was an imperial liability and he acted quickly. The curtain-raiser to the drama is the speech he gave to the Commons on 31 January 1799.[19] Later, he would modify the speech slightly and have it printed for an Irish audience.

Ten thousand copies of the speech were distributed there.[20] His arguments for Union as a necessity for protecting the Empire are a crucial source for understanding everything that follows – his own and his government's determination to pass the measure and the methods used to secure that end.

A recurrent theme is that Union was absolutely necessary for the 'power, stability, and the general welfare of the Empire'. Pitt's vision, one could say, was one of a great imperial legislature, capable of healing wounds and restoring tranquillity after the crisis years.[21] He insisted that Ireland had a vital role to play in this larger scheme of things. It was indeed a 'mighty limb of the Empire'. The closer connection between the two countries, once it was made legislatively permanent, would be advantageous, indeed 'essential to the interests of both'.[22] He was also very keen to present the imminent dangers of dissolution. His point always seemed to be that they, the British and the Irish, must act now or the whole imperial project, a force for good in the civilisation of the world, would collapse.[23] The alternative would be the 'destructive principles, the dangerous projects, and the unexampled usurpation of France!' Was this just imperial bluster so that he could browbeat opposition into submission or was there a genuine risk of the demise of British imperial status as a result of Irish problems? It is probably more likely to be the former. There is no doubt that he was deliberately stirring things up. He challenged the Commons' sense of complacency by asking rhetorically: 'Can we really think that the interests of the empire, or of its different branches, rest upon a safe and solid basis at present?'[24] But, it was truly a crux moment. Pitt's political memory was sharpened by having taken over the reins of government just after the American colonies had been squandered – obviously he did not want another haemorrhaging of power, least of all in the context of the international war in which Britain was playing a central role.

Pitt proceeded to push home the point that a disorderly and rebellious Ireland was a liability when conducting a war with Napoleonic France. The House of Commons was likely to feel this acutely. Ireland, with a population half that of Britain, was important, even if just in a rudimentary head-counting way. Whatever the rhetorical exaggerations, Pitt did indeed have a point in insisting that trouble in Ireland would have a knock-on effect on Britain. Memories of the aborted French invasion in the Irish rebellion were still fresh. There was thus a general feeling that Ireland could not be allowed to 'continue to pose a threat to Britain's western flank in time of international crisis and war'.[25] Pitt made the most of this powerful argument. He even went so far as to conjure up, provocatively, a situation in which the Irish legislature had voted to oppose the British war effort.[26] What if that had happened? What if it were not just native Irish rebels but the 'respectable' Irish parliament that decided to withdraw support from Britain for reasons of their own? Carried along by the momentum of a war which he had been leading since 1793, Pitt's attitude and language in this celebrated speech imbued the Irish Question with a gravity and an urgency that is only properly interpreted by situating it within the highly charged political, military and imperial context of the 1790s.

Other Reasons for Union

There were other reasons why Union was advocated. For an age fascinated with new orthodoxies of political economy and international trade, a solid economic case had also to be made for Union. In short, it had to be presented as something both useful and profitable, as well as something necessary for imperial reasons. This was a project very dear to Pitt's heart, in particular, and the debate took the tone from him. Inspired by Adam Smith's treatise *On the Wealth of Nations*, he had once tried to introduce a scheme for closer reciprocal commercial connections, effectively free trade, between the two countries in 1785 and had failed. Now he confidently announced that Union would be 'the most effectual means of increasing her [Ireland's] commerce and improving her agriculture', and that England's influence and capital would promote Ireland's economic growth. It would end the commercial jealousies consequent on having two independent legislatures and bring parity to the two countries.[27] The principle of 'connection', as he crisply put it in a letter, was primarily economic and Union gave Ireland 'equal participation of all commercial advantages'.[28] This is classic Pitt, never more buoyantly plausible than when talking matters economic. But perhaps it was his one huge economic mistake. Perhaps his confidence in the workings of both economies in tandem was misplaced. A mere act could not create parity in two such unequal partners, although it is possible that the Union was not the economic blow to Ireland as is sometimes depicted.[29]

Among the other reasons given for Union were those targeted specifically at powerful interest groups in Irish society. The key here was to make it as attractive as possible to as many of these as possible. The Anglo-Irish would be the hardest to win over; they had created the 1782 settlement, after all, and were aghast at the thought of losing it. The Lord Chancellor, Lord Clare, simply sought to persuade the endangered Irish parliamentarians on the ground of self-interest and self-defence. What was their security, he argued, if not the power and might of Great Britain? A negligibly sized, disproportionately privileged elite, their continued status depended on binding themselves to the powerful British establishment. Otherwise, they were at the mercy of the arbitrary whim of natives whom they did not much like.

Their property would be in danger and perhaps also their lives. Who was to protect them from the lawless men of the hills? Had not Wexford in 1798 proved enough of a warning? There was also an attempt made to appeal to the elite's Protestantism. Irish Protestants would always feel insecure, the argument ran, if isolated in a country overwhelmingly Catholic. They would benefit by being united with their coreligionists across the Irish Sea. Pitt further sought to appeal to them by employing the conventional argument that change was necessary in order to stay the same. He spoke of the value of preserving for Ireland 'all those blessings arising from the British constitution, and which are inseparable from her connection with Great Britain'.[30]

Catholics, too, needed to be wooed. Some of them were now able to vote and hold civil and military rank and there was, as we have seen, a growing middle-class lobby.[31] Pressure was coming from the Whigs to grant full Catholic emancipation at this point and, in any case, Pitt himself supported the notion. Better to make Catholics loyal subjects than alienate them by continuing the unreasonable, impolitic and outdated hostility of former, more religiously bitter times. He had already extended the franchise to eligible candidates. But no British establishment figure wished to see hordes of Catholics running an Irish parliament, which is why Union seemed such a fiendishly clever plan because, in making Ireland a subordinate partner in a union, the difficulty subsided. Emancipation could be granted and, it was hoped, the alienated majority would become a quiescent minority in Westminster. McDowell emphasises Pitt's mathematical approach – in Ireland, the Catholics outnumbered the Protestants three to one; in a United Britain, they would themselves be outnumbered three to eleven.[32] It seemed like a neat solution and the perfect sop to the bishops, clerics and middle classes. Because of this informal understanding, Catholic opposition to the measure was muzzled. Not particularly well served by the 1782 settlement, they believed that they could look forward to a better future where getting office might be easier. Westminster would be a more gracious environment than a Dublin parliament dominated by illiberal Protestant landowners whose fears about Catholics were more immediate and therefore more acute.

Opposition to Union

Even the 'seductive allurements of [Pitt's] amorous sportive imagination', as Richard Brinsley Sheridan described them,[33] could not drown out the voices of the critics. The opposition, from the day the scheme was first mooted to the last, was very pronounced indeed. A veritable pamphlet war took place from 1798 to 1800, which a recent research project has now placed within the public domain.[34] There was, as was said at the time, a 'fury upon the subject' in the capital. Critics argued their case on many grounds – patriotic, economic and, never lurking far below the surface, pure self-interest. The most passionate arguments came from the ranks of the Ascendancy class. For obvious reasons, members of the endangered Dublin parliament such as John Foster and John Parnell, speaker and chancellor of the exchequer, respectively, were the most vocal of all.

Patriotic self-awareness was central to the opposition's polemic. This was articulated above all in their polemical language drawing heavily on earlier traditions of thinking about political liberty. It was a language developed first in the English Civil War period during the radical protests against arbitrary Stuart power. It was then appropriated and adapted by certain factions of Whigs, especially in the lean decades of the end of the eighteenth century when they were out of power and trying to construct a moderately liberal image. Their slightly smug motto was 'fast friends to liberty alone'. More recently and potently, it was a language, radically tinged, which had informed the American colonists in *their* titanic struggle for liberty. What happened in 1798–1800 was that this Anglo-American discourse about liberty became an Irish one.[35] Notably, this was not the same 'liberty' as that invoked in revolutionary France. It was not so much ideological as practical, not so much abstract as particular. Opponents of Union argued that liberty was necessary in order to pursue energetic commerce, enterprise and, indeed, civilisation. Being 'enslaved' politically would mean a sort of moral enslavement and that, in turn, would make the country regress into barbarism.

It may well be asked whether or not this patriotism of theirs was a form of nationalism. There are two broad schools of thought regarding the birth story of nationalism. The first traces a modern tale memorably exemplified by Benedict Anderson and further explored by Ernest Gellner and Eric Hobsbawm and emphasises mass politicisation and the media of communication.[36] As against the modernists, there are those who have proposed that we look further back for the origins of national sentiment and even of nationalism itself.[37] It does, of course, depend on what one means by nationalism. It is certainly true that the Protestant Ascendancy was not in the vanguard of nineteenth-century nationalism, but harkened back to earlier traditions. For them, nationalism was not a movement of the masses. There was nothing proto-democratic about their polemic in 1800. Theirs was essentially a form of educated civic consciousness which set a value on liberty, freedom from arbitrary interference and carefully constructed rights surrounding representation. Subsequent forms of nationalism that we shall have occasion to examine will be monopolised, in the main, by Irish Catholics. But at the start of the period there are residual traces of Protestant, specifically Anglican, nationalism. They had an identity at once separate from the Irish natives and mainland Britons, hostile to the former and resentful of the dominance of the latter. The key to this identity lay in the fact of having a parliament of their own. John Foster made sure to clarify the issue of dependency. Ireland was dependent, it was true, but on the 'crown and not on the kingdom'. The distinction was an important one and he went on to qualify it still further by claiming that theirs was 'a theoretic dependence' but 'a practical independence'.[38]

They were outraged at the idea that they were now deemed somehow incapable of self-government. Foster described how 'painful' it was 'as an Irishman' to hear proponents of the Union 'degrade the character of their native country' and depict the Irish as historically 'a savage and restless people, devoted to eternal feuds with uncivilized manners'.[39] He and others emphasised the great positives which had come out of the settlement of 1782. In a speech made on 17 February 1800, he claimed that the country had advanced in civilisation, wealth and manufacture.[40] A barrister, John Collis, writing an *Address* to fellow citizens, also emphasised the track record of Grattan's parliament – 'from that moment, the age of your prosperity may be dated'. And with prosperity went the diffusion of comfort and happiness, the very fruits of independence.[41]

Institutional pride is evident at all turns of the debate. One of the great set pieces was the return of Henry Grattan 15–16 January 1800 to the Commons. Having withdrawn from parliament a few years previously, he came back, dressed in his Volunteer uniform, and proceeded to declaim for two hours. Too weak to stand, he was allowed to sit. This was the man who was associated more than anyone with the 1782 dispensation and his appearance spoke something of the collective pride taken in the achievement. Addressing his fellow parliamentarians, he accused Lord Castlereagh, the then Irish secretary, of seeking to 'destroy the body that restored your liberties and restore that body which destroyed them'.[42] It was a moving and an eloquent speech, a grand statement of Irish Protestant patriotic feeling.

Defenders of the status quo could also point out that the Irish parliament had even helped to put down the 1798 rebellion. Why emasculate the Ascendancy classes, 'the natural and capable guardians' of society, by depriving them of their own assembly?[43] It was Foster's reproach: '[A]re we for this to be punished, and our parliament transported like a felon for its extravagant efforts to maintain the British connexion by maintaining the cause of Britain?'[44] Surely it did not make sense, surely it was hypocrisy and, worse still, impolitic to get rid of the one institution which could acquire the requisite data on native problems and deal with them accordingly?[45]

Critics all painted a dire picture of decline and fall were Union to be carried out.

> [W]e shall be brought back to the miserable state in which we were, when governed by the laws of another parliament sitting in another land, ruled by their will, not by our own; our purse, our trade, our properties, our very liberties at their disposal and under their control.[46]

In particular, it would be a retrograde step economically. Pitt might talk lyrically of actual benefits to be gained but opponents believed none of it at all. It was a 'palpable delusion'; the real economic outcomes, Foster said darkly in March 1800, would be 'ruinous'.[47]

The motivation of self-interest is not hard to detect. What the Ascendancy feared, as the subtext reveals, is the prospect of being *déclassé*. How much this influenced them is open to debate but, undoubtedly, it was an element in their thinking. The eighteenth century had indeed been their gilded age, as Roy Foster describes it, and, with Pitt's proposals, they had an inkling that the good times were coming to an end.[48] They envisaged – quite rightly as it turned out – a 'twilight of the gods'. Undoubtedly, they knew that Dublin would no longer have the same cachet. It would not be the magnet that it had become. The social 'season' would be replaced, if one had the money, by the more glittering 'London season'. They feared that worst of social fates – that of waking up one morning and finding themselves *provincial* and relegated to second-rate status. Collis puts this into words – he writes of the 'reduction of your country to the situation of a province subject to foreign dominion'.[49] Of course, not all the elite would be equally affected by this sudden loss of status. The grandees who had more direct connections with Britain would be less vulnerable. Lesser gentry, the clergy, the lawyers and the miscellaneous others who loosely constituted the 'elite' would suffer a much more perceptible loss of status. It is no surprise that Collis writes as a barrister. Pitt, in his January speech, put their opposition to the proposed Union down to 'mistaken' national pride, showing at once his recognition of and his dismissal of the phenomenon. Maybe it *was* mistaken, maybe their real guarantee lay with the British establishment. Time alone would tell. For now, they were just the single obstacle in the way of a Pittite imperial juggernaut.

Chapter 2

DAWN OF A NEW CENTURY

A Closed Subject?

The actual passage of the Act of Union is an extraordinary episode in Anglo–Irish relations and its dramatic historiography illustrates well the necessity of continuously probing research. Once a subject deemed 'closed' and comprehensively understood, it has only recently come to light through the discovery of Home Office secret service files just how involved, weighty and indeed corrupt the whole process was. G. C. Bolton's thorough and complacent account of *The Passing of the Irish Act of Union* (1966) has been seriously undermined by David Wilkinson's intriguing 1996 findings in a way that turned around debate on the issue and forced historians to confront realities which had been hidden for almost two centuries.[1] The story of the legislation must be told before an attempt is made at interpretation. The bill had, firstly, to pass the British Parliament, but that was relatively straightforward. There was very little opposition – a mere 26 members of parliament (MPs) voted against, whilst 208 voted for; in the Lords, it was a mere 7 against 75. Now came the difficult part. A draft Union bill, sent to Dublin in 1798, made no headway, failing to pass – albeit narrowly – on first being submitted to the Commons. The celebrated debates on 22 January 1799 and 15 January 1800 lasted 21 and 18 hours respectively. These were marathon sessions. It was, however, only a matter of time before attrition wore down opposition and so it proved. At the third reading of the second bill, on 7 June 1800, it passed 158 votes to 115. The bill received assent in London in July and on 2 August, the Irish parliament was dissolved. Five months later, on the auspicious day – 1 January 1801 – the Act of Union took formal effect.

That is the story simply told. But there is also a hidden story to unearth. It is an intriguing one, especially after recent research discoveries.

The three people most responsible for getting this bill through were Pitt himself, Lord Cornwallis, the Lord Lieutenant, and Lord Castlereagh, the Irish secretary. They had to ensure firstly that the parliament at College Green did obligingly vote itself out of existence, and, secondly, that the episode did not turn into an embarrassing and politically damaging failure. So how did they manage the situation? Management indeed is a crucial concept in examining how British politicians sought to control Ireland. It goes without saying that all the usual 'lubricants' of eighteenth-century politics were employed to full effect. That meant, in effect, distributing favours. Patronage was lavished on a large scale, evidence of serious intent. There were, as a result, 21 new peerages or elevations total from a lower to a higher rank.

The question is whether or not this was a corrupt process. The traditional account would have it so. Simply, the rhyme of the day went:

> How did they pass the Union?
> By perjury and fraud;
> By slaves who sold their land for gold
> As Judas sold his God.[2]

This served as a sort of nationalist catechism later in the century, but it was not merely a jingle. Many well-informed voices, at the time, accused the British government of using shabby means to get the bill passed. Richard Brinsley Sheridan, himself Irish-born and an ardent Whig, responded to Pitt's speech in January 1799, by criticising the system of 'corruption and intimidation' by which the measure was to be carried.[3] Subsequently, this was the story taken up by W. E. H. Lecky in his celebrated A History of Ireland in the Eighteenth Century (1892).[4]

And thus the matter rested until Bolton's The Passing of the Irish Act of Union. Bolton made the case that this was very much an act of its day and could not be accounted corrupt by contemporary standards. Patronage was a legitimate way of securing favours in the absence of a tight-knit party system – the 'hose of royal favour', as Boyd Hilton memorably describes it, could be turned to effect in any direction.[5] To say that there was something unusual about the Union episode is to forget the extraordinary outpouring of patronage in 1784 that enabled the young Pitt to cling onto power against the powerful Foxite faction. Such things were done on a large scale, when necessary. It was typical, conventional and not in any way out of order. Bolton claimed that the traditional tale of corruption was a supremely exaggerated one and that, in fact, there was little or no direct bribery.

A 1996 Discovery

Intriguingly, the post-revisionist story gives more credence to the traditional account. In 1996, Home Office secret service files were released and David Wilkinson was thus in a position to give substance to the story of bribery.[6] After 1792, the secret service under the guidance of Pitt was a growing counter-revolutionary network, involved in information gathering, intelligence and infiltration – one of the more controversial aspects of his time in power.[7] Ireland was always one of its main areas of focus – although they had an official cut-off point of £5,000 to spend on Ireland in 1799–1800. What Wilkinson found was that a balance, separate from the regular amount, was paid out in that same period, amounting to £32,556.6s.11d. This sum, over £1 million today, was paid out in five instalments.[8] Pitt clearly did not do things by halves. So even by the standards of the day, the proceedings were deeply problematic. No doubt, as Paul Bew says, the government felt justified by circumstances, in 'breaking its own rules'[9] – national security was all. Although money was not the only reason why parliamentarians changed sides (nor the most important one), it was clearly significant nonetheless and should be seen as part of a battery of government methods used to secure consensus.

Impact of Union

Ireland was now one with Great Britain, forming a United Kingdom. What did the Union achieve? There is little consensus among historians about its effects. At one extreme, there is the darkly dramatic picture. Ireland, claims MacDonagh, 'lay inert in the aftermath'.[10] Geoghegan also speaks of 'political paralysis'.[11] At the other extreme, Foster, in his iconoclastic way, claims that the impacts were 'ostensibly minimal'.[12] Both interpretations have a measure of truth in them. Life did go on, in some respects, as before. But other aspects had been radically changed. Physically, the effects were outstandingly obvious. The Dublin parliament was no more. The fine parliamentary buildings would be used first as a garrison, later as an art gallery and even later (as it still is now) as a bank. Vanity of vanities. Upon selling it, the British government insisted that the building be so adapted that it could never act as an assembly hall again. The loss of an effective claim to political stature brought with it, as critics had said it would, a loss of civic identity. Ascendancy Dublin was hushed. The 100 MPs, 4 Lords Spiritual and 28 Lords Temporal representing the Irish electorate would now travel to Westminster, adding to the crush in the old houses of Parliament. Yet, the erstwhile Anglican opponents did tend to come around to the point of view that the Union was a good thing, a bulwark against growing Catholic power. They did adapt, and turned their backs increasingly upon Ireland which was changing out of recognition. Even Grattan, as McDowell slyly points out, spoke of the Union in 1815 as 'firm and lasting'.[13]

As it was an essentially imperial measure, it is well to gauge its effects on the metropolitan power. On Britain, the political consequences itself were initially not benign. It is true that it revealed Pitt's 'overwhelming strength at Westminster'.[14] It is true also that he was trusted as the 'pilot' who was weathering the European storm and respected as a man who knew best how to deal with the choices facing the Empire. However, it is equally true that the issue showed his limitations, particularly in regards to that careful tip-toeing around the monarchical will. The British monarchy plays an intermittent part in the history of Ireland, 1800–1922. At certain moments, such as in 1801, it comes to have a real bearing on the story.

The problem was that all the Hanoverians had sworn in their coronation oath to protect and preserve the Protestant religion in their domains. Having envisaged a measure of Catholic emancipation to accompany Union and indeed soften the blow, Pitt now found himself thwarted by George III, who was adamant that no such measure would be enacted whilst he had any hold on power. He had even gone so far as sending a message to Cornwallis on 31 January 1800, announcing that 'though a strong friend to the Union of the Kingdoms, I should become an Enemy to the movement if I thought a change of the Situation of the Roman Catholics would attend this measure'.[15] He even wrote to Pitt, telling him that he was bound by a 'religious obligation [...] to maintain the fundamental maxims on which our Constitution is placed, namely the Church of England [...] and that those who hold employment in the State must be members of it'.[16] That much was sure. When Pitt began to talk of introducing a plan for Catholic relief, the king got wind of it and firmly put a stop to any such move. With a taste for politicking that recalled his earlier days, George III announced at one of his royal *levées* that those supporting such a measure were to be considered 'personal enemies'. That was a strong statement and no government, at the time, felt confident if the king withdrew his trust. Pitt bowed out, tearfully if gracefully, in February 1801. The Union had, perhaps fittingly, made its architect its first victim, although perhaps a more grateful one than might be imagined, for Pitt was deathly tired.

His resignation has puzzled historians. Was he really that attached to the cause of Irish Catholics? Or did he use it as an excuse to resign from power for a while? It is likely that his reasons were mixed. Perhaps strongest of all was the fact that he felt that he had lost the confidence of the king and thus that his constitutional position as the king's minister was undermined. Geoghegan sees it as a distinctive moment 'in which, depressed and tormented, Pitt acted instinctively, in the decision that was the culmination of his life, his oratory and his character'.[17] This might be too rosy a view of Pitt's aloofness from lesser considerations like self-interest. In any case, he did resign and that made him, as Hilton notes, the 'first of seven nineteenth-century prime ministers to fall as a result of the Irish question'.[18] It became something of an occupational hazard.

A more general point of analysis emerges from the nature of Pitt's debacle which will be important to bear in mind throughout the subsequent narrative. The state of Union meant that British prime ministers and parties, superintendents of the new dispensation, were themselves potential victims of the vagaries of the Irish Question. Far from simplifying matters for them, it complicated them. They were more involved, more responsible and therefore more vulnerable. Not only did they have to become more knowledgeable about Irish affairs and attend to Irish voices, they also had to bear in mind the effects of their decisions on their own parliamentary standing and party following. This would be a very difficult line to tread, as Robert Peel and William Gladstone, in particular, would learn to their cost. Of course it is possible to criticise, as Beckett does, British statesmen of the period for culpable ignorance of Irish affairs – a double ignorance of both facts and of the nature of the people and their habits of thought. It is an ignorance which he describes as 'almost universal' among the British ruling class.[19] Gladstone was an exception, but even then he only visited Ireland once in his long career. Some, it is true, had experience in Ireland – Wellington, Peel, Melbourne and Derby as chief secretaries, Russell through visitation and Palmerston through landownership – but still the limitations of their knowledge were marked.

Long-Term Effects on Ireland

Whether or not the Union was a good thing for Ireland as regards the economy is contested. Certainly the Union put in motion three processes that would play themselves out in the long term.[20] First, in creating a single market between Britain and Ireland, it established a free-trade zone, an important precedent in the gradual progression of economic liberalism that had started carefully but decidedly in Pitt's first decade in power. In fact, one could go so far as to say that, as far as the Board of Trade was concerned, this was a fine testing ground for the gospel of free trade that it would be so zealous in promoting from the 1820s onwards. Ireland, as would often be the way in legislative matters, was a 'test case'. Second, one may point to the start of the process of the harmonisation of taxation, a process which would be completed in the 1850s by Gladstone in his capacity as chancellor of the exchequer. Initially, there was much unevenness because Ireland retained its own exchequer and its own debt until 1817. After that point, the equalisation of taxes took off. Third, the Union shifted the hub of the economy from Dublin to London and thus led to the subordination of Irish interests to British interests. This would not become evident just yet for, in the years of the Napoleonic Wars, there was a certain amount of prosperity. Nor would it be especially evident in the years immediately following 1815, which were economically traumatic ones on both sides of the Irish Sea.

But in the late 1820s when Britain's economic state was improving, Ireland's troubles became more noticeable and criticisms were increasingly voiced in the '30s about the role of the Union in this. There was indeed a full-blown debate between repealers and economic unionists. Irish cotton, for example, suffered against competition from the thriving and industrialised north of England, especially Lancashire. Linen was another casualty in the south (although the north adapted). Daniel O'Connell made political capital out of the fact that the 'bounty on imported linen yarn operated to shift the trade from Ireland to Scotland'.[21] The picture is not quite as simplistic as he makes out but it is fair to say that Ireland and Britain were very unequally matched and that the two horses did not run as a pair.

There is much recent historiographical debate, however, about this last point. Was Union really such a bad thing for the Irish economy? Did it have a bearing on the gravity of the Great Famine in the 1840s? The traditional case would say that it did not help. Beckett shows the Irish economy lagging behind its British counterpart and points out that British capitalists failed to invest in the country, even though they invested in South American ventures.[22] The revisionist case, by contrast, as presented by Liam Kennedy and D. S. Johnson, maintains that the Union conferred substantial economic benefits. To illustrate this, they ask, counter-factually, what would have happened if Ireland had been left to her own devices in the 1800s. The picture that they paint is not favourable and the conclusion they offer is that a hypothetical independent Ireland would have had 'very little to commend it on economic grounds during the first half of the century'.[23] Some have even suggested that economic Union did not go far enough. This is the argument in Joel Mokyr's *Why Ireland Starved* (1983).[24] Kennedy and Johnson also mention this and venture to say that perhaps, had there been a closer union, there would have been more resource sharing and fewer deaths from famine. The point they reach is a rather radical one, albeit tentatively phrased: 'From the perspective of the welfare of the most vulnerable people in Irish society, several million cottiers and labourers, the process of union may not have gone far enough.'[25] In short, they argue that there was too little union, not too much.

As regards long-term developments in politics, the Union brought a fundamental shift. In abrogating the career of a certain kind of constitutional

Irish leader, the measure of 1801 left a leadership gap which would need filling and which would, indeed, be filled in due course by a very different type of man. This is a point worth dwelling upon. Grattan and the patriots of 1782 had been naturally friendly to the Whigs – indeed, it was '[t]he co-operation' between the two that 'enabled English influence to survive'.[26] But the Patriot Party was now ejected to the dustbin of history. A radical and thwarted leader *did* emerge from their ranks in the immediate aftermath of the Union, but he was easily crushed. This was the charismatic 25-year-old Robert Emmet of a well-to-do Protestant background who sought to stir up rebellion in 1803. It was over in a few hours and he was captured and executed. His most important contribution to the 'cause' of the nation was not practical, but rather romantic – particularly his speech from the dock which would thrill future nationalists with its prescience of grandeur. 'When my country takes her place among the nations of the earth, then, and not until then, let my epitaph be written.'[27] In him died the last of a kind of Anglo-Irish radical leader.

Instead, the leader that would emerge was far more matter-of-fact. The emphatically Catholic and unambiguously middle-class Daniel O'Connell would serve a very different constituency of the country's population and in a very different manner. Like members of the Patriot Party of the 1780s, he too would work with mainstream British parliamentary politics from the 1830s onwards but it was much more of a convenience than a deep-seated bond. Union made O'Connell possible, especially as it was an unfinished Union, lacking a complementary measure of Catholic relief. According to Pocock, Union also made a new kind of parliamentarianism possible – that of Parnell later in the century. This was 'more effective and deeply rooted than any achieved by the parliament of the pre-Union kingdom'. He would make a large single-handed contribution to the evolution of party politics in and outside Britain.[28]

Evaluation

Perhaps the biggest failure of the Union from a majority Irish point of view was the failure to pass a measure of Catholic relief at the same time. Without this, the Union, in the words of Geoghegan, 'endured rather than flourished'.[29] Although the temptations of the counter-factual must be resisted, it is plausible to argue that, had the Catholics achieved full political rights at this point, it would have constituted a new era in Anglo–Irish relations and would have brought into the establishment the grateful body of the new middle classes. First impressions were important and Catholics felt betrayed. Nevertheless, this point can be overstated. As O'Connell would prove, relief was something one could work toward. Besides, even if Pitt had had the political will to push through this issue at all costs (and given the king's position, the costs would have been high), one has every right to doubt its political practicality. Considering the savage opposition to the measure in 1829, it is impossible that it should have been any less raucous in 1801. Quite probably, the measure would have been ejected unceremoniously from both houses. Perhaps it is fairest to conclude, as J. C. Beckett does, that the Union 'might have been a great measure' but had serious shortcomings.[30] Still, the Union proved a more flexible instrument than at first appeared. It proved to be compatible with the later measure of emancipation and even with Gladstone's disestablishment of the Church of Ireland and with the various projects of land reform of later in the century.[31] But all that was far in the future. In 1801, it looked rather inflexible – a testament to reaction and a barrier to reform. The Protestant Ascendancy, transplanted for several months a year to Britain, had ostensibly survived. Catholics were given a new reason to mobilise.

Chapter 3

CATHOLIC MOBILISATIONS

Context

Into post-Union Ireland, Daniel O'Connell strode. The state of the nation was deeply problematic, an account that revisionist historians have not seriously dented. Rural poverty was supremely evident in the hundreds of thousands of miserable one-room cabins dotted across the country. Beggars were, as travellers noted consistently, omnipresent. The population was especially vulnerable to bad weather and harvests – the poor summer of 1816, for instance, caused an outbreak of typhus which in the following three years killed 65,000 people. Cycles of rural violence led by groups with eccentric-sounding names like the Threshers and Caravats, the Shanavests and the Ribbonmen were particularly prevalent in the first three decades of the century. This was one form of Catholic mobilisation far removed from O'Connell's populist initiatives but significant in another way. Instead of regarding them merely as evidence for disorder, the importance of these secret societies, for Bartlett, lies less in their purpose and activities and more in the experience of politicisation and socialisation that they provided. They were a focus for the articulation of grievances and the organisation of protest. They brought their members (all male) 'face to face with the power – or more commonly the powerlessness of the state'.[1]

From the top, there was the often vain attempt to restore order. Transportation to Australia was a convenient solution and one increasingly employed by a government determined to export the danger to the other side of the world. Taking the figures in total up until 1853, when transportation ended, a disproportionately large 25 per cent of all those deported were Irish, of whom 1.5 per cent were political rebels, 20 per cent social rebels and 80 per cent ordinary criminals of varying degrees.[2] But not all unrest could be solved by transportation. Arthur Wellesley, taking a short break from his military endeavours, became Irish chief secretary in 1807 and had an act for a Dublin police force passed, thus making it the first city of the Empire to be properly policed. Later, in 1814, Robert Peel, one of his successors in the job formed rural constabularies too.

Historiography Surrounding O'Connell

In this context of predictable disorder and attempts at order, O'Connell stands out in a wholly unique way. His folk-hero status covers and occasionally conceals a complex individual and, like all folk heroes, he represents a historiographical challenge. As Donal McCartney points out, he is to Irish historians what Napoleon is to the French – 'argument without end'.[3] There was, in fact, a dazzling succession of O'Connellite incarnations – as radical deist, as eminent lawyer, as pious Catholic, as popular agitator and as parliamentarian. Which had the upper hand at any one time is worthy of consideration. We are dealing with a man who had a larger-than-life image throughout his public career and, rather than simply dismissing this, it demands commentary. Applicable to him is a comment that Paul Smith makes about Benjamin Disraeli: '[i]f that risks taking him at face value, it avoids the grosser error of ignoring the value which attaches in human transactions – and which he certainly attached – to face'.[4] His public life is political theatre at its most dramatic.

Boisterous, rambunctious and irrepressibly himself, he inevitably looms large in any modern Irish history, although his changing status is an indicative barometer of Ireland's own political ambience.[5] Hailed as 'The Liberator' in his own day, the man who rolled back the most severe aspects of constitutional anti-Catholicism in Britain and Ireland, he was also despised as an uncouth Gael, the 'scum' of an Irish 'bog', 'ruffian, coward, demagogue' as the *Times* ungraciously put it on 26 November 1835.[6] We would not expect anything different from the *Times* but, more surprisingly, there was also a certain Irish animus against him which remained a part of nationalist historiography. Even before he died, he witnessed his brand of middle-way politics go out of fashion in favour of something more radical, revolutionary and romantic. He has thus always been a misfit in the nationalist canon of historiography. Of late, in keeping with wider trends in the academy, there has been much more interest in his very complexities. The revisionist story, developed by MacDonagh and Dudley Edwards, among others, recognises that he *had* to play the role of 'a Janus-faced politician' and is curious about how he used various registers, populist and parliamentary, in making himself at once a folk hero and a force in high politics.[7] Questions have been asked about his political thought,[8] his role in helping to create modern democratic politics[9] and his impact on the development of sectarianism and the exacerbation of the north–south divide, despite his beliefs in and professions of cross-cultural unity.

The Background of a Catholic Middle-Class Lawyer

An understanding of his background is critical to all this. He inhabited what a biographer calls 'a series of overlapping cultures', which helps to explain his ease in a variety of contexts whether mixing with the Whig *ton* or Irish peasants.[10] It also helps to explain his ambiguities. Although Catholic, and therefore suffering the disabilities of the majority in a Protestant state, his family laid claim to noble Gaelic lineage and he spoke English as his main language, a clear sign of middle-class progressivism. His father was a combination of farmer and merchant. His uncle, Maurice, known as 'Hunting Cap', owned Derrynane House in Co. Kerry and, being childless, made Daniel his heir. Another uncle worked his way into the graces of the Bourbon court and became a count. O'Connell was, therefore, in a comparatively privileged position with respect to most of his other coreligionists. But there was also a streak of the populist. He was fostered to a herdsman's family for the first four years of his life and there learned to speak Irish as his mother tongue. Perhaps it is too much to attribute his subsequent popularity among the 'ordinary people' to this early experience but it must have marked him in a powerful way. Education followed locally, and, as a teenager, he was sent to the English colleges at St Omer and Douai where high-status Catholic boys would traditionally go.

His formative years were thus spent largely on the continent and O'Connell found himself in France until 1793, leaving a mere two days after King Louis XVI's execution. The experience of revolution had two important impacts upon him. Firstly, it caused him to find violence repellent – the 'altar of liberty totters when it is cemented only with blood'.[11] Later this belief would be articulated in the celebrated maxim that the freedom of Ireland was not worth the shedding of one drop of blood. This belief would become more engrained with the passing of the years, thus making him, as McCartney put it, 'the nearest thing to a convinced pacifist' in Irish history.[12] In a country scarred with political deaths which number many thousands, this is distinctive (and admirable) in itself, but it should not be overstated. His pacifism was not, in fact, absolute – he later supported the South American wars of independence in the 1810s and '20s and also the Belgian Revolution of 1830.

But hatred for revolutionary violence did not make him a conservative. On the contrary, he flirted with radicalism in his London years – 1793 to 1796 – when, as well as receiving training in the law, he joined one of the progressive debating clubs in the lively capital. He mixed with artisans and freethinkers and became a religious sceptic for a while. It was in London that his political thought was forged. Two books in particular were critical in his intellectual development. The first was William Godwin's *Enquiry Concerning Political Justice and its Influence on Modern Morals and Manners* (1793). The second was that *succès de scandale*, Thomas Paine's *Rights of Man* (1791). From the former, O'Connell adopted a belief in the perfectibility of humanity and the futility of violence to achieve it. From the latter, he picked up a superficial deism, which he would later drop, and an idiom of rights, which he would adapt at leisure.

The picture that emerges of him in the formative period of the 1790s, therefore, is that of a middle-class youth with some radical tendencies, but never extremist ones. His awareness of the stirring times and shifting contexts led him to see the value in 'war upon every form of civil discrimination – all handled "moderately"'.[13] Moderation meant one thing for him – changes in the law. He was, after all, the direct beneficiary of a 1792 act which enabled Roman Catholics to practice as lawyers.[14] He moved from Lincoln's Inn in London to King's Inns in Dublin in 1796, and, although moved by the rousing times of rebellion in 1798 (historians have never quite been able to reconstruct his role), he remained sufficiently devoted to his legal career, attaining the rank of barrister in the Easter term of '98. Professionally, O'Connell was hampered by his religion. He would have taken silk (i.e. been awarded the King's Counsel) but this was debarred to him. This would add impetus to his involvement in the wider Catholic cause.

O'Connell's Vision

O'Connell's political vision could be summed up in the phrase he often used: Justice for Ireland.[15] This meant, for him, legal equality between Catholics and Protestants, the revocation of the Act of Union, and the restoration of a national parliament under the aegis of British authority. Two aspects of this vision are particularly noteworthy. One is its non-sectarian character; the other is its relative conservatism. Although principally associated with the Catholic cause, O'Connell was not sectarian. He assumed (wrongly as it turned out) that sectarian divisions were 'irrelevant to national identity and equality'.[16] He resented the 'wretched sections and miserable sub-divisions' tearing communities apart and he claimed that they had been fostered by the 'enemies of Ireland'.[17] The language of sectarianism was spoken by many and his refusal to speak this language did much to commend it. This did not mean, however, that O'Connell had a commitment to trying to woo over those who had a fundamental problem with his political vision. Did he underestimate the power that religious divisions had in practice?

It is possible. In reality, O'Connell probably never grasped the full extent of the attachment which many Irish Protestants, especially in the north, were beginning to feel towards Union. In a trip to Belfast in 1841, he tried to allay their fears of repeal with reassurances that there was 'not a Protestant more opposed to Catholic ascendancy than I am'.[18] The fact was that divisions in Ireland were becoming more entrenched in the first few decades of the 1800s and that O'Connell found himself on one side of the divide.

His vision for Ireland's future was also reasonably conservative; it was emphatically not republican and it would be misleading to see him as nationalist in that sense. He was not a new-look member of the Society of United Irishmen. He had a great respect for the British monarchy, which he sometimes went to deliberate lengths to show off. He was, it could be said, a loyalist, not a Unionist. The distinction would look increasingly anachronistic as the century wore on, but then, his monarchism was in no way unusual for one of his class and background. This benign feeling toward the throne is an important corrective to our general view of Ireland's relationship with the British monarchy in the nineteenth century. As James Murphy has shown, the monarchy was often spoken of as a 'golden bridge' linking Britain and Ireland, providing symbolic continuity which could 'disguise the high degree of autonomy' it was hoped would come through repeal or, later, home rule.[19] No doubt this was O'Connell's brand of monarchism. He was there in 1821 to honour George IV on his state visit to Ireland and later, in 1837 when Victoria came to the throne, he used the opportunity to stress his monarchism and attended a royal *levée* in February 1838. This was a genuine expression of loyalty on his part but it was also political: Victoria favoured the Whigs and O'Connell was then linked with them in government. Indeed, support for Queen Victoria may have been widespread, as we have records of many Irish ballads hailing her as the 'millennial deliverer'.[20] In this attitude, they were entirely at one with Orangemen and Tories and it could have proved a bridge between them. It never did, owing to the deeper disagreements about religion and politics already discussed.

Early Campaigns

O'Connell's developing career had two strands: that of lawyer and that of the popular agitator. They were combined remarkably effectively. In his legal capacity, he championed the cause of Irish tenants, earning for himself legendary status as counsellor. In the Magee trial of 1813, he turned the tables on Dublin Castle, insolently, and used the opportunity to decry misgovernment. This sort of subversive ability convinced the castle that he was a man to watch. He also appeared to court trouble. In 1815, he got involved in an argument about the Dublin Corporation, was challenged to a duel and shot dead his opponent, a noted duellist. Later the same year, it was he who issued a challenge to the young Robert Peel, who was cutting his political teeth as Irish chief secretary and had injured O'Connell's honour in the Commons. Fortunately, owing to the intervention of the authorities, the duel was never fought and O'Connell and Peel were left to engage in vicious professional duels later on.

He was disappointed, as were others, with the sterility of Union without emancipation and entered the Catholic Committee in 1804 and, soon making his mark, established the Catholic board in 1811, which agitated for the redress of legal prejudices. In contrast to some of the older and more traditional Catholic gentry, O'Connell was not in favour of a 'softly softly' policy. He was angry as well as energetic and resilient and, when the organisation was suppressed in 1814, he revived it in 1817. The infusion of new vigour had significant consequences. It was at this point that he discerned his real vocation – that of popular leader. In a public meeting in Fishamble Street, Dublin, on 15 June 1813, he announced the principle of public agitation. If O'Connell is to be credited, as O'Ferrall maintains, with the founding of Irish democratic forms,[21] then this is an extremely significant moment – the fact of invoking the power of the national public in the service of a political cause. Immediately, he had brought into play new rules of the game. He had made the discovery that, in the absence of a parliament, public theatre was a way of doing politics. As long as it could be kept legal, the authorities would just have to stand back and observe.

The Stories of the 1820s

The 1820s offer a striking juxtaposition of both 'high' and 'low' political narratives in relation to the Irish – more particularly the Catholic question. In high politics, there was some appetite for reform, especially from the Whigs and liberalising Tories, but progress was intermittent and hampered by internal opposition. In 1821, another emancipation bill was introduced by Whigs in Westminster. It had become a ritual for the last 20 years and each time it had failed to get through. The political appetite was never really there. This time, a limited bill had passed the House of Commons (a first since 1813) but was subsequently dismissed by the Lords. The speech of Irish member William Conyngham Plunket in the Commons was notable in its assertion that emancipation was inevitable: 'it is impossible to mistake the feeling of […] the enlightened part of the country on this subject, or to doubt that it is a growing one'.[22] Perhaps he did indeed overestimate the decline of prejudice against Catholics in Britain, but he had observed what turned out to be true – a change in the spirit of the times. It was time to act. O'Connell noted, 'We have lived, another year, the victims of causeless injustice. Our lives wear away, and we still continue aliens in our native land.'[23] He decided to harness that resource that every government feared but no government could absolutely control: the public. The Catholic Association, established in 1823, represented a new departure in popular politics. D. G. Boyce goes as far as to say that it 'broke the mould' of political life in Ireland which had been stagnating since 1808.[24]

The most compelling feature of the association was its law-abiding nature – it was organised as a pressure group which would have recourse to all legitimate means in seeking its end, or in its own words, to use 'all such legal and constitutional means as may be most useful to obtain Catholic emancipation'.[25] It was deemed important to emphasise the constitutional dimension because a powerful argument against emancipation maintained that it was deeply unconstitutional. The Glorious Revolution of 1688–89 and the Succession to the Crown Act of 1707 had rubber-stamped the Protestant character of the realm. Any change could be thought of as violation. Of course, there was another way of reading the matter, which O'Connell made use of. This was to say that British constitution would be strengthened by securing the loyalty of Catholics. Better that than leave them a disaffected body. So, using liberal theories of contractual government then fashionable, the association worked 'with the grain of the British Constitution'.[26]

This was not its only strength. It scored because it was a genuine mass movement, something that looks ahead to other later mass movements in Europe in the late nineteenth century. It had popular appeal. Its way of securing it was through the newspapers and O'Connell showed himself canny in exploiting this resource. It is here that he shows the charismatic's Midas touch, turning a political cause into something epic, even, in the words of one historian, 'millennial'.[27] He could be faulted for exaggerating the benefits of emancipation – it became a struggle between, not only good and evil (terminology well suited to his peasant audience), but modern enlightenment and blinkered bigotry (language to discomfit his 'liberal' listeners). He was willing to speak in all registers. There is no doubt but that he had a real understanding of the power of the masses. Reynolds rather condescendingly styles him as a mob leader although a later generation of historians, notably O'Ferrall, see him as the progenitor of modern democratic forms.[28] O'Connell's own views are worth probing. Undoubtedly he was aware that people liked to hear his particular brand of eloquence and he inflated every possible aspect of emancipation to good effect. But he was also a subtle observer of the new power of public opinion, maintaining that there was a certain 'moral electricity in the continuous expression of public opinion concentrated on a single point'.[29] Such moral electricity could be dangerous and it was this implicit danger behind a mass movement, frustrated and unappeased, that created the conditions for the concession of Catholic emancipation in 1829.

Another notable feature of the association was its capacity to function on several different levels. It was para-political not just political. It was an agency for evicted tenants, a real problem when there was no control of rents. It vetted would-be MPs for their support of emancipation. It tried to get legal redress for Catholic victims of Orange Order violence. Most importantly, it organised meetings and collected funds. As a fund raiser, indeed, it was tremendously successful. The so-called Catholic rent was the penny a month collected at Mass on Sundays. It not only gave the association much-needed money for its activities, but there was no surer way to bind people to its mission, thus transforming 'sentimental support into real commitment'.[30] The political education of Catholics en masse had begun. O'Connell was also particularly successful in harnessing the goodwill and indeed the active participation of the Catholic clergy, although it has been averred that Richard Lalor Sheil, another leader of the movement, was even more instrumental in involving the priests.[31] Priests, allowed to join free of charge, gave the campaign warm support from the pulpit and elsewhere. It was a powerful statement of unity. O'Ferrall's theory is that his wooing of church figures enabled him to solve the dilemma of how to build a national organisation on the one hand and be able to control it at will on the other.[32]

To what extent did emancipation attract Irish Protestants? It is certainly true to say that the more liberal Protestants were emancipationists. Conyngham Plunket, who, as we have seen, delivered a celebrated oration on the subject to the Commons, was one such. But many opposed it. In particular, there were hard feelings due to the Unlawful Oaths Act of 1823's suppression of the Orange Order (it was later revived in 1828) and they watched angrily at the successes of Catholics as they wormed their way into the good graces of the Dublin administration. Religiously, an evangelical revival among Methodists and Anglicans saw the establishment of organisations like the London Hibernian Society and the British and Foreign Bible Society which tried to convert the Irish Catholics. Some evangelicals concentrated their efforts here. The sting would be taken out of emancipation if most of them were to 'see the light' and become good Protestants instead.

The decade wore on. Emancipation bills introduced into Westminster once more failed because of the Lords' opposition. The then first minister, Lord Liverpool, was emphatically against emancipation himself and did not want the issue to be made a subject of policy. His cabinet was much divided but, whatever they might think in their conscience, he was determined that it should never become a government sponsored measure. In a letter to the king in 1826, he reiterated his position that the Roman Catholic question was not 'to be considered as a question of government, but that […] all persons in office, should be at liberty to take the course in Parliament upon it, which they might think proper, according to their own individual opinions'. Liverpool's resignation in favour of George Canning in the spring of 1827 could have opened the way for change. The latter, a Pittite, had long been in favour of concession. But, oddly, the tide seemed to be turning against emancipation. The arch-Tory Duke of Wellington and his friends refused to serve under the so-called 'Catholic' premier. In the general election of 1826, an anti-emancipation stance had been a popular platform. A few weeks after Liverpool had had his stroke and before the announcement of Canning's new ministry in April, a motion for Catholic relief had not even passed the Commons. The last time that had happened was in 1819. There was hardly anything in it, a mere four votes, but it was enough. Canning did not live long enough to try again. He died in August. Emancipation now seemed further away than ever.

Chapter 4

THE ACHIEVEMENT OF EMANCIPATION

Interpreting Emancipation

The achievement of Catholic emancipation in 1829 is an episode at once simple and complex to assess. It is simple in the sense that it is regarded as an unambiguous achievement for the Irish people and for English Catholics who had been kept in a political outhouse since the Reformation and subsequent penal legislation. The achievement was, as one biographer has observed, 'immense'.[1] In the words of G. I. T. Machin, who situates the act as part of a series of emancipatory measures and processes, it was the 'main legal advance made by Irish and British Catholics' in the 1800s.[2] In particular, its peaceful and public nature has been noted and contrasted favourably with other developments in Irish society.[3] Historians of Victorian Britain consider it a 'constitutional revolution'.[4] It was, moreover, a catalyst for further systemic change: Wendy Hinde quotes J. S. Mill in the subtitle of her study of the measure, saying that it was 'a shake to men's minds', something which dislodged the reflexive prejudices of centuries.[5] It could be seen, in context, as the high crest of the wave of liberalism in the 1820s and also as a herald of change to come. It certainly prepared Britons for the reform measures of the following decades.[6]

Yet the central paradox is that it was passed by a resolutely Tory government and that it was given grudgingly and with a restrictive measure. It is highly questionable if 1829 represented a genuine conversion on the part of the government and was an example of constructive unionism. It seems more likely that pragmatism and the fear of civil unrest were behind its passage. Yet, even if that interpretation is correct, another question emerges. If it were a real crisis, why did they take so long over it? The hostile attitude of the king was crucial, as Richard Davis points out.[7] The delay was politically damaging as opposition had time to mobilise. And opposition certainly did make itself felt, a fact which raises important questions about the role of minorities and majorities in influencing or failing to influence legislative decisions. Although one could say that the Catholics were a majority in Ireland, they constituted a minority within the United Kingdom and thus acceding to their demands was felt particularly controversial. The idea that government was giving into undue Irish pressure was highly unpopular at home. It is not the least paradoxical feature of the measure that it was 'almost certainly against the wishes of a majority in the country [United Kingdom]'.[8]

From a wider perspective, Catholic emancipation is seen as progress for the cause of civil liberties in the nineteenth century: it is a moment when the majority pressed for reform and were listened to. Rainer Liedtke and Stephan Wendehorst edited a volume in which Catholic emancipation is integrated within the context of multiple European emancipations in the same time period – British Jews, French Protestants and Jews, German Catholics and Jews and Italian Protestants and Jews.[9] This is an important corrective to an overly parochial account of the measure. In the summative essay of the volume, Wendehorst sets emancipatory measures within the context of nineteenth-century nation building and modernisation – they are seen as being part of the process whereby the old, corporate structures of the *ancien régime* give way to abstract, formal and impersonal law.[10] It could also be interpreted as a move away from the confessional state narrowly defined to the ethical state, which had broader moral parameters.

Yet, despite its undoubted significance, several questions remain debatable. Does O'Connell deserve a larger reputation as the founder of Irish democracy as a result? It has been claimed for him, for instance, by Fergus O'Ferrall in his *Catholic Emancipation: Daniel O'Connell and the Birth of Irish Democracy, 1820–1830* (1985). For O'Ferrall, the means of achieving it was the achievement itself. The claims he makes for him are large. He became the creator of the 'first modern political party' and even the 'pioneer of modern democracy' for Europe.[11] Yet, the claims must be assessed in context. Were all the innovations his doing? How far was it *his* achievement or that of the public whose opinion he harnessed? Bartlett underplays his role somewhat in order to emphasise the long-term democratic processes at work since the granting of the franchise to middle-class Catholics in 1793 and also the increasing militarisation of society (one in six adult males had spent time in uniform) which accounted for the discipline that made the Catholic Association such a success.[12] Nor should the role of the clergy be neglected. It is debatable whether or not they were more important than the lay leaders of the Catholic Association: J. A. Reynolds believed that they provided the movement with their 'most energetic leadership'.[13] More recently, O'Ferrall has brought out the importance of liberal clubs, made up of the lay middle classes who organised the movement at the grass-roots level.[14] The clergy, in his account, are fundraisers and supporters.

Political Context

Irish politics depended so much on the vagaries of who was in power. The succession of High Tory Wellington as first minister and Robert Peel as home secretary and leader of the House of Commons in 1828 did not bode well for emancipation. Neither favoured the cause or its leader; neither liked the prospect of appearing to cave in to popular pressure. Both were quite adamant that concession should not happen under their watch. Furthermore, both were alive to the divisive effect it would have on the Tory Party still trying to find itself in the rapidly changing contexts of industrialisation and urbanisation and looking particularly fractured since the resignation of Lord Liverpool in 1827.[15] It is 'not possible to entertain a worse opinion of any Administration than I do of the present', O'Connell wrote grimly.[16]

Yet he soon realised that they could be forced to change. That was the lesson of the first few months. John Russell, a Foxite Whig and future prime minister, introduced a motion to repeal the Test Acts (1673) and Corporation Act (1661) so as to give civil liberty to non-Anglican Protestants, erstwhile termed the 'dissenters'. Fifteen Ultra-Tories changed sides, hoping thereby to stave off their real bugbear – Catholic emancipation – and the bill passed.[17] Now that he had forced 'the enemy to give up his first line, that none but Churchmen are worthy to serve the State', Russell was confident that there was every likelihood of making them 'give up the second, that none but Protestants are'.[18] With increasingly enthusiastic Whigs and divided Tories, it is likely that emancipation would have come about sooner or later, but it was events in Ireland that brought it about with such speed and made a government *volte-face* necessary – and embarrassing. It would result in the very surprising paradox of an unimpeachably Anglican establishment passing a liberal, pro-Catholic measure.

The County Clare By-election

The happening in question was a by-election in Co. Clare which pitted the government-backed candidate William Vesey Fitzgerald against O'Connell himself. The idea of contesting an election as a Catholic, a dazzlingly simple one, had not been tried before, although the idea had been mooted. It had the merits of being both impudent (and thus unignorable) and legal (and thus undeniable). O'Connell, initially tentative, had to be persuaded into contesting the seat, but, once committed, he launched into the campaign with his usual verve.[19] It was a risk, but a calculated one, for by mid-May he could smell victory, writing to Charles Sugrue that 'I will be likely to have a great triumph'. [20] Fitzgerald was known to support the Catholic cause so it is somewhat ironic that O'Connell should choose to contest him. But every government candidate was a target in the new phase of campaigning. The fact that Fitzgerald had also just become president of the Board of Trade and thus would be in cabinet would give a victory against him undeniable public éclat. Politics shaded into religion as many priests called on the electorate to support O'Connell. One does not need to go quite as far as Reynolds does in regarding the priests as local despots;[21] it is, however, undeniable that their influence was disproportionate to their numbers. The hopeful candidate made his way to Clare amid public ovations and an atmosphere that could only be described as euphoric – 'an unprecedented carnival of popular politics'.[22]

The election campaign thrust O'Connell's political rhetoric to the foreground. He was accused at the time of mere demagoguery – now, we are in a position to be more objective. There is no doubt that his public utterances were extremely effective. There is more than a little of the *impresario* about O'Connell: he knew his public and what they wanted to hear and he worked upon mobilising even the most inert. There was something compelling about the mixture of progressive liberalism, almost provocative constitutionalism, loyalism and popular piety in his pre-election rhetoric. He emphasised, as indeed he had a right to do, the constitutionalism of his position. He had to persuade potential voters that a vote for him would not be wasted.

> I entertain a confident hope that, if you elect me, the most bigoted of our enemies will see the necessity of removing from the chosen representative of the people, an obstacle which would prevent him from doing his duty to his King and to his country.[23]

He was careful to tread the fine line between defiance and loyalism, thus avoiding the accusation of sedition.

He also exploited to the full the electorate's horror at the anti-Catholic nature of the oath required for entrance into Parliament. It was, he emphasised, blasphemous; it outraged all the doctrines that Catholics held dear. And, to stir things up further, he pointed out that his opponent had sworn it a full 20 times. Warming to the subject, he claimed that he himself would rather be 'torn limb from limb'[24] than take it – clearly he was relishing the heroic self-depiction as an early Christian martyr. He must have known that he held the trump card in this test case – his incipient triumphalism seems to indicate it.

He knew that, if he were to be denied entry into Parliament after legitimately winning a political contest, the echoes of that denial of constitutionalism would be heard all over Europe. It would 'create a sensation',[25] he declared; it would be a blow at Britain's much-trumpeted political integrity. It would raise such a furore of indignation against Britain that Wellington and Peel simply could not withstand the pressure.

Does he deserve the charge of demagoguery or is his performance in 1828 better regarded as a fine exercise in democratic politics? His speeches are certainly full of exaggerations and bravura, but the overblown and the exaggerated are both crucial to the kind of politics he sought to develop. He was the greatest populariser of his day who, in this moment, instigated a kind of active mass democratisation, not only gaining the trust and faith of crowds but endowing them with an agency to change an inequitable system. Peel grudgingly recognised the potency of this model of participative politics and observed of the by-election that there were 'tens of thousands of disciplined fanatics, abstaining from every excess […] and concentrating every passion and feeling on one single object'.[26] It is no surprise that Gladstone, later to become 'The People's William', would admire that quality in the Irishman. Occasionally, it is said that Gladstone himself resembled an evangelist preacher in his relationship with crowds. There was something about the preacher in O'Connell too, but also something of the storyteller. It is notable that his pacifism did not stop him from drawing examples from Ireland's often violent past. For those who wanted to read violence into his speeches, there was just that subtext of threat. Political rhetoric, an acute sense of timing and brilliant tactics were enough to win him success. The results of the polling put him considerably ahead of his rival – 2,057 votes to 982. The majority of the 40 shilling freeholders had become converts to O'Connell. He had cocked a snook at the British political establishment *and* become part of it at one and the same moment. It seemed like a trick, but an impeccably legal one. He could be execrated, alright, but not faulted.

To Emancipate or Not?

There was a stark choice now facing the British executive. 'They must crush or conciliate us',[27] O'Connell told the Catholic Association. Peel, watching on in dismay, knew that the writing was on the wall. What followed, as he put it in a confidential memorandum to his leader, was a 'choice between different kinds and different degrees of evil'.[28] If they ignored the result, they were ignoring the implications of a legitimate election based on lawful procedure. No law said a Catholic could not contest an election, the oath merely made it impossible for a Catholic to follow up on an electoral victory. If they tried to stifle the electoral mandate, then O'Connell would be a loose cannon and thus more dangerous than ever. They even may have contemplated the dire possibility of a 'secessionist parliament constituted of mandated but unlawful Catholic MPs'.[29]

Even if this did not happen, worse could. Whether or not violence would have resulted from the failure to grant emancipation in 1828–29 is debatable. It seems plausible that it would have. In any case, the fear of it was potent. The initiative could pass from the admittedly moderate O'Connell to the hands of radical separatists, to the men of violence who always lurked close below the surface of Irish life. There had been secret societies, most often rural, aplenty for decades. Their discontent could spread. British neglect of the results of the by-election would seem to prove the point that concessions could never be lawfully gained from a repressive British government, and that more robust methods than O'Connell's were necessary. It was this last, more than anything, that convinced the government of the necessity of conciliation. As Peel stated in the same memorandum, the dangers 'resulting from this union and organisation of the Roman Catholic body and the incessant agitation in Ireland' were fraught 'with prospective and apprehended dangers to the constitution or religion of the country'.[30] As often was the case in Anglo–Irish relations, fear proved the most powerful motivator behind legislative change. Any interpretation of deep government conversion on this issue would be a falsification of the truth.

Thus precisely to preserve the Union and to prevent the outbreak of civil unrest, it was necessary to do something. But should *they* be the ones responsible? And what should they do? How could they ensure stability? Peel felt the matter so distasteful that he considered resigning. Wellington persuaded him not to on the grounds that he, as leader of the Commons, was absolutely necessary to secure the passage of whatever bill emerged. And so he was. His loyalty to the ministry did not, however, gain him favour with the High Tories who saw this as a glaring betrayal of principle, one of the many occasions in the nineteenth century when Irish issues would poison relations within a British party. On the back benches, they were struck horrified at this apostasy of their hopeful young 'favourite'. He frankly confessed his unwillingness to yield on this issue, but it did him no particular good. He insisted that he was only supporting the measure as he was 'unwilling to push resistance to a point which might endanger the Establishments that I wish to defend'.[31]

He put to the Commons the stark choice between granting concession or countenancing civil war. The subtleties of his opinions did not interest the majority of his party: Orange Peel had become 'lemon'. His donnish constituents at Oxford University were so angry that they nailed 'No Peel' onto a door at his old college, Christ Church, which can be seen to this day.

Brunswick Clubs were formed in vociferous opposition to the measure.[32] Doubtless, as the coming man, Peel had more to lose from this episode than Wellington. But, despite this, the measure was sure of success. With Wellington and Peel lending their weight to the measure in both houses, respectively, and with the support of the Whigs, the Catholic Relief Bill[33] could not but pass, although it soured the 142 Ultra-Tories who voted against it. The measure was granted with a particularly bad grace. The king, who had declared that he would return to Hanover and never come back, remained to grumble that 'everything was revolutionary'[34] and that his own position was reduced to that of a 'Canon of Windsor'.[35] His opposition helps to explain the delay. The most bizarre demonstration of hostility came from the Duchess of Richmond, who hosted the cabinet to dinner at Goodwood, subsequent to the passage of the act and had 200 rats stuffed as room decoration for those who had 'ratted' on the Protestant cause. Whether the legislation caused the breakup of the Tory consensus is controversial. Divisions on liberalism had been forming since the start of the 1820s, so the Catholic crisis did not emerge from a vacuum. Davis maintains that it certainly hastened the break-up.[36] Its effect on Peel's reputation amongst party diehards was very significant in the long term.

O'Connell was delighted with legislative success. The bill, he wrote to a friend on 6 March 1829, is 'good – very good; frank, direct, complete; no veto, no control, no payment of the clergy'.[37] What he had feared was that emancipation would be granted with strings attached, and that the clergy would not like being subordinated to the government. But, there was nothing in the bill to dampen anyone's spirits. Fortunately, Peel declared that the government had not the power to make arrangements with the Court of Rome. As it stood, proponents could be thankful that it was, in essence, a remarkably straightforward measure. Catholics were henceforth to be allowed to enter both houses of Parliament and hold all offices except those of Lord Chancellor, Regent and Lord Lieutenant of Ireland.

The Irish Parliamentary Election Act

Its generosity was marred by a parallel measure. A comparative approach is particularly useful here, as Liedtke, in the study of various European emancipations, concludes that emancipation generally did not come 'unconditionally', but was based upon some sort of *quid pro quo*.[38] The *quid pro quo* here was the Irish Parliamentary Election Bill and it was Peel's cynical attempt to limit some of the harm emancipation could do. O'Connell must be borne, but an Irish-Catholic political elite must not be allowed to swamp Westminster. How was the establishment to be preserved? One needed to be able to control the flow quite strictly. The election itself had suggested an obvious 'solution'. Given traditional ideas about the necessity of deference, the disobedience of the 40 shilling freeholders who had defied their landlords and voted for O'Connell was not to be tolerated. Well-conducted landlord–tenant relationships were vital to the maintenance of the sociopolitical system upon which Britain's authority in Ireland was based. That relationship ought to mean deference not defiance. Accordingly, they and others like them must be punished – they could not be allowed any weight in the new political dispensation. The new bill swiftly, ruthlessly disenfranchised them. The 40 shilling freehold (£2) in the counties was no longer a qualification for the vote, it was now £10. At one fell swoop, this cut the Irish electorate to one-sixth of its size – from 216,000 to a mere 37,000 adult males. It was, as even the usually temperate Foster notes, a 'drastic' change.[39] Even this did not satisfy the Ultra-Tories – how dare the government tamper with the 'mystical beauties of the unreformed constitution'?[40]

But it did satisfy Peel. The Whigs were also in favour of it and, although their Irish credentials were traditionally more liberal, this was only when it suited them. There was a good deal of the *gauche caviar* attitude about the Whigs. They were far too establishment to be really radical. They liked to flirt with liberalism but, beneath, their traditionalist credentials were safe. One aspect of the matter had caused them great alarm – the defection of free-holders. The potential mass defection of their own tenants was an issue that struck fear into the heart of even the greatest of landowners. Many of them, we must remember, were landholders in Ireland, too – often absentee. So the Whigs satisfied the needs both of conscience and self-interest during 1828–29, supporting emancipation and disenfranchisement at the same time. Irish issues were rarely *purely* ideological concerns for British politicians: there were many vested interests that counted, too.

It is somewhat surprising, at first blush, that this measure should have aroused no civil discord in Ireland. O'Connell was certainly distressed and petitioned against it. 'We must put on record our decided hostility to it in every shape and form, so as to enable us hereafter, *and soon*, to do battle in favour of a restoration of this right.'[41] Yet, he did not press the issue, and perhaps could not at this point – there was very little he could do. More oddly, it must be added that some middle-class Catholics and gentry did not feel very strongly about the disenfranchisement of their less well-off coreligionists. In fact, some of them, overtly or tacitly, supported it. Two interpretations suggest themselves. First, it is often notable that newly established groups mark themselves out by their gratitude and their determination to prove their loyalty. Acceding to the franchise alteration without demur made middle-class Catholics feel secure in their newly acquired privileges. Secondly, it is another notable trait of the newly established that they actually enjoy being part of an exclusive establishment, even though, by the very fact of their joining it, it has become less exclusive. Having so recently been outside the pale, they now could enjoy one of the more malicious pleasures of being established – that of excluding others. It was easier now to distance oneself from the Catholic Association (such a 'mob concern'); it was easier to acquire the trappings of respectability. It was far better to quietly accept the disenfranchisement of lesser associates who would lower the tone, anyway.

Evaluation

Clearly, the limiting legislation did detract from the achievement of emancipation and did perceptibly lessen O'Connell's triumph. Nevertheless, for all its subsequent caveats, the Roman Catholic Relief Act of 1829 represented a magnificent achievement for O'Connell. 'We had our own Waterloo', he wrote. 'We chained the valiant duke to the car of our triumph, and compelled him to set us free.'[42] It had an enormous impact on O'Connell personally. His reputation was now firmly established as that of 'The Liberator'. This unlikely man had rolled back the prejudice of centuries by unleashing the power of mobilised popular opinion. Not since 1688 had a Catholic been appointed as a MP. Now that once impregnable system of sectarian exclusion had ended. Money tributes flowed in so that he was in a position to give up the practice of the law and devote himself to politics. It could be seen as the height of his achievements.

However, the matter does not reflect credit on him entirely. He has been faulted for his exaggeration in promising that all good would follow emancipation.[43] Some peasants began to believe that it would usher in a social utopia and he certainly did nothing to undeceive them. There were those who thought, naively, that they would never need to work again once O'Connell poured gold into their pockets.[44] Whilst he cannot be accused of anything more than political exaggeration of the kind very familiar to us through election manifestos, it does show a casual attitude towards accuracy. There are other negatives that historians have drawn attention to. According to Hinde, the measure did not bring 'peace, prosperity, and an end to sectarian discord'.[45] On that last point, O'Ferrall slyly points out that, whilst it may have answered the 'Catholic question' for some, it did not do so for northern Protestants.[46] Nor did it do much for the divisions between Ireland and Britain. The manner of passing it was so ungracious that it left a very sour taste.[47]

Nevertheless, despite these caveats, this one act changed the complexion of the Union completely. Some would now regard the settlement as fully complete. What had been lacking in the original was now added. Catholic loyalism now had a basis upon which to build. Ulster Unionism had a further reason to stay close to Britain, for all that Britain had shown favour to its enemies. But there was a sense in which the Emancipation Act undermined 1801 and made it somehow more unfinished than ever. Did it make it seem, Boyce asks, as if the Union were on some 'permanent [and public] trial'? Was it never to be 'taken for granted [...] but always in question, a matter for debate, an arrangement that could or should be subject to perpetual review'?[48] What did the decision of 1829 commit the government to? If Catholics were now fully fledged subjects of Her Majesty and entitled to take office and enter Parliament, why should there be legal disabilities against them in other ways? Why should the state church exact tithes? Why should Catholics not be permitted higher education? And so on. The questions with which the British establishment would have to deal were more numerous and controversial than ever before.

One person who let himself reflect upon this was Robert Peel. His grudging acceptance of the necessity of emancipation is most often read as the triumph of simple pragmatism over deeply held belief. Alternative interpretations are possible. Most notable is Hilton's who argues the possibility that Peel did indeed, as a result, change 'his whole approach to Irish governance, as well as his language and tone'. It became part of his liberalising process in three ways. First, in using language like 'the time has come', he began to adopt a fashionable language of progress and posed as a moderate force in ensuring that it did not occur too quickly. Second, his conversion was liberal in the sense that he showed a new commitment to getting the 'mechanism of Irish society right' rather than falling back on the old-fashioned methods of patronage and management. Lastly, he began to think about how the situation of Ireland might be improved through freeing the economy. In 1829 he also repealed the last of the penal laws against Catholics owning property.[49] So, in all these ways, it is possible to refute the conventional wisdom about Peel, or at least heavily problematise it. Although not a conversion of the heart, perhaps it was an intellectual one.

In Britain also, the methods O'Connell had used to achieve victory proved widely influential. His deft usage of constitutional means to reform what he saw as the abuses of the constitution was a lesson for Britons of a reforming hue. Certainly, the networks of connection between British and Irish reform initiatives of the period would be unthinkable without the achievement thus attained by the Irishman. Thomas Atwood, a banker from Birmingham and founder of the Birmingham Political Union in the 1830s, hailed the 'great and bloodless revolution' that he had brought about.[50] Jewish emancipation followed in 1858. Perhaps J. S. Mill was correct in calling it a 'shake to men's minds' in weakening 'all old prejudices'.[51]

A distinction should always be made, as Machin does, between 'formal' and 'informal' emancipation.[52] The fact that the former was achieved does not mean that the centuries of prejudice and the structures of exclusion gave way so easily. Anti-Catholicism would remain a key component of many British attitudes towards the Irish. But there was a further point and that concerns the peculiar snobberies of upper-class English Catholics. Although they had been liberated (and indeed the Earl of Surrey was the first to enter Parliament), they retained their snobbery towards their Irish coreligionists. No political triumph could gain O'Connell social credibility among the English-Catholic elite, who, ironically but perhaps predictably, seemed to resent being indebted to an 'uncouth' Irishman. Not for the first time did liberation come at the price of vulgarity – the whole thing lacked tone. On seeking membership into their exclusive Cisalpine club, O'Connell was blackballed. It is a testimony to him that his reaction was, though a little puzzled, both generous and humorous. 'I heartily forgive them all', he wrote to a friend, 'But it was a strange thing of them to do; it was a comical "testimonial" of my services in emancipating them. It would be well, perhaps, if I could *un-emancipate* some of them.'[53]

Chapter 5

IRELAND UNDER WHIG GOVERNMENT

Historiography of the 1830s

The years 1830–45, although often overlooked, are, as one historian has noted, a 'little era in their own right'. It was this period rather than 1801–30 which set the 'pattern for Anglo–Irish relations in the later nineteenth and earlier twentieth centuries'.[1] They are therefore utterly crucial. Three features are especially notable. The first is the dominance of O'Connell. One way of interpreting this period is to see it as his age.[2] It was he who secured reforms from successive governments – Whigs and Conservatives – and, as traditional accounts would have it, he also summed up the aspirations of a people until 1843, wielding unambiguous popular authority.[3] Or was it entirely so? Revisionists have seen in him more limitations and divisiveness than the conventional narrative might suggest.[4] How successful was he lobbying for concessions in Parliament? Can we attribute to him anything more than undramatic bread-and-butter efficacy? There is a distinct possibility articulated by Dudley Edwards that he was politically emasculated by being in Westminster, that his 'significance became greater in England than in his own country' and that he lost touch with common people back home.[5] Furthermore, a rosy view of his pan-Irish status is difficult to maintain in the light of his failure to cultivate a meaningful rapport with Ulster Protestants. He claimed to 'hate bigotry of every kind, Catholic, Protestant or Dissenter' but that did not necessarily mean that he was good at or even willing to understand those of a very different politico-religious persuasion.[6] This argument has been made pointedly by Dudley Edwards and Foster, among others, and serves to complicate his status as a unifier and as a force for good after 1830.[7]

The second feature of note was the formation of a liberal alliance in Westminster between Irish Catholics and a Whig and Radical complex. It was the first of such combinations and would foreshadow later developments.

Of debate is both the nature of this connection – whether principled or pragmatic – and its political efficacy – which side stood to gain more? Interpretations vary. Undoubtedly, there were needs on all sides that drove them into each other's open arms. The 1830s were a high point for Whiggery and the reforming rhetoric of its grandees often sounded high minded: they claimed to act upon liberal principles. However, it is possible to read below this rhetoric and see them, as Boyd Hilton does, as arch-pragmatists.[8] This reading gives a certain colour to their attitude to the Irish MPs and sees the connection as more one of convenience than of commitment. Macintyre talks of them as having to fulfil 'embarrassing obligations' to the Irish in return for support for their own agenda.[9]

The often progressive-sounding statements of the Whigs should not, therefore, be taken entirely at face value. Ian Newbould emphasises their aristocratic paternalism throughout the decade which made them keep the excesses of the radical interest at bay. In this reading, they are classic 'middle-way' politicians concerned, above all, with keeping the country in a balanced state.[10] Peter Mandler, however, insists that many of them retained a populist instinct, in the tradition of Charles James Fox, and were constructive social reformers who believed in government intervention to solve social and economic problems. Their government was still aristocratic but there was a genuine impulse for reform which distinguished their record.[11] Their cultivation of the Irish MPs and their interest in the Irish Question thus could be said to owe something to both principle and pragmatism – in what measure, each may be debated.

The third feature about which there is much debate is the combination of reform and repression offered to or imposed upon Ireland during the two Whig periods in office, 1830–34 and 1835–41. Traditionally, the focus has been on Peel's reforms in the 1840s and the Whig contribution has been unfairly sidelined. O'Connell, himself, grumbled on one occasion that it was 'stingy, restricted and insulting'.[12] Hinde agrees that he did not get very much out of it.[13] However, the facts may bear a very different interpretation. The Whigs put forward 19 bills to solve Irish social and economic problems in the realms of education, public works, policing, workhouses, municipal government and religion. As a record, this looks commendable, particularly in the context of years of legislative inactivity and passivity; scholars such as Newbould have supported a reasonably favourable interpretation, referring to their sense of 'administrative fair play'.[14] Hilton sees their municipal reform as offering the 'best opportunity for the development of a non-sectarian urban middle class'.[15] However, as Macintyre rightly points out, the Whigs did not dare tackle the land question directly because of vested interests, thus showing their innate and inflexible conservatism.[16] Moreover, their reform often came simply out of a desire, expressed by the Marquess of Anglesey, Lord Lieutenant since 1830, to render 'O'Connell harmless [...] by anticipating him' and prevent anybody but themselves having the 'advantage of the initiative in all healing measures'.[17] If they were (sometimes grudgingly) reformist, the Whig establishments were also exemplars of government by force. Their usage of coercion reflected habitual and unquestioned assumptions about the natural unruliness and disorder of the Irish people. In the light of the facts, it may be hard to avoid Hilton's conclusion that their methods of coercion were draconian[18] or at least unimaginative. As a result, the Whig cocktail of reform and repression is a peculiarly complicated one and permits no simple evaluation.

The Role of O'Connell

Aged 53, the popular agitator now had to adapt to a new role as a parliamentarian and channel his persona and agenda to a very different context to the ones than he had hitherto known. MacDonagh has it that he was something of 'a born politician'; this reading would suggest that the challenge of adaptation was minimal.[19] However that may be, O'Connell had been learning the arts of politics for several decades now. He had even experienced attending a debate on the state of the nation in Westminster on 24 March 1795 and had there admired the rhetoric of William Pitt and the policies of Charles James Fox.[20] Now he was a member of the Commons himself and the political play consequent on such a state was his lot. This was more especially true in his case because all thirty or so of his followers – there were 39 after the general election of 1833 – became a coherent voting bloc in the Commons and thus a tight-knit group to be reckoned with. This gave O'Connell a certain strategic advantage from the outset. However, he and they had the drawbacks as well as the advantages of such a position and it is to O'Connell's credit that he grasped them fully. Bew has it that he duly became a 'force in British high politics', although how much this was actually the case remains open to question.[21]

The Westminster that he entered was dominated by the Whigs on the government benches and the Tories in opposition, foundering in the wake of the emancipation crisis and the prospect of parliamentary reform. O'Connell quickly learned that neither party would sponsor repeal of the Union. In fact, a motion asking for a committee to enquire into the effects of the Union was resoundingly defeated in 1834 – 528 against a mere 38 votes; 37 of the 38 votes, be it added, were O'Connell's own followers, the other was a British radical, a lone voice and not representative of any particular interest. It was implausible to expect this to change in a political generation.

not a practical proposition. Understandably, therefore, he settled
nding a middle ground. What does this deliberate strategy reveal
? It illustrates, above all, his realism and what Hilton describes
as his pragmatic willingness to pursue alternative strategies'.[22] It may even,
in the words of Adelman and Pearce, show him as an 'opportunist', ready
to seize upon whatever opportunity came to hand, even if his long-term
goals were far more radical.[23] Dudley Edwards refers to him as 'playing to
the Whig gallery' and undoubtedly, there was an element of tempering his
principles to the political climate.[24] There is a further complexity, though.
O'Connell remained ideologically and rhetorically committed to the idea of
repeal. He still doughtily declared to his Irish following that his 'ultimate
object' was repeal and, in his 1830 *Letter to the People of Ireland*, he urged
them to agitate against the Union as never before.[25] This is evidence of the
flexibility of the man. He was able to keep more than one ball in the air
at any one time. But he was sensible enough when it came to choosing his
battles in Westminster and would not fight the already-lost. His attitude may
also have been a reflection of the fact that the Irish public had no political
energy for another mass campaign so soon after the last one. The masses had
been overexerted; a period of calm was needed. Middle-class Catholics were,
meanwhile, consolidating their gains and making advances in the professions
throughout the 1830s.[26] In short, nobody of any status in Ireland especially
wanted another fight.

Earl Grey and Ireland

Although both parties were adamantly anti-repeal, it was more natural that
O'Connell should find common ground with the Whigs. They had a long
reformist and indeed populist tradition harkening back to the charismatic
persona of Charles James Fox.[27] O'Connell, observing this, had said to a friend
in 1829 that he wished to out-Whig the Whigs, to become one 'des plus
prononcés'.[28] This was indicative of a desire to challenge the liberal pieties
of the Whigs with more substantive claims and a more radical agenda. Earl
Grey's ministry was the first Whig ministry since 1806–7, and the first of any
note since the Rockingham days, unless, of course, one counts Pitt's ministry
as that of an independent Whig, which he certainly had done. Presided over in
the Lords by a sextegenarian Earl Grey, this government (1830–34) was keen
to tackle meaningful legislation and their cooped-up energy lavished itself
on parliamentary and Poor Law reform. The Irish Question was important
to Grey, as it always had been in the Foxite tradition, but in no way was it
the major part of his agenda. Still, O'Connell's support was politically useful
and there is no doubt but that it helped to secure the passage of the Great

Reform Act of 1832. This act redistributed seats quite radically and increased the franchise from 13 per cent of adult males in England and Wales to 18 per cent. It was meant, in Grey's words, to be 'large enough' to satisfy the middle-class public and provide a bulwark against demands for further change and innovation.[29] It was a piece of legislation of prime significance, the herald of a new age of representative politics.

The parallel measure which applied to Ireland, however, was much more timid. There was no new enfranchisement. The disqualification of 1829 was retained, meaning that only 5 per cent of Irish adult males could vote. If things had been proportionate, Ireland would have got 100 MPs in addition to the ones that they already had. As it was, it only got five – ones for Belfast, Limerick, Waterford, Galway and Trinity College. It was also particularly striking that no rotten boroughs were disenfranchised in the Irish Reform Act. This surely is a measure of how useful political patronage was to the Ascendancy elite. O'Connell was understandably disappointed, but what could he do? No doubt he put his hope in the fact that the reformed Parliament would bring in a more liberal elite, ready to countenance change in Ireland. But this belief was, as we have seen, dashed by the failure of the 1834 motion to reconsider the state of the Union.

Early Whig Reforms

It is worthwhile noting that the various factory and transport reforms introduced in Westminster in this period applied as much to Ireland as to Britain. But some measures were distinct and peculiar to Ireland. The most notable, surely, lay in the field of education. Edward Stanley, the chief secretary for Ireland and a conservative Whig, was responsible for the development of a national school system in Ireland.[30] In 1831, he wrote what came to be called the Stanley letter, which is still the legal basis for primary education. The following year, the government set up a Board of Commissioners for National Education, consisting of three Church of Ireland members, two Catholics and two Presbyterians. Their job was to support the creation of local schools on lines that would be acceptable to all denominations, an innovative approach. They would be in receipt of a government grant in order to do this. The set-up was a daringly enlightened way of neutralising religious division. The number of children in primary school increased from 107,000 in 1833 to 355,000 ten years later. Despite its shortcomings, Macintyre concludes that the measure was 'vital' in securing the 'education of peasant Ireland'.[31] It is also notable that in this crucial index of modernity – mass education – Ireland was decades ahead of Britain. The application of such a planned scheme is an important qualification to the stereotypical view that Britain lacked imagination in dealing with Ireland. Ireland was, on this occasion at least, a place where new ideas could and should be tried out – it was an experimental ground for progressivism. Whether the system managed to make Irish children into 'happy English children' is more doubtful. Certainly, it helped to foster the English language and destroy the usage of Gaelic as a means of communication. But if education could win people over to the establishment, it could also give them the wherewithal to reject it. Literacy would be a powerful weapon in the armoury of the subsequent nationalist movement.

The Whigs also began to tackle much-needed reform in the Church of Ireland. This institution was, as Gearóid Ó Tuathaigh has remarked, 'both over-staffed and over-endowed for an establishment ministering to the needs of less than a seventh (800,000) of the population'.[32] For some of the front-line Whigs interested in the theories of Jeremy Bentham, the institution obviously failed the test of utility.[33] The Irish Church Temporalities Act of 1833 accordingly purified some of the excesses of the established system. The act reduced two archbishoprics to the status of bishoprics and amalgamated ten bishoprics to adjacent sees. It also redistributed funds and allowed tenants on church lands to purchase their holdings at a fixed annual rent. What looked like rationalisation for some seemed like the erosion of due privilege for others. A group known as the Derby Dilly (including the Dukes of Richmond and Stanley) resigned from the cabinet over the proposal to redistribute confiscated church revenues to poor relief and education.[34] Traditional Church of Ireland members felt particularly aggrieved and regarded it as a predictable consequence of Catholic emancipation. For O'Connell, it represented a move in the right direction and he expressed his satisfaction with these modest measures, showing once again a characteristic streak of political realism. At times, he gave the impression of being the wagging 'Irish tail' to the Whig dog, of playing to the 'Whig gallery' as Dudley Edwards said.[35] Yet this view must be modified somewhat in light of the facts. Although he gave conditional support to the Whigs, he adopted a strongly hostile reaction to the coercive measures which the government also sought to employ.

Whig Coercion, Irish Troubles

The long series of coercion acts introduced by Westminster for Ireland in the nineteenth century could well make the subject of a book.[36] At first it is tempting to pass over them without much comment – they were, after all, short-term responses to crises situations – but it is worth probing a little deeper to assess what lay beneath the habitual exercise of coercion from above.

Recently there has been much interest in Britain's usage of political violence and the mechanisms of control.[37] Max Weber's classic theory about official violence is useful in general terms. In his essay, 'Politics as a Vocation' (1919), he defines a state as that body which possesses a monopoly of legitimate violence.[38] Authority cannot be maintained in the long term without power and power implies the claim to control by violent means. Certainly, the British state throughout this period was ready (one might almost say *unduly* ready) to lay claim to this power in regard to Ireland. 'You may trace Ireland through the statute-book of England, as a wounded man in a crowd is tracked by his blood' wrote a contemporary.[39] But the insight that must emerge from this is that, however immediately efficacious it may be, coercion is a double-edged weapon and the more it is used (rather than just threatened), the less it looks legitimate. Coercion was not government. Indeed, coercion implied, to some extent, the failure of government and the necessity of resorting to force. Put another way, excessive use of coercion, in the absence of other sources of legitimacy, tends to weaken authority rather than strengthen it.

But hard-pressed governments did not always think about the long-term consequences of the regular exercise of force. Domestic experience had not prepared them for this. In contrast to unrest in Britain, which tended to be confined to short periods and caused by very particular urgent problems (1815–20, 1830–32, 1848, 1866–67), Ireland had an endemic subculture of agrarian violence that rumbled on throughout the century. Ireland was, above all, regarded as a law-and-order problem. The British masses, essentially, were not. Accordingly, the Whigs passed the Peace Preservation Act and Suppression of Disturbances Act in 1833 which gave the Lord Lieutenant power to declare districts in a state of disturbance, impose curfews and detain suspects without trial for up to three months. Meetings, even those petitioning Parliament, were banned unless permission had been granted by the Lord Lieutenant. These were particularly draconian measures and O'Connell disparaged them as 'Algerine' in their severity.[40] More constructively, in 1835 they introduced a constabulary bill that united the forces existent in the country, regularised the hierarchy, provided for professional training and did much to ensure impartiality. Newbould maintains that it was 'one of the lesser known but more successful measure of the Whig attempt to pacify Ireland'.[41]

But Ireland still refused to be pacified. Throughout the 1830s, there was, in fact, an alarming increase in agrarian violence. The administration in Dublin Castle was constantly concerned by the proliferation of Irish banditti, with various names such as the Ribbonmen, White Feet, the Rockites and the Shanavests. For some British observers, the reason for such lawlessness lay in the Irishman's native disposition, 'a natural predilection for outrage', according to Peel, which 'nothing can control'.[42] The assumption of innate

Gaelic disorder was a common one among the political and social elites of Britain. L. P. Curtis has charted the evolution of the 'idea of a dichotomy' between Celt and Anglo-Saxon and a 'crude and inflexible stereotype of Irish character' which had 'political as well as psychological significance'.[43] We would thus do well to interpret the policy of official coercion partly in this light.

Such assumptions helped to prevent politicians from either seeing the profound reasons for unrest or taking them seriously enough. The most fundamental cause of unrest was the vexed question of proprietorship in the land. This was more than simply a confused feeling that land was in the wrong hands. The course of the nineteenth century made it more obvious than ever that contractual landlord–tenant relationships, brought about through centuries of imposition, had never taken deep root in Ireland and that they were under increasing pressure from below. There were two claim-rights being articulated, or, in MacDonagh's words, 'two mutually exclusive and antagonistic versions of the meaning of property in the land'. The Ascendancy version was based on absolute landlord ownership; traditional Irish practice advocated more communal forms.[44] The British government took crimes against property notoriously seriously both at home and abroad. It has been noted that its rate of execution in the period was far higher than in Prussia and that a majority of people were executed for property crimes rather than homicide (unlike in Prussia).[45] Given their beliefs, they naturally regarded crimes against property in Ireland as anarchic behaviour rather than as protest against perceived illegitimacy, so their attitude to change was bound to be conservative. Some more astute observers, like Alexis de Tocqueville (the French political theorist who visited the country in 1835 and wrote up his observations) and Nassau Senior (the Whig economist), recognised that Ireland was a multi-legal society with mismatching codes and provisions. The Whig government was not, however, able to recognise this.

Another particular focus of hatred among these agrarian radicals were the tithes required by the Church of Ireland, a 'spectacularly inequitable' system, in the words of Foster.[46] Tithes seemed even more problematic after the granting of emancipation in 1829. A veritable tithe war from 1831 to 1838 saw a breakdown of law and order in the country with hundreds of murders, attempted murders and arson attacks. Nor were the new Catholic landlords exempt from punitive reprisals.[47] It would be wrong to assume that this violence emanated from the most miserably poor areas of the country. On the contrary, the strongholds of violence were Roscommon, Tipperary, Clare and Limerick – notably *not* the poorest areas of the country. Disproportionately, with only 16 per cent of the island's population, they were responsible for 60 per cent of agrarian crime. Although Stanley had shepherded the Tithe

Act through Parliament in 1832 whereby tithes could be commuted by a money payment, many of the problems remained, unabated. Later the Tithe Commutation Act of 1838 reduced tithes by 25 per cent and made the remainder payable to the landlord. This pacified them somewhat, although Whig conservatism is once again noteworthy.

In the meantime, the crack of the whip was the obvious short-term 'solution'. Perhaps more than anything else, the eager recourse to coercion was a failure of political imagination. It is an indictment of many governments in the nineteenth century that they showed greater energy in repression than in reform. That fact alone reveals that Ireland was seen, first and foremost, as a police problem more than as a partner in Union. Already in the 1830s, Westminster was establishing a pattern that would eventually mean that they have more troops garrisoned to keep Ireland quiescent than in the whole of India.[48] It would be a very costly exercise.

The Lichfield House Compact

Coercive policies reveal just how uncomfortable O'Connell's connection with the government was in the early 1830s. In terms of his reputation at home, it did him no particular favour as he was seen to have thrown his lot in with the oppressor. Personally, he found agrarian violence disturbing and quietly agreed that soldiers were necessary to curb it. However, he reacted strongly against the excessive use of repression and attributed it to the 'base, brutal and bloody' Whigs.[49] It is interesting that O'Connell, despite his 'establishment' status in politics never lost his capacity to stigmatise those he opposed in belligerent terms. Dudley Edwards faults his 'offensive expressions against public men' and claims that they roused hatred against the English amongst some of his Irish followers, which did not make for peaceable relations.[50] Even the generally laudatory MacDonagh comments on his 'unscrupulous' oratory at times which tended to alienate one community from the other.[51] This further problematises his achievements post-1829.

Despite the discomfort with coercion, O'Connell still found the Whigs preferable to the 'Orange' Tories under Peel and he fought the January 1835 election campaign with the somewhat desperate slogan 'No Tories, No Tithes'. In February 1835, he had 'officially' teamed up with the Whigs to defeat a fragile Peelite government. What brought them together were the events of 1834. O'Connell had long realised that the reformed Parliament would be just like the unreformed Parliament in its implacable opposition to repeal. He now desired a closer alliance with the Whigs so as to gain winnable concessions. The party grandees were also coming to the realisation that they needed Irish support. Partly their need was purely pragmatic and there was an irony in their needing it at all. It was, after all, the controversial Irish church reforms which, in alienating some forty backbenchers and two cabinet ministers, made some sort of overture to O'Connell necessary.[52] Furthermore, they realised that they were now up against a Tory Party newly resurgent under the brisk leadership of Peel.[53]

The overture took place when the Whigs were out of power and the Conservative Party, under Peel, were unconvincingly in. The Earl of Lichfield presided over a gathering of Whigs, Irish and radicals and the gentlemen's arrangement resulting became known as the Lichfield House Compact. It foreshadowed, to some extent, the creation of the Liberal Party in 1859. It was always more of a marriage of convenience than of affection and, as Bew notes, proved to be a 'frustrating partnership for both sides'.[54] Nevertheless, everyone had something to gain – their joint forces combined to defeat Peel after a 100-day premiership, ironically, also on Irish issues. Lord Melbourne, that suave specimen of the aristocracy, was now prime minister and John Russell his home secretary. The latter was determined to use the 'language of conciliation' to make Irish Catholics feel that they were 'free subjects of a free country'.[55] This was a fresh note. The administration at Dublin Castle was also a reforming one. In particular, Thomas Drummond, the undersecretary, was a force for change on the ground. It was he who laid down the crisp principle that property had its duties as well as its rights, a gauntlet thrown down to the unregenerate patricians of the land.[56]

Later Whig Reforms

There were further Irish reforms of mixed significance in the latter half of the decade. Here, Ireland was not the testing ground; it was, rather, made to imitate modernising English legislation. An act of 1838 sought to rectify the tithe situation. O'Connell accepted it with a 'display of reluctance'.[57] The Irish Poor Law Act (1838) sought to imitate the 1834 English original, in providing for workhouses in each district under boards of guardians. Yet, controversially, it was not based on the commission report of 1835 because that had recommended a level of government intervention that offended their laissez-faire principles. The government may be faulted for ordering an English Poor Law commissioner to do a later rushed investigation lasting a mere nine weeks – obviously the resulting report recommended what they wanted to hear. The Municipal Corporations Act in 1840 sought to reform Irish civic government along the lines of an 1835 act for England. The connections between the polities are particularly obvious here, but there were important differences. The Irish act was a more limited piece of legislation and control of police was left centralised. Nevertheless, Catholics began to reap the benefits of official *détente*. Local councils were made non-discriminatory and O'Connell's followers made gains here. Catholics were encouraged to join the police and the magistracy and act as sheriffs and Poor Law board guardians. O'Connell himself became Lord Mayor of Dublin in 1841. Stiff Orangemen might object to this creeping popery of the country, but the atmosphere was certainly healthier and the Union began to look more like a 'flexible instrument' for reform. These were five years bristling with systemic change.

In the atmosphere of official *détente*, the Irish Catholic Church flourished and the seeds of its dominance in Irish life were sown. Already, in the 1820s, a pro-cathedral in Dublin in the Greek revivalist style had opened up and the first episcopal see since the Reformation was reinstated. A huge programme of church building began in the 1830s, making up for years of hiddenness and persecution. The seminary at Maynooth was attracting many vocations and a new generation of priests was sent out to minister to parishes around the country. Bishops had great importance among the flock. Teaching orders of priests and nuns were thriving and making the most of the new dispensation of primary education. There was even a Catholic version of the largely Protestant temperance movement, launched by Fr Mathew in Cork in 1838. It was claimed that, as a result, rates of violent crime in Ireland fell considerably. In short, what we have is a picture of a newly confident, assertive church and much evidence for what could be called a devotional revolution. Emancipation and concession had allowed Catholics the latitude to flourish.

Protestant and Unionist Ireland

It is worth dwelling on the reaction of Protestant Unionists to the Whig reforms of the 1830s. Although Unionism had emerged among the rural poor, it had quickly gained strongholds in the towns, most significantly among the working classes in Belfast.[58] There was a real sense in which they felt that their cherished monopolies were being eroded and their status completely undermined. They also increasingly felt a sense of grievance at the hearing given to O'Connell in British political circles and resentment that he was considered to be the mouthpiece for the views of the country. After 1829, in particular, conservative Irish Protestants felt threatened by the rise of Catholics, especially by their entrance into previously intact strongholds such as the law, politics and the constabulary. Hilton refers to a 'bonanza of jobbery' for Catholics following the Irish Constabulary Act of 1836.[59] Opinion began to mobilise under the Presbyterian minister, Henry Cooke. His particular contribution was to unite both established church people and Presbyterians under the banner of traditional Protestant politics.

The Unionist Orange Order waxed strong in this new context. There were 1,500 lodges by 1835 and the Whigs, despite the opposition of King William IV, sought to dissolve them and exclude their members from government service. There was some Unionist feeling in the south of the country, too. The Dublin Protestant Operative Association was a working-class organisation, aimed at reversing the perceived decline of the Protestant cause. It later merged with the Orange Order.[60] It is important to emphasise how newly vulnerable these groups began to feel and how they began to harbour an admittedly partially unreasonable (but nonetheless potent) suspicion that they were being shuffled along by the establishment. Their own convictions about Union hardened as attempts were being made to make it a more conciliatory arrangement.

Although Unionist movements were proactive in setting an intransigent tone, O'Connell himself must be held partially to blame for this increasing polarisation of the religious communities on the island. Although professing a non-sectarian approach to politics and genuinely supporting civil and religious liberties, he did not show, at any stage, a willingness to reach out to the Protestant communities of the country, most obviously concentrated in the north. Although he had a certain following among liberal Protestants, he was 'anathema' to conservatives.[61] He did little to assuage them and this could be said to complicate his reputation after 1829. His failure here may have been due to his insensitivity to their traditions which bound them more to Scotland and the industrial revolution than to the Gaelic past. His assumption of a basic unity of experience was too crude to work. In any case, despite his blithe confidence that sectarian divides were ultimately of secondary importance in political allegiances, it is hard to avoid Foster's conclusion that, after 1829, Irish politics 'set hard into a sectarian mould'.[62] The communities were increasingly at loggerheads with long-term political consequences.

Interpreting the 1830s

As the decade came to a close, the connection between the O'Connellites and the Whigs was also reaching its end. It had been politically convenient for a time, giving the Whigs a body of support for their legislation in the Commons and O'Connell some shelter in the parliamentary jungle. 'Parliamentarian *par excellence*' he may have been, but it was becoming increasingly clear that the Whigs were going to lose power in the near future and that, in any case, he had not really succeeded in making them tackle reform on a large scale.[63] Accordingly, he turned to the old idea of repealing the Union, something that would even further alienate traditional Protestants. Nevertheless, the Union was a respectable target –

there had been petitions for repeal as far back as 1810 and petitions were, evidently, the most loyal form of protest.[64] The framing of a petition was an explicit recognition of legitimate authority in the very act of seeking the redress that only it could grant. By a peaceful and legal campaign, reformers could thus advocate change without appearing to be revolutionary. O'Connell, with his curious combination of traditionalism and radicalism, found that he could still loudly profess loyalty to the king and constitution, (from 1837 onwards, the queen and constitution), whilst arguing for the *status quo ante* 1801. However, for protest to turn into something more forceful and more effective, he would need to turn, once again, to the people.

Chapter 6

THE CAMPAIGN FOR
REPEALING UNION

Historiography

The 1840s, which began with the formation of the National Association for
Full Justice or Repeal, mark O'Connell's final seven years of political activity.
It must be asked whether or not those years were the culminating point of his
public life and whether, on the basis of this last campaign, he was more of a
force for good than otherwise for Irish society and for Anglo–Irish relations
in general.[1] Undoubtedly, he failed to achieve the desired repeal of the
Union, but, as historians have pointed out, he may never have believed this
concession possible in the first place, his reasons for the campaign being more
about securing interim concessions. In the sense that his activities led to
Peel's reforms, he could thus be said to be indirectly successful.[2] On attitudes
in Britain, his impact was, most often, a sour one. By 1846, *Punch* magazine
was calling him the real potato blight.[3] Undoubtedly, he personified for many
the epitome of the feckless, dishonest, semi-civilised 'Paddy', a stereotype
increasingly potent in the Victorian worldview.[4] But he cannot be faulted
for the prejudices of others. Of greater moment is his effect on his country of
birth. There, his agenda continued both to unite and to divide – ambivalence
is once again a hallmark. Although the repeal campaign was explicitly and
emphatically non-sectarian, it was largely a Catholic movement and the few
Protestants who attached themselves to it were 'eccentric or ultra-liberal'.[5]
Once again, the accusation of divisiveness may be made.

None of this was new. What was new in this decade was his fairly sudden
fall from public favour in the south after 1845. That O'Connell's status sharply
declined before his death in 1847 and even more noticeably thereafter was
in part due to the inevitable cyclical nature of public feeling, his failure to
read the new public mood and the catastrophe of the Famine. Ironically, it

has been suggested that, if his proposals on tithes, municipal reform, land and the Poor Law had been attended to, some of the tragedy of the Famine might have been averted.[6] As the country collapsed in disastrous circumstances, O'Connell saw his vision of a loyalist and free Ireland doomed. This ultimate failure must be weighed against his earlier successes and achievements in summing up the contribution of the man and his overall impact on his country and on Anglo–Irish relations more generally.

The Nature of the Campaign

O'Connell's campaign of the early 1840s happened against a hostile background of Conservative government. In 1841, the Conservatives had swept to victory in an election which had been based around the traditional grounds of economic protectionism. The Conservative Party now had a majority with 76 seats. The candidates endorsing repeal had not fared brilliantly well – there was a mere 18 of them, compared with 47 Irish Whigs and 40 Tories. O'Connell, who became Lord Mayor of Dublin the following year, took the opportunity to reach out to the masses. The 1840s campaign was reminiscent of the popular mobilisation for emancipation in the 1820s. It possessed the now familiar hallmarks of the charismatic maestro – rousing oratory, widespread appeal, support of the clergy (Archbishop MacHale of Tuam was a notable member) and an atmosphere that was part political evangelisation, part street drama, wholly carnivalesque. Like the Catholic Association, it was a focused entity, with a clear mission and populist methods. O'Connell was superlatively good at stirring up the population and also, as we shall see, at controlling them. But he faced a British political establishment adamant not to concede repeal and determined not to be frightened into doing so.

Repeal of the Union was ostensibly a simple call, but it was not quite so straightforward a matter as the collocation might suggest. MacDonagh goes so far as to call it a 'paradigm of ambiguity in constitutional terms'.[7] What would it mean in practice? What did O'Connell believe it to entail? How conservative or radical an idea was it? Historians have debated the possibilities. Did it really mean a return to the *status quo ante* 1801? Some have put this forward quite strongly. Dudley Edwards sees him as harkening back to Grattan's 1782 experiment in parliamentary independence.[8] However, there are some problems with such an interpretation. A genuine return to the past was impossible and nobody knew it better than O'Connell – Catholic emancipation and Whig reforms had thoroughly reshaped the country. Half the judges, stipendiary magistrates and police inspectors appointed from 1835–41, for example, were Catholics.[9] A revived national assembly would inevitably have a new and a very different character to Grattan's gentrified and

Protestant parliament. What can be said in deference to both points is that O'Connell could play the card of traditionalism and restorative change when he wished. These were the cards to be played most effectively in Westminster. It also suited his conservative instincts. He was a devoted monarchist and could make the scheme sound reassuringly traditionalist. Repeal, he insisted, was not to be a prelude to social revolution: the Anglo–Irish connection would be maintained and indeed enhanced thereby. 'They say we want separation from England, but what I want is to prevent separation.'[10] So far, so conservative.

The most original interpretation of this conservatism is that of Boyce who claims that what we find in the 1840s is an example of a revived form of Irish Jacobitism. After all, who more devotedly loyal to the last of the Stuarts than the Catholic Irish in the Battle of the Boyne in 1690? In the 1840s, the phrase 'For God, Queen and Country' was a profession of loyalty that could be held by many without any seeming contradiction. Queen Victoria was reasonably popular.[11] A huge shift would occur in the coming decades, but, for now, loyalism did not sit awkwardly in the minds of many Catholics. In fact, so adamant was O'Connell to prove the point that he would make his listeners applaud Her Majesty's soldiers who were there at his meetings to supervise proceedings.

Yet the traditionalism of the repeal agenda must be heavily interrogated. O'Connell's wider vision of the United Kingdom was more radical, modern and even progressive than the above suggests. Daringly, he advocated three parliamentary institutions: one British, one Irish and one Imperial. This would solve the problem of necessary independence within a context of unity. Gladstone, decades later, would propose just such a solution to the constitutional problems vexing the British Isles in his Midlothian Campaign of 1879, suggesting further that Scotland and Wales should have their own representative institutions. If, in 1879, people were still not ready for that idea, it was far ahead of its time in 1841. Nevertheless, the originality of such a political idea is striking and indicative of the sophistication of O'Connell's political thought. Still more radical was the language O'Connell used when speaking to mass Irish audiences. 'My first object is to get Ireland for the Irish' he said to a mass meeting on 14 May 1843.[12] He spoke, in Galway, of a 'peasant cavalry' ready to be conducted in the 'peaceable battle' of 'law and national exertion'.[13] He fully expounded on the practical benefits of repeal for Irish manufacture, commerce and agriculture. There was no denying the far-reaching potential of such language, whatever the modesty of the actual objective. Besides, as MacDonagh shrewdly observes, the idea of restoration could mask 'perhaps even from himself the essential radicalism of his objectives'.[14] Isaac Butt, the future 'Home Ruler', said at the time that 'repeal was revolution'.[15] There is no doubt that some people, particularly Protestants, saw it so and, when a futile rebellion did break out in 1848 (which had nothing at all to do with repeal), it was nonetheless labelled as the Repealers' Revolution.

O'Connell's Tactics

A possible reading which might make sense of these ambiguities is to regard O'Connell as playing a sort of double game in this campaign. He was deliberately ambivalent, sometimes sounding conservative and at other times defiantly radical. He was, indeed, a master of ambivalence – so too, in a different way, were Parnell and de Valera, later leaders of the Irish cause. It is fair to say that ambivalence is a tool suitable for those who find themselves having to juggle widely different contexts. By this point, O'Connell had realised that flirtation with the Whigs had nothing substantial to offer and that the real strength of his hand lay outside Westminster and that, as Foster says, the 'trick was never to define what Repeal meant – or did not mean'.[16] With mass support, stirred by rousing rhetoric, what pressure might not be brought to bear on Westminster? It had worked, he knew, before on an unlikely government.

Even if it did not work to the desired end, it would be efficacious in securing some sort of reform. This is another possible interpretation of the whole campaign and perhaps more plausible, given O'Connell's political realism. The experiences in parliament in the 1830s taught him that repeal was highly unlikely in the current political climate. There was implacable opposition among all sectors of opinion in Parliament and Peel's position was very strong, ostensibly at least, after 1841. Furthermore, O'Connell's own was weak – his followers had now fallen to 19 MPs. He also knew that some middle-class Catholics were ambiguous about or even hostile towards repeal. Yet, he was determined to stir things up, saying in 1840 that 'if we get the justice we require, then our Repeal Association is at an end, but I know we will not get justice'.[17]

Mass Politics

O'Connell's reputation as a democratic innovator rests largely on his formidable ability to gather, mobilise and control massive crowds in public. The crowds that attended the association's monster meetings and paid their 'Repeal Rent' were peaceful for now, but numbers had their own potency. It is estimated that 3–4 million may have attended the meetings in this period, a much greater number than for the Chartist demonstrations, then active in Britain. The British government, preferring to count pockets, not heads, may have dismissed numbers as criteria for political rights, but it could not dismiss their power. Numbers were an argument in themselves. Put simply, the government had seen nothing on this scale before – it dwarfed the mass meetings that had been an intermittent phenomenon since the 1810s. It is estimated, for example, that there were 300,000 people at Castlebar, 350,000 at Roscommon, one million at Tara. So the O'Connell who presided over the repeal campaign of the 1840s should not be seen as a disappointed parliamentarian who, in losing touch in Westminster, sought refuge in popular politics, but rather as a canny tactician who used the very public repeal campaign as a 'mode of intimidating governments', indeed as a way of bargaining with them.[18] He might talk big in Ireland and call 1843 'the Repeal Year' but he would close with a lesser offer, if indeed a lesser offer was forthcoming. It was, in lawyers' parlance 'an invitation to treat'.[19]

The Clontarf Non-event

The repeal campaign left Peel in a real dilemma. It made his policy of benign neglect no longer an option. If he did nothing, the Orange Order (banned in the 1830s) might be stoked into life and there might conceivably be a civil war. So he announced a policy of coercion, passing the Irish Arms Bill in May 1843, allowing for increased recruitment. By October, 34,000 troops were stationed in Ireland, the largest number in 16 years. This was a potentially inflammatory situation. The showdown occurred in the decision to ban a final monster meeting, scheduled for 8 October in Clontarf, just to the north of Dublin. This would have been a dramatic set piece indeed, but true to his constitutional beliefs and showing a formidable level of control over the movement he had set up, O'Connell turned back the crowds who were already thronging into the city. They followed his lead and Clontarf was a non-event, perhaps the most spectacular non-event of the generation. This was brinkmanship of the highest order and, for the government, a 'damned close-run thing'.[20] With all his fastidious sense of legal niceties, O'Connell was on the right side of the brink, although just about. If he had gone ahead, Dublin Castle would have used the force it possessed and there may well have been violent eruptions.

Then the government over-reached itself. Truly worried at this level of mass mobilisation, it arrested O'Connell, his son John and some others on the charge of conspiracy. It was all deeply unfair and could indeed have been politically unwise, as O'Connell's status as popular hero was high. But it never became a *cause célèbre*, curiously enough, although he was sentenced in May 1844 to a year's imprisonment and a £2,000 fine. We may speculate as to the reasons why not. One might be that O'Connell's popularity had waned somewhat when he had cancelled the meeting at Clontarf. The movement was in disarray and remained confused as to the purpose and procedure, although this has been overemphasised. Secondly, one could suggest that it lacked the subversive undertone of the typical *cause célèbre*. It was not remotely rebellious to support O'Connell at this point. Nor was it a distinctively Irish cause any more: by sentencing him unjustly, the cause of *English* liberty and *English* justice were at stake. The House of Commons recognised this by giving him a standing ovation when he visited London between his trial and sentencing. Banquets and demonstrations were held in his honour in major English cities and finally, and most conclusively, the House of Lords vindicated him and caused him to be released from his admittedly rather mild imprisonment in September of that year. Ironically this erstwhile outsider, once blackballed by an exclusive London club, had become an establishment cause.

Historians have sometimes seen in this non-event the beginning of the decline of the repeal movement. This case has been somewhat overstated, as Foster notes.[21] Yet the incident does have significant implications, principally on O'Connell's status. It could be said that he was particularly unlucky. First, the campaign was clearly having no success in its aim, despite its impeccable constitutionalism and O'Connell's genuinely impressive control over a mass movement. But nor had O'Connell the advantage of emerging from the episode a martyr to the cause or, preferably, not emerging at all. If a long-term victim of corrupt English proceedings, his status would have been sanctified as heroism. As it was, he was left to suffer the indignity of political old age. After 1843, neither O'Connell nor his repeal movement would have quite the same momentum as before.

Interpreting the Repeal Movement

To say that the repeal campaign failed is to tell only part of the story. It was an important movement and its significance can be explained in four ways. Firstly and most importantly, according to Kevin Nowlan and Maurice O'Connell, there was distinction in the fact of its existence and *modus operandi*. It constitutes, in their words, 'the first effective expression of constitutional and moderate nationalism in nineteenth-century Ireland'.[22] Naturally its immediate effectiveness was limited, but it could be argued that it left an important pacific legacy which was taken up in subsequent decades in the Home Rule movement. Both were movements of the *via media* and both successfully managed to keep at bay the violence endemic to so many political expressions in nineteenth-century Ireland. Secondly, it was a fine exercise in crowd politics and proved to be an inspiration for groups like the

Chartists. This is a good antidote to the lazy view which sees the influence as all one way (from Britain to Ireland) rather than as reciprocal. As regards popular protest in the Victorian period, Irish movements had and, to some extent, retained the initiative. Thirdly, the repeal campaign fathered a rather wayward child in Young Ireland, professing a more vibrant nationalist creed. Lastly, although it never dislodged Peel's commitment to the Union, it did make him take the Irish Question seriously and seek to placate and reform, where the placatory might do good. Without the realities of a potentially unstable mass movement in Ireland, it could be argued that Peel may not have proposed the package of reforms that he proceeded to do in 1844. Paradoxically, O'Connell got more from Peel through enmity than he did from the Whigs through alliance. These latter two points must be considered in a separate chapter.[23]

Evaluation of O'Connell

O'Connell died in May 1847 on his way to Rome, having lived long enough to realise the impact of famine on his country. Already a dying man, he had made a moving speech on the subject in the Commons in February. It was a tragic end for a man who had been so buoyantly confident about Ireland's prospects for decades and who had done a great deal to put 'Justice for Ireland' on the British political map. How are we to sum up his contribution and evaluate his legacy? There are many points of contestation. His greatest achievements were undoubtedly political and the most unambiguous of them all was Catholic emancipation. Despite the caveats, it was truly a constitutional revolution. Through it, the Catholic Irish now had the capacity to make themselves heard by the political establishment. It was also a significant achievement in giving the Irish a taste of constitutional redress of their grievances within the context of Union. It heralded wider social, economic and political changes. In O'Ferrall's analysis, the manner of its achievement foreshadowed 'modern democratic parties in almost every respect'.[24] Insofar as O'Connell forced the hand of Wellington and Peel in passing this one piece of legislation, his reputation as a radical constitutional reformer rests secure.

After 1829, however, his success was much more debatable and restricted. He did not use his authority to unite his countrymen, he failed to achieve repeal of the Union and he failed to convince the government to act energetically at the outbreak of famine. There is a sense in which he cannot be held fully responsible for any of these things, but, nevertheless, the fact remains that after 1829 he becomes a much more problematic figure. There is even a sense in which his focus may have become too political.

There is a telling comment about the level of socioeconomic distress, elicited by a priest in the 1830s from an agrarian troublemaker who saw no solution to eviction and poverty other than actual resistance. 'To whom should we address ourselves?' the man said, 'Emancipation has done nothing for us. Mr O'Connell and the rich Catholics go to Parliament. We die of starvation just the same.'[25] Perhaps O'Connell had put too much faith in the enabling possibilities of emancipation. Perhaps also it was naive of him to believe that the simple restoration of a national parliament would solve Ireland's economic woes – he never worked through the economic question in any great depth.[26] His implacable enmity with Peel blinded him from being able to recognise that this leader may have done a better job managing the Famine than the Whigs, whom he always supported.[27] His stinging insults – whether calling Peel and Wellington 'filthy state apothecaries' or the English aristocracy 'pigs with soaped tails' – were extreme and unlikely to bring palliation to the often-poisonous nature of Anglo–Irish relations.[28] O'Connell both achieved and failed by being, essentially, a political animal.

In the long term, his political legacy was ambivalently received. Perhaps somewhat surprisingly for somebody who knew such popularity in his lifetime, his reputation in nineteenth- and twentieth-century Ireland was tremendously problematic. He turned out to be the most curious anomaly of all in the nationalist pantheon. Although a hagiography always existed around him among constitutionalists and Catholics, there was a very powerful school of thought that held him in disregard and even in scepticism. To the Young Ireland movement, which sprung up in the 1840s, and to subsequent militant nationalist organisations, to the Fenians and Sinn Féin and to the leaders of 1916, he was very much a *persona non grata*. He would appear to them as calculating and self-centred, his agenda as antiquated and redundant and his commitment to doing business with Westminster evidence of hateful compromise. His monarchism was embarrassing to later generations. In the celebrated and notorious words of Young Ireland, he was, after the British government, 'the worst enemy that the Irish people ever had'.[29]

Culturally, as well as politically, he was viewed with much disfavour by nationalists. He was accused, despite all his 'greenery' motifs, of being a covert Anglophile, although this case has been much overstated.[30] However, it must be said that he did coin the collocation 'West Briton', subsequently a term of derision for those of dubious national credentials. His support for the Empire soon looked to be treachery for some. He had assured the Commons in 1832 that 'the people of Ireland are ready to become a portion of the Empire, provided they be made so in reality and not in name alone; they are ready to become a kind of West Briton if made so in benefits and justice; but if not, we are Irishmen again'.[31] The whole smacked of too much fraternising with the enemy for later nationalists to stomach. Both philosophically and politically, he was far removed from such 'elevating' notions as blood sacrifice, having proclaimed that Ireland's fate was not worth blood-shedding. The nation was a legal, not a sacral, cause and the struggle must only happen at that level. Such pragmatism fit ill with later romantic nationalists. As the twentieth century progressed, however, his very lack of transcendence and his eschewal of physical force methods, having seemed so tame to generations of hot-blooded revolutionaries, looked newly attractive. That which the nationalist leader, Eoin MacNeill had dismissively labelled his 'ultra'[32] constitutionalism was a quality not to be despised. It was a rare achievement in itself. O'Connell's reputation was thus salvaged from the nationalist dustbin of history.

Another point of historiographical contestation lies in his usage of identity politics and whether or not he was more of a divisive than a uniting force in his country. There is no doubt but that he was perfectly at ease in his Irishness, with MacDonagh going so far as to say that '[b]eing Irish was merely being himself'.[33] The part he played was, in that sense, natural to him. But, again, his personal identity construction was also part of his sense of public theatre. The performance aspect of his self-presentation, although mocked by some contemporaries as vulgar, was crucial. He clearly enjoyed the display of the green silk handkerchiefs in 1829 and the symbolism of the twining shamrocks. He relished laying claim to old traditions of Gaelic leadership – he was the *Rí gan Choróin*, the Uncrowned King, in popular mythology. One could almost say that he was, if not the 'stage', at least the 'staged' Irishman of the day, conscious of being larger than life and at ease in the cult which built up around him. However, his autocratic streak may not have been entirely healthy and has been seen as helping to create a culture of 'boss' politics, especially among the Irish-Catholic diaspora to America.[34]

His identity politics have also been criticised for being superficial and unreflective. He may have worn green, but he did very little, it has been said, to restore a sense of cultural nationhood amongst the people of Ireland. By *not* endorsing such a sense, he may indeed have contributed to its decline. The romantic posture, as conceived especially by the Germans, was one which espoused the native language as the most precious treasure of a people, that which showed off the inherent character of the *Volk*. Famously, despite being a native speaker, O'Connell did not defend the cause of the Irish language. Nationalists deplored this, seeing him as influential in the catastrophic decline of the language in the nineteenth century. The proportion of monolingual Gaels fell from 50 per cent to a negligible 0.5 per cent in its course. Although to blame O'Connell solely would be to overstate his influence and although he did become patron of national historical and antiquarian associations, it does reveal something about his cheery cultural insouciance and even, as some would suggest, his utilitarianism. Irish was not a useful language for the social and political advancement of the Irish therefore, as far as he was concerned, it could die unmourned.[35] This would have been philistinism for the ardent romantic, wedded to ideals of the mother tongue and to lost or all-but-lost causes. In fact, with his lawyer's mental habits, Irishness seems to have been more about birth and residence, not about language nor, for that matter, religion.

Yet, ironically, it was he who did more than anything to identify the Irish cause with the Catholic cause. The achievement of emancipation in 1829 perhaps made this inevitable. But there was more to it than that. O'Connell's deliberate cultivation of the clergy brought a powerful force into Irish public life that would continue throughout the nineteenth century with its admixture of strengths and problems. He could not have foreseen all this but, nevertheless, the clericalisation of society came about, in part, as a result of his successful politicisation of this influential sector. Whilst few contemporary historians would agree with Reynolds that the priests 'controlled the Catholic population', their influence was highly disproportionate to their numbers and would increase throughout the nineteenth century.[36] It is possible, as O'Ferrall argues, that his own liberal Catholicism was 'compromised' by clerical dominance over his repeal movement.[37] Even more problematic was his failure to acknowledge the specific problems and issues faced by Ulster Protestants and his disregard for the seriousness of their opposition to repeal of the Union. Sectarianism was a fact of Irish life and, if O'Connell had not existed, it still would have put a wedge between the island's communities. Nevertheless, it is hard to avoid the ironic conclusion that this non-sectarian ideologue, so focused on achieving a fairer condition for Ireland, did help to exacerbate the politico-religious divide.

The last area of evaluation concerns the question of his modernity. How far was he an old-fashioned conservative and how far a modern innovator? There was much of the old about him. Religiously, after a fling with deism, he returned to the devout practice of traditional Catholicism. Politically, he harkened back to the parliamentary traditions of the 1700s and emphasised government by social contract based on legal rights. In that sense, he may be seen in lineal descent from the American revolutionaries and from Grattan. His kind of patriotism was in an eighteenth- rather than a nineteenth-century mode.[38] Boyce, as we have seen, sets him up as a revived Jacobite in the 1840s.[39] Ideologically, he was not in tune with voguish romanticism, nor yet with the new logic of industrialisation.

Yet, he was in other ways amongst the *avant-garde* of his generation. Four features in particular stand out: firstly, his political philosophy, secondly, his charismatic practice of public politics, thirdly, his espousal of all kinds of liberal causes and, lastly, his synthesis of Catholicism and liberalism. If O'Connell fits rather uncomfortably within mainstream nationalist tradition, he is much better situated, as Thomas Duddy in his *History of Irish Thought* (2002) makes clear, in the tradition of pragmatic Benthamism, emphasising as he did the principle of utility and greatest happiness of the greatest number.[40] Although this case for his theoretical coherence and consistency can be exaggerated, it is nonetheless vital in our understanding of the contemporary underpinnings of his political thought and his reformist aspirations.[41] A greater sensitivity to what K. Theodore Hoppen calls his 'complex and often profound' political ideology yields results.[42]

The second – and in some ways the most striking – sign of his modernity lies in his development of a new mode of charismatic politics. By this, he was doing something that the new contexts of the nineteenth century, with its growingly important transport networks and media coverage, newly enabled. A new sociology of leadership was emerging. O'Connell could be considered a kind of prototype of a plebiscitary democratic leader in what was still, in many ways, an age of oligarchy. Having won the favour of the masses, he was carried by them into Westminster; he distanced himself from them in the 1830s only to re-engage with them in the 1840s. He was a politician whose power was based on crowds. Hoppen sees a mixture of the contingent and the constructed at work: it was 'partly by accident partly by foresight and design' that 'he invented an entirely new form of politics'.[43] The man matched his context – this is a better explanation of success than attributing it to his political genius alone. Strikingly, his movements remained committed to the usage of moral force and did not ever resort to physical force, something of an achievement in a context where recourse to violence was rather more common than not. Does his success at public politics mean that he deserves a reputation as the 'greatest innovator in modern democratic politics'?[44] Is it fair to maintain, as Reynolds does, that in the first half of the nineteenth century the 'public life of Ireland revolved' around this one man?[45] Gladstone himself described O'Connell as 'the greatest popular leader whom the world has ever seen [...] who never for a moment changed his end [and] never hesitated to change his means'.[46] Superlatives are somewhat problematic, however. He was certainly one of the greats and the context proved particularly propitious. However, it might be averred that he over-concentrated on politics and political causes to the detriment of agrarian issues[47] and that, in his public performances, he lapsed into crude dichotomies and unsophisticated viewpoints which exacerbated the divisions between Britain and Ireland rather than smoothing them over.

He was also a man of his time in the sense of being a liberal of European stature. Take him, for one moment, out of a narrowly Irish context and an unambiguously progressive image of him emerges. In the history of popular protest, he provided inspiration for the radical Chartists in the 1840s. His methods also inspired the free-trade Anti-Corn Law League. He pursued his beliefs to their logical ends, by giving advice to the Jewish community after 1829 about how to secure their own emancipation, which they did in 1858. His opposition to slavery went as far as not accepting funds from US slave-owning states, a mark of unambiguous integrity. In the words of Bew, he became something of an 'international humanitarian'.[48] In these senses, he was certainly ahead of his time.

Lastly, his modernity is perceptible in his politically and socially engaged Catholicism. A devout believer from 1808 onwards, he ought to be read as part of the international liberal Catholic scene, which included Hugues-Félicité Lamennais, the French Dominican Jean-Baptiste Lacordaire, the Count of Montalembert and Giocchino Ventura. He offered, in his way, something of a synthesis between burgeoning liberalism and Roman Catholicism, a larger strand in the nineteenth century than is sometimes recognised.[49] Irish Catholicism is often accused of narrowness, parochialism, excessive conservatism and clericalism. O'Connell certainly does not deserve that criticism. European Catholics of a liberalising hue found him an interesting and significant figure and talked about him in their journalistic writings. And it looked as if things might be turning that way in the church when the conservative Pope Gregory XVI died in 1846 and Pope Pius IX, who began by being much more interested in this liberal synthesis, succeeded. Unfortunately, that was just before O'Connell, himself, died. He left his heart, fittingly, to Rome, not such an unromantic after all.

Chapter 7

THE AGE OF PEEL

Interpreting Young Ireland

Peel and O'Connell had been enemies since the 1810s. Yet, despite their very real differences, they held in common a belief in constitutionalism and in traditional monarchy which never wavered. A much clearer opposition may be seen between the hotly nationalistic Young Ireland movement, which sprung up in the 1840s, and both O'Connell and the Conservative prime minister. It is debatable how much Young Ireland owed to O'Connell and the repeal campaign. Foster claims that it was a 'splinter' of the repeal movement,[1] a self-consciously youthful splinter as its name suggests. Some would see the distinction between O'Connell and the Young Irelanders as that between pragmatism and principle – the latter 'kept the question of principle strictly in the foreground', writes Dudley Edwards.[2] The matter, however, is rather more nuanced. Born in the same context and supporting the same agenda, Young Ireland did adopt an ideological and culturally radical tone; soon it became tinged with combativeness. Publicity became an end in itself. Its principal organ was a newspaper, the *Nation*. Its leadership, Thomas Davis, John Blake Dillon and Charles Gavan Duffy were all of them lawyers with a keen nose for publicity. They were incurably verbal with a remarkable capacity for the kind of rhetoric that sold papers. Their extraordinary popularity is testified to by the fact that up to 250,000 people may have been reading the *Nation* in 1843.

Was it that Young Ireland had something new to say or just a new way of saying it? There was a mixture of the familiar and the novel in their agenda. Historians have often failed to observe that it was most unlike O'Connell's associations in that it was an evolutionary movement with no 'set' agenda from the start. Davis holds that it was not a 'clearly articulated movement'.[3] They, too, supported repeal, but they began to accuse O'Connell of selling out and agreeing to piecemeal reforms. They were more overtly non-denominational in their view of the nation and came to disagree with O'Connell's eschewal of violence at all costs. What was new, also, was the tone that set the Irish struggle in transcendent even rapturous terms, emphasising that a spiritual rebirth of the nation must be achieved through the sword, if necessary. Hilton also points to their heightened sense of cultural nationalism, shown by an emphasis on 'emotion and ethnicity'.[4] All this looked very different to O'Connellite rational pragmatism and much more like radical revolutionary nationalism, rather *völkisch* in the manner of the German romantics. Some scholars draw much from this distinction. MacDonagh sees it as 'probably the most fundamental of the great dichotomies of later Irish politics'[5] – the constitutionalists *versus* the revolutionaries. If so, the 1840s are a crucial decade in bringing both of these strands to the fore.

However, this view needs to be qualified. Foster shrewdly observes that, in 'many ways, the spirit of the *Nation* was as modern and utilitarian as O'Connell'.[6] They had more in common than would appear. Some of them were still conservatives at heart and most of them would not know what to do with any weapon other than a pen. There was an amount of posturing. Naturally, they did not see it that way and came to distance themselves from him and what they rather snobbishly called the 'Donnybrook Fair school of Irish patriotism', Donnybrook Fair being known for its uproarious, knockabout, drunken antics. They, by contrast, sought to 'spiritualise' the national struggle, even intellectualise it. They saw the nation as something organic, not primarily as a legal construct. It may be somewhat reductive but there is a sense in which the distinctions between O'Connell and the Young Irelanders were due to an inevitable generational gap. O'Connell was born in 1775 and, in some respects, remained in the eighteenth-century lawyer's mould. By contrast, Davis was born in 1814, Dillon and Duffy in 1816. Perhaps, also, it was a conflict of different sorts of public charisma. O'Connell's very presence was charismatic; their writing was compelling. He had hearers, they had readers.

For all that bound these youthful hotheads together, Young Ireland should not be regarded as a homogenous unit. Davis even has it that the divisions within were greater than those between Old and Young Ireland.[7] Lyons posits a distinction between the theoretical revolutionaries and the practical ones and between those who sought primarily political change and those whose focus was more on root-and-branch social and economic transformation.[8] It was the latter that began to take initiative under the influence of James Fintan Lalor in 1847. Believing that the Famine had transformed the situation completely, he urged that there be a general strike against rent. His views influenced John Mitchel, a radical Presbyterian solicitor. By this point, most northern Presbyterians had become, more or less, fervent Unionists – but not Mitchel.

He harkened back to the republican creed of 1798 and looked forward to a holy war against baleful British influence, stances that proved embarrassing to more moderate voices in the movement. After failing to make his point in the Irish Confederation (founded by Young Ireland in 1847), he branched out on his own, founding a weekly newspaper called the *United Irishman*. The language was extremely militant and the paper boasted articles on street fighting and pike drills. Although he adopted socially radical positions, a biographer notes that he could not be considered a true socialist because he focused more on an independent peasantry than on the urban proletariat.[9] He blamed the Famine on British misgovernment and looked to European example, something that recalled the international revolutionary mood of the 1790s more than the parochial focus of agrarian rebels.

Europe's revolutionary year was 1848 when, inspired by Paris, many cities boasted more or less serious revolts against the cosy *ancien régime*, as resettled in the Congress of Vienna, 1815. Mitchel's advocacy for 'spontaneous revolution' in Ireland did bear fruit, but spontaneity was no recipe for success. When the aborted rising did take place in July 1848, Mitchel was already in prison, convicted under the new Treason Felony Act. Instead, William Smith O'Brien, a Harrovian-Cantabrigian, was its unlikely leader and paid the price – sentenced to death and later commuted to life transportation.[10] The usual interpretation is that the rebellion was a shoot-out in a cabbage patch. More recently, however, Kinealy sought to argue that the conventional wisdom is misleading. She argues that revolutionary plotting was of major concern for the government, particularly because of the links with France, and that its leaders were 'brilliant' and their vision an 'inclusive' one.[11] Nevertheless, the fact remains that the revolution itself was very damp indeed. Yet, the potency of Mitchel's extremist rhetoric remained and in that laid its importance.

The Legacy of Young Ireland

Young Ireland was a movement whose words were more significant than their actions and whose legacy was far more important than their life. They were amongst the first political associations to put 'Celticism' to political use, to harness culture (especially language, literature, ethnicity and symbology) in the service of their agenda. Thomas Davis advocated a 'nationality of the spirit as well as of the letter' and F. S. L. Lyons, for one, admires the nobility of his ideals of cultural and non-sectarian Irishness.[12] More problematic is their allowance or even advocacy of violent means to secure their ends. For the more moderate amongst them, like Davis, this was merely an unwillingness to rule out physical force methods if necessary. For the more bellicose, like Mitchel, violence was a legitimate response to criminal British rule.

The criminalisation of England was central to his political theory; Lyons criticises him for his 'generalised concept of oppression to which he gave the name England'.[13] The third aspect of their legacy is their revival of the tradition of republicanism, dormant since Wolfe Tone's era. After this, there would always be some groups who believed that the only solution to Ireland's ills was complete independence.

Perhaps their most important legacy lay in their words. Their capacity to master the new media in the popular press was especially impressive. The very motto of the *Nation* was 'to create and foster public opinion, and make it racy of the soil'.[14] Many of their phrases, such as 'Ireland's right', 'educate that you may be free', 'a nation once again' became general currency. Anglophobic sentiments were also expressed and given greater legitimacy not only by the experience of famine but by Mitchel's fiery journalism and his subsequent writings, notably his bitter *Jail Journal*.[15] Could he be regarded as the 'unacceptable face of Irish nationalism'? Does the rot start with him?[16] It is a question well asked. It is certainly true to say that his bitterness of tone left its mark on nationalist political culture and proved to influence later leaders directly, such as Arthur Griffith and Patrick Pearse, both of whom saw themselves very firmly in the tradition of Young Ireland. Cultural nationalism, Anglophobia, popular sovereignty and separatism – one could thus conclude, as MacDonagh does, that, by 1850, the 'ideological infrastructure of modern Irish nationalism' was formed in its essentials.[17] Young Ireland had given it a new vocabulary.

Historiography of Peel

Robert Peel has been given good press in twentieth-century historiography. He is regarded as one of the very ablest prime ministers of the nineteenth century and the architect of the country's mid-Victorian boom. Norman Gash, the writer of his classic biography, sees him as the father of modern Conservatism and regards the 1830s and 1840s as his age. Gash brings to the fore his adaptable pragmatism especially in his forging of a connection between the landowners and the new urban middle classes. He comes across as a great consensus politician with an admirable flair for administration.[18] Looking 'not to programmes but to national expediency', he approached government with clear-sightedness and realism.[19] Hilton's Peel, by contrast, is a much more doctrinaire and inflexible type. He admits that he might have been politically pragmatic at times but that he held his ideas dogmatically and that, in a crisis, he tended to become more intransigent rather than compromising.[20] These broad interpretations have their role to play in understanding Peel's government over Ireland. The consensus view of historians on the subject is generally favourable; nevertheless, his motivations and assumptions present a more complex picture. Furthermore, the price he paid for his Irish reforms (the breaking-up of his own party) may well be questioned.

Motivations for Reforms

Peel's motivations for reform in the 1840s may be variously interpreted. Hilton's thesis about his liberal conversion has already been remarked upon.[21] In his celebrated Tamworth Manifesto of 1834, Peel announced that his party would henceforth carefully 'review [...] institutions, civil and ecclesiastical' as well as correct 'proved abuses' and redress 'real grievances'.[22] It is unlikely, however, that he would have acted without the weight of context. Faced with such stirring movements in Ireland early in the decade, Peel was astute enough to see that the British government could not rely upon 'mere force' to solve Irish ills and that concessions must be granted for the sake of stability. He may have talked boldly in May 1843 of the possibility of going to war over the maintenance of the Union. Much as he claimed to dislike the idea, he declared anything 'preferable to dismemberment of this empire'.[23] But he was not genuinely considering this except as a final resort and Clontarf showed him that there was no immediate danger of military confrontation.

Yet the repeal campaign was a warning sign and accordingly, in early 1844, he prepared a programme of reforms for cabinet consideration. All the sensitive matters were in evidence: the franchise, the land question, education and religion. Can we say that Peel's aims in all this were entirely pragmatic? He certainly does not appear to have had an imaginative vision of Ireland's future. When looking across the water, he saw only problems – he never saw Irish discontents in any other way than as, in Evans' words, a 'haemorrhage draining away the life blood of national prosperity'.[24] He was always supremely pessimistic about resolving the situation and confessed to rejecting coercive responses merely for fear that the 'instrument will break short in our hands'.[25] What he wanted to do was also negatively framed – he desired to break the 'formidable combination'[26] of O'Connell and the Catholic clergy, that potentially disruptive nexus of alternative power, flexing its muscles so very publicly in the repeal campaign.

Winning over the Clergy

His analysis of the Irish situation took into account – and perhaps exaggerated – the importance of the Catholic priesthood. Priests in Ireland were very much of the people – they were well loved and respected and it is true that they possessed much moral authority. Peel hoped to win over the clergy to the

British government and, in gaining their loyalty, get a greater hold over the people. Hilton regards this as an 'elegant' but problematic approach because it was based on rather naive assumptions – firstly, that the Irish were controlled by their clergy and, secondly, that clerical loyalty could be 'bought' so easily.[27]

Nevertheless, Peel brought about the Charitable Bequests Act of 1844 in the hopes of achieving those aims. Existing laws meant that Catholic testators could not be sure that their bequests went to Catholic institutions. The act changed all this, for the first time allowing Catholics to leave money and bequests to the church in their wills. Some bishops, notably MacHale of Tuam and Paul Cullen of Armagh, opposed the measure, but that was more because of internal clerical wrangling than principle – they disliked the Archbishop of Dublin, Daniel Murray, and dubbed him a 'Castle' Bishop. The MacHale faction, however, were reprimanded by Rome for their opposition. It was not unreasonable to suppose that the Bequests Act would have its effects. Although some of his assumptions were a little naive, they were not entirely so. Peel was already aware that the bishops and higher clergy, drawn from more socially elevated ranks than the humble priests, tended more towards establishment values. He was also aware that up to one-third of the bishops had not supported the Association for Repeal. He was convinced that, with a little graciousness, he could widen this gap and detach the 'priesthood' from the 'mob'. Even if he could not win them all over, at least he would try to depoliticise them – hence the overtures to Rome, extraordinary in their way, seeking a papal condemnation of priestly political activity. Rome issued a mild reproof to the clerics involved, not at all what Peel had hoped for.[28] That Peel's government went to this length shows just how seriously they regarded the question of clerical loyalties in Ireland. The attitude of the church mattered for the survival of the Union. One could say, of course, that he was uncannily right in this, as the clerical 'conversion' on the cause of independence in later decades would prove.

The Franchise and the Land Question

Some other Peelite projects met with little success. A franchise bill, seeking to scale back the £10 threshold to £5 (still not at its pre-1829 level of £2), failed at its first hurdle in the Commons. Of no immediate effect, but of long-term significance, was the establishment of a Royal Commission into Land (the Devon Commission) within weeks of the Clontarf episode. Peel chose commission members carefully, for the last thing he wished was to 'strike a fatal blow at property'. Heading the commission was a liberal Conservative, the Earl of Devon, and their instructions were to enquire into the state of land not to commit to reform. The ministry did not want to be compromised by reckless promises. O'Connell was convinced that the whole project was an empty 'bubble'. The commission reported in 1845 – a huge endeavour consisting of three volumes, a report and voluminous correspondence. The central point was that the landlord–tenant relationship was such that it impeded improvement and progress. It recommended legislation, although, in a cautiously optimistic tone, it did emphasise that improvements were already being made. The report was an official recognition that the land situation in Ireland was unique. Merely yoking the two countries together in a Union did not help to achieve parity. Now, at least, there was an awakening of consciousness.

However, it was a still-birth. A bill which would have compensated Irish tenants for improvements made to their holdings when they were evicted was dashed in 1845 and again in 1846 and was lost definitively upon the fall of Peel. There were too many vested British interests in Irish land, especially in the Lords, to countenance even a modest measure of change. The report's recommendations may have been adopted had circumstances been other, but the Great Famine intervened and brought everything to nought. Hilton, in fact, maintains that the commission and bill may have done 'more harm than good by raising false hopes that peasant proprietorship might shortly be on the agenda'.[29] The government actually lost more credibility in proposing reform and not delivering it than in not proposing it at all.

Maynooth Crisis 1845

The most controversial aspects of Peel's Irish programme were those dealing with education, both lay and clerical. This brought together issues of control, funding and curriculum, as well as treading on the sensitive issues surrounding the established church. As regards lay education, he passed the Provincial Academical Colleges Act in 1845, which established non-denominational colleges in Belfast, Cork and Galway. This was clearly an attempt to open up university education to non-traditional, that is to say non-Anglican, sectors. Belfast was targeted at the Ulster Presbyterians, the other two would cater more for Catholics. The Houses of Parliament passed this readily, but the Catholic hierarchy objected to the lack of academic chairs in theology and philosophy. O'Connell snorted that the new institutions were 'godless colleges',[30] although this was partly because he was likely to oppose Peel anyway, thinking ahead to a possible Whig succession. In any case, it appeared that Peel could not win. The Irish university question moved thereafter on three tracks as F. S. L. Lyons describes.[31] Trinity College Dublin still served, as ever, the Anglo-Irish elite. The Queen's Colleges, Peel's ventures, stumbled along, with Belfast proving to be the most successful. Finally, the Catholic

University of Ireland was set up in 1854, showing just how little Peel's educational reform had satisfied that increasingly vocal middle-class sector. That Archbishop Paul Cullen of Dublin managed to secure that doyen of Anglican converts John Henry Newman for its first rector, only adds to the irony.[32] University education remained denominational, despite Peel.

Funding for clerical education was the most controversial issue, however. Historically, the Irish-Catholic clerical elite had been educated abroad: after the Reformation, Irish colleges had sprung up across the continent. As part of the policy of *détente* in the 1790s and as a consequence of anti-clerical disruptions in revolutionary Europe, the Irish parliament had set up Maynooth College outside Dublin as a seminary for Catholic priests. Westminster quietly granted it a yearly grant of £9,000 from 1808 onwards as a gesture of good will. The college's financial difficulty in the 1840s was Peel's opportunity. He would raise the grant to £26,000 per annum and give the institution a one-off grant of £30,000 for new buildings.

His logic was straightforward and pragmatic. It is perhaps a little too crude to say that he wished to buy the loyalty of Irish priests, but he certainly hoped to foster a disposition among clerics and the hierarchy that the British government was their friend and protector and that it was in their interest to support the Union. From his position, what he had observed in the Catholic Association and again in the repeal movement was a priesthood 'embittered rather than conciliated' and far too much concerned with the lower orders. Let them be placidly middle class. He sought to detach from the cause of repeal and 'agitation and disaffection a considerable portion of the respectable and influential Roman Catholic population', and that meant, first and foremost, the priests.[33] There were no strings attached, no effort to extend government control over clerical appointments – the measure relied on the expected gratitude of the Irish clerical caste. It was a bold move.

The problem lay not in Ireland this time, where the act was welcomed, but rather in Britain, most especially among members of Peel's own party. His rebranding of the party in the 1830s in the direction of a moderate Conservatism, or pragmatic progressivism as it has been called, did no more than temporarily conceal the deep divisions between old-style Tories, reactionary gentry for the most part, and newer-style Conservatives. The Maynooth crisis showed how deep these divisions were. For the Tory core, most of them backbenchers, any concession to Roman Catholicism was un-English, immoral and a body blow to the establishment of church and throne. For evangelicals, too, it was unacceptable. It was also a matter of money: Sir Richard Inglis criticised him for funding the Church of Rome out of the pocket of British taxpayers. The feeling was wider than mere party, of course, and Hilton suggests that perhaps 'as many as one in twenty of the entire population of Britain and Ireland registered opposition'.[34] The *Times* accused him of forcing 'Romanism' on the nation. Even people who had supported the 'grace and favour' donation before 1845 objected to the fact that it was now made into official yearly funding.

In this case, the old cliché that Ireland was the graveyard for British politicians has some truth in it – the High Tories felt that Peel had betrayed them twice, once in 1829 over emancipation and now in 1845 over Maynooth. They were now baying for blood. Despite their opposition, the measure passed, with Whigs and Irish all voting for it. But the Tory Party was horribly divided – on the second reading, 159 voted for and 147 against; by the time of the third reading, 149 were against and 148 for. Truly it was a party 'shivered and angry', as Sir James Graham, the home secretary, reported in the aftermath of the legislation.[35] Irish issues exacerbated British divisions. Imperial and colonial fates were inextricably linked.

Peel's arrogance waxed high and he wrote to his wife dismissing the vacuous opinions of those 'who spend their time in hunting and shooting and eating and drinking' and who presumed to know better than those (like himself) with the best access to information and with responsibility for 'public security' very much at heart. After 1845, his position was supremely vulnerable. Peel's reputation as an Irish reformer cost him his reputation in his party. Hilton maintains that Peel regarded this as a price worth paying.[36] However, having become so convinced of the necessity of reform, he perhaps had not read the signs of implacable opposition early enough and found himself embroiled much more so than he had envisaged. The Maynooth crisis thus brings out very well the fraught contexts in which Irish problems were enmeshed after the Union and it shows the dilemma facing generations of British politicians in having to appease their own parties and constituents as well as adopt what they felt to be the appropriate legislative solution for Ireland.

Enter Gladstone

There is one further point to be made – the issue was a 'Rubicon' (the word is Foster's)[37] not merely for Peel, but also one for a young, able Tory, William Ewart Gladstone, whose very practical efforts at the Board of Trade could not dull his keen nose for religious affairs. His beliefs were High Anglican as evidenced by his book, *The State in its Relations to the Church* in 1838, followed two years later by *Church Principles Considered in their Results*. Believing that the state had a primary duty to maintain Anglican Christianity, he presented his case in a very old-fashioned and reactionary way. Peel threw his eyes to heaven at this, thinking it a possible ruination of the young man's career. Indeed, he had precisely appointed the awkward but talented young man to the Board of Trade as an antidote to high theocracy. But the Maynooth crisis awoke the young man's conscience and made it impossible for one of such sensitive theological disposition to carry on. In a somewhat tortured but quite typical way, he resigned from the cabinet over the issue but voted with Peel, thus satisfying the needs both of moral conscience and party loyalty. Afterwards, he planned a tour of Ireland to study the problems more closely – family circumstances arose to prevent this and it would be many decades yet before he would cross the sea.

It is, in retrospect, fitting that Gladstone should emerge in a dramatic way in the context of an Irish issue. Nobody would have imagined from the seeming inflexibility of his beliefs that his first major act on becoming prime minister in 1868–69 would be to disestablish the Church of Ireland. From high-establishment values to disestablishmentarianism, there was quite a road to travel. And yet, as Hilton forcefully notes, the 1840s were a crucible for his future development. Peel, in putting a 'moral energy at the centre of the state', may be seen as a 'progenitor of Gladstonian liberalism'.[38] Hilton focuses on the economy, but it is not difficult to see how this could be true, in part, as regards the Irish Question. Gladstone's Irish mission owes something to his political father, as will be seen.

Ireland and the Repeal of the Corn Laws 1846

We shall have occasion to consider Peel's response to the Famine at a later point. Here it is important to note that it served as an occasion for the great parliamentary drama that dominated the first half of 1846 – the repeal of the protectionist Corn Laws. It certainly explains the timing. It was just when reports of the gravity of the subsistence crisis were filtering back to Westminster in autumn 1845 that Peel presented his four cabinet memoranda on the issue. At first he proposed suspending the laws by order in council, thus obviating the need for parliamentary debate. By early December, he was determined to push ahead with the gradual abolition of the laws, despite the controversy that it was already awakening among his party. There is no doubt that Ireland provided a convenient background for repeal. It was possible to play the empathetic card and to say that, in removing these laws, one was making bread cheaper and thus more accessible to a starving people.

However, it is hard not to avoid Hilton's conclusion that Ireland was a 'red herring'.[39] Other motivations were stronger. If Ireland had been the only reason, he might have chosen to suspend the operation of the laws for the duration of the Famine rather than phase them out over three years.[40] As it was, he had come around to the position that the future lay in free trade and that the laws were a shibboleth which had long ceased being either prudent or practicable. Peel's own summation of the role played by Ireland in his motivations is, on the whole, fair. 'I do not rest my support of this bill merely upon the temporary ground of scarcity in Ireland, but I believe that scarcity left no alternative to us but to undertake the consideration of this question'.[41] In short, the Famine provided the pretext for the immediate passing of the bill. The repeal of the Corn Laws was the issue that crushed Peel's career and broke the party definitively, but, as we have seen, he had already 'betrayed' his traditionalist backbenchers by his double *volte-face* and relations had been increasingly sour since 1843. The actual issue upon which Peel resigned in June 1846 was a proposal designed to deal with possible food riots. A 'blackguard' combination, as Wellington would have it, defeated him and thus another prime minister fell because of Ireland.

Evaluations of the Peel–O'Connell Era

It is entirely fitting that the era of Peel and O'Connell reached its end at a similar moment and ironically fitting that it should be in the context of Irish disaster. In late 1846, O'Connell had urged on the House of Commons an outlay of £40 million to 'ransack the world for food and buy it at any price'. His plea fell on deaf ears. He died in 1847, a tragically disappointed man as he watched 'his long decades of gargantuan political effort and achievement [...] turned to dust and ashes by a natural catastrophe'.[42] Peel died tragically and unexpectedly after a riding accident in 1850. Both had defined, in different ways, a new phase in their own countries and both could claim that they had brought about new departures in ways of doing politics. Both were acutely subject to the tides and eddies of public opinion and were aware of how, at times, it worked so much in their favour and, at other times, beat them back. Theatre is an appropriate image for nineteenth-century politics and the dynamic between these two men provided for much of the vibrant colour in late Hanoverian, early Victorian political culture. It could also be said that the very antagonism between them had led, despite itself, to a more constructive phase in Anglo–Irish relations. There is also a sense in which the whole period 1830–46, bizarrely, prefigured the future. MacDonagh describes it as 'a sort of matinée performance of 1880–1906'. Present are features like the mobilisation of 'the Irish masses, of the church-in-politics, of the avatar-leader and the leader lost, of the Liberal Alliance and killing Home Rule by kindness'.[43] The duo of Peel and O'Connell presaged that of Gladstone and Parnell.

An overall evaluation of Peel's proposed and actual reforms for Ireland must pay tribute to their reasonably constructive nature. Most would tend to congregate around this middle-way position. He was prepared to use the

Union, not as a battering ram to suppress dissent, but as a flexible instrument to alleviate or even fix Irish social ills. There was no easy solution, of course, and much of what he wanted to put in place was badgered by opposition from within and without. Moreover, his pessimism and his false assumptions were not conducive to a genuine understanding of the Irish situation. Yet, he laid out the principle of legislative change under the Act of Union more convincingly than any other prime minister since 1801 and, although aborted, he at least established the precedent of setting up a commission of enquiry into the land question. As regards his own aims, however, was he successful? Did he succeed in eroding that dangerous united Catholic front? Superficially, it would seem so. It is true that the Catholic united front presented in the early 1840s in the repeal campaign disintegrated. It is also true that some of the hierarchy, for now, became more firmly Unionist in sympathy and thus, as he would have it, well disposed. Yet, his strategy of dividing and conquering was only partially successful. Kerr emphasises these limitations when he says that the Irish-Catholic bishops would remain in a position to pressure the government in subsequent decades.[44]

The main charge that one could lay against the government in this period is a lack of openness and political imagination. This is the point behind Kerr's criticism that Peel was 'legislating *in vacuo*' as it were, without consulting those supposed to benefit.[45] These were measures coming from the 'outside' in – they were not perceived as Irish solutions. But perhaps the biggest failure of Peel's reforms has more to do with context than with the reforms themselves. No reform, undertaken in the short duration of a ministry, could have resolved the deep problems in Irish society, particularly in relation to land. There is an *avant le deluge* quality to the modest efforts made to improve Ireland before the catastrophe of the Famine, 1845–51. Like rearranging the deckchairs on the *Titanic*, they were ultimately exercises in futility.

Chapter 8

EXPLAINING THE FAMINE

The Arrival of Blight

The Great Famine is, by virtue of its catastrophic nature, guaranteed a central place in any account of modern Ireland. The narrative may be simply recounted. A warm summer in 1845 gave every sign that there would be a good harvest of potatoes that August. 'The doomed plant', wrote Fr Mathew in retrospect, 'bloomed in all the luxuriance of an abundant harvest.' Nobody reckoned on the appearance of a blight, *Phytophthora infestans*, which within months had destroyed three-quarters of that year's yield. Stores were quickly used up and the prospects for those dependent on the potato began to look bleak indeed. 1846 brought no improvement – the fungus throve in the mild moist climate. The realities became even bleaker as thousands succumbed to starvation and disease. In 1847, there was a small yield but in 1848–49, the blight struck again and the burden fell, heavier than before, on a debilitated population. This was a subsistence crisis on a catastrophic scale, leading to over a million excess deaths. The Ireland of 1851 was a much reduced place.

Famine as Heritage

The Famine's status as global calamity has been confirmed by the proliferation of 'places of memory' – Canada's Grosse Île in the St Lawrence River which acted as quarantine station for the thousands entering Quebec, the good ship Jeannie Johnston, the National Famine Monument in the shape of a sculpted coffin ship and the yearly Famine walk in May from Doolough to Louisburgh. The event still has the capacity to be political as witnessed by Tony Blair's apology in 1997 for the failures of the British government. It is the thesis of Pierre Nora in his important work on *Les Lieux de Mémoire* (1984) that history is written under the pressure of collective memory and that the subject itself is often confused with the national memory of it. It can be its own prisoner.[1] Few things are historiographically more challenging than writing about an episode for which collective memories are so fraught and so painful.

Historiography of Famine

Practically speaking, this episode presents the historian with a number of difficulties. First, it is morally repugnant to deny the extent of the trauma and the deep scars it left on Ireland and on the Anglo–Irish relationship. On the other hand, it is tempting for the historian to de-sensationalise the popular version with its accounts of unbearable Irish miseries and a criminally inept British response. It is certainly easier, in every circumstance, to take the event apart and study the economics, the administration or the sociology of the phenomenon. Yet, this is to fall short. As a foremost historian on the subject, Cormac Ó Gráda has written, there is still no definitive history on the Famine for this reason.[2] Perhaps there cannot be. It is difficult to describe the Famine in the totality of how it was experienced.

There is a certainly a most popular history of the Famine, that provided in Cecil Woodham-Smith's *The Great Hunger: Ireland 1845–1849* (1962). She clears the British of the accusation of genocide but not of other blame.[3] At its most extreme, the notion of genocide is raised and the Victorians take their place in the pantheon of imperial villains through the eras, whilst the Irish take theirs in the pantheon for colonial victims. A. J. P Taylor once claimed controversially that 'all Ireland was a Belsen'. The fact that the genocide claim has been made is, as Donnelly says, 'one measure of how radically mistaken were the actions and inactions of the politicians and administrators'.[4] It is a story which has had its supporters, often among Irish Americans. At the time of writing, it forms part of the Holocaust and genocide curriculum of the state of New Jersey.[5] We would do well to tread carefully, however. There was an undeniably important strand of British opinion which welcomed the Famine as a sort of providential purificatory process for the feckless Irish, but this, although morally abhorrent, is not the same as a campaign of systematic annihilation of a race.

But even the less extreme version of this narrative, which lays the blame heavily on the British government, has come under fire from revisionist historians for several reasons. First, it is seen as far too simplistic in its imputations of blame – another case of British-bashing by angry nationalists. There is also a rather derisive sense that this story is too full of wild oversimplifications, too full of embarrassingly over-emotional content to constitute real history. The myths need puncturing, and this would seem to have been the logic behind the history honours paper at University College

Dublin in 1963 which invited students to discuss the following essay title, 'The Great Hunger is a great novel'.[6] Revisionists see the traditional accounts as rather too presentist in that they risk judging past actions and inactions by the ever-supercilious standards of the present – another case of the enormous condescension of posterity. They stress, by contrast, that Britain could not have been prepared for such a disaster and some would even suggest that they did well, considering.

More positively, what revisionist historiography has done since the 1940s and '50s to the debates surrounding the Famine can be divided up in four ways. Firstly, they have significantly repositioned the debate and reframed the questions. Instead of concentrating on overall responsibility, they have focused on the surrounding structures and the administrative problems hampering any sort of response to a disaster of such magnitude. Secondly, such interpretations, whilst acknowledging the victim, studiously refuse to name the villains. On the contrary, theirs has been the task of empathising with the policymakers and the administrators of the day, overwhelmed as they undoubtedly were by the nature of the catastrophe. If their responses were timid and half-hearted, that was only to be expected in an age when it was not considered a moral responsibility of the state to intervene in the economy in a time of crisis. If adjudged lacking by the perspective of more recent times, they cannot be judged so by the standards of their own. They were prisoners of their systems not stage villains.

Thirdly, revisionists have sought to remove the event from its sacral place in the history of world victimhood. This may be necessary in some ways, because, as noted above, the episode's transcendent status does, at times, detract from understanding it historically. They have sought to de-emphasise its uniqueness by placing it in national and international contexts. It was not the first potato famine of the century in Ireland – there were 14 episodes of varying degrees of severity between the years 1816 and 1842. There were also potato famines that took place contemporaneously, in Scotland and Belgium for example.[7] Against this, one may say that this episode was distinct both for its geographical extent and its temporal duration, that is to say, it affected the entire country – albeit to different degrees – and it lasted over four years. Nevertheless, it is important to see the Famine in context.

Fourthly, revisionists have queried the way in which the Famine is seen as the great turning point of the nineteenth century. Undercutting the usual story of the Famine being the *fons et origo* of subsequent socioeconomic realities, they have presented a picture of much more underlying continuity, seeing the episode as a catalyst for existing sociocultural trends such as emigration. From an economic point of view (and much of the fine revisionist work has been economic) some historians like L. M. Cullen maintain that 1815, not 1845, represents the key transitional moment.[8] Part of the claim here is that the transition from tillage to pasture, which was often attributed to the Famine, began at the ending of the Napoleonic Wars. The influx of foreign grain into Britain brought about a decline in Irish grain exports and thus promoted a change in the habits of agriculture.

Much excellent work has been produced along these and other lines. In social and economic terms, we have a much clearer picture of the complex realities governing Irish life and a surer grasp of population, marriage, health, agriculture, social mores and emigration before and after the Great Famine. Nevertheless, it is an approach which is not without its own problems. A post-revisionist generation, with all the welter of information provided by the revisionists but no necessary axe to grind against particular modes of understanding the past, is more comfortable raising them. The first problem is the tendency to present a rather bloodless account of the event as if it were merely an administrative hiccup. Somehow it is safer to write about administration than to write about communal emotions and experienced disasters. It may, of course, be ventured that professional historians are not, traditionally, very good at writing about emotions or about trauma, because of a lurking von Rankean belief that history is only 'history' with the drama left out. But one cannot merely write a de-traumatised history of such an episode without undermining the event as it was experienced. The most extensive work on the subject is an example of this. Commissioned by Éamon de Valera in the 1940s, to commemorate the centenary, *The Great Famine* (1956), edited by Owen Dudley Edwards and T. D. Williams, represented a significant advance in historical reconstruction. And yet, there was something a little lacking and it was revealed, for example, in the helpless comment in the book's foreword about the number of casualties: '[W]hat is certain is that many, many died'.[9] It all falls rather flat. Perhaps something of this criticism was apprehended by Dudley Edwards, himself, who noted in his academic diary that there was a danger of writing a 'dehydrated history' of the Famine.[10]

This problem has been raised, notably, by Brendan Bradshaw in his general critique of revisionism.[11] For him, the attempt to cerebralise and deny the trauma is not an especially helpful one for a number of reasons. Firstly, it is reductive – a history without a real recognition of the ordeal which was the Famine and a genuine intellectual engagement with it is inadequate.[12] Secondly, it makes a virtue of the clinical and is at its most lame when treating the extent of the tragedy. From the point of view of the history of ideas, it may also be a problematic approach because it fails to do justice to the immense impact that the episode had on 'the communal memory [that] retains a keen sense of the tragic dimension of national history'.[13]

Bradshaw is not the only one to point out the limitations of revisionist historiography in treating of this subject. Cormac Ó Gráda concurs when he describes that a central shortcoming of the Dudley Edwards and Williams volume, is the way in which it is confined to telling the account 'of the politician, the poor law administrator, those who controlled passenger movements, and the medical practitioner'.[14] Only in rare moments does one gets a 'true sense of what the tragedy was like for those on the receiving end'.[15] He also questions its claim to being apolitical. As revisionism aims to undercut all grievance narratives, the matter is approached with some bias, just as problematic in its way as those politicised traditional narratives which take British guilt for granted.

His most powerful accusation is a weighty one. It is that the revisionists have refused to take seriously the lines of enquiry proposed by the celebrated Indian economist and Nobel Prize winner Amartya Sen in his seminal study, *Poverty and Famines*, of 1981. Sen makes a distinction between people 'not *having* enough food to eat' and 'there *being* not enough food to eat'.[16] The distinction is a critical one because, whilst the latter is a simple story of scarcity, the former is about entitlement or lack thereof. Based on the former, the tragic paradox of famines emerges; although there is sufficient food in the country, people still starve because it is not available to them. They are, in short, not entitled to it and the question then becomes why not? For Sen, famine is not an inevitable tragedy, but an avoidable one. The causes of the Great Famine may be much more systemic than revisionists have liked to portray. An already established political-economic system severely disadvantaged Irish inhabitants, not just short-term policies – something that is worth bearing in mind in the narrative which follows.

Beyond Malthus

To explain why famine occurred when it did entails examining population, land ownership, agricultural usages and eating habits. According to the then fashionable theories of Malthusian catastrophe, the Famine was an inevitable result of population outpacing agricultural growth. Famine provided a sort of check on growth, a necessary – if ugly – outcome that could have been predicted in advance and avoided altogether if the birth rate had been lower. Malthus's deterministic theory is no longer seen as a powerful explanatory tool for understanding the causes, however. It has a superficial plausibility, yet it is too glib. However, agriculture and population growth are all involved at some level and any understanding of the causes must take their interconnections into account.

Agriculture

The system of land tenure in Ireland which developed over several centuries of British rule and plantation had a number of features which were to prove deeply problematic. Ownership of land belonged mainly to the Protestant elite, although that, as we have seen, was a diverse body. Although it would be a mistake to subscribe to the cliché that all major landlords were absentee, it is true to say that some of them were for much of the year and thus that a model of mutually supportive landlord–tenant relationships did not develop as it had done in England. This had profound consequences. The socioeconomic hierarchies in rural areas were largely unmediated by personal connections that often built up around the Great House across the sea. There was a very real sense of alienation from the landowners' religion and customs. The system also permitted corrupt middle-men and estate agents to flourish. This did not bode well for a time of crisis.

That said, agriculture was not in a universally bad way in the pre-Famine decades. The traditional story presented it very much in a state of terminal decline, but, as Ó Tuathaigh observed, actual output consistently increased in the 50 years preceding 1845.[17] Produce was fetching very good prices on the British market and the years of the revolutionary and Napoleonic Wars proved something of a boom time for farmers. Agriculture was also diversifying – the dairy and tillage sectors were both expanding and exports of pigs and pig meat notably increased. In short, the picture was, ostensibly, a healthy one. But, crucially, the profits were not evenly spread and neither was the diversification universal. Landlords certainly made gains in the period, partly from the boom and partly from higher rents. Tenant farmers also made gains and with increased profits went higher living standards especially in places like Munster and Leinster. The higher rents, however, made some inroads into their profits. Moreover, landlords were suddenly less keen to grant long leases when so much more money could be made from short-term tenants. So this had an unsettling effect. Then there was the negative impact of the international situation of peace. The year 1815 brought an end to the easy times and the value of grain exports fell by 50 per cent.[18]

The real problems, however, lay further down the hierarchy. Population growth meant high competition for land. It meant dividing and subdividing holdings until they were very tiny indeed. The cottiers, an important subgroup, rented their modest plots of one to five acres from the tenant farmers. These accounted for 24 per cent of the land holdings in the country. There was a far higher concentration of these poor cottiers in the west, a region well known for its barrenness. By contrast, they were least in evidence in the more prosperous east of the country. Needless to say, the cottiers did not benefit in the least from the thriving agricultural sector. It was quite a grim picture for them. Rising prices and rents often meant having to sell the family cow, which meant that they could not manure the potato patch for themselves, nor could they sell a calf or make butter or buttermilk. They were a very vulnerable class of people.

Nor did the million or so landless labourers fare any better. Their situation was, if anything, worse. They worked on the farms, especially in the labour-intensive sector of tillage. They may just have been able to scrape a small patch of land. Daly puts an account of their condition in very stark terms: '[i]f we assume £5 as the cost of a cabin, turf, garden and an acre of unmanured potato ground, the labourer would have to work for 200 days at the higher rate [6d a day] or a virtually impossible 300 days at the lower rate to pay the rent.'[19] Unsurprisingly, many migrated to England for seasonal work.

Population

A precariously balanced society such as this was also a growing one. The Irish were proving very fecund. The classic theory about demography and famine is K. H. Connell's 1950 study, *The Population of Ireland, 1750–1845*. According to his thesis, falling marriage ages led to more births.[20] This is not an altogether unproblematic story as more recent research has shown. First, there was much more regional variation in population growth than is suggested by the general theory of increase. Secondly, the evidence of early marriage patterns is quite anecdotal and fails to reveal a truly representative picture. It has been suggested that average marriage ages were actually rising from 1800 to 1841 so that, by the latter date, women were 26 and men 29.9 when married.[21] Nevertheless, it is indubitable that the population *was* growing – estimates put it at 4.8 million in 1791 and 8.1 million in 1841.[22] Various other interpretations have been suggested. Daly contends that large families were welcomed because children 'cost little to rear',[23] and, one might add, there was a certain absence of middle-class aspirations which might have limited family size. One might also impute to them Christian beliefs in the value of a large family. It has also been suggested that the death rate was declining in this period. This, if true, was not dramatic and average lifespans remained comparable with elsewhere – 37/38 years.[24] If one lived past the difficult first year of life, one was likely to reach 50.

The Potato

The fundamental fact about these millions of people was that their diet relied heavily on a single crop – the potato. It is plausible that reliance on this crop facilitated reasonably early marriage and raising a large family. The potato, indeed, was an ideal crop for wet and poor lands. It was also a highly economic use of the land available, providing the maximum amount of feeding on the minimum amount of soil. It suited insecure cottiers to grow such a crop – if one were evicted tomorrow, there was no point diversifying. Furthermore, the Irish poor had intuitively discovered what modern science has subsequently proved – the humble potato was an exceptionally nourishing food, in fact the 'only single cheap food that can support life as a sole diet'.[25] The oft-quoted fact that Irish recruits were valued in the British Army because they were taller than their counterparts across the Irish Sea has been attributed to a healthy daily diet of potato (12–14 lbs), supplemented by milk, oatmeal and fish.[26] If the potato was a success story in the sense that it enabled large and poor families to survive off bad land that they rented for high prices, in what lay the problem? The answer is over-reliance. By 1845, potato acreage had reached 2 million. Although the better-off farmers maintained a balanced diet of grain, milk, butter and meat, the diet of cottiers and labourers was very restricted and the rhyme, *Prátaí ar maidin, Prátaí um nóin, Is dá n-éiróinn istoíche, Prátaí a gheobhainn*, was likely to have rung true for many of them.[27] There was no possibility of escape for these people in the event of the failure of the crop. Famines had happened before but a crisis on the scale of 1845 was, in the way of these things, unthinkable until it was upon them. The wet summer of '45 swept everything away.

Chapter 9

RESPONSE TO FAMINE

Interpretations

It is conventional in the historiography to distinguish two broad phases of response to the Famine – that over which the Conservative Party presided and the period from 1846–52 in which the Whigs were in government. Peel's response is generally viewed favourably by historians, albeit with caveats. Kinealy notes that he was constricted by his assumption of Irish exaggeration and his conviction that the crisis would be short lived.[1] Still, he has generally got off relatively lightly. The Whigs' period in office under the premiership of John Russell is, by contrast, often viewed with some disfavour.[2] Russell was a believer in the necessity of modernising Ireland in the long term and is accused of having his eyes too much on the distant scene. The passivity of his comment that 'some kind of hope may be entertained that some ten or twelve years hence the country will [...] be in a far better state' shows a certain lack of urgency, a certain lassitude which did not bode well for those who were in dire straits.[3]

However, instead of regarding the Whigs as the simple villains of the piece, it is necessary to give much more attention to the complexity of their attitudes and to the importance of the civil service as well as the politicians in determining the nature and limitations of the response. It has been a fairly recent development in historiography to consider the systemic and structural flaws of an economic mindset that refused to interfere in the market even in such exceptional circumstances as there were in Ireland. David Nally, for instance, insists that the 'violence of hunger' is not accidental but systemic, that it can result from colonial policies, corporate food control and market crises.[4] This is in keeping with the fine work on the nature and aetiology of famines done by Amartya Sen.[5] So the overly complacent revisionist account of fair effort overwhelmed by circumstances appears increasingly dented. Besides, the differences between the two regimes, Tory and Whig, may be exaggerated. Although the context was more dire by the time the Whigs took over in 1847, can it be truly said that Peel had a different mindset about Ireland, that he would have laid to one side his dogmas about political economy and gone all out in an effort to save lives? David Nally observes that Peel's economic thinking would be the 'decisive force in shaping the direction of relief', thus seeing a continuity between Peel's and Russell's policies.[6] Perhaps it might be averred that Peel, who had more political talent than his successor, might have been more adaptable, but what he would have done had he remained in power is in the realm of the counter-factual.

Peel's Response

There were three main directions in Peel's response to the news of the failure of the potato crop. The first was designed to be a short-term boost. Immediately upon hearing reports, he undertook to buy £100,000 worth of Indian maize from America. Its source was kept quiet so that it would not set a precedent of massive state intervention and thus discourage local effort. Food depots were set up in three of the four provinces (not in Ulster). Although a commendable gesture, it did not have quite the desired effect as the maize was difficult to process and, if eaten uncooked, only exacerbated diarrhoea and dysentery. Its recipients showed forgivable thanklessness by calling it 'Peel's brimstone'.

Secondly, Peel's government turned to the landlords in the expectation that they would make the most major contribution to resolving the crisis. This was entirely in keeping with government practices of *laissez-faire* economics and reliance on traditional mechanisms of socioeconomic control. The landed elite had the biggest stake in the country and, accordingly, stood to lose most from a crisis if it spiralled out of control. Peel, that least paternalist of Tories in some ways (he had clashed, memorably, with Lord Ashley over factory reform in 1843), was now advocating landlord paternalism on a large scale. This principle represented governmental consensus – Irish property must support Irish poverty. They must take ownership of the problem. It was with this in mind that the government endorsed the creation of local relief committees and by the summer of 1846 they numbered 650. They were the 'eyes and ears' of the government, active in collecting information and funds, in reporting back on the various problems arising and in making suggestions for what needed to be done. Not all of them were quite so proactive – the poorer areas of the country were ill-served and, sometimes, not served at all.

Thirdly, it was Peel's conviction that the Irish could work themselves out of the crisis. The Irish Board of Works, which had been created in 1831, was given the task of providing employment for the destitute able-bodied. A grant from the Consolidated Fund covered half the expenses of each scheme; the other half was to be paid by the local landlord. This was the logic of self-reliance at work again; Peel did not want the crisis to become an excuse for over-dependence. Thus, between the autumns of 1846 and 1847, a daily average of 100,000 men were being employed on public schemes. The idea was definitely commendable, but the schemes were riddled with problems from the start. The huge numbers involved were difficult to organise and feed and, moreover, there was a distinct lack of national coordination, which meant that much-needed schemes were neglected and unnecessary schemes put through. There were roads which led nowhere and improvements made to unimportant piers and harbours – dispiriting and fruitless labour that did not contribute to the betterment of the economy. It was all rather redundant. It is odd, given their belief in the importance of landowners, that they did not ensure their co-operation in such schemes by making it profitable for them. There seems to have been a general unwillingness to interfere in ways that were not strictly necessary – they believed that the landlords ought to feel moral compunction and ought not need financial incentive. Yet, greater imagination here may well have improved the functioning of the schemes. Ó Tuathaigh speculates that '[h]ad the poor rate been devoted to schemes aimed at improving the productivity of the land the land-owners would not perhaps have been quite so parsimonious'.[7] The schemes were, in effect, politically cosmetic but, in reality, *culs-de-sac*.

Despite these drawbacks, Peel's response to the Famine has generally been cautiously commended by historians. At least, as has often been noted, nobody actually died from starvation in 1845–46. However, there are two caveats to this. Firstly, the blight of the first year did not affect the whole country and, secondly, people survived the first year because there were some food reserves. Death consequent of starvation, debilitation or illness was only a matter of time. The number of the destitute had risen worryingly to 750,000 in late 1846. By the time the harvest that year had revealed the grim truth, Peel was out of office and John Russell's Whig government was in.

The Whig Response

The Whig government has received serious criticism for their handling of this crisis, but that, as we have established, might be a function of the fact that they were in power during the worst phase of it. Russell had long been interested in Ireland and, as home secretary under Melbourne's administration 1835–41, he had sought to speak the 'language of conciliation' and reach out to the Catholics. Neither his talents nor his cabinet proved equal to the task of governing effectively in such a crisis, however. Charles Wood, Russell's chancellor of the exchequer, was an unhelpfully timid figure as regards the economy and his horror of deficit financing made him loathe to spend more on relief in Ireland than could be helped. Saving the British taxpayer was a more pressing aim than saving the Irish peasant. What the situation needed was some bold, imaginative handling. It did not get any. Just as important as the actual politicians were the civil servants upon whose views, competencies or, indeed, incompetencies the administration of the relief effort would rest. In fact, this episode casts a somewhat unholy light on these people, who, although often overlooked, were utterly vital in the formulation of policy. So much of what we consider policy was dictated by administrative needs and attitudes. Thus Whitehall, as well as Westminster, is a crucial context for any consideration of the Irish Question and nowhere more strikingly than during the Famine years.

The spotlight falls on Sir Charles Trevelyan, assistant secretary to the Treasury. His dominance had predated the Famine and would continue until 1859. 'No civil servant', claims his biographer, 'did more to place the Treasury in its modern role of watchdog of the whole of the civil service'.[8] His gods were political economy, cheap government and retrenchment. Although recognised as one of the architects of the mid-Victorian boom in Britain, his particular role in administering relief policies in Ireland would be highly problematic. The third 'wing' of the response emerged from the administration at Dublin Castle. Lord Bessborough was the first resident Irish landlord to be appointed to the job of Lord Lieutenant for a long time. He urged the government for more intervention, but in vain. His death in 1847 saw the post taken by Lord Clarendon. A member of the Political Economy Club, Clarendon was committed to *laissez-faire*, but not blindly so; he saw the need for intervention and chaffed against what he called 'harsh Trevelyanism'.[9] Nevertheless, he shared the conventional view that the Celt's native laziness was a contributory cause of disaster – the idle fellow would 'sooner starve [...] than prosper by industry'.[10] Such attitudes reflect the widespread establishment view that the Famine was an inevitable and even a divine visitation on a superstitious and feckless people.

Russell's Early Decisions

The Russell government got off to a poor start. A surprising decision was taken in August 1846 to close most of the food depots. By December, they were opening up again in the impoverished country west of the River Shannon. What few there remained in these autumn months sold food at increasingly high prices – in Cork, for example, a tonne of Indian meal cost £11 in September and £17–18 in October. A delay in its arrival in the bad winter that year caused further suffering. Meanwhile, corrupt practices of profiteering among importers and dealers created something of a scandal. The obvious question is why, in such exceptional circumstances, the government refused to regulate the market and control prices. It is important to realise that their decision was a principled and considered one. It is not too much to aver that *laissez-faire* economic liberals of the day believed in the sacral nature of the market and that any interference would be deeply harmful and indeed counter-productive. The most striking example of this was a decision taken in 1846 to allow exports of grain from Ireland to continue in the teeth of massive subsistence crisis. These were perhaps the most infamous moments of the whole famine, when hungry hoards of people watched shiploads of grain leaving port. Trevelyan's words indicate that this was no accident. He could see no possible short- or long-term justification for interference in the market. 'The discouragement and feeling of insecurity to the [grain] trade from such a proceeding would prevent its doing any *immediate* good; and there cannot be a doubt that it would inflict a permanent injury on the country'.[11] The raw dictates of the market he saw as 'blessings in disguise'.[12] Entitlement to food was secondary to the moral imperative of the market. Thus, for the sake of the purity of political economy, Irish peasants were left to perish in the hideousness of their hovels. Of course, it is permissible to wonder whether, even if Trevelyan had been willing to interfere more in the market, the Famine's effects would have been alleviated. It is safe to say that nothing that the government could have done with the resources it had and the nature of Ireland's infrastructure could have 'solved' the problem in 1847. However, that is not to say that interference in the market would have had no effect. J. S. Donnelly concludes that, although it would not have averted disaster, it would have mitigated it somewhat.[13] That is probably the fairest statement.

Under the Whig government, there was also a change in how the scheme of public works functioned. Trevelyan had become convinced of the wastefulness of the previous dispensation and decided that, in the future, all projects would be funded through local taxation. The government would no longer provide half of the funds, it would merely loan money to be repaid. The public work scheme became increasingly swollen in the first few months of the ministry. In early October, 26,000 were being employed daily and by March 1847 this had reached a staggering 714,390 persons. No system could support such a sudden weight. A particular controversy surrounded the practice of payment by task and by quality of work. Could debilitated workers be expected to be really productive? How could they produce quality work without the requisite tools? Why should they be held responsible for delays which were often caused by administrative hiccups further up? The schemes were riddled through with scandals of late payments, deaths at work and outbreaks of disease. In one case, at least, the Board of Works was accused of gross negligence in its treatment of an employee. Clearly the schemes were now a colossal failure and, in recognition of this, they were phased out.

The Second Phase of Whig Response

Instead, the Temporary Relief Act, the so-called Soup Kitchen Act, was introduced and began to have an effect from the second quarter of 1847 on. Soup kitchens were established and, although it was a slow start, they were feeding up to three million people a day by June. Still, not all the people dismissed by the Board of Works and their dependents were provided for and able-bodied labourers in receipt of wages were not allowed free food, they had to buy it. Despite this, it did avert or postpone starvation in some cases and must be counted as a comparative success. However, the scheme, which was only designed to be a temporary palliative, was brought to a close in September 1847. In short, it only lasted for a few months.

Health care as well as food provision was, by now, a huge concern. Oedema, scurvy, anaemia, heart failure, fever and dysentery were rampant. After an appallingly bad winter, the government re-established the Board of Health in 1847, which they had allowed to lapse in the previous August. Temporary hospitals were set up over the country, but they were not able to deal with the hundreds of thousands who came and the good that they could do was inevitably limited. Alongside the government were the various voluntary organisations, often religious, which sought to give relief. The Religious Society of Friends and the British Relief Association were notable in this respect. An occasional whiff of proselytism, making aid conditional on conversion, damaged their reputation somewhat.[14]

The Last Phase of Whig Response

In a move very much endorsed by Trevelyan, the Irish Poor Law was reorganised and extended in June 1847. This was to be the basis of the last phase of the Whig response to the calamity, a response that lasted from 1847 to 1851. A special Poor Law Commission was established with a fully paid inspectorate. The law had several important features and sought to make distinctions between absolute and relative destitution. For the absolutely destitute (those who were not able-bodied), relief could be administered in the workhouse or outside. For the able-bodied, relief was *only* available in the workhouse. This was supposed to function as a test of how desperate one was – the administration did not want the able-bodied sponging off scarce resources.

This reflected the usual Victorian preoccupation with distinguishing between the deserving and the undeserving poor. The infamous Gregory Clause, named after a Dublin MP, laid down that those who had more than a quarter acre of land could not enter the workhouse (despite the fact that the land was of no use to them and their need was as great as those who had less). This clause had its own circumscribed logic – Sir William Gregory's aim was to rid the land of the pauperised holders and start over. There followed a spate of evictions – surely one of the most hideous features of the catastrophe – and the cottier and labouring classes were utterly decimated by a combination of natural disaster and disastrous policy.

Indeed, landlords often did quite well out of the Famine. They used the opportunity to consolidate their holdings and to clear the land of the least productive tenants. From 1849–54, there were at least 48,748 permanent evictions. With the average size of such a family being five, this meant that about 250,000 people were affected. Landlords sometimes actively assisted tenants to emigrate through goodwill or self-interest. In the worse cases, they presented them with the stark 'choice' of emigration or eviction. Most shamefully, they sometimes took away all semblance of choice by unroofing their dwellings and levelling their cabins while they were seeking temporary relief, thus making it impossible for them to return. As a result of consolidation, 15-acre-plus farms went from being a third of all holdings in 1845 to a half in 1851.

The workhouse system, meanwhile, creaked under the sheer weight of people. There were 930,000 inmates in 130 institutions by 1849. It is a true measure of the nature of the crisis to reflect on the fact that even this hated institution for the average Victorian Briton became, for some desperate Irish people, a morbidly respectable refuge – many delayed their entrance until they were about to die so that they would get a decent burial at public expense. Money again bedevilled the matter. Irish rate payers (the landlords and the prosperous farmers) were largely funding such relief operations as there were and, all too soon, many of the Poor Law Unions which administered the workhouses were bankrupt. The Treasury doled out some help, but not enough. Meanwhile, the rate payers were evicting tenants from their land to solve *their* problems and turning it from tillage to livestock. There was a very practical reason for this. The law laid down that the more tenants one had, the higher the rates one had to pay and, of course, tillage farming demanded more workers than livestock did. It was a fault of the system that it was often more profitable to evict.

As well as the phases in the relief programme proper, Russell's government also passed the Crime and Outrage Act (to prevent forces of lawlessness from taking over) and the Encumbered Estates Act. It was hoped that the latter would encourage British capitalists to invest in Irish property and improve estates, but, in fact, only 4 per cent of encumbered estates were bought by Britons. The new Irish mercantile classes and the gentry tended to buy them instead. Thus, ideas for a new social plantation were dashed and the *Times'* genial optimism that 'a Celtic Irishman will be as rare in Connemara as is the Red Indian on the shores of Manhattan' was not exactly fulfilled in the way they had hoped.[15] The Celts had disappeared from the west in their thousands, alright, but they were not replaced by 'civilised' planters. In a move that resembled Peel's overtures to Rome several years previously, the Whigs did what they could to stave off Catholic discontent by passing a Diplomatic Relations Act, thus reinstituting diplomatic ties between the courts of St James and Rome. This was to be a fundamental prerequisite for fully re-establishing Catholic hierarchies in the UK.

Evaluations

By 1850, the worst of the Famine was over and poor relief shrunk to one-fifth of its level in 1849. The debts incurred by state loans were finally remitted in Gladstone's budget in 1853, a belated recognition that Irish property could no longer pay for Irish poverty and that they might as well seek to regain the money in alternative ways. It can be no exaggeration to say that the five years of famine represented demographic disaster. Attempts to quantify the casualties are varied. Joel Mokyr has convincingly argued that the figure stands at 1,082,000 or indeed 1,493,000, if one takes averted births into account.[16] There was a heavy regional bias in the number of deaths. Connaught, predictably, was the most affected, Leinster least. The stark fact remains that over a million people died in excess of the normal mortality rates in the course of this period. This one fact inevitably colours all attempts to assess the relief effort under the Whig government. Varying interpretations are possible. In contrast to a traditional story which blackened the government completely, the revisionist story has been a comparatively generous one. The contention here is that the relief effort was valiant and imaginative, but limited by the inevitable constraints of its time. Ordinary and extraordinary means were tried and the very variety of methods is indicative of a government seeking to come up with creative solutions. Failures there were, assuredly, but the government cannot be held responsible for failures in dealing with such a crisis – it was overwhelmed by needs on a scale that was truly unimaginable. The civil service had never been designed to cope with such eventualities.

This story makes many fair points, but it is all a little too cosy, as post-revisionists have contended. For one thing, it could be said that the government schemes happened in such rapid succession that the very breaks meant jarring disconnects in provision. For another, the Whig government was consistently too optimistic in thinking the problems were solved. The schemes were deliberately temporary. It was, for example, clearly a mistake to close the soup kitchens in August 1847. Then, the point has been made that government expenditure was, even by the standards of the day, unimpressive. The government spent £8 million on Ireland, but contrast this with the £16 million averaged on defence per annum since 1815, the £20 million given to West Indian slave owners to compensate them for emancipation in the 1830s and the £69 million spent on the Crimean War in the following decade. Parsimony is relative, surely. It is hard to avoid the conclusion that, in the greater scheme of things, Ireland's famine never became the grand economic priority of the government. It just did not exert them enough.

A rather intriguing line on the subject which is not always given due consideration in the historiography is the refusal of the Whig government to entertain the February 1847 programme of Lord George Bentinck, a conservative Tory and leader of the protectionist faction. Bentinck, for all that he is most associated with securing the downfall of Peel and obsessing about horses, showed a remarkable aptitude for thinking constructively about the Irish dilemma. In some ways it was the most remarkable aspect of his thinking. In his programme, he suggested endowing the Catholic Church, taxing absentee landlords (the latter, something that O'Connell had also proposed earlier in the decade) and, most importantly of all, the building of railways. He proposed that the Treasury loan £16 million to railway companies repayable over 30 years. This would employ people purposefully, build an Irish transport network and stimulate Britain's own industrial production and capital investment in Ireland. Russell wanted to battle against what he saw as the 'general distrust in the English market respecting Irish lines'.[17] At first, this scheme, which he deliberately put forward as non-partisan, was well received amongst reformers in both parties. Yet, this ambitious and imaginative plan – one might say the most imaginative plan to have come from a British statesman in this period – was defeated by political considerations. This was partly because Bentinck's party, riven from the Peelite split, was unwilling to risk taking over government again. But it was also because Russell made it into a confidence issue. Instead of considering it on its own terms as a non-partisan programme, he made it a party one. The altercation between the two on 4 February is interesting. Whilst complimenting Bentinck's 'sincerity', goodwill and 'patriotism', he did not think Irish distress would be relieved by the 'expenditure of this money'. Spending money on systemic change like the railways would not, in his words, be 'wise'. 'What is necessary for them is food.'[18] This shows Russell at his most limited.

All this seriously detracts from the story of energetic government commitment. But neither should we revert to a story of 'willed genocide', of a government determined to rid itself of a subspecies of humanity. What then? The most sensitive reconstruction of the *mentalités* that allowed the Famine to happen in the way that it did is that provided by Peter Gray in *Famine, Land and Politics: British Government and Irish Society, 1843–1850* (1999). His central thesis is that the reaction to the Famine cannot be understood merely in terms of relief policies, but must be positioned in the context of the history of certain powerful ideas. These ideas had been hegemonic before the Famine and they, in turn, determined both the kind of policies imposed and those omitted. He writes that, although the Famine called for a specific response, the 'broad lines of response had already been sketched out'.[19] The Procrustean 'iron' bed to which Irish problems had to be fitted was a *laissez-faire* theory of political economy. According to this theory, first articulated by Adam Smith in his 1776 *An Inquiry into the Nature and Causes of the Wealth of Nations*, the market was better left to its own devices and the government's role was to foster the market rather than check it. Long decades of implementing free trade incrementally since Pitt entered power in the 1780s had made their mark on the dominant mindset in the Treasury and in government and, thus, it was that the Famine found them set in certain habits of thought which were not dislodged even for a crisis of this ilk.

There was another complementary strand of thinking at work which Hilton has called the practice of soteriological economics – that is to say, the mapping of religious values onto the market.[20] Insofar as this *laissez-faire* theory had moral overtones, it led to a sort of meticulous respect for the workings of the market, a belief that the free play of market forces was conducive to prosperity and also to active virtue in citizens. There was a disinclination to interfere in case that very interference, however good willed, would destroy the delicate balances of the system. In this model, dependence was bad morality as well as bad political economy. Trevelyan saw dependence as a 'moral disease'[21] and thus that the Famine was a 'judgement of God on an indolent and unself-reliant people'.[22] Catastrophe was read both positively and negatively in this period – negatively, because it was deemed inevitable and, as Hilton has suggested, this thought was something of an obsession in early nineteenth-century Britain, but positively, also, because good could and would be drawn out of it.

Subscription to these ideas, at some level, was near universal in all those who held office or sought to hold office. It is from this cold logic that the oft-quoted comment by Nassau Senior springs – that a million deaths in the Irish Famine would 'scarcely be enough to do much good'.[23] Senior was the 'court' political economist for the Whigs since the early 1830s and, to do him justice, he had then recommended government investments in Ireland which had never materialised. But the 'good' that Famine would do now was to make the Irish market a level playing field again and, by taking out the economic parasites, enable it to be more prosperous and virtuous. For Anthony Trollope in his novel *Castle Richmond* published in 1860, the whole story was one of ultimate blessing. In fact, there were three stories, all interwoven: one of famine, one of pestilence and one of exodus. 'These three wonderful events, following each other', he wrote, were nothing less than 'the blessings coming from Omniscience and Omnipotence by which the black clouds were driven from the Irish firmament.'[24] At the very least, he was wrong as regards the Anglo–Irish relationship, as coming decades would reveal. He was surely wrong in other ways, too.

If one could map Dante's distinction between hot and cold sins onto the British establishment in this period, they would fall guilty, not of the former, but of the latter. This is why the accusation of genocide is not born out. They were not guilty of rampant race murder – theirs was the more complex guilt, in Cormac Ó Gráda's words, of a flawed 'commitment to their vision of a better world'.[25] Undoubtedly there were practical limitations to what a government, however willing, could do to resolve the situation, but it may well be that the tightest constraints under which administrators were operating were not so much practical as ideological. Mental blinkers and rigid economic beliefs determined the response and confined the nature and administration of aid. Gray is right to dwell on the deadly games played by liberal moralities in this period.[26] Ironically, it was their moralities that were at fault, not their immoralities. Their moralities meant, to put it bluntly, that more Irish people died than needed to because of an excess of economic zeal. The confidence that came from these moralities meant that confirmed Whigs never really saw themselves as acting except in the interests of the greater good. Most tellingly of all, in 1848 Trevelyan received a knighthood for his work on behalf of the Irish.

The Irish Famine was, in every sense, a tragedy.

Chapter 10

POST-FAMINE IRELAND

Two Mid-century Narratives

There are two powerful ways of considering Irish history in the mid-nineteenth century. One is to regard it simply as post-Famine Ireland. The other is to see it, in a much more buoyant way, as mid-Victorian Ireland. Both approaches are important although angled very differently. The former is the traditional strand, very much emphasised by classic general histories and also in histories of agriculture and rural life. F. S. L. Lyons' magisterial *Ireland Since the Famine* (1973) takes the event as its point of departure, not only because of its severe immediate effect which was 'to impose an overwhelming burden of suffering upon an impoverished and defenceless people' but also – and in his reading, more importantly – because of its profound 'psychological legacy', which consisted, he claims, in a deep-rooted and long-lasting hatred for the English connection.[1] For scholars focusing on agricultural history, the Famine is the dividing line between two land economies.[2] Moreover, an interpretative emphasis on the legacy of the Famine lends itself to studying the politicisation of the Irish diaspora and also to studying the groundwork for a politics of discontent, which surfaced in the emergence of the separatist Fenian movement.[3] Both are highly interconnected because the radical initiatives often came from the Irish living outside Ireland. The narrative of near-universal exile discontent has been questioned by Akenson, however, who interrogates the conventional wisdom that the exiled Irish always bore hatred for British institutions when they went abroad. As settlers, soldiers, administrators, policemen and clergy, they have been among the 'greatest supporters' of the British Empire.[4]

The portrayal of 'Victorian Ireland' is a relatively new emphasis in the historiography. Propounded by scholars such as Peter Gray and R. V. Comerford, it serves as a sharp corrective to the more usual narrative of gloom, hatred and depression.[5] Not everything was affected by the long shadow of the Famine. Or, perhaps it was affected so as to modernise.[6] It is a reminder that Ireland also experienced something of the benign revolutions in transport, leisure, culture, infrastructure and middle-class life that are familiar to us from studying English history in the same period. Nor were all of these developments imposed. There is an argument that pre-Famine culture was 'dismantled ruthlessly by the people themselves' and that they were trying actively to come to terms with the 'overwhelming culture and power of imperial England'.[7] It is also the case that Irish history was not inevitably channelled into a politically separatist mode at this point. James Murphy notes the popularity of Queen Victoria – as many as 1 million people coming out on the streets of Dublin to welcome her in 1853.[8] Although there is no full-length study of Victorian Ireland to date, strong cases can be made both for the existence of a 'post-Famine' and a 'Victorian' Ireland. They are not, of course, mutually exclusive, but it is worth telling each narrative separately.

Post-Famine Ireland

The impacts of the Great Famine are greatly contested. Traditionally, it was seen as a clear, brutal line of demarcation, disrupting and transforming traditional patterns of agriculture, social mores, cultural norms and religious habits. This view has been modified somewhat, as we have seen, by economic historians who view 1815, rather than 1845, as the major turning point.[9] There have also been those who detract from its significance as a national phenomenon. Controversially, Cullen asserts that the Famine was 'less a national disaster than a social and regional one'.[10] For all that it was socially and regionally varied in effect, it did not stop being a national disaster. It has also been emphasised that the Famine did not create a culture of emigration, it merely accelerated it. For all these reasons, the idea that the Famine constituted a great turning point at the time, is somewhat dented. Nevertheless, it is still defensible to regard the period 1845–51 as a major watershed in many significant ways.

Ireland outside Ireland

First, the growth of an 'Ireland' outside Ireland is the most obvious corollary of the mass exodus in the period. This was a diaspora of a particular kind – the 'push' factors were, initially and perhaps always, stronger than the 'pull' factors. There was no future for many in Ireland if they remained. There was a great sense of hopelessness about their situation and a lack of will and ability to put it to rights. 'All we want is to get out of Ireland. [...] We must be better anywhere else than here', said a contemporary.[11] But the 'pull' factors were there too, revealing the attractions of powerful nations: industrialising countries and labour-needy entrepreneurs were calling out for workers in their thousands. In fact, Irish migration should not be seen as an exceptional story, as it is often portrayed. It is true that the Irish case is particular in some ways, but it should be put in the context of the massive population movements of the nineteenth century. In total, 55 million Europeans left their native lands in the century following the 1820s. Ireland's experience is unique, in a way, but also forms part of a wider pattern of migratory movement.

The figures for emigration are particularly stark in the Famine decade. Between 1845 and 1855, 2.1 million people left the country. The majority of these (1.5 million) went to the United States, 300,000 went to British North America and another 300,000 to Britain. Others went to Australia and New Zealand. The demographic haemorrhage did not stop. By the 1920s, as Terence Brown established, a staggering 43 per cent of Irish-born men and women were living abroad. These numbers are much greater than other notable emigrant groups. The next, the Norwegians, only count as 14.8 per cent.[12] The connection with other parts of the British Empire or with former colonies remained strong, although a certain number went to South America at this time, too. As Lyons notes, this was a largely 'irrevocable movement' – most of those who went never returned.[13]

When the Irish migrated, they most often took up residence in the big cities, perhaps a rather peculiar choice given that most of their backgrounds would have been agrarian. But the cities boasted the advantage of anonymity, ethnic solidarity and plenteous employment. In the United States, New York, Boston, Philadelphia and Pittsburgh were prime destinations. In Britain, London, Liverpool and Manchester increased their Irish residential clusters. About 750,000 Irish people lived in Britain in the decades after the Great Famine, although statistics are notoriously difficult to come by.[14] The census of 1861 records a peak number of 806,000 Irish-born residents living in Britain – no doubt there were more.[15] There were different reasons which pushed some people towards the United States and others to Britain. The United States were a definite breaking point with the past, whereas going to Britain meant that one could 'keep one's options open'.[16] It was cheap and quick to get there and get back. By mid-century, it might only cost five or six pence, or nothing at all from Cork to Bristol if one was prepared to act as ballast for the ship. Compared to this, the transatlantic fare came out at about £10. So migration to Britain was a more casual phenomenon than a move to the United States.

Emigration affected gender and class in different ways. As regards gender, it is notable that the Irish were the only emigrant group to America which consisted of more than 50 per cent women. Clearly many women felt that they would be better off having an independent life abroad than remaining at home unwed and unprovided for. There is an often-talked about the strain of Jansenism in Irish Catholicism which may have facilitated celibacy. Akenson points out that some of the most able women became nuns and went on missions abroad.[17] However, the point should not be overplayed: many women married in their new abodes. Women very often found work in domestic service, a growing sector throughout the century as even the modest middle classes were more likely to employ a maid. Thus the stereotype of the 'biddy' was born. Socially, emigration hit the lowest classes most, especially the labourers and servants. The very poorest went to Canada because the journey there was cheaper than to the States. As these people tended to be Gaelic-speaking and illiterate, one of the effects of the Famine was to cause illiteracy rates to decline. The proportion of native speakers of Irish dropped sharply from 47 per cent in 1851 to 33 per cent in 1871. Linguistically, this was an irreversible shift.

The character of migrant occupations was as varied as places of settlement. By the 1850s, for example, there was a 'spectacular increase' in migration to Australia and New Zealand largely because of the gold rush – a high proportion of the gold diggers were Irish. At the start, Munster men tended to dominate and, from the 1880s onwards, Leinster men.[18] A special case has to be made for the seasonal migrants, mostly male, who made their way to Britain at particular times of the year for farm work (e.g. reaping) or industrial work (classically, on the railways). These were more likely to be welcomed and appreciated as they came to do a specific job and generally avoided some of the stereotypes that vagrants had earned – that of being feckless and lazy, although drunkenness and rioting were not uncommon complaints. More positively, they were often described as thrifty and hard working – high praise, indeed, in an age which sought to model itself on the work ethic of the beehive. Sometimes, they carefully planned their visits so that they could move from place to place, fulfilling different functions at different times of year – the hay, then the corn, followed by the turnips and potatoes. They generally sent their wages home to Ireland to pay the rent, but sometimes it was used to pay for the steamship to America.

Apart from the emigrants to Britain, the chances of seeing their homeland again were slight for most of those who left the country for distant shores. Despite or perhaps because of this, the migrant communities would maintain strong home ties. A mystical veneration for the homeland developed through the songs and poetry of the exiles and those who remained. One of the most celebrated was John Locke's *Dawn on the Irish Coast* (1877), which described the emotions of the returned exile in strongly sentimental terms. The 'one short hour pays lavishly back / For many a year of mourning'.[19]

He portrayed himself as the archetypal western rover. Emigration had, for centuries, been a prominent feature of the island's history and its sense of itself, but this was indeed a new chapter. It is plausible that from the late 1840s onwards, those who left brought with them not merely a nostalgia for the old country but a residuum of hatred for British rule, which would express itself in political organisations and movements, notably Irish-American Fenianism. The memory of the Famine helped to forge a radically nationalist expatriate community who would remain in touch with their homeland through correspondence, associative life, newspapers and, crucially, giving them money.

Where the Irish went, stereotypes abounded. They were portrayed as dirty, belligerent, improvident and illiterate; their Catholicism made them even more suspect. One obstacle that they faced, particularly in Britain and America, was a kind of three-layered prejudice. As regards the history of ideas, the study of the genealogy and structure of a prejudice is of fundamental value, for it reveals a society at its most unreflective and instinctive. Curtis, in his investigation of anti-Irish prejudice in Victorian England, distinguishes three kinds: that based on race, on class and on religion. In practice, this meant that the Irishman was stigmatised as Celtic, lower class and Catholic.[20] He met with something of the same reaction in America, although class had fewer historic underpinnings there. To make matters worse, it so happened that the Irish exodus occurred about the same time as the enthusiasm for 'scientific' ethnography and anthropology, which classified the races according to a hierarchy where the Anglo-Saxon was superior and masculine and the Celtic very lowly indeed.

The first thing to say about the Irish diaspora of the nineteenth century is that it was not a homogenous entity and stereotypes of laziness, drunkenness and inability to rise above their lowly stations are problematic. It is true that many of the immigrants lived in ghettoised conditions and had serious and persistent social problems. Frederick Engels, observing the Irish worker in Manchester, noted that, when he got money, he got 'rid of it down his throat'.[21] But neither problems nor prejudice, however much they might circumscribe, would entirely define the Irish experience abroad. In the United States, despite the need to overcome anti-Catholic prejudice and even bigotry (notably in Boston), the Irish began to make headway in popular politics and in jobs such as the police force. They provided one possible model of collective action and egalitarianism and were heavily involved in the nascent labour movement. Later in the century, they would become increasingly associated with urban political machines for the Democratic Party. In Britain, their situation was often healthier than imagined. Evans takes the stereotypical picture of the Irish in Britain (i.e. extremely poor, often criminal and unable to adapt to urban living) and undercuts it. There was more social mobility than often imagined and the censuses of 1851, 1861 and 1871 reveal that fully one-third to two-fifths of the Irish-born inhabitants in Liverpool, Hull and York were in professional or skilled labour.[22] The Irish thus proved to be important in the countries to which they went – in Britain, contributing to the mighty Victorian economy and, in America, constituting, as David Doyle says, a 'huge importation of manpower, skills and consumers'.[23]

The Rise of the Small Farmer Class

Although rural poverty was not eradicated by the Great Famine, many of the rural poor had been. In their place rose the small- and middling-farmer class. These were the great beneficiaries of the disaster. Their holdings were between 20 and 30 acres and worth about £15. But this alone is not a sufficient measure of their importance. There is a compelling thesis, articulated by Foster and others, that a 'small farmer ethos' was emerging in the latter half of the nineteenth century, influencing culture and beliefs more widely.[24] What might such an ethos entail? It was essentially a conservative phenomenon that placed a value on self-advancement, prudent marriages, dowries, education and orthodox practices of piety – in short, on the trappings of respectability, a quality deemed lacking in the pre-Famine masses. It is not difficult to advance reasons for the growth of a new *mentalité* at such a time. There may have been, understandably, a desire to distance themselves from the miseries of the past as the much reduced population sought out a more stable future. They were the survivors – the inheritors – and they were determined not to make similar mistakes. The thesis is an alluring one and it is born out in a variety of sociological developments. Marriage patterns were affected – there were fewer than before. No longer, as Terence Brown shrewdly notes, was there the 'agreeable carelessness' of improvident pre-Famine life; instead, there was much 'calculating sensitivity to the economic meaning of marriage'.[25] Fathers held onto the land as long as possible and there was plenty of encouragement to extra children to leave the country and find a role for themselves elsewhere. Rural society was not the idyllic prelapsarian, pre-materialist paradise as later middle-class urbanites would like to have pictured it – the focus on money and profit and prices was 'meticulous'.[26]

   Those who stayed and prospered in their humble way had the modest powers of newly comfortable men, determined to better themselves and convinced of the merits of Anglicisation. The most notorious example of this was the *bata scoir* or 'tally stick', a stick on a piece of string that children would wear. Every time they spoke Irish, the stick would be notched and several notches meant a beating. This was how determined some parents and educators were to stamp out what was perceived as a sociocultural badge of failure. As these farmers became more comfortable in their manner of life, they might have been able to afford the status symbols of the day – a reaping machine, meat for dinner several times a week, a trap for the ride to church, a parlour for visitors and even, that most essential of Victorian bourgeois acquisitions, a piano. Perhaps they might have been able to keep money in the bank.[27] By now, there were several branches of the Bank of Ireland throughout the country; the financial sector was becoming increasingly important, in tandem with developments elsewhere. The small farmer ethos may also have had political implications in the mid-nineteenth century. A more deferential attitude to authority was patent. Some had reason to be grateful. The Representation of the People Act for Ireland in 1850 gave tenants with holdings of £12 (that is to say about 12 acres of good land) the right to vote. This was a first for the United Kingdom and it established the precedent of allowing mere tenants into the electoral franchise. Once again, Ireland was a sort of experimental ground. Southern Ireland responded in kind by generally voting for what would become, after 1859, the Liberal Party. A surface political calm reigned for the present.

Agricultural Change

As regards agriculture, the Famine is often said to have brought about a shift from tillage to livestock farming, although the point can be overstated. It is true to say that cattle farmers gained as the price of land fell. The ratio of cattle to people grew from 22 per 100 in 1841 to 74 per 100 in 1871, totalling 4 million cattle. The biggest growth period was from 1847–59, but the expanse of the cattle industry persisted until 1914. More people were eating meat more often. Moreover, the declining population meant that tillage was no longer as popular as it was a more labour-intensive work. Acreage under wheat decreased catastrophically from 750,000 in 1847 to 48,000 by 1910. Oats and barley were still needed for animals and brewing so their decline was less notable. However, the turning away from tillage and the growing vogue for livestock was not merely a result of the Famine. The boom times from the 1850s to 1873 made for very favourable prices for animal products. More and more effectively, the Irish were providing the resources for the growing meat market in Britain. Cattle exports were a huge source of revenue. Fashions in food consumption changed so that the fat cattle gave way to the less bulky varieties which were more easily reared and exported.

The new agricultural orthodoxy was dubbed 'flocks and herds' and was endorsed by officials and administrators who were very ready to see the positives of the post-Famine transformation. A classic example is provided by

George Howard, the seventh Earl of Carlisle, who was the popular, if hardly energetic, Lord Lieutenant during Lord Palmerston's Liberal premierships 1855–58 and 1859–64.[28] At the big annual cattle show in Athlone, organised by the Royal Agricultural Improvement Society of Ireland, Carlisle brought an imperial perspective to bear upon the new concentration on livestock. He told his audience to 'bear in mind what nature in her wise economy seems especially to have fitted this island for is to be the mother of flocks and herds – to [...] be the larder and dairy of the world – to send rations of beef and bales of bacon to our armies wherever they are'.[29] Howard lyrically described Irish beef as contributing to the strength of the imperial army and thus sought to encompass Irish agriculture in the project of British global dominance.

One feature of the new dispensation which was less palatable to elites was the growth of tenant leagues.[30] It represented a more determined and concerted effort from below to lobby for tenant rights which were felt to be increasingly threatened. The growth began in Ulster, where Presbyterians sought legitimation of the so-called Ulster Custom which gave them more security in their holdings and more rights when it came to selling their right to occupancy. Another initiative, the Callan Tenant Protection Society, sprang from two Catholic curates in 1849. Although small scale, it lobbied to restrict the power of landlords over substantial tenants. By the following year, this sort of association had cropped up in many other districts in Munster and Leinster. The composition was petty bourgeois, consisting of shopkeepers, farmers and priests. They were adamantly non-violent, wanting to distance themselves from the Ribbonmen and Whiteboys of decades past.

By August 1850, unity was achieved between all these societies with the establishment of the Irish Tenant Right League. It sought to put pressure on Parliament to achieve legal change in the land question. Papers such as the *Nation* and the *Freeman's Journal* propagated the cause more widely and the Representation of the People Act of 1850, which more than doubled the country electorate to 135,245 men, opened up new opportunities for politicisation of the question. The emergence of the Independent Irish Party in the 1850s was a consequence of this. There was a sense in which this phenomenon was a new form of O'Connellism, but now directed towards agrarian matters. The same 'moral electricity in the continuous expression of public opinion concentrated on a single point' would eventually become too powerful to ignore.[31] For Beckett, its real importance is that it constituted a 'first experiment in using the land agitation as the basis of a national party'. Certainly the effort to recruit both Catholics and Protestants from north and south was notable.[32] For now, although there was some success at the 1852 election (where 40 of their candidates were returned) and much lobbying (250,000 signed the league's 1856 proposals), nothing was conceded by Parliament. The initiative soon collapsed.

During its lifetime, the Tenant Right League brought attention to many abuses. A particular case involved a Galway landowner called Alan Pollock. He was a beneficiary of the Encumbered Estates Act of 1849 and thus a much-disliked new landlord. Progressive, modernising and in step with the trends towards cattle farming, he got into trouble for trying to clear some of his many tenants from the land. He did manage to eject 300 families, but there was outrage as a result. As Bew notes, what is most striking about the incident is not the angry reaction from predictable sources but the outrage from the media establishment, namely the *Times* of London.[33] If there is a post-Famine attitudinal shift, this is an early sign of it. The feeling of 'wrong done' in the 1840s and the idea of moral reprehensibility for the suffering of the Irish was taking root in some powerful strands of British opinion.

Although the Famine helped to change the nature of agriculture and attitudes towards it, it did nothing to turn people away from agriculture and towards new industrial ventures. The Industrial Revolution remained the story of the north of the country; the south did not participate to any considerable extent. It was Belfast which primarily continued to grow. It was officially given 'city' status by Queen Victoria in 1888. Industrialisation was also a primarily Protestant phenomenon – the capital and the skilled jobs belonged to them. The outbreaks of religious tensions in the period should also be seen to involve these economic factors. The 10 days of serious sectarian riots in Belfast in July 1857, sparked by Orange parades, prompted the government to enquire into the causes and nature of such violence.

The Devotional Revolution

On the subject of religion, it has often been suggested that the Famine brought about a devotional revolution, a kind of Catholic revivalism in the latter half of the nineteenth century. This was combined with institutionalisation and reform from above.[34] Various explanations for the devotional revolution from below could be proffered. People may have turned to their spiritual lives as a means of transcendence in a time of desperation. Death and resurrection was the central Christian theme, it could be held metaphorical for a whole people. There are more mundane reasons also. After the Famine, in the shattered and fragile 1850s, the church was left standing, a spiritual and institutional point of reference, comfort and support. During the Famine, clerics and religious had done impressive relief work for the population and bishops had come out strongly on the side of the poor, supporting the right to life over the right to property and denouncing the practice of 'legal' evictions.[35] The story of sudden religious revival consequent on the Famine is perhaps a trifle too abrupt, however. Signs of vigour had already been visible in the pre-Famine years. Fr Mathew's alcohol abstinence movement reached its peak immediately before the outbreak of the Famine. Nevertheless, it remains abundantly clear that belief helped people to cope with the traumatic disruption of the 1840s and the profoundly altered conditions of life afterwards. Rural superstitions, such as those surrounding holy wells, declined (their main practitioners, after all, fled or were dead) and a more organised and orthodox popular piety took hold, manifesting itself in public practices such as associations, confraternities, processions and pilgrimages and private devotions such as the household use of pious images and the family rosary. Sunday Mass attendance leaped from a mere 40 per cent in the 1840s to 90 per cent in the 1880s.

This culture of piety was fostered by the clergy, who had emerged from the episode with an enhanced moral status in a society so severely jarred as it had been. It was a golden age of religious vocations – in 1850, Ireland had one priest for every 2,100 people; 20 years later, it had become one priest for every 1,300 and one nun for every 1,100. On the latter note, nuns were heavily involved in education, charity and managing institutions. Archbishop (later Cardinal) Cullen of Armagh and later of Dublin set the tone for the whole religious revival. He was made a cardinal in 1866 by Pius IX. He, in the words of Comerford, would homogenise the Irish church.[36] He also made it more Roman. Politically, he mattered too, as he energetically lobbied the government on various issues. Indeed Emmet Larkin's thesis is that the corporate unity of the bishops and their engagement with social, political, educational and spiritual affairs in the 1860s was crucial in consolidating Irish Catholicism.[37] The effects of the dual Catholic 'revolution' were to cement the relationship between the church and a growing sense of Irishness, whether abroad or at home. Brown identifies this when he claims that the church provided people with a 'way to be Irish [...] meeting the needs thereby of a nascent Irish nationalism at a time when the Irish language and the Gaelic culture of the past were enduring a protracted decline'.[38]

The Politics of Hatred

Lastly, the question of whether the Famine cemented a newly fresh hatred for the British among the Irish must be considered. There is little doubt that, for many, it certainly did. Those 'calamitous years', wrote Lyons, 'burnt themselves deep into the imagination of the people and have haunted their descendants ever since'.[39] Folk memory was unlikely to forget the more scandalous abuses of the period and a sense of grievance, especially among the emigrants, was unlikely to be dislodged. In fact, one could say that, by putting themselves outside of Ireland, it could not be dislodged. Many never came back. The Ireland that they remembered was frozen in the mould of the tragedies of 1845–50. Songs and ballads record the wrenches and the trauma that was felt and orally transmitted to the next generation. Akenson insists that Irish migration must be understood as the whole 'multigenerational phenomenon' that it is and not merely a one-generational matter.[40] The relationship between the Irish people, understood in this widest sense, and the British government could not but be soured as a result.

Chapter 11

MID-VICTORIAN IRELAND

The Problem of Victorian Ireland

It would be a mistake to think that Ireland had no 'Victorian' era, properly speaking. This would be to lapse into the common trap of thinking that the Irish experience is entirely summed up by recounting a tale of ruralism, poverty, emigration and opposition to the British state. An understanding of the varied Irish experience in the mid-century wards against the 'ruin, decay, rags and misery' school of history.[1] It is the contention of some recent work, notably by Gray and Comerford, that Ireland should be placed within the context of the mid-Victorian period of stability, economic growth and sociocultural transformation.[2] An obvious point of departure is Queen Victoria's four visits to Ireland – the first in 1849, the second in 1853, the third in 1861 and the final one in 1900. In all, she spent five weeks in the country during a 63-year reign. Her visits were, on the whole, magnificently successful and lend at least surface credibility to the notion of a Victorian Ireland.[3]

More meaningfully, to talk about mid-Victorian Ireland is to situate the country very much within the framework of contemporaneous developments in Britain. A boom period from the 1850s to 1875 saw general levels of prosperity inch up and the quality of life enhanced by a multitude of converging developments in transportation, technology, domestic appliances, food stuffs and leisure. This story cannot, however, be unproblematically mapped onto Ireland. As architectural historian Christine Casey has it, Dublin's commercial and industrial architecture is much less impressive than Liverpool's, Manchester's and Glasgow's, a clear sign that the Victorian city (and, by extension, the country) failed 'to expand as a manufacturing centre'.[4] There was also unrest underneath the surface calm. The underbelly of Victorian Ireland was Fenianism. If southern Ireland fails on some of the main criteria of successful Victorianism, it would be a mistake to think that there were no correlations. The key is administrative, technical and social rather than political – one of the reasons, no doubt, why the story is often neglected. The political is not entirely missing. Alvin Jackson holds Conservatism to be the 'unsung success story of mid-Victorian politics' and notes that the reorganisation of the Irish Tories happened long before equivalent English or Scottish initiatives.[5] The Tories reached out to commercial and professional classes: its attractiveness is evidenced by its popularity in the well-to-do new suburbs outside Dublin. The suburb of Rathmines, for example, voted for a Unionist candidate as late as 1918. So much for the background political narrative. A remarkably efficient team at the castle, manned by a very capable undersecretary from 1853–68, Thomas Askew Larcom, set the tone for administrative reform. He was responsible for regularising the Poor Law system. A new system of medical dispensaries was established to deal with public health, sewerage was improved and, in 1854, the Towns Improvement Act sought to sanitise and beautify the drab urban environments.

Gathering detailed information about the country so as to govern it more effectively was another aspect of Victorian Ireland. The Victorians were passionate collectors of information. Partly this was because of a belief in the march of progress and their desire to master the world. Partly, also, it was for the pragmatic needs of the expanding civic sector. Work had already begun in the 1820s on Ordinance Survey maps of Ireland (six inches to a mile); by mid-century it was brought to its completion. At the cost of £1 million, a team of surveyors led by the Royal Engineers mapped the country in more detail than any other country in the world before. The project employed the antiquarian George Petrie and was quite a hub of scholarly and literary activity for many years.[6] Between the years 1852–64, the 202-volume *General Valuation of Ireland* appeared – a vast compendium about land usage. The state wished to inform itself: it was a kind of modern doomsday book. The Public Records Act of 1867 set up a state paper office in central Dublin, a clear sign of the growing politicisation of information in the period. Before, records were in 'several hands' and in 'unfit buildings', now they were to be handed over to the master of rolls for safe keeping. But change was not merely driven by the Victorian craze for counting and quantifying and preserving. There was a genuine desire to enhance the means of self-improvement and make them more accessible to the discerning public. The Royal Dublin Society (RDS) had hosted industrial and arts exhibitions in the 1830s and '40s and provided inspiration for the Great Exhibition in Britain in 1851. In 1853, the Dublin Great Industrial Exhibition showed that the public had such an appetite for art that the National Gallery of Ireland was founded at once and opened its doors in 1864. Generous funding and art bequests from wealthy patrons made it a great success. The Public Libraries Act in 1855 mirrored British developments five years previously.

The Transport and Communication Revolution

There were parallel revolutions in transport and communication. These would have enormous effects not merely on the social habits of people but also on their way of doing politics and in their awareness of the wider world. Benedict Anderson's point is that such developments in the nineteenth century made nations smaller. There was a 'skein of journeys through which each state was experienced' by its inhabitants.[7] The Italian-Irish entrepreneur Charles Biaconi had been the first to capitalise on the horse-coach business after 1815 and soon acquired over a hundred vehicles, linking the main towns to one another. The Grand and Royal Canals were by now thriving thoroughfares linking the Liffey and Shannon rivers. Ireland, too, had its railway age – its engineers, navies and travellers. The story goes back to the early 1830s and, by 1850, work was in progress along 400 new miles of track. The connections between the main cities (Dublin, Belfast, Limerick, Cork) were followed by connections to the secondary urban centres like Galway, Killarney and Omagh. By 1870, the 2,000 miles of track catered to 14 million passengers per annum. The sociology of travel began to change as fares for third class were, by parliamentary order, kept cheap at one penny a mile. This led to a certain democratisation in modes of transport which could not have failed to have its effect in changing how people used space and thought about travel. The railway is also always credited with shrinking the nation, enabling the construct to be imagined more easily.

Certainly, whatever its impacts on a sense of nationalism, it did encourage a nascent tourism and the seaside at Bray, the Lakes of Killarney and the Giant's Causeway were great draws. Victoria's enthusiastic reaction to the scenery of Killarney inspired many others. Photography from the 1840s and postcards from the late 1800s played up the image of a wild rural paradise, remote, unspoiled and beautiful. Not only tourism but scholarship was facilitated by the new modes of transport. Celticists, emanating first from Germany in 1847 under the training of Johann Kasper Zeuss, began to come to Ireland to study the language and mores.[8] The railway age brought in a number of other major changes. First, it caused the regularisation of time. Dublin Mean Time was introduced in 1880; GMT (Greenwich Mean Time) would be observed in 1916. Moreover, it brought to the fore a new type of man: the engineer. One of the most notable was William Dargan – he was of fundamental importance in the growth of the network as well as being a member of the RDS and the main patron of the National Gallery. But he was also a nationalist and refused a baronetcy from Queen Victoria. The Irish mid-Victorian capitalists were sometimes less Victorian than one might imagine.

Communications were also a vital component of change in this era. On the ground, newspapers were flourishing. From 1853–60, Gladstone's budgets had repealed all duties on ads and paper. With no more 'taxes on knowledge', it was cost-effective to reduce prices and reach a wider audience. The *Irish Times* was launched in 1859, three times a week for a penny a week. It developed a Unionist stand point. The *Morning Post* was the first penny daily. The 100 papers in 1852 had become 140 by 1871 (22 of them Dublin based), ample evidence of a reading public, engaging more and more with the issues of the day, whether locally or nationally. What were the effects of increased newspaper reading? Undoubtedly the main effect was to politicise. There was also an appetite for the sensational and the 'martyrdom' of the Fenians in 1867 awoke just such a sympathetic response in the reading public. On another note, there was a huge demand for novels and Charles Dickens's three visits during which he performed his celebrated public readings were immensely popular.

The nineteenth century became an age of inveterate letter writers. The Uniform Penny Post was introduced across the UK in 1840, thus ensuring the delivery of mail anywhere in the archipelago for the uniform price of one penny. Previously, the mail had been a complex system whereby distance had a bearing on price. Comerford has come up with some interesting statistics. In 1839, one letter per head was sent. In 1870, it was 12 letters per head – that is to say, 65 million letters in total. This is a significant increase (although less than half that of England and Wales) and denotes growing comfort with literacy. The percentage of illiterate people had fallen from 53 per cent in 1841 to 33 per cent in 1871.[9] The figures also denote the significant levels of geographical mobility which required letters to be written in the first place.[10] The American missive – money included – was a staple of many an Irish cottage. All told, the American money sent in this period was extraordinary. People were also now able to send telegrams. Four hundred towns had telegraph offices by 1870 and thus new and immediate ways of sending and receiving vital information.

Ireland also became a strategic place in the Anglophone communications revolution when it came to laying the transatlantic cable. In 1858, Valencia Island, off Co. Kerry, received its first message from America as the eastern terminus. The message read: 'Glory to God in the highest; on earth peace and goodwill towards men.' Teething problems meant that cabling was not properly effective till 1866. It was a major commercial success after that, only shutting down in 1966. Communications that would have taken a matter of 10 days by ship could be given and received within minutes. Eight words a minute was the initial speed and it kept getting quicker. It is hard to underestimate the importance of this development in making the world smaller. Ireland thus had its part to play in wider global stories of the communications revolution. It is an important antidote to a story of parochialism.

The Growth of Markets and Consumption

What of the market? Having been victims of unregulated market forces in the 1840s, the picture in the 1850s was rather different. There was a massive increase in traffic of all kinds – ships, goods, exports and imports. Dublin Port was thriving. The linen industry of the northeast had adapted supremely well to industrialisation and, by 1870, employed 55,000 people. Retail expanded. Department stores opened up, notably Hugh Brown's Grafton Street store, Brown Thomas, in 1848 and Arnott's on Henry Street, when the successful entrepreneur, John Arnott, took the shop over in 1865. People wanted more things. Although less obvious than in Britain, the idea of a mass market did take hold in this era in Ireland, too, and the availability of more made people desire to have more. Asa Briggs has charted the extraordinary plenitude of 'things' at this time.[11] There was, as Comerford notes, a 'spectacular rise' in the consumption of tea and tobacco after the Great Famine.[12] In this regard, the development may have favoured women who had control over household management. Like their counterparts in Britain, middle-class women were increasingly likely not to work outside the home during this period. The little luxuries were within the means of all but the very poor (of which, it must be added, there were still many). Indeed, as Casey points out, Ireland actually lagged behind England and Scotland in the provision of public housing.[13]

Of course, Ireland, like Britain, had its *nouveaux riches* – a capitalist and entrepreneurial class which did extremely well in the second half of the nineteenth century. The spectacular success story was, of course, Guinness Brewery. Their rise is a classic example of how, with forward-looking market ideas and the use of new technologies, fortunes could be made and, indeed, peerages achieved. Unlike William Dargan, the engineer, the Protestant Guinness family did accept a baronetcy and thus entered into the mainstream British aristocracy. From 1855–70, the volume of Guinness sales increased threefold in the capital and, thanks to the effective usage of new railways, fivefold everywhere else. The horse-drawn carts, with their wooden barrels full of the stout, became a familiar countrywide sight. This could be considered a small instance of, what Michael Billig has called, 'banal nationalism' – that is to say, the small, everyday representations that remind one of a national product or identity. Guinness became an Irish story.[14] Small breweries were squeezed out, unfortunately, as a result. By 1914, brewing was the country's largest industry – an intriguing fact in itself – and beer consumption per capita had increased sevenfold since 1850.

Mentalities

To turn from facts of change to attempt to reconstruct mentalities of the era is rather more difficult. To what extent had the Irish made their peace with the British system and all it entailed? There seems to have been a large degree of quiescence. We have already discussed the 'small farmer ethos' and what it connoted. This point could be further developed by suggesting that certain portions of the Irish middle classes self-consciously acquired or aspired to a veneer of Victorian 'respectability' and an interest in the social proprieties which had not been visible before. Evidence for this is intuitively compelling, although it is a subject upon which very little has been written. The infamous Donnybrook Fair was summarily brought to an end in the 1850s after a committee had been set up to campaign for its abolition. Some of the old traditions and superstitions – holy wells, for example – were frowned upon by those newly conscious of a dignity to maintain. Initiative also came from further up. In 1851, it became an offence in law to leave turf, dung or timber on the roads and to let swine wander freely. In the same act, carts were made to display their owner's names. Increasing regularisation of social habits and mores was a feature of the Victorian era in Ireland.

As regards language and changing sociocultural habits, it would be interesting to study high-status Dublin accents in the period to see if these were changing to reflect a growing sense of class, thus mirroring what was occurring in Britain. Certainly, it seems likely that at least some Victorian Irish benefited fully from *embourgeoisement* and would have cultivated the snobberies that distinguished them from those they deemed social inferiors. Jackson, emphasising the political, sees this as part of a surprisingly 'rich Dublin unionist culture'.[15] It also had sociological implications. An elite culture of masculine associational life took root. The gentlemen's club, established in the 1700s, took off in the mid-nineteenth century: the Kildare Street Club was a bastion of the Protestant Ascendancy, whilst the Stephen's Green Hibernian Club developed out of the initiative of Daniel O'Connell and attracted Catholic liberals and, later, Home Rulers. The *beau monde* tended to want to build new houses a little away from the increasingly down-at-heel city centres. Georgian house were left to decline whilst smart suburbs grew in Blackrock, Clontarf, Drumcondra and Rathmines in Dublin, Montenotte in Cork and the Malone Road in Belfast. Terraced gardens and the latest products of craft and industry were very much in demand. Vacations to the seaside resorts of Blackrock, Bray, Howth and Dalkey became very popular. The Victorian Irish, like their British counterparts, did like to be beside the seaside.

There was also a growing consciousness of the necessity of preserving native heritage that fits in with wider international trends. The Dublin Museum of Science and Art was founded in 1877 by an act of Parliament and its new buildings on Kildare Street were opened to the public in 1890. It showed off to an excitable new public the treasures of Gaelic antiquity, just as the museums in South Kensington were doing for the cultured classes of London. The same act also established the National Library of Ireland, one of the earliest to use the Dewey Decimal System. Heritage thus began to be packaged, institutionalised and commodified in a way that it had never been before – a clear reflection of the growing comfort of middle-class society and their liberation from more basic concerns like food and shelter.

Urban spaces began to be used more creatively and even democratically. A good example of this is the growth of public parks. St Stephen's Green, a 22-acre space in the heart of the city, had been open only to residents and subscribers since 1814 but was in much disrepair. When Albert died, Queen Victoria suggested it be renamed Albert Green, but the Dublin Corporation brusquely refused, a sign of the disjunction between the city and its monarch. By the 1860s, there was a campaign to make it a public park. The *Nation* newspaper thought it a 'hateful relic of barbarous feudal distinctions and arrogant class exclusiveness' and insisted that it ought to be the public property of the citizens.[16] Sir Arthur Guinness was keen to support it as long as the government would do its share. One of the arguments he made was that the Phoenix Park, whose People's Flower Gardens had opened in 1864, was too far away for artisans to make use of. He pointed to the success of the National Botanic Gardens to show that Irish workers could be trusted not to destroy the flowers. In 1877, an act was passed to re-open the Green and, by 1880, the public could make use of the attractively laid-out lawns, water features, benches and rockeries. A bandstand was set up, perhaps to mark the Queen's Jubilee in 1887 or perhaps rather earlier, and that great Victorian staple, the brass band, provided musical entertainment for the city dwellers. It was noted that children increasingly frequented the park and it was hoped that it had a positive effect on public health.

Cultural life was vibrant. A college of music was established in 1848 and it became the Royal Irish Academy of Music in 1871. Within ten years, it had attracted the Italian composer Michele Esposito, who revitalised the musical scene in Ireland and established the 70-piece Dublin Orchestral Society in 1899. This was a national first. Theatre was given a boost when The Gaiety Theatre of South King Street opened its doors in 1871.

The Lord Lieutenant attended the opening night. Designed by C. J. Phipps, The Gaiety, with its Venetian façade, red and gold interiors and tiered balconies reflecting all those nice social distinctions, was an archetypal Victorian setting. So too, in their way, were the conspicuous new Catholic churches, the most notable by the Briton, Augustus Pugin, who gave the country some very fine neo-gothic structures, notably St Mary's Cathedral in Killarney, which happily combined Irish and English medieval features. Some formidable Victorian mansions were constructed also – Muckross House in Kerry (1839–43) where Queen Victoria would stay on her visit in 1861 and Kylemore Castle in Connemara (1867–71). The latter was paid for by Mitchell Henry whose father had made his money in the Manchester cotton industry.

The world of leisure was expanding. The Irish had, for many centuries, obsessed over their horses, but it was only in the mid-nineteenth century that meets and races were more formalised. Fairyhouse opened in 1848, Galway in 1869 and Leopardstown in 1888. The Dublin Horse Show, which rapidly became an annual society event, began in 1868. The first Irish Grand National occurred in 1870. Elite Dubliners, in particular, also kept up to date with the up-and-coming sports of the day. In fact, there is a rather unusual back story to that most typical of all upper-class nineteenth-century games, croquet. A game called 'crookey' was played in Ireland in the 1830s and, by 1852, it had migrated to England where it became rapidly very popular, not least among the Victorian court. Soldiers in the Curragh brought golf to Ireland mid-century and, by the mid-1890s, the Golfing Union of Ireland and the Irish Ladies Golf Union had established themselves. In 1877, the Fitzwilliam Lawn Tennis Club was founded and, two years later, an Irish Lawn Tennis Championship had been established, making it the second oldest in the world. One of the minutes condemns the disastrous practice of letting women play upon the courts in heels. The Victorian Irish, like their British counterparts, were earnest about amusing themselves and about making rules to regulate those amusements.

Policing

Against this background, it may come as something of a surprise to be recalled to the reality of a negative British vision of Ireland. This is manifested, above all, in the unusually high concentration of police – armed and centralised from 1836 onwards. There was one policeman for every 425 people. Put more strikingly, this meant that Ireland was 'twice as heavily policed as England and Wales and two-and-a-half times as heavily policed as Scotland'.[17] Still, the subculture of rural unrest remained. It is a comparison not often drawn out but still worth making that the 1860s also saw the birth of the Sicilian Mafia. Although in many ways a very different entity, there were parallels between this and contemporaneous Irish movements. It was not just that these movements were secretive and criminal. It was not just that both came from a society with very close familial bonds. It was that both were, essentially, pre-modern, their very existence proof that the state was failing its job. Of course, as Vaughan points out, the government had not been doing a very good job of controlling arms. Arms licensing had been brought in from 1843 onwards; by 1870, even revolvers had to be licensed. But, he insists, this was more an excise measure than a political one. 'For a country that was supposed to be plagued by disorder, the control of arms was poor, to put it mildly.'[18]

The Fenians and the Irish Republican Brotherhood

By the 1860s, new revolutionary movements were making themselves felt, which showed the British government just how tenuous their control could prove. These new revolutionary currents were embodied in the Fenian brotherhood. Fenianism's role in the nationalist canon was quite clear: it was the direct precursor to the revolutionary movements of the early twentieth century. Revisionist thinking is keen to place it in its socioeconomic context and interpret it as a particularly vociferous reaction to Victorian change. Tom Garvin makes the point that the real enemy of the Irish rebel was not the British soldier or the police but rather the 'continuing steady adjustment of Irish society to commercialized, capitalist, modern civilization'.[19] It was this drip-drip of growing societal complacency that explains their nostalgia and their disruptiveness, even though they relied on modern methods.[20] Instead of focusing on its continuity within a tradition of nationalism, Townshend points to its novelties, its inspiration from freemasonry and continental anti-clericalism and the fact that it had no scruples at all about violence.[21] Some of its personalities have even been deemed fanatical by Garvin.[22] It had a vague programme and, unlike the Young Irelanders, was not particularly interested in culture, although, like them, it gave importance to rhetoric. Many of its members were drawn from the artisan classes who were newly disturbed in an age of industrialisation. That the Fenian influence is remembered rather than the equally worrisome social discontent in England in the same period is not because they differed in gravity but because they differed in legacy.

That the Irish revolutionary tradition needed to be reborn was clear. It had been morally and politically defunct since 1798 with inconsiderable spurts of life in 1803 and 1848. Now it was the Irish-American communities that gave the push-start. Fenianism, indeed, was the 'decisive proof that a greater

Ireland beyond the seas now existed'.[23] In fact, there were brother movements that are grouped under the same umbrella. One James Stephens set up the Irish Republican Brotherhood (IRB) on St Patrick's Day in 1858; a year later, the Fenian Brotherhood under John O'Mahony emerged in America. For all that the name recalled the ancient Irish warrior caste, the organisation was not merely or even mainly introspective in orientation: American political tradition and Second Empire France were huge influences on their thought.[24] Secrecy was a feature, but it was not absolute because, in 1863, they began to publish a paper called the *Irish People* which earned them the praise of no less a person than Karl Marx for being a socialist lower-class movement. Marx wrote about the Irish Question in the *New York Daily Tribune* and thus brought his analysis to a transatlantic audience.[25] Marx and Engels both took a great interest in the country and were the first to, in the words of Anthony Coughlan, pioneer a 'systematic analysis of the country's social class relations', their collected writings on the subject amounting to 500 pages.[26]

Irish Socialism

Indeed, Ireland's connection with the growing phenomenon of socialism is an interesting one. Historians have been rather slow to integrate this into mainstream accounts of the period. Fenians had links with the First International movement (1864–76) and participated in its Geneva Congress in 1866. For Karl Marx, the Irish Question was not simply one of nationality but also one of 'land and existence'. He envisaged a choice between '[r]uin or revolution' and even predicted that Irish emigration patterns could lead to a war with America.[27] He articulated this in a speech to the German Workers' Educational Society in 1867. Yet, the connection should not be overstated. Although popularly considered anti-clerical, most Fenians were, in fact, reasonably Catholic and their motto 'no priests in politics' might indicate nothing more than an instinct to keep the spheres separate.[28] It should not be taken as an automatic sign that they were rabidly anti-clerical and proto-communists. Later, the disconnection was made further evident when Karl Marx and Friedrich Engels both condemned the paltry Fenian attempts at a rising in 1867. The former thought it 'very stupid'.[29] There was also a way in which the Irish impeded the emancipation of the working class in Britain. This was because the national antagonism between English and Irish workers in Britain had prevented them coming together in a common cause and overthrowing their exploiters. Marx would read British repression of the Irish international in the light of an attempt to put down the first effort at pan-working-class solidarity.

Fenian Rising 1867

The year 1865 was key because it brought to an end the American Civil War. The British government feared that Irish-American officers would migrate back to Ireland in droves, so they decided to organise a pre-emptive round-up of all the usual suspects. John O'Leary and Jeremiah O'Donovan Rossa were both imprisoned. In this context of repression, the Fenians made two admittedly paltry attempts at a rising.[30] In February, Kerry rose up and was easily crushed. The 5 March episode was squalid, not least because of appalling hail and snow. The following day, the rebels fled, those who were captured had their belts and braces cut and had the humiliation of holding up their trousers as they were marched to prison. Damp though the risings were, they put fear into the British establishment. Two factors made it particularly acute. Firstly, 1867 was a disturbed year in Britain, too, with the controversy surrounding the Second Reform Act. Secondly, this sudden outbreak of Fenianism upset the cosy *Pax Britannica* which had been pretty much secure since 1848. It reminded people that there *was* a real Irish problem and that the mid-Victorian boom had not made it go away. It is also important to dwell on the Irish reaction. On the whole, respectable Irish opinion was quite hostile to the Fenians. They were felt to be an unrepresentative minority. The Catholic clergy, in particular, deplored the criminality of the acts. Later that year, after the Manchester trial, a bishop from Kerry would speak the resounding words of judgment: '[W]hen we look down into the fathomless depth of this infamy of the heads of the Fenian conspiracy, we must acknowledge that eternity is not long enough, nor hell hot enough to punish such miscreants.'[31]

The reaction of the clergy is a point worth emphasising. The matter was a complex one. The doctrine of the church was carefully nuanced when it came to using force to resist an unlawful authority or an authority overstepping its mandate. The notion of justified resistance had been in place since the Middle Ages. There was a theology of resistance, formulated by Augustine first and then by Aquinas. This was the *jus ad bellum* – the right to make war. However for that to happen, certain conditions had to be met (e.g. just cause, right intention, good authority, proportional gain) and there seems every reason to believe that, for the present, most clerics did not feel such conditions were applicable to Anglo–Irish relations. They were grateful for the benefits of the British connection and found it morally a better position to lobby for reform rather than side with the revolutionaries. That would change – many in the church would put their weight behind the national struggle – but never unambiguously so, especially among the higher ranks. The secret societies were excommunicate by virtue of being in secret societies and they often went to confess to certain religious orders that were willing to bend the rules on their behalf in the interest of the care of souls.

From Miscreants to Martyrs

Then events occurred to change the status of the Fenians from heartily disliked criminals to highly venerated heroes in Irish eyes. On 18 September 1867, two leading Fenians were being transported to gaol when the police vehicle that they were in was attacked as part of a rescue. The prisoners did indeed escape but the policeman was shot dead. As a result, five Fenians were convicted of murder and three were sentenced to death by hanging. Exemplary public hangings had fallen somewhat out of fashion in recent years due to changing attitudes – an increasing embarrassment with this aspect of the criminal justice system and a desire to 'hide it away' from prying media eyes. But, at a makeshift execution venue outside Salford prison, in front of a crowd of up to 10,000, William Phillip Allen, Michael Larkin and William O'Brien met their end. It was a public spectacle and the media dwelt upon it. For Robert Kee, the executions illustrate the level of the government's 'obtuseness' and failure to read the signs.[32]

More was to follow. In November 1867, the wall of a prison at Clerkenwell was blown up by gunpowder to help Fenian inmates escape. Twelve people died and 120 were injured. Now the fact that this was a terrorist act on the greatest capital of the world struck anger not just into the very heart of the establishment, but into the working-class English, too. They were outraged and old anti-Irish prejudices were once again reworked. Whether this incident endangered the wider socialist cause is debatable. Marx certainly believed that it had seriously damaged the prospect of solidarity between the working-class Irish and Britons. Of more immediate importance was the change in public attitudes towards the Fenian 'martyrs'. Michael Barrett, the man responsible for the explosion, was hung at Newgate on 26 May. His was the last public hanging ever in Britain, a dubious distinction in itself. Once again, some Irish newspapers stirred up popular sympathy. Public moods are one of the most unaccountable factors in history. Why the attitude of a critical mass of people suddenly changes seems, at times, out of all proportion with the causes. Historians have sometimes been rather behindhand compared with social scientists in studying conformism as a reason for massive opinion shifts. And yet, this is undoubtedly what occurred. The formerly execrated Fenians began to be thought of as martyrs. There was a growing consensus on this. People sympathised not with the manner of their struggle, but with some of their aims and, most of all, their frustration with British rule. The popular song commemorating them, written by T. D. Sullivan and entitled

'God Save Ireland' (1867) became an unofficial national anthem.[33] With its rousing lyrics containing reference to the 'vengeful tyrant' and the 'cruel foes' and the heroism of death for one's country, it could be said that the seemingly cosy sense of *Pax Hibernica* had ended. Contented Victorianism had been punctured. There was a faint stirring in the blood as Irish opinion became unsettled again. Was this the beginning of an Irish revolutionary impulse? Garvin even believes that 1867 marks a peak in the first revolutionary phase that began in 1858 and ended in 1879; he believes the other revolutionary phases continue to 1923.[34] But whether or not this does indeed deserve inclusion within a revolutionary history, it is certain that it caused some trouble to the minority Conservative government under Lord Derby and Disraeli that was presiding at the time of these incidents. Disraeli took the reins as prime minister in 1868, but his government was precarious in the extreme and only lasted a matter of months. One man, newly taking over from Russell as the leader of the opposition, was watching on with unusual levels of interest and an uncanny exercise of the imagination – William Ewart Gladstone.

Chapter 12

GLADSTONE'S FIRST MISSION

Historiographical Interpretations

However differently historians judge the impact of Gladstone's four premierships (1868–74, 1880–85, 1886 and 1892–94) on Ireland, their momentous nature is never questioned. To do so would be to deny the constitutional revolution that he instigated by his conversion, during his second period in office, to Home Rule. Nevertheless, there are some very definite areas of contestation and historiographical debate. The first set of these pertain to his motivations. Were they, as traditionalists have argued, coherent and evolutionary throughout? Was his Irish policy reflective of a moral drive to restore justice, a true manifestation of his liberalism? This was the classic thesis of his early biographer, John Morley and also that of J. L. Hammond, the latter defending the noble 'spirit of his faith in moral forces and the reconciling power of freedom'.[1] Revisionists have cut across this account. They have emphasised motivations that were more pragmatic and party political, and thus subject to all the vagaries that circumstances might imply. John Vincent makes him look more calculating in his approach to Ireland and claims that he adopted Home Rule because there was 'no other available position'.[2] Michael Winstanley constantly problematises Gladstone's self-presentation as a 'man in politics' rather than a politician and insists that pragmatism was his hallmark, particularly from the 1860s onwards.[3] His very liberalism has been called into question – Richard Shannon argues that he became a 'kind of Liberal' but did not give up on his more traditionalist credentials.[4] Shannon, in particular, brings out the complex effect of his religious views on his Irish policy. On the one hand, his belief that he was an instrument of providence committed him to reform. But, on other hand, that very belief made him a 'passionate partisan; a theologian of the dogma of reform, rather than a careful politician', rationally working out what Parliament might grant and what the Irish might accept.[5]

Then there are questions which pertain to the nature of his Irish reforms. Should they be seen as exceptional, best considered apart on their own terms of reference? Studies emanating from Ireland often understandably approach it in this way. There are some justifications for this: Gladstone did not want Ireland to be a testing ground for what might work in Britain. To an extent, he always regarded Ireland as a special (and increasingly puzzling) case. But this approach has its limitations; it is necessary to situate the Irish legislation not only as a constituent part of a wider project of Gladstone's systemic reform in Britain and indeed as part of a broader Gladstonian agenda to reshape the Empire along more liberal lines. This being so, how do his Irish policies compare – can they, in any sense, lay claim to being his most experimental policy, his most inventive, his most ethical? Do they show off Gladstone, as it were, at his most Gladstonian? Do they, as some would argue, form his 'finest hour' politically speaking?[6]

All these questions need to be asked and yet there is one even larger one to keep in mind throughout the investigation and it concerns the less tangible issue of reputation and mythic status. There is a certain status clinging to Gladstone among Irish people to this day, that of a great reformer, indeed the greatest of all British statesmen in his relations with Ireland. It is a reputation largely uninterrogated by those outside the community of academic historians and even in scholarship, as Boyce has noted in his excellent review of the historiography, Gladstone has gotten off relatively lightly.[7] But how to separate the legend from the reality? We are not helped in the least by Gladstone's own ability to make his role seem epic, to present himself as a folk hero – in a celebrated incident, he presaged this in the very moment of his accession to power. The telegram announcing the victory of Liberals in the 1868 election reached him as he was felling trees on his estate in North Wales, a habitual leisure activity for this titan among Victorians. Pausing in his vigorous labours, he leaned on his axe, and, turning to his companion, said with a barely containable sense of drama, 'My mission is to pacify Ireland.'[8] Then he turned back to chopping his wood. Grandiose this sounded, indeed; he would soon be deluged in numbing levels of detail – not that any detail could be too numbing for Gladstone's extraordinary energies. But this incident, with its self-conscious dramatisation shows a politician acutely aware of the new media which could and did repeat this story to a mass audience. Winstanley makes the point that Gladstone was more aware than any prime minister before him that reputations were increasingly made outside Westminster.[9] Thus we must approach Gladstone on more than one level and interrogate that fine dynamic between private conscience, political pragmatism and public persona which he exemplified in his dealings with Ireland.

Early Motivations

Gladstone's general interest in Ireland predated 1868 and, in some respects, may be traced back to his sense of himself as Peel's political inheritor. This was an important background for the early evolution of his thought. For Eugenio Biagini, a historian of political thought, the influence comes down to two key points. Firstly, Gladstone learned from Peel the benefits of neutralising 'the state in its dealings with various religious bodies'. Secondly, he gleaned from him the habit of encouraging 'cross-community integration in the training of a new professional middle class'.[10] In short, Biagini maintains that what Gladstone took from Peel was his progressive pragmatism. Although acknowledging the value of this interpretation, it must be averred that there was something distinctively Gladstonian about the form his interest took. For Peel, Ireland was (and remained) a practical problem; for Gladstone, she was essentially a moral one, even religious. That was the crucial difference between the two and it is to be gleaned from an early comment of the young politician's. 'Ireland, Ireland: that cloud in the west, that coming storm, the minister of God's retribution on cruel and inveterate and half-atoned injustice.'[11] He had said this in 1845, on the cusp of the Famine disaster. This was not the language of Peel, but rather of a visionary who saw apocalyptic times ahead not only for a victim Ireland, but also for Britain, who would be held accountable for her neighbour's woes. Ireland, in this scheme of things, was to play the role of an avenging angel. There was something Old Testament–like about this statement and, indeed, about many of Gladstone's subsequent statements on the subject of Ireland. The role of charismatic prophet suited him quite well – it was a part he played to perfection. How best to understand this? Hammond offers the quite sensible interpretation that he had 'a larger imaginative understanding' of the Irish Question than other British politicians.[12] Political (and moral) imagination is key. He was very often thinking of the transcendent, roaming the outlying frontiers of the terrain where few had gone before. To his opponents, this smacked of fraternising with the enemy and, increasingly, Gladstone would find himself alone in the stances he took. Nevertheless, it took time for the Irish Question to come into sharp focus; despite the prescient pronouncements, his evolution was a slow and gradual one. Even in 1862 he could only say that 'among other objects in the distance' Ireland was 'again slowly growing into a political difficulty'.[13] Six years later, it had become the central plank of his election campaign. How did this shift come about it?

The evolution from occasional to obsessive interests clearly needs to be uncovered. One could argue, of course, that, even aside from Peel's inheritance, Gladstone's passion for great causes would light upon John Bull's other island sooner or later. A sense of divine mission was fundamental to much of his thinking throughout. Shannon, in his study in *Gladstone: God and Politics* (2008), investigates the multiple ways in which religion was a (or even *the*) 'crucial explanatory power' in Gladstone's political thinking and action – the conviction of divine election never left him.[14] Furthermore, a complex and tortured character such as he no doubt found something fascinating about the very complex and tortured nature of the Irish problem and it proved to be a fitting focus for the truly inordinate energies of his middle and old age. The wry dictum in *1066 and All That* (1999) that Gladstone spent 'his declining years trying to guess the answer to the Irish Question; unfortunately, whenever he was getting warm, the Irish secretly changed the question' has a degree of truth in it.[15] The Irish Question was fugal and elusive and, with a characteristic perversity, Gladstone chased it to the end of his career, baffled to the last.

Imperial Motivations

He had, of course, other reasons apart from the religious and heroic which prompted him to full-scale engagement with Ireland: there were imperial and political motivations at work, too. On the subject of empire, it is a good idea to approach Gladstone as a student of the great eighteenth-century Irish Whig political philosopher, Edmund Burke. Gladstone's vision of the British Empire was very much in Burke's mould, something that distinguishes him in the context of the hungrily imperialistic elite of the latter half of the nineteenth century. Unlike many others of his political generation, Gladstone was not an eager imperialist.[16] He did not subscribe to the 'wider still and wider' view of the British Empire. Although his governments presided over expanse, he was uneasy with it; expanse, in any case, largely happened outside direct control from London through the initiative of men on the spot.

However, all this does not mean that Gladstone was anti-empire. He *was* obsessed with the question of how to run the existing empire well and how to avoid the pitfalls of excess, extravagance, misrule and corruption. There was enough in that to occupy legislative energy. He was very aware of the sorry lessons of the past. A century before Gladstone first took prime ministerial office, the situation of the American colonies had arrested Burke's attention and he had eloquently urged the establishment to a course of conciliation rather than unreasonable antagonism 'Deny them this participation of freedom', Burke wrote, 'and you break that sole bond, which originally made, and must still preserve the unity of the empire.'[17] The government of the day had not listened, the colonies had rebelled and the rest was history. But this idea that the Empire was best governed by attaching the colonies to the mother country by the bonds of affection and freedom struck Gladstone forcefully. The British Empire should be one of liberty, not arbitrary power. Eventually, these ideas pushed him into considering greater levels of self-government for colonies. From this point of view, Ireland was, clearly, a policy priority. Her condition was a litmus test of the health of the Empire. If she was unhappy, then something was rotten indeed at the very imperial core. In short, Gladstone's Irish interests were not an eccentric luxury tacked onto his general political profile: they must constantly be placed in this wider intellectual context.

Political Motivations

Electorally, too, there were reasons to engage. The nature of the Liberal Party meant that it attracted the 'fringe' elements in society such as non-conformists and Irish Catholics.[18] This meant that it had more of a British than an English support base and it always needed to use the leverage this provided. Winstanley brings out the full force of this point when he says that '[r]eputations, as Gladstone well knew, were increasingly made away from Westminster'.[19] Politically, there was thus every justification in seeking to keep the Irish Catholics on side. This was made even more urgent by the context of the late 1860s, when, as we have seen, Fenianism was gaining sympathy, less for its violent agenda than for the shabby treatment of prisoners. Gladstone must have realised that there was something to be practically gained in championing the Irish cause, in driving it down the channels of legitimate reform rather than letting it drift, as it was then doing, so very dangerously. This is a good example of what Comerford describes as his active conscience, never running ahead of 'his pragmatic political practice'.[20] The need for votes was a very sensible reason for pledging himself to justice for Ireland. One could turn this point the other way around, of course, and say that the Irish were ready for what Gladstone had to offer in 1868. Stirred by the sufferings of the Fenians and in a state of political commotion, they were prepared to meet the premier half way, seeing in him someone who would be readier to govern Ireland with 'Irish ideas'. It is to be noted that the voters, encouraged by the clergy, voted overwhelmingly for the Liberals in the 1868 election. This lent Gladstone momentum from the bottom up.

There was another political motivation that we can attribute to Gladstone, and this is a more narrowly party-based one. The enmity between Gladstone and Benjamin Disraeli is a legendary one and provides many examples of one-upmanship over the decades of their co-habitation at Westminster. The year 1868 brought an opportunity for Gladstone to trump his discordially despised opponent. In dramatically bringing the Second Reform Act through in 1867 in a minority-Conservative administration, Disraeli had stolen the initiative back from the Liberal leader on one of the big questions of the day – electoral reform. Almost, it seems, in riposte, Gladstone announced to the House of Commons his scheme for Ireland in March 1868 and laid out his conviction that the Conservatives had failed lamentably in this regard. A week later, he moved that the established Church of Ireland should cease to exist as an establishment. Thus, whilst still in opposition, he sought to create a political opening for himself to win back the initiative from the government. Ireland then became one of the main planks of his subsequent election campaign. He was accused, at the time, of political one-upmanship, a charge which he studiously refuted. Nevertheless, it is not hard to see that party advantage could accrue from tackling an issue so much in need of legislation. It could not have been a more inaccurate instinct – he would neither pacify the Irish nor the Liberal Party. Rather, he stirred things up.

Early Reform

The years 1869–71 represent a crucial watershed. Vaughan sees it as one of the short periods when Ireland was utterly central to British politics. In this respect, it was akin to 1829 and foreshadowed 1881 and 1886.[21] It was, nonetheless, a very distinctive moment which changed the rules of the game entirely. It was also a very controversial moment that divided more than it united and, arguably, unsettled more than it achieved. The matters arising, fraught with complications by their very nature, absorbed much legislative time and energy: sessions on Ireland were exhaustingly long and Gladstone oversaw them at some cost to himself. Whilst it is more common in recent historiography to qualify the magnitude of the change that took place, it must be stated at the outset that change was indeed substantial and systemic and was concerned, like Peel's before him, with the three major areas: church, land and education.

On coming to power, the deliverance of the Irish Church Act was first on his agenda and convention would regard this as the most straightforwardly successful of all his early reforms. It was, moreover, achieved with 'apparent ease'.[22] In a sense, this was inevitable because it was a root-and-branch change, disestablishing the Church of Ireland and unlike the land question, it was clean cut. That said, it did not lack for controversy and it will be seen that Gladstone's methods of driving through change could alienate. Back in Peel's day, the disestablishment of the Church of Ireland would have been truly unimaginable. But times had changed, as had Gladstone. A vocal and educated Catholic middle class looked askance at such arcane legislation. The 1861 census had confirmed the existence of an overwhelming Catholic population of 4.5 million and a comparatively tiny establishment one of 0.75 million. The established status of the Church of Ireland was thus a more gigantic anomaly than ever. The principle of elementary justice was rudely offended. It was a 'hideous blot', Gladstone had acknowledged in a private communication in 1865. He wrote a chapter in his autobiography, explaining his change of mind.[23]

His readiness to do away with systemic injustice was born out in the decision, upon taking office, to take the formulation and the safe passage of the bill upon himself rather than leave it to any other minister. This indicates that something more than pragmatism was at work and lends support to an interpretation of great personal commitment to Irish issues, something that would remain characteristic throughout all his periods in office. He spent hundreds of hours crafting each measure. With extraordinary commitment to the minutiae and a deliberate emphasis on the heroism of the measure – he called it 'the most grave and arduous work of legislation that has ever been laid' – Gladstone began to tackle the matter at once. The first part of the bill established the principle of disestablishment, undoing this symbol of the Ascendancy from 1 January 1871. The change was systemic and, because systemic, revolutionary. Historians, although recognising the importance of the law, have often failed to do justice to the nature of the change in its broadest historical context. For that we need to look back to the sixteenth century. In 1560, the Irish parliament had acknowledged Queen Elizabeth as supreme governor and adopted the Acts of Supremacy and Uniformity. Just what was being undone now in 1869, by a few legislative strokes, was the entire Elizabethan settlement in relation to Ireland. Gladstone had torn up one of the legitimating politico-religious documents of Britain and Ireland's shared past.

The more complex (and less ideologically interesting) parts of the bill dealt with disendowment and the redistribution of funds and properties. The bill could have run aground on the admittedly convoluted details, but eventually a compromise was hatched whereby £10 million would compensate and pension off Church of Ireland clerics who lost out and £13 million would go to poor relief and education. The old Maynooth grant, erstwhile a subject of such controversy, was replaced by a permanent endowment. An 'ash-pale', Gladstone brought the bill through Commons with the implacability and the confidence of somebody who had already won. His momentum was seemingly inexorable. The House of Commons 'moved like an army', he duly noted; indeed, at this point, he was acting more like a commander than a politician, something that, again, seems to point to an absence of pragmatism in his parliamentary behaviour. The Lords gave way and an exhausted prime minister went back to his estate that August to recuperate. The Irish Church

Act became law, and Vaughan's summation of the whole as a 'masterly exercise in the constitutional dismantling of a great and complicated vested interest' is plausible.[24] Boyce offers a rather different perspective in evaluating it as a 'brilliant political manoeuvre against the Conservatives'.[25] It was, in short, a triumph, relatively speedily achieved and of incalculable consequences for the future. One of those consequences would be, as Jackson notes, that it broke down the division between Protestants and paved the way for an 'inclusivist "Protestant" identity'.[26] There was a flurry of protesting organisations – for example, the Central Protestant Defence Association and Ulster Defence Association. In many ways, the act and its aftermath functioned as the necessary preface for what followed in terms of both reform and resistance.

The Land Question

That said, Gladstone did not see what followed until well into the debates of 1869. Trying to pin on him a coherent 'programme' of reforms from the start is thus an untenable view. Nothing was inevitable. Nevertheless, his views about what might be done evolved rapidly through the study of the issues and debate. By the end of 1869, he had come to the conclusion that, although the church question was also indirectly a question of land, the latter had to be tackled separately with legislation of its own. A great deal of legislative tip-toeing would be required as he would have to try to deliver enough so as to satisfy the various Irish interests but had to be careful to avoid offending the Whigs who were still big landowners in the country and an important part of his own cabinet. Compromise was inevitable.

The most serious of the extra-parliamentary pressures facing Gladstone's government were those of the Tenant Right League, which was established as a nationwide organisation in 1850. It campaigned vigorously for tenant rights, summed up in a neat formula known as the Three Fs: fair rent, free sale and fixity of tenure. Prominent leaders became Irish MPs, forming the Independent Irish Party. In tackling the matter in the bill, Gladstone did not go quite as far as they would have liked, but he was acting under his own ideological constraints as well as internal political pressures.

The Landlord and Tenant Act

No historian believes that the Landlord and Tenant Act of 1870 was a huge success, although they divide upon whether Gladstone himself was to blame for this. Shannon faults Gladstone for too great a conservatism. Comerford, more understanding, points to Gladstone's inability to create a solution for problems that had been centuries in the making.[27] Hammond paints a picture of an earnest Gladstone, with 'characteristic courage and energy' fighting single-handedly in cabinet for his proposals.[28] There were three features of potentially great significance in the act itself. Firstly, the 'Ulster Custom', which had given tenants rights of sale and tenure, was given the force of law in the north but it was not extended any further to the rest of the country. The second clause of note was that evicted tenants were to be given compensation for improvements that they had made to their holdings. This, Gladstone felt, would make unjust evictions less common or, as he poetically (and hopefully) put it, it would cut the landlords' hands 'with the sharp edge of pecuniary damages'.[29] Thirdly, the bill allowed for the tenant purchase of holdings in certain circumstances. The landlord, of course, had to be willing to sell and the tenant had to be able to advance one-third of the price of purchase; the state would loan the rest and he would pay this back over 35 years at an interest rate of 5 per cent. These were clearly the most radical clauses of the bill and functioned as a shy advance towards the ideal of peasant proprietorship. It must be immediately noted, however, that Gladstone only reluctantly agreed to their inclusion. They were promoted by John Bright, a prominent radical whom Gladstone was keen to keep on side – a revealing insight into Gladstone's own limitations as leader and as reformer. The two houses were in agreement with the general principles. By the second reading, Gladstone had convincingly carried his case in the Commons and the Lords passed the measure in July. It was another personal triumph for the premier but, as regards its desired effects, an indubitably flawed one.

The bill was necessarily convoluted, all 73 sections of it. In fact, it may be said that few people understood the details and that it lacked the bold simplicity of the Three Fs solution. It did not advertise itself. No attempt was made to control rent prices so that eviction would still occur despite Gladstone's hopeful belief to the contrary. The courts had a way of interpreting the word 'exorbitant' rent in a way that militated against Gladstone's good-willed intentions. Finally, few tenants were in a position to afford advancing any money to buy their land; the offer of a state loan was, therefore, in most cases redundant. Such flaws are enough to make it, in Biagini's eyes, a missed opportunity.[30] Naively, Gladstone himself thought it would be a success. The fact that a coercion act had to be passed alongside, followed up by another in 1871 must have shown him just how wrong he was, although he still continued to hope.

How to interpret Gladstone's role in all this? Both this act and the Irish Church Act indicate that Irish issues were 'special case' scenarios for Gladstone. Disestablishment in Ireland was not meant to act as a precedent for an equivalent measure in England. That would have contradicted his deeply High Anglican sympathies. So also the land bill was an exceptional measure – it was not meant to give radicals in Britain ideas, despite what John Bright might want. There was a large element of the 'constructive traditionalist' about Gladstone as Winstanley has said.[31] So whatever else he was doing, Gladstone was certainly not using Ireland as a testing ground for what *might* work in England. Rather, it was the other way round. Ireland was made to try what supposedly *had* worked in England, where 'residence', 'personal familiarity' and 'sympathy' were all hallmarks of the landlord–tenant relationship, at least, according to the premier's somewhat rosy views. Ireland was to be allowed to 'catch up', to emulate a better model of community to that which it had known for centuries. Because of this, it is customary to judge Gladstone's act in 1870 as a failure to reach out to the Irish electorate by governing with Irish ideas. He dresses up as a liberal reformer but, as Shannon powerfully argues, one can still see in him the traditional desire to 'legitimate the government of Ireland in terms of the assumptions of the Liberal tradition'. And the assumptions of that Liberal tradition were conservative. The all-too-ready assumption of a 'community of interests between the legitimate and natural ruling classes of Britain and Ireland which would in turn legitimate the Union' was a problematic one.[32] Gladstone, in such a reading, was as yet politically immature in his attitudes towards Ireland.

Not all interpretations emphasise his failure quite so harshly. Considering the fraught context, what is striking is that a first real attempt was made to tackle the matter on a national and systemic level. The land situation was staggeringly complex. There had been whole centuries of exploitation and legislative neglect. One act could do no more than skim the surface. Realistically, it could be argued that the 1870 act was about as much as could reasonably have been achieved at the time. Comerford makes a very plausible point about the difficulty of 'creating' immediate solutions in such a field. He holds that the 'successful working of a commercial landlord–tenant relationship requires the existence of a complex of understandings and usages' and that these understandings and usages were non-existent in the Irish case. An effective working relationship is, he argues, a 'sociocultural accomplishment that cannot be conjured into existence by even the most sophisticated legislation'.[33] There could be no Gladstonian miracle, therefore, and the myth of unabated success is already deconstructed. That said, there was much hard thinking, great commitment and a real attempt to bring about legislative reform.

Education

The third plank in Gladstone's Irish mission pertained to universities. No doubt Biagini is right in pointing to Peelite influence in his desire to woo the professional middle classes to the British establishment.[34] No doubt, also, this was the most pragmatically motivated of his early reforms, but it was also extremely ambitious, showing a readiness to ruffle yet more vested interests. And this, unsurprisingly, is where he finally came aground. In 1873, he had begun to tackle the issue, proclaiming to the Commons that higher education for Catholics was 'miserably' and even 'scandalously bad'. The state had failed a sector of the population that they could not choose to ignore. His object here was to create an umbrella-like structure under which Trinity College, Newman's Catholic University, Queen's University Belfast and various other colleges would function. Once again, the Irish situation left him freer to imagine far-reaching solutions – it would never have occurred to him to try to incorporate the fiercely independent British universities. Yet, the freedom of his imagination met with the more constricted views of a variety of opponents. In the Commons, the motion was defeated on a second reading by a mere three votes. His opposition came from some Liberal secularists in his party and the Irish Liberal MPs who were ambiguous about the endeavour. Outside Parliament, the Irish Catholic hierarchy objected to the fact that there would be no theology, philosophy or history chair, which would, in their opinion, take the good out of the whole project. With this fresh example of the government advancing 'English' solutions for Irish issues, many priests now began to support the emerging Home Rule movement. For Gladstone, the defeat was bitter enough. Having proclaimed this to be a 'confidence' issue, he resigned briefly after the vote went against him but was persuaded to resume office upon Benjamin Disraeli's strategic refusal to serve. Let the Liberals peter out, was the latter's logic, they were already 'exhausted volcanoes'.[35] They limped on for the best part of an inglorious year – clearly the Irish Question had sapped Liberal energies. Gladstone called a surprise election in early 1874 and, rather to his surprise, lost, retiring (for now) from his position as leader of the Liberal Party. The 1874 election was a rather damp end to Gladstone's first mission, but there is no question that something major had been achieved and even more left lingering in the political air.

The Rise of Irish MPs

By now, things were definitely stirring in the Irish political cadre, however, and Gladstone was not responsible for it. The movement that was to cause such disruption to the British Parliament had fairly innocuous beginnings under the aegis of an MP called Isaac Butt. Conventionally, he was viewed as a fairly minor character and, in the nationalist canon, he gets very little attention. He pales in comparison to his political inheritor Parnell. But a recent interpretation attributes to him more significance than heretofore.[36]

Born in 1813, he was educated at Trinity College and called to the Irish bar in 1838. He started his career as a sort of Protestant patriot in the eighteenth-century mould and evolved to the point that he was a fervent supporter of religious toleration, tenant rights and the protection of Fenians from harsh treatment. He was a late convert to the idea of a separate legislature for Ireland, having become convinced that the Union was not working. He sought for a measure of 'independence without breaking up the unity of the empire' and without impinging on the sovereignty of the monarch.

On 19 May 1870, he gathered some like-minded, mostly Protestant, gentlemen together to discuss his plans. This was the nucleus of what became the Home Government Association and from 1873, with Butt's reluctant consent, the much more popular Home Rule League. They were essentially federalists. Unlike O'Connell, its founder was no great populist and it was *despite* rather than because of him that it gained popular momentum. Yet Butt, like O'Connell, was a parliamentarian and was elected for Limerick in 1871. The first sign of influence of the more general influence of his 'party' was the election coup in 1874. Whilst Liberal Party votes in Ireland plummeted from 66 (in 1868) to a mere 12 seats, 59 candidates (loosely) supporting Home Rule were elected. Forming a powerful bloc in the Commons, they constituted the heart of a new party, although discipline was as yet lacking. The Irish Question was about to be formulated anew by Irish MPs. British politicians would have to sit up and take notice.

Conservative Government 1874–80

But under Disraeli's Conservative government, it was asked in vain. Irish issues were not given the same oxygen as they had been before. They were simply not foremost on the prime minister's imperialist agenda. Interpreting Disraeli's attitude towards Ireland is a much simpler task than interpreting Gladstone's, for he thought and talked about it far less and got away with the minimum amount of legislation.[37] In the 1860s, he had tried to woo Irish Catholic MPs as he thought that their religious principles made them natural Conservatives. Before Gladstone came into office, he had been planning a scheme whereby both Roman Catholicism and Presbyterianism would be endowed.[38] But, in the 1870s, he was increasingly concerned that the Irish were trying to sever the ties with Britain and, with a subversive Liberal Party on their side, were set to 'challenge the expediency of the imperial character of the realm'. From 1874–80, Irish issues were thus put to the background. In these circumstances, there seems to have been something of a decline in morale among Irish MPs themselves – perhaps it was inevitable after the heady promises of Gladstone's ministry.

Butt was criticised for his unduly mild leadership – he insisted that his followers should continue to present the case but seek, all the while, for more immediate practical reforms. This approach was too polite and ineffectual for some. It was one of his nominal followers, Joseph Biggar, a doughty northerner and MP for Cavan, who developed the much more combative strategy of obstructing parliamentary business so as to make the mainstream parties take cognisance of the Irish Question. With long speeches, questions and motions for adjournment, these MPs made havoc with parliamentary etiquette but stayed always within the bounds of the strictly legal. 'What is that?' asked Disraeli witheringly when Biggar rose to speak for the first time. But such snobbery was impossible when faced with the rising light of the movement, Charles Stewart Parnell, whose social background was far above Disraeli's own.

For the young Meath MP, the strategy of obstructionism looked particularly attractive and he soon became most adept in its usage. Not only that, but he also claimed that it was a form of principled opposition not just opposition for its own sake. In a speech in Killmallock in September 1876, he described the duty of the Irish members to 'demand, and if we will not get what we ask by demanding it, then our duty is to show them that they must give it'.[39] Such tactics brought him into conflict with the increasingly sidelined Butt but this was a generational mismatch as much as anything else. Parnell was in his early 30s and Butt was ailing and did indeed die in 1879. It is common practice to overplay the distinctions between the two characters and their policies. Distinctions there undoubtedly were, but the underlying belief in self-government, the primacy of the House of Commons as a focus of debate were points in common. In any case, the advantage clearly lay with the younger man and, by the middle of 1877, Parnell had established himself as the effective leader of the movement.

Chapter 13

PARNELL AND THE LAND LEAGUE

Persona and Interpretations of Parnell

Who was he? Parnell was that most difficult of all types for a British politician to pin down – a member of the Irish-Protestant landed gentry with all the manners of a gentleman on the one hand, but possessing sympathies that were wider ranging than his own class and creed might conventionally dictate on the other. He had all the traditional traits of the Ascendancy: he hunted, played cricket, attended society balls at Dublin Castle and enjoyed horses. He was, in short, among the British elites, but not of them, a kind of *enfant terrible*. His contemporary Michael Davitt says of him that he was 'an Englishman of the strongest type, moulded for an Irish purpose';[1] Bew that he was a conservative with a radical tinge.[2] From a family established in the seventeenth century, he had an estate in Avondale, Co. Wicklow. His education in England had bestowed upon him an upper-class accent and a social circle which put him on an equal plane with those he interacted with in Parliament. But he had also developed a sort of interest in the plight of the Fenian martyrs, a luxurious eccentricity for an undergraduate at Cambridge in the late 1860s perhaps, but one with long-term political consequences.[3] These paradoxes surrounding the persona of Parnell have often been remarked upon. Yet, according to Conor Cruise O'Brien, these very ambiguities gave him credibility both at Westminster and in Ireland. His stature in Ireland, for example, placed him 'above the resentment which men feel at the advancement of their equals'.[4]

Although not a man of the people in his origins, he would cultivate that interest in them which, as has been seen from O'Connell's career, was inevitably the hallmark of those claiming unofficial leadership of a country so peculiarly situated as Ireland. Indeed, in that sense and in others, he may be compared with O'Connell. Parnell's original biographer ended his two volume biography in 1898 stating provocatively that O'Connell (rather than Parnell) was the 'greatest Irishman of the century'.[5] However that may be, Parnell's reputation has certainly remained higher in the public domain, Boyce and O'Day noting that he has been given a mystique 'usually reserved in Ireland for the martyred dead'.[6] Whether this is largely due to the tragically romantic nature of his fall from power or his personality and his achievement is another question. Certainly the romanticism of his end and of his persona has proved irresistible to some.[7] But revisionist scholars tend to nuance this image somewhat and see more reasons than pure martyrdom or stubbornness in his decision to cling to power until the end. Philip Bull sees him not so much as a 'victim' (the view of hagiographic accounts) but as a 'moulder of destinies'.[8]

Apart from the drama of his fall, there has been much historiographical debate about his contribution to the Irish Question. Comerford takes issue with any kind of hagiography, pointing to the limited nature of his achievement. He was successful in an area in which 'nineteenth-century Ireland excelled', that of party political mobilisation, but less than successful in guiding the country towards 'any of the more substantial bases of self-respect, such as economic enterprise, intellectual achievement or cultural enrichment'.[9] For all his talk about land, Comerford says that he did not do anything to inspire farmers 'to find out how two blades of grass might be made to grow where one grew before'. His support for the land war may have helped farmers, but the cost was to reduce the overall capital value of Irish land.[10] Bew claims that the much-vaunted unity that he created was superficial. How could there be real alliance between Catholic peasants and a squire, keen to salvage his own class (southern Protestant gentry) from the 'ravages of history'?[11] These criticisms are well made, but not all approach the man with such qualification. His original biographer saw his main achievement as the 'herculean labour' of combining church, constitutionalists and radicals in a united front and indeed this was an extraordinary moment of national consensus.[12] Alternatively, Conor Cruise O'Brien regards his mark of distinction to be his insistence on the 'primacy of the parliamentary principle'.[13] Indeed, as a politician he was at his most impressive and as a parliamentarian he made a huge contribution to British party politics.

The irony is that he went into politics by default. When other career options did not seem to tempt him, he turned to patriotic politics and began, as we have seen, to make a name for himself in Butt's Irish Tenant League. Susceptible to nervous illness, he was neither as robust a figure as O'Connell, nor as robustly populist, but he would learn to speak slowly and clearly on open-air platforms for maximum impact. There is a certain immediacy in his oratory which must have had its effect. He was particularly scathing in speaking of the injustices of English misrule but, at the same time, confident and reassuring, declaring that 'we shall beat the oligarchy in this country [...] without the shedding of one drop of blood'.[14] There was, furthermore, an achievement of self-control, even self-effacement in public which had its own attraction. T. P. O'Connor noted that it was a 'joke among his intimates that to Mr Parnell the being Parnell does not exist'.[15] The mercurial, the elusive and the ambivalent are all habitual descriptions of the man in both contemporaneous and historical accounts. Parnell left no diaries or memoirs, which makes interpretation even more challenging. F. S. L. Lyons, trying to reconcile the seemingly irreconcilable, goes as far as to say that there were four different Parnells: the country gentleman, the political genius, the companionable, if rather neurotic, eccentric and the dark, passionate figure who could breathe ice and fire at the same moment.[16] That he was a formidable figure is, at least, incontestable. In a very different sense to O'Connell, the British government would soon realise that they had someone to deal with. He was the proverbial loose cannon.

Context of Agricultural Depression

Cometh the man, cometh the hour. By the late 1870s, Ireland was in the throes of a vicious agricultural depression. The depression was European-wide and Ireland was hit especially hard. Meagre harvests, falling food prices and an outbreak of famine in the west precipitated a crisis of great magnitude, all the greater because of the higher expectations that some of these farmers had come to cherish. Foster's point is that the farmers were newly angry because, at last, they 'had something to hold on to'.[17] It was misery coming after a modicum of success and prosperity. As tenant farmers struggled to make ends meet, there followed the inevitable increase in eviction. In 1877, 2,200 families were forced out of their homes; by 1880, that figure had mounted to 10,500 and a staggering 100,000 tenants were in arrears and, from this disarray, a vicious land war ensued from 1879–82.[18]

Against this background, a new type of agrarian leader emerged – Michael Davitt, a Mayo man. In contrasting Parnell and Davitt, Paul Bew has seen them as representing 'two contrasting philosophies of Irish development' – Parnell's the social conservative, gentry-led vision, Davitt's the socially radical one based on peasant proprietorship.[19] This distinction is an apt reflection of their divergent background. Davitt's family had been evicted for non-payment of rent back in 1850, so he had a first-hand grudge against systemic inequities. Brought up in the restricted circumstances of an Irish immigrant community in Lancashire, Davitt had joined the Fenian movement and had been imprisoned for seven years. Upon release in 1877, he energetically threw himself into the most urgent matter of the day and championed the cause of the Mayo tenants. Just as significant is the fact that, in 1878, he visited the United States to meet John Devoy, the charismatic leader of Irish-American Fenianism who had gone into exile in 1871. The Irish-American Fenians had, since the late 1860s, regrouped under a new organisation known as Clann na nGael. It boasted a healthy 10,000 members by 1877. Their ultimate aim was insurrection, but they were quite ready to do business with Parnell, especially on the land question. It is difficult to offer an adequate explanation for this, but it seems that Fenians took hope from Parnell's bold public statements and the rhetoric in which he so clearly flirted with the language of aggression. At a speech on 24 September 1876, Parnell acknowledged that '[n]o amount of eloquence' could achieve 'what the fear of an impending insurrection – what the Clerkenwell explosion and the shot into the police van had achieved'.[20]

Devoy, who passionately believed in the abolition of landlordism, clearly thought that a crucial moment had arrived in the struggle and that some imaginative combination would be necessary at this juncture to drive things forward. Accordingly, both he and Davitt cultivated Parnell, who, although tentative at first, began to see the possibilities of a new sort of parliamentary-populist manoeuvre. On his own, he lacked popular credentials; with these men he might attain them. It was Devoy who telegrammed him on 25 October 1878, suggesting a 'New Departure'.[21] In using the weight of public pressure to increase pressure on Westminster, the new departure was, in some respects an old departure: O'Connellite precedents were still in public memory. But this was principally an agrarian cause and campaign, not a religious or a constitutional one.

Besides, it was novel that there was to be a close connection between widely differing strands – the agrarian radicals, the revolutionary nationalists and the constitutional nationalists would now all work together to the one end. Parnell, typically laconic, made no public response to the telegram but within days he had accepted an invitation to speak at the Ballinasloe Tenants Defence Association, a clear indication of acceptance. It is not always predictable that a leader will find himself suddenly popular before the tribunal of public opinion but it certainly happened here. The time was ripe and the man, impressive. Thus did a discontented public learn to welcome and later worship the unlikely figure of Parnell, a different type to O'Connell but with his own sense of dramatic style. His words spoke of moral combat. Keep a firm 'grip of your homesteads' he told Limerick peasants in August 1879. It was what they wanted to hear. Maybe it helped to hear it said by a Protestant gentleman. It made resistance seem 'safer' somehow. He gave them a new sense of powerfulness and entitlement. '[N]o power on earth could prevail against the hundreds of thousands of tenant farmers' campaigning together.

And he assured them that whatever happened, they would not be exterminated as they were in 1847. Times had changed.[22] A meeting in Dublin between Devoy, Davitt and Parnell cemented the connection, proving, once again, that shared grievance had its own binding power.

The Irish National Land League

What was now needed was a national organisation to harness this feeling. Although the agrarian basis needs to be stressed, the outcome was also, according to Comerford, a 'political movement that was to overturn Gladstone's and everyone else's assumptions about Irish politics'.[23] Accordingly, in August 1879, Davitt founded the National Land League of Mayo and, two months later, the Irish National Land League equipped with the emphatic slogan 'the land of Ireland belongs to the people of Ireland'. It was funded mostly by Irish Americans. If anything was to be achieved, the leadership had to be plausible to a British audience and so Davitt, even against some voices in the Irish Republican Brotherhood (IRB), persuaded Parnell to step up to the task. What was in it for the latter? In the first place, it provided him with a ready-made public platform and a way of wooing both lay and clerical castes. 'Ireland for Parnell' became the common cry. The priests had held him in suspicion previously, now he garnered their favour and that helped to establish his reputation all the more. As C. J. Woods makes clear, the favourable opinion of Archbishop Croke was crucial and Parnell courted this deliberately. But Woods also notes that Parnell remained in control – the priests only joined the league on 'invitation and on his terms'.[24]

He was also now able to conduct a riotously successful public speaking tour of America in 1880. This part of Parnell's career is indicative of the extent to which the Irish Question was internationalised by the latter half of the nineteenth century and projected as a universal humanitarian cause. O'Connell had never received funding from America, but now, with a proactive and politicised diaspora as well as closer media networks, this was made possible. Parnell thus visited 62 cities and travelled 16,000 miles. In Philadelphia, he announced that '[w]e must push the cause in Ireland, in England, and in America. We must push it everywhere, for all the world over are to be found our countrymen'.[25] He had certainly found his mature public voice. This sort of publicity lent him a new *éclat*, besides gaining for the league and for the destitute some valuable funds – an impressive £72,000 was collected in two months. The exiles gave supremely generously to a country most of them would probably never see again in their lifetimes. As regards his party, his status as president of the league gave him a moral mandate for his more aggressive tactics and allowed him to sideline the moderates even further. Moreover, somebody as coolly intelligent as Parnell could not but be aware of the advantage of riding the tiger of mass agitation. It was a way of ensuring that the government of the day would sit up and take notice. And it did.

By then, of course, the Land League's activities had extended in scope. Despite some vagueness about its aims and a 'shaky structure',[26] it had indeed become, within months, a mass movement of tenant defence, very western in orientation, and, what is more, wielded a moral authority which had a potency all its own. The story of its immediate popularity has been questioned – Comerford claims that it took off countrywide in 1880, the first year of good harvest, as that was the time when landlords were trying hardest to recover their arrears of rent.[27] Its methods were non-violent but certainly confrontational and, according to some, belligerent.[28] The term 'boycotting' emerged in this context from a Captain Charles Boycott, a land agent for a 12,000 acre estate, who had had the temerity to evict some tenants. People simply refused to work under him. They scattered his cattle and would not sell food to him. They spat and hooted and treated him as a 'leper of old'. Was this sort of intimidation seen as being morally legitimate? It was a question well asked. This social ostracising had been encouraged by Parnell, who urged the creation of 'a moral Coventry' for those who bettered themselves from other's misfortune. But even here his influence was a moderating one. At the very speech in Ennis when he announced this tactic, somebody had cried out from the crowd that the real solution was to shoot the traitors. Shunning rather than shooting was Parnell's method and it worked, to a certain extent.[29] The practice also developed of only paying 'rent at the point of the bayonet' which aggravated the overstretched Royal Irish Constabulary still further.[30] Although the Land League itself was officially against violence, these were violent times and lines were consequently blurred. There were outrages of various degrees of gravity, from mutilations and attacks on persons to damage to property and animals. The statistics indicate a massive increase in such incidents, from 266 in 1877 to 4,439 in 1881, and this made the new Gladstonian government, which had taken over from Disraeli's ministry in 1880, smell conspiracy and insurrection behind the whole phenomenon.

Coercion

The government reacted, then responded. William Forster, the chief secretary, had the unhappy task of dealing with the situation on the ground. Nicknamed 'Buckshot' Forster, he was a sensitive man who became depressed about his role, but, although his reputation was only partly deserved, he did encourage Gladstone to respond by coercion. There were two acts in 1881 which allowed the castle to imprison those whom they reasonably suspected and also practically suspended *habeas corpus*. There was a fine line between constitutional and unconstitutional protest and Davitt, with his advocacy of rent strikes, was deemed to have crossed it; he was duly imprisoned. This sort of crackdown is long familiar to us, but times were changing rapidly and public opinion was, by now, much easier to mobilise against such harshness. Surely, it was argued, a military establishment of 21,000 soldiers and 11,000 policemen was excessive? A particular bone of contention was that the policemen had bayonets, rifles, bullets and buckshot – that is, that they served as a covert army. It was dishonest, argued Parnell passionately, a mere pretence at a civil force. The government might at least be honest in the pursuit of coercion and shoot down the Irish with 'all the insignia of organized oppression' rather than relying on the so-called civil force.[31]

The government's reaction was a godsend for Parnell. He used the opportunity of the debates in Parliament to articulate his own distance from the violent wing of the movement but also his hostility towards undue means of repression. By this, he managed to remould the Irish Parliamentary Party; this transformation of a group of followers into a super-disciplined party is sometimes regarded as his most characteristic achievement.[32] The debates about coercion were a rallying point and they demanded from Parnellites a level of assertiveness, aggressiveness and, above all, unity. Those who may have felt more than a little ambiguous about the revolutionary potential of the New Departure were now arguing on the safer grounds of *habeas corpus* and constitutional rights. A Parnellite army was being tried out for the first time. It is true that the coercion bills went ahead in spite of them, but his followers could now be considered, properly speaking, a party. It was a development of profound significance for the decade.

The Land Law Act

The spry 71-year-old Gladstone had come to power again on the back of a spectacularly successful campaign in Midlothian, Scotland in 1879 where he had lambasted Disraeli's government on every score. In the decade just gone, he had come to have more refined doubts about the way the whole British imperial project was being conducted. He objected to aggressive Disarelian diplomacy and fumed over the shallow triumphs of the Congress of Berlin. He was uncomfortable with emerging popular jingoism. He felt that the Christian credentials of Britain were being undermined. He wanted, with more solid justification, the British Empire to be a fairer, more just and more humane entity. Only then would it survive. As against the logic of a so-called 'forward policy' of empire, what was needed was true reform of the territories already possessed. Oddly enough, the intensity of the problems in Ireland struck him almost by surprise at the end of the 1870s. It seemed as if, despite his systemic reforms in his first ministry, the situation required new treatment. A lesser politician might have shrugged his shoulders, but not Gladstone.

He had been reluctantly convinced that coercion was necessary in 1881 but he was only too aware of the limitations of such policies. They were, at most, a temporary expedient, expensive, controversial and even morally repugnant when not combined with positive measures of reform. The Burkean empire did not depend on force. Thus did the Land Law Act of 1881 come about. It was essentially a political measure, designed to make the Land League redundant. Of enormous complexity and provoking longer debates than any measure since the Great Reform Act of 1832, it took 58 sittings, 15,000 speeches and 93 amendments in the Lords to pass. This was a legal marathon.

What did it do? Simply put, it effectively enshrined the principles of the Three Fs – thus, despite the deficiencies riddling the bill, it constituted a big concession. The act also established a Land Commission to which tenants could apply and their rents could be fixed for 15 years, long enough, it was thought, for them to make improvements to their holdings without fear of arbitrary rent increases. Furthermore, greater legal protection was afforded to the tenant so as to discourage eviction practices. The major fault of the act was that it excluded those who were already in arrears for rent. The number of debtors was not negligible, consisting of 150,000 leaseholders and 130,000 occupiers. It would do them no good in the least. Still, it is possible to interpret this act as 'one of the most momentous pieces of legislation in the history of modern Ireland'.[33] A measure of its success is the attitude of many farmers towards it. They were very grateful that the fixed rents were far lower than heretofore and, thus, did not continue the agrarian agitation. Still, it did not fully heal the woes caused by the agricultural recession. Emigration rose from 7.7 per 1,000 in 1878 to 17.6 in 1880 and a high of 21.6 in 1883.[34] Those figures tell their own story.

The Passage of the Bill

In the course of the passage of the bill through Parliament, Gladstone and Parnell locked horns, with Parnell behaving in his characteristically ambivalent fashion. He had much to juggle. He did recognise the magnitude of the concession and the satisfaction it would create among moderates in Ireland. He also comprehended the disappointment of more radical types, the agrarian left wing. Accordingly, as Lyons remarks, he 'solved his problem by balancing between the two extremes, thrusting in either direction as circumstances seemed to demand'.[35] Once he could ensure that the act would go through the Commons, he began to weigh in *against* the government and promote continued agitation for further reforms. In particular, he suggested that the Land League should bring certain test cases before the 'new tribunal' to see what stuff the act was made of. His game was deep and a bewildered government read it as opposition to the measure, pure and simple. Little about Parnell was simple.

The dramatic showdown between the two leaders occurred in October of that year. In Leeds, Gladstone publicly accused the Irish leader of arresting the bill, standing 'not as Moses stood, to arrest but to extend the plague'.[36] He then compared him unfavourably with the honourable Mr O'Connell. Parnell's riposte was swift. Two days later, in a public speech in Wexford, he accused the prime minister of being a 'masquerading knight-errant'.[37] The implication of incompetent blundering do-gooding was particularly cutting. He also referred scathingly (and very unfairly) to Mr Gladstone's power of trampling 'on the aspirations and rights of the Irish nation with no moral force behind him' and told his audience that he was bringing 'fire and sword into your homesteads'.[38] He had certainly happened on the 'go to gaol' square. Four days later, he was arrested and imprisoned under the very coercion laws he had opposed and lodged in Kilmainham Gaol. Every radical leader had, at some stage or another, ended up there at one period or another. Parnell, being a member of the upper classes, was made quite comfortable in his arrangements and not treated like a common-or-garden criminal.

A Gentleman's Agreement 1882

Historians have mused upon why Parnell was so clumsy as to get himself imprisoned at this point. Was it mere rashness on his part? Was it a desire to gain even more credibility, being aware of the 'aura of martyrdom that prison confers on patriots'.[39] Historians, such as Lyons, have sometimes seen him playing a deeper game.[40] The convenience of being in prison at such a time was not lost on Parnell. It is sometimes suggested that he deliberately went about having himself imprisoned because he felt that the end of the Land League was nigh and that striking out a new departure would be once more necessary. It allowed him to part ways with more radical agrarians like Davitt and Devoy once the marriage of convenience was over.[41] If he did calculate on being there, that does leave the puzzle as to how he expected that prison would do him any concrete good rather than just the negative advantage of keeping him from public visibility for a while. In any case, the time spent in Kilmainham, it is often argued, gave him valuable thinking time. By the spring of 1882, both leaders were in a position to let bygones be bygones. Parnell happily discovered that he could, after all, accept the land act with some qualifications; besides, the anniversary of Grattan's parliament turned his mind towards parliamentary political channels once again. He was never more than a superficial agrarian. Gladstone, for his part, was quite ready to do business with Parnell: the latter was the one obvious person whom it would be dangerous to punish too heavily.

The result was the so-called Kilmainham Treaty. It provided amnesty to the imprisoned leaders and relaxed coercion. It engaged Parnell in the campaign against lawlessness. He now promised to lend the weight of his support to the Land Law Act. As regards modifications to the actual act itself, although they did not go as far as Davitt and the more radical agrarians would have liked, some flexibility was introduced into the provisions so that leaseholders, too, would benefit and there would be protection given to the tenant in arrears. It was a surprising, but not unimaginable, turn of events. It showed Gladstone willing to compromise still further to fulfil his vision of a contented Ireland. For Hammond, this is one of those extraordinary marks in Gladstone's favour, showing that, once Parnell had accepted the Land Law Act, Gladstone, however much he might disagree with him on some issues, recognised him as somebody who should 'take his part in solving the largest problem before the British Empire'.[42] Biagini also has high praise for Gladstone at this point, claiming that he turned a 'semi-revolutionary situation' into one where 'grievances were voiced through legal and political channels'.[43] The compromise seemed remarkably simple.

There was a bitter aftermath however. Forster resigned his position in the castle immediately on hearing of such a shameful compromise, whereupon, Lord Frederick Cavendish took over. He was the husband of one of Gladstone's nieces. He had no sooner arrived when he and his undersecretary were set upon in the Phoenix Park by an extremist group called the Irish National Invincibles and stabbed to death. It was a horrifying murder which shocked the majority on both sides of the Irish Sea. It could have shaken the settlement to its foundations; it is a testament to Gladstone's forbearance that it did not. What it did was make both sides more desirous than ever to seek solutions.

Chapter 14

THE IRISH LIBERALS:
A UNION OF HEARTS?

Historiography

The 'solution', as laid down by Parnell, was Home Rule. Home Rule was to remain a dominant political motif until 1916, awakening deep passions on both sides and eventually threatening the whole institutional structure of the British state. The ultimate failure of Home Rule as a policy does not mitigate its importance in the least, both for Ireland and in the long term, for Britain. It is possible to see Home Rule as the first articulation of British federalism and to trace its descendants in Scottish and Welsh movements to this day.[1] Expanding upon this interpretation, Boyce has suggested that 1885, the year of Gladstone's conversion to Home Rule, represented a political and ethical turning point in the history of the UK and the British Empire.[2] Far from seeing it as a mistaken Gladstonian obsession, Biagini even claims that Home Rule served to strengthen and expand Liberal politics and that the 'synergy created by the "Union of Hearts" reshaped popular expectations of liberty and citizenship in both Britain and Ireland'.[3] Thus it is deemed an important subject in intellectual history. At the time, the Home Rule agenda sounded modern and O'Day has argued for its parallels in other parts of Europe.[4] But it also, as Alvin Jackson astutely notes, wore an air of tradition. It harkened back to a legacy of seventeenth-century patriotism and to the constitutional emancipation campaign. Besides, the collocation of Home Rule was itself a 'superb manifestation of Victorian marketing skills, parcelling some negative or ambiguous connotations within a formula redolent of family values and fireside comfort'.[5] It was well adapted to the spirit of the age, a focus for popular liberalisation and point of convergence for the desires and aspirations of a critical mass of people for at least 30 years.

There are many areas of historiographical debate. One concerns the motivations and role of Gladstone. Whether he pursued this agenda more for reasons of principle or pragmatism and whether his blind spot over Ulster was just a 'tactical blunder', as Fleming has suggested, or something more serious may well be questioned.[6] Ostensibly, Gladstone presented Home Rule as a matter of overwhelming principle: there was a dramatic conversion moment, a media moment, be it added, when Gladstone's views were 'outed' in the public sphere. Biagini remarks upon Gladstone's insistence that 'policy should reflect moral imperatives' and that this enabled a culture of moral politics to flourish.[7] But this does not mean that party calculations were unimportant. Cooke and Vincent in *The Governing Passion: Cabinet Government and Party Politics in Britain 1885–86* (1974) have explored this dimension and needled the traditional accounts.[8] Then again, Gladstone's own role in the sponsorship of Home Rule is ambiguous. Doubtlessly, without him the agenda would have got nowhere. Still, his methods and his obsession with the question turned some people off and succeeded in fracturing his own party.[9]

Another great debate concerns the revival of Unionism. One might wonder whether Unionism needed to be revived. It had become quite engrained by the 1880s, proof of the success of Irish conservatism and appropriation of the advantages of the Victorian revolution. Jackson paints a picture of a 'luxuriant' and vibrant Unionism which had bound together the southern middle classes and the northern industrialists, Dublin and Belfast working classes, as well as attracting the intellectuals in Trinity College Dublin and Queen's College, Belfast.[10] Generations had grown up within the framework of Union and all but the most radical took it for granted. The prospect of self-government convinced its most ardent defenders that the Union itself was in danger. Typically, this is seen as an Ulster phenomenon and it became primarily so. Two factors are particularly compelling in its evolution. First, the speed with which the phenomenon of Unionism was 'pruned down to a northern core' was striking.[11] Secondly, the methods used, paradoxically a militant kind of *rebellious* loyalism were new. The new Unionists would become revolutionaries of the *status quo*. Townshend makes the point that, though they spoke loudly about the symbols of the Crown and the Empire, their fundamental loyalty was to themselves and to their Protestant way of life.[12] However narrow Unionism became, it was not entirely homogenous. Boyce warns against overdrawing the distinction between Anglo-Irish (southern Protestant) and Ulster Unionism. He also contends that regarding the latter as a solely Presbyterian phenomenon is erroneous: Anglicans were found in the ranks of the Orange Order, for example.[13] Still, however, the perception of the new, belligerent Unionism as primarily a northern and a sectarian Presbyterian phenomenon is largely accurate.

A Matter of Party and Expedience?

One of the strongest arguments for the importance of party politics in the introduction of Home Rule lies in the confusion surrounding who would sponsor it. It was not inevitable that it would be the Liberal Party. Parnell himself thought it might be the Conservatives, whilst Gladstone very much hoped it would be the Conservatives as they stood a better chance of getting it through the two houses. The Conservatives were obviously unwilling to contemplate such a radical change, but conscious that something must be done. The Lord Lieutenant, Lord Carnarvon, gave Parnell some intimations that his party might be induced to consider the matter, having in mind a measure of local government. He was suitably vague as to what this might entail in practice.[14] Parnell clearly thought this a good bet (or feigned to believe so) and backed the Tories in the 1885 election. The results were as follows: 335 Liberals, 249 Conservatives and 86 Home Rulers. That meant that the Irish members were now in a strategic position.

Luckily for them, Gladstone saved them from the necessity of a *volte-face* by adopting Home Rule in 1885. How major a turning point this was for him may be questioned. There was something of a slide from ideas of devolved local government to full-blown Home Rule. In the Midlothian Campaign, he had put forward the idea of devolution all around, i.e. for Scotland and Wales and England also. Certainly, he did say a great many things in his 1879 campaign speeches which were not meant to be pragmatic policies. He was, after all, contending merely as a member of the Liberal Party, having for a few years resigned its leadership. But what we *can* say for certain is that he was ruminating on such ideas as a possible (and cheaper) way forward for the United Kingdom. Gladstone was always one to worry about cheese parings and candle ends in government, on the principle that good government was thrifty. Ireland, as it was, was a drain on the exchequer.

A more radical interpretation of Gladstone's pragmatism is possible. In Cooke and Vincent's *The Governing Passion*, it is suggested that this new agenda was Gladstone's way of retaining his dominance over a fractured Liberal Party, a party increasingly keen to oust him.[15] In this reading, Gladstone pursued the policy for his own executive ends: there was no 'happy or generous note about it'.[16] The 'Grand Old Man' felt that he needed a transcendent cause to rule his party through the people. This narrative runs counter to the usual story of Gladstone's overwhelming sense of mission in 1885–86 and reformulates it instead in terms of party calculation. The focus is not on political imagination but on control. It is a plausible interpretation up to a point. The Liberal Party was an eclectic mix of incompatibles and Gladstone's charismatic leadership was sometimes resented. At this stage, they did have their doubts about the sanity of their leader. The queen had some, too, be it added. His rages and passions were quite something to behold. However, this interpretation is not entirely justified, not least because it fails to do justice to the fact that Gladstone almost always had to believe in and rationalise a policy before he brought it through. Moreover the idea that Ireland would enable him to unite his own party was a far-fetched one which the experience of the 1870s had already taught him.

Gladstone's Rational Conversion

It seems likely that Gladstone had become rationally convinced that a substantial measure of self-government had become necessary for Ireland in its present state and convinced, also, that he was the divinely ordained means to bring this about. His epiphany may have preceded 1885. He had visited Ireland for the first and only time in October 1877 for four weeks and there he had a very positive experience, although that was before the agrarian crisis, which disturbed him greatly.[17] In a thoughtful letter to the chief secretary in 1882, he recognised that until 'seriously responsible bodies' represented Ireland, every scheme came to Irishmen as a distasteful 'English plan'.[18] Boyce contends that the motivation was more personal than political. Home Rule appeared to him as a fitting project for a statesman of the kind he most wanted to be. It gave him the opportunity 'to capture public opinion, to mould and direct it, and all towards some great and even good end'.[19] He had also become convinced that the grant of 'enlarged powers' to Ireland would not be a 'source of danger, but a means of averting it' and that it would guarantee peace, unity and cohesion.[20]

His rational conversion was, of course, facilitated by new circumstances in the political scene. He had witnessed the precocious success of the Irish National League, founded in the autumn of 1882. Its electioneering machine had brought desired success in the 1885 election where the 86 party members, led by Parnell, were returned to Westminster, holding the all-important balance of power. These were not temporary blow-ins, but men 'at home in the best-club in Europe, in the smoking-rooms as well as on the floor of the house'.[21] They were there to stay. Parnell played a politically flirtatious role, as well he might, and, although he recognised that the chances of getting a successful measure lay more with the Tories, the chances of getting any measure at all lay with the Liberals. It was to be a fateful choice of alliance. It is even possible to aver that it may have doomed Home Rule from the start because the Tory-dominated House of Lords would never be bludgeoned into agreeing (as they had been over emancipation in 1829). Still, it was the only alliance then possible.

The Home Rule Bill

Gladstone's conversion to the policy of Home Rule was floated before he became prime minister in an incident known as the Hawarden Kite, named after the site of his country house. The latter half of the Victorian period was very much an age of new media and it is no surprise to learn that, before he brought the matter to Parliament, his views were 'aired' in the national press. Whether he wished the publicity or not, (it may have been his son who leaked the news to the press without consulting him) it committed him to bringing forward a bill upon taking office in February of 1886. He shook hands with Parnell on 5 April, crisply describing him as 'very clever' in his diary. From hindsight, the bill appears to be a moderate one, but that there *was* a bill at all on such a matter at such a time was, for some, the height of Liberal radicalism and represented a genuine parting of the ways between Unionist and Home Ruler. The prospect of undoing the United Kingdom was anathema to some, including Joseph Chamberlain. O'Day maintains that, whilst everyone was prepared for some concessions, the idea of a proper Dublin parliament was a sort of 'political bomb'.[22]

The bill made the following proposals. There would be a Dublin legislature under the queen consisting of two orders, one of peers and the other of elected representatives. Executive power would rest in the Lord Lieutenant, acting on behalf of the queen. This position could now be filled by a Catholic. The civil service would be under Irish control. Control of defence, foreign policy, coinage, the law of trade, post and telegraphs would remain in Westminster. It was an explicitly non-denominational settlement: the Irish legislature was not allowed to endow any church, restrict any religion or impose religious tests.

Debates in Parliament were particularly vigorous. The British public was surprised, even shocked, professing grave doubts about the viability of such large constitutional change. The *Times* denounced the proposals. Not all opposition was particularly well reasoned. Beckett holds there to be a façade of rationality but regards it, at root, as fruit of an 'irrational determination to maintain the integrity of what it regarded as the national territory'. He further notes the paradox of the British having supported the idea of self-government in other parts of the world, for example among the Greeks, South Americans, Serbs, Italians and Poles.[23] Much has been made of the secession of Liberals, but Graham Goodlad offers an important antidote by pointing out that the vast majority of the Liberal Party and its supporters went along with Gladstone's bill, many because of their trust in Gladstone as a statesman. Joseph Chamberlain pointed out that, if Gladstone's 'great authority were withdrawn from these bills, I doubt if twenty persons outside the Irish Party would support them'.[24] It is, of course, possible to see this as 'atavistic tribal loyalty' as O'Day does, rather than any deeply held belief.[25] Opinion in southern Ireland varied from wild enthusiasm to a more grudging approval. The *Western News* welcomed it as the re-emergence of the 'sun' of Ireland's freedom. The *Connaught Telegraph* hailed its divine mandate.[26] There were undoubtedly inflated expectations as to what the bill would entail and uneducated opinion saw it, at least initially, as the promise of social as well as political regeneration. Parnell, less naively, held it to be the 'first cup of cold water' offered to a desperate nation and his opinion was echoed by many. But, although prepared to split hairs, he was not likely to oppose such a grand concession.

The fiercest opposition came from Unionist opinion, Conservatives and from conservatives within his own party. Gladstone's bill did not make any special provision for Ulster. It has even been claimed by N. C. Fleming that, for Gladstone, there simply was 'no Ulster question'.[27] Others are more nuanced – O'Day quotes Gladstone as saying that the 'Protestant minority should have its wishes considered to the utmost practicable extent'.[28] Among the reasons for his implacability that have been suggested are his firm conviction that his settlement was the right one and thus his unwillingness to countenance any change; moreover, he may have felt, based upon past precedent, that opposition would melt away and that time would reconcile Unionists to the new dispensation. No doubt his alliance with Parnell and the Irish Party was another factor in his failure to make Ulster a special case. In any case, this failure was a gross error of judgement.

What he found was that he had unwittingly stoked into life Protestant conservatism. They argued that Ulster was a distinct entity with a separate history, that its success depended on its connection with the British and Atlantic markets and that its religion was only safe in the context of the Union. Home Rulers sought to reassure their fears, claiming the settlement would help to recreate Ireland along non-sectarian lines, but to no avail. Protestant conservatism began to mobilise in defence of the *status quo*. The militancy of the Irish Loyal and Patriotic Union, with its northern version the Ulster Loyalist Union, was notable from the outset – one of their members proclaiming that they would resist the dictates of an Irish legislature 'at the point of a bayonet'.[29] Lord Randolph Churchill visited Belfast and spoke at a Unionist gathering there on 22 February, uttering there the memorable words 'Ulster will fight; Ulster will be right'.[30] Just as notable was the level of support for their cause not merely among Tories but among various strands of the Liberal Party as well. This explains the quip in Oscar Wilde's *The Importance of Being Earnest* where, as Lady Bracknell points out to Jack, the Liberal Unionists count as Tories – a fine joke for the crowds who flocked to St James's Theatre, London on St Valentine's Day 1895 for the premiere. The fact that it was riotously funny in

1895 just shows how unimaginably divisive the issue was for the Liberals in the long term. Joseph Chamberlain saw it as 'tantamount to separation' for he would not countenance more than limited local self-government; Lord Hartington predicted that it would cause civil war. It was the start of the story whereby Ireland would become one of the big reasons for Liberal decline. The secession of key Liberals in 1886 has traditionally been interpreted at face value as the result of the rejection of the Home Rule settlement. But the sources of conflict and tension went further back and 1886 was merely responsible for bringing these to the surface and exacerbating them.

The Fate of the Bill

Debates lasted from 8 April to 7 June. The Liberal drift was enough to swing the House of Commons against the measure so that 93 Liberals voted down the bill on the second reading on 8 June, causing the dissolution of Parliament and the accession to power of a new grouping, the Conservatives and Liberal Unionists. That end was predictable but not inevitable. Gladstone made some critical mistakes – he may have introduced the proposal too early in the session and antagonised his colleagues by trying to railroad the measure.[31] Yet, for all that, he made his mark. What we find during these parliamentary debates is something new, something emphatically Gladstonian. The momentum and drama of the Irish Question carried him to new heights of fervour and, indeed, to a sense of urgency. This old man really *was* in a hurry, as Randolph Churchill once wryly commented. In his justly celebrated plea before the vote was taken, there is no doubt but that he had set the issue of Ireland at the very centre of the British stage. No first minister before him had done so in quite such a way. No first minister after him could ignore that he had done so.

> 'Have the honourable gentlemen', he asked, 'considered that they are coming into conflict with a nation? Can anything stop a nation's demand? Ireland stands at your bar expectant, hopeful, almost suppliant. [...] We hail the demand of Ireland for what I call a blessed oblivion of the past'.[32]

It was a lyrical and passionate speech in which he sought to set the issues beyond the reach of narrow party politics and turn them into a cause for moral right and justice. There is, however, a paradox in his very sponsorship of the Home Rule bill of 1885. Hammond points it out quite nicely.

> It may be said of him that nobody else could have gained for Home Rule anything like the support it received in the House of Commons

and in the country in 1886 [...]. But it may also be said that a man with gifts far inferior to his could have obtained a second reading for his Bill if once that Bill had reached the position that the Home Rule Bill had reached by April 1886.[33]

The point has been reiterated by Jackson in a different way. He maintains that the prime minister's 'evangelical self-assurance' and his propensity to regard the issue as a 'divinely ordained act of political justice' scared his colleagues off and did the cause no ultimate good.[34] Gladstone himself sometimes stood in the way of Gladstonian reform.

The Second Home Rule Bill

There was another Home Rule bill (the second Government of Ireland Bill), which Gladstone introduced in his last ministry in 1893. This is the least studied of the three bills and is often treated as a repetition of 1886. Yet, although there was continuity, not least in Gladstone's own intentions, it was not merely a replay. It was a better bill than before and Gladstone had gone to the effort of consulting both factions before introducing it.[35] The lapse of time had made the public both more aware of and more comfortable with the notion of Irish self-government. The most striking dimension of the 1893 episode was Gladstone himself. An octogenarian (the only British premier ever to begin office over the age of 80), he nonetheless threw himself into the matter with great energy. His biographer notes that he 'personally took the bill through the committee stage in a remarkable feat of physical and mental endurance'.[36] We have seen British premiers sometimes uninterested in Ireland, sometimes intermittently concerned, but on no other occasion throughout the whole period is there any evidence of similar levels of sustained commitment. Discussions lasted 82 days and almost a thousand speeches were made in opposition. Gladstone may not have succeeded in solving the Irish Question, but there can be no doubting his good will and devotion, as evidenced in these, his twilight years. Not all historians view this favourably. From the perspective of the health of the Liberal Party, Winstanley is particularly scathing of what he sees as Gladstone's hopeless obsession. After 1885, he became a 'liability' to the party and brought it about so that the Irish Question 'hung like an albatross round the party's neck'.[37] Any summation of Gladstone's role needs to take into account these complexities.

Having only a small Liberal majority in the Commons, however, he had had to lower his expectations of what could be achieved. Jackson here discerns a more 'pragmatic' and less enthusiastic approach than for the First Home Rule Bill, the result of an acceptance that 'Providence had assigned him a more humble role in Ireland than he had hitherto envisaged.'[38] Many of the provisions were much the same as in the first bill, but this time 80 Irish MPs would remain in Westminster with limited voting rights. No exception was made for Ulster. Once again, Unionist opposition sprang to life, this time in the form of the Ulster Defence Union; Arthur Balfour spoke at a rally in Belfast. Although the bill passed the Commons with a slim majority of 31 after an extraordinarily gruelling 82 sittings, it was rejected by the House of Lords after four days of discussion by an unambiguous 419 to 41 votes. Gladstone was once again baffled and foiled – 'that confounded Bill', he fumed.[39] He retired in March 1894, knowing that his final mission was incomplete.

The failure of the second bill had the effect of sidelining the issue for almost twenty years. The Liberals, after Gladstone, professed themselves uninterested. His political inheritors, Lord Rosebury, Sir William Harcourt and Sir Henry Campbell-Bannerman shied away from full-on engagement with the question for reasons obvious. Parnell's party had splintered badly and had little lobbying force. Even the Irish public seemed to become somewhat apathetic. Alternative paths presented themselves – cultural renewal, micro-politics, socialism and extreme nationalism. The Home Rule 'moment' had passed for now. Despite that, Gladstone's proposals had become the 'standard by which subsequent self-government schemes were measured'.[40]

Evaluating Gladstone

To attempt an overall interpretation of Gladstone's impact on Ireland is a complex task. His premierships were undeniably crucial for the development of the Irish Question. His record was not always positive: false assumptions, unfortunate methods, technical lapses and the intransigence of his own personality played a part in undermining his efforts at reform. They also played their part in undermining the vibrancy and credibility of his own party. To say, however, that it damned the Liberal Party to a slow torturous decline is a wild over-exaggeration. It did not help party unity and exacerbated existing conflicts, but the Liberal Party had always been a fractious entity in an unusual position and it would carry on till the 1920s. Nevertheless, if Irish matters showed Gladstone's weaknesses and his party's disunity, they also showed his considerable political strengths and the stature of his party and supporters. He was the first prime minister to approach the matter with real (and unflagging) commitment. He was the first to see that solutions must come across as 'Irish' not 'British-imposed' ones. Hammond, an admirer, acknowledges that his knowledge of Ireland was not absolute, that J. S. Mill understood the land question better and Joseph Chamberlain, the matter of Irish resources. What is distinctive about him, claims Hammond, is that 'from first to last he thought of the Irish as a people' and that he passed his policies through the test of whether it would help the people gain self-respect.[41] He brought imagination and a capacity for minutiae to the formulation of policy from disestablishment and education to self-government. He put the question in moral terms and brought it, through some tooth-and-nail struggles, into the forefront of British political life. Above all, he recognised an opportunity – an opportunity for resolving an urgent constitutional question. Whether 1885 was one of those 'golden moments of our history; one of those opportunities which may come and may go but rarely return, or if they return, return at long intervals, and under circumstances which no man can forecast', may be questioned.[42] But the fact was that he presented it as an opportunity. Perhaps that is why Boyce is right in noting the paradox that, despite the manifest failure of both Home Rule bills, they are seen as his finest hour.[43]

The Fate of Parnell and Parnellism

But we must retrace our steps and reconstruct what had happened to Parnell and his following in the years between the first and the second Home Rule bills. The narrative is one of dramatic downfall, although opinions differ about Parnell's responsibility for this. With the accession of a Conservative Unionist government after the general election in 1886, the Gladstonian Liberals and Parnell had entered a phase of united opposition, although the much-proclaimed 'Union of Hearts' was more superficial than it sounded. The demands on Parnell were heavy. He needed at one and the same time to oil the connection with the Liberals, to downgrade the level of Unionist opposition (*that* he could not do) and to monitor the situation in Ireland to prevent it from going in too radical a direction.

William O'Brien clashed with him over a renewed land agitation, the Plan of Campaign. The Plan of Campaign adopted the usual strategies of communal intimidation and resistance to unreasonable rents.[44] For Parnell, the conflict should not be fought in that way anymore and the Land Law Act should be allowed to function properly. He was also afraid of putting too much pressure on the all-important connection with the Liberals. Personally, Parnell's reputation was attacked by some infamous articles in the *Times* which linked him with crime. He showed admirable *sang-froid* when dealing with this and thus stood to gain when the documents were exposed in 1888 as forgeries. It seemed to cement his moral victory.

It was superficial. Very soon he was to be embroiled in a personal crisis of a more politically fatal nature, although Lyons has suggested that power was already slipping from his grasp.[45] A Captain O'Shea filed for divorce at the end of 1889, citing Parnell as co-respondent. Parnell had lived with Mrs Katharine O'Shea for many years: they were the most devoted of adulterous couples. Bew calls the affair 'reckless' but it was not out of the common way for politicians to have a mistress – Parnell was perhaps unusual in being entirely faithful.[46] O'Shea, quietly cognisant of his wife's position, had chosen a moment to strike when there was a prospect of getting some money out of it, Katharine's wealthy aunt having recently died. So Parnell's career took on what Tim Healey called 'the stench of the divorce court'.[47] Victorian penny papers obsessively followed the divorce court proceedings of the rich or famous. Parnell had not expected a verdict of guilty, but the court was adamant. The subject, with all its tawdry details of subterfuge, was now in the glaring light of the public. The matter in itself need not have caused his downfall. The attitude of the Liberals and the Catholic hierarchy would be significant. Gladstone's reaction was guided by pragmatism: he had his eyes fixed on the opinions of the non-conformists and knew that he would lose support if he continued to associate with a disgraced adulterer. The Irish Party reacted in some confusion. At first they voted him back as leader, some on the silent expectation that he would do the honourable thing and resign of his own volition.

It was then that Parnell made perhaps his most serious and egregious error of judgement. He stayed to become a bone of contention in his own party. He who had brought them together divided them painfully. A Liberal ultimatum put them in the unenviable dilemma of choosing between a respected leader and the possibility of securing Home Rule, between a person and the policy. At the final bitter vote in 1890, 45 voted against him, 27 with him. Parnell, with inborn astuteness, said that, if they were to sacrifice him, they should at least extract beforehand a firm promise for a more liberal Home Rule settlement. They did not. The aftermath was still more acrimonious. Parnell did what all charismatic leaders might do in such circumstances – he went to the people. He put himself – or rather, his candidates – before them in three infamous by-elections, all of which he ignominiously lost. The defeat was not just political, it was personal. An exhausted and gaunt Parnell caught chill and returned to Katharine, who had by now become his wife, to die. And die he did on 6 October. It is hard to underestimate the importance of the drama of his sudden demise, both political and actual. Had he shown the 'self-centredness, ruthlessness, and brilliance' Comerford says? If so, it seriously backfired.[48] For Lyons, the whole episode shows his degeneration as a leader and disfigures the last phase of his career.[49] The fall of Parnell was at once dramatic and lamentably sordid. He was romanticised in death and even his fiercest enemies recognised the potency of the myth surrounding him, Tim Healy lamenting tellingly that 'we have the voters but Parnell has their sons'.

The Fallout

The fallout was particularly divisive and the Parnellite party, cultivated with such care as to discipline, became a fractured entity. Disunity would dog it until 1900. And, even after, it would never regain the magic that it had under Parnell. Yet, his divisive legacy does not blind us as to his achievements. He was the first popularly recognised leader of the Irish since Daniel O'Connell, commanding a loyalty and a following that could not but be recognised by the British establishment. They had had to do business with him. He was unavoidably large in the scheme of things. And in his death he remained so. The hillside men mythologised him – his sacrifice was deemed important. This unlikely champion had sacrificed himself, it was said, for the great national cause. Second, he put Home Rule on the political map; he attached it firmly to the Liberal Party. This was the only practical option, although it did doom it to failure as long as the House of Lords had veto power. Thirdly, he was responsible for the creation of a disciplined parliamentary force. In the hands of such men, the logic went, self-government was conceivable. He had made an interest group politically plausible, a force to be reckoned with. It was his – and their – tragedy that his death divided them for years. Yet, the agenda, the force and the energy which he brought to the Irish Question was not all 'dissipated when he himself died'.[50] In some respects, it was just rechanneled. Receiving the Nobel Prize for Literature several decades later, Yeats said that modern Anglo-Irish literature began with Parnell's passing in 1891. It is an alluring thesis even if it only represents a half-truth in claiming that the disillusioned turned from grubby politics to 'ennobling' culture. About Parnell, one is left wondering whether his myth is not more important than his record.[51]

Chapter 15

CONSTRUCTIVE UNIONISM, 1886–1906

Interpretations

The Irish *fin de siècle* has often been seen as culturally rich but politically uninteresting. However true the former, the latter is rather unfair as it fails to do justice to what some historians have described as a silent revolution, no less significant for being comparatively discreet. The Conservative government's legislation certainly lacks Gladstonian fanfare and overt 'missionary' drive. Parnell's demise left Irish leadership with a charisma crisis. There is, it could be argued, a relative lack of surface drama whenever the Conservatives are in power, which was for much of the period 1885 to 1906. This was perhaps because change was effected tactfully and cautiously by the very party who were disinclined to trumpet change at all. Even as it was, many of their efforts met with 'little praise' and won them 'no new friends' in Ireland, according to O'Halpin, whose focus is on the decline of the Union.[1] Not all historians would see it so. Lyons points to the 'steady and undramatic, but nevertheless profound, social and economic change' which made people more prosperous and more content with their lot.[2] Gailey, among others, has set the roots of Ireland post-1921 in this very period.[3] At root, one could see the Conservative policy in these years as a practical effort to pacify Ireland. It could even be read as an attempt to depoliticise the Irish Question – if that were at all possible – by killing Home Rule with kindness. Of course, kindness is only a half-truth. Curtis claims that it was not until Arthur Balfour arrived in 1887 that the programme of killing Home Rule began in real earnest, and that was only possible through a fusion of both coercion and conciliation. Curtis presents a generally positive interpretation of constructive Unionism.[4] Lyons sees it as a real 'philosophy of government'.[5] That said, some scholars regard the concept of a Tory programme for Ireland as inherently problematic: Cooke and Vincent describe the 1885 package of legislation as 'unrelated fragments of widely different origins'.[6] Andrew Gailey believes the phrase 'killing Home Rule with kindness' to be a 'static formula' which in no way sums up the complex and fluctuating motivations of British objectives in Irish affairs in this period.[7]

Lord Salisbury and the Conservative Government

Disraeli's death in 1881 put Lord Robert Salisbury in the leadership position, a role which he would retain until his resignation in 1902. His biographer, Andrew Roberts, notes that he 'intensely disliked Ireland and the Irish'.[8] Over the years, he had been known for his sometimes acute, often flippant and invariably reductive comments on the country. In 1857, for example, he noted wryly that Ireland had 'given us foreign invasions, domestic rebellions; and in quieter times, the manly sport of landlord shooting'.[9] He blamed the relative lack of capitalism in southern Ireland on the endemic levels of violence which deterred even the commercially greedy. Why wouldn't capitalists prefer 'peace and 3%' over '10% and the drawback of bullets in the breakfast room'?[10] From bons mots such as these, his deeper attitudes are readily apparent.

His alternative to Gladstonianism was summed up in a simple phrase in a speech in St James's Hall in 1886. What Ireland needed and craved was 'government – government that does not flinch'.[11] Much of the problems over the last hundred years had stemmed from too much conciliation. Although Salisbury was not a rampant imperialist he had long held the view that race was hierarchical and that, whilst self-government was admirable for the Teutonic races, it was not viable for others. His conviction was that the Irish and the Indians were much better off under British rule. In his Quarterly Review article in 1872, he laid down that Ireland must be kept 'like India, at all hazards; by persuasion if possible; if not, by force'.[12] His vision became more elaborately imperialist as time went on – the fully fledged prime minister who arrived on the scene in the 1880s was unlikely to evolve any further. The castle administration as much as the cabinet was vital to what ensued – Ashbourne's longevity as Conservative Lord Chancellor provided a sense of continuity. Sound government meant thorough administration rather than flagship measures which would be hostages to the fortune of the moment. The brothers Balfour, who became chief secretaries 1887–91 and 1895–1900 respectively, agreed, broadly, with Salisbury's approach. Arthur declared in 1887 that he would be as 'relentless as Cromwell in enforcing obedience to the law, but at the same time [...] as radical as any reformer in redressing grievances'.[13]

The Land Acts

Were he and the Conservative Party more generally justified in making the latter point? In relation to land, there was continued evolution towards native proprietorship. The Land Law Act of 1881 had left unfinished business and so obvious was this sense of incompletion that the Conservative Party felt compelled to tackle the matter once again. The advantages of creating a prosperous farming community of owner-occupiers were not lost on the government. They hoped, not unreasonably, that it would stabilise the country economically, dampen political ardour and undermine the campaign for devolution. A well-fed and deferential peasantry who did not meddle in politics was desirable and possibly achievable. Moreover, these classes could well express their gratitude in voting Conservative and taking on all the traditionalism of a newly established and legitimised social group. This was indubitably a party political motivation. It was hoped that agricultural Ireland would turn Tory.

The first act of significance was Ashbourne's Purchase of Land Act of 1885 (the Ashbourne Act). Edward Gibson, the first Baron Ashbourne, was the new Lord Chancellor of Ireland, the highest judicial officer in the land (and remained so in every Conservative government until 1905). Of reforming temperament, he proposed that the aspirant tenant should be given an advance of the whole price of the farm, which he would then pay back over 49 years. The impact of this one act was considerable. If their idea was to give more people a stake in the land (and thus in the country), they succeeded, although the effects would be gradual. It provided no 'instant panacea' and there was a revival of the Land League in its aftermath.[14] If it was aimed at political pacification, it was more limited in the long term. Within three years, however, 25,000 tenants had made use of the scheme and there were further sums voted for the fund in 1887, 1888 and 1889. By 1890, the scheme was so successful that Arthur Balfour, chief secretary from 1887, even thought of compelling landlords to sell. Although this idea was summarily dropped, an 1891 act advanced another £33 million for the land-purchase scheme. The Conservatives were clearly convinced by their own success into granting more concessions.

The Plan of Campaign and Balfour's Reaction

The government was also convinced of the necessity of constructive measures by other, more threatening matters. Evictions were on the increase again and sympathetic Irish MPs – namely John Dillon, William O'Brien and Timothy Harrington – had launched the Plan of Campaign, a group pressurising landlords to reduce rents. If landlords refused to fall in line with demands, tenants would quite simply pay the reduced rent to their landlords and the difference to the plan's trustees instead, who would then distribute the funding to those in need. By the spring of 1887, the running of 116 estates was being sabotaged in such a manner. In its mischievous methods, it very much recalled the first land war – the boycott and 'shadowing' (the practice of dogging the footsteps of collaborators) were some of its key methods of intimidation. It was a veritable war of attrition on the landed. As such, it earned the condemnation of the Holy See, but the resulting papal rescript was ignored by the hierarchy and condemned by campaign leaders – a clear rejection of 'Rome rule' by orthodox Irish Catholics. The results of the campaign were distinctly mixed. Sixty estate owners immediately gave in; 24 subsequently followed suit. Others failed to win through or the matter resulted in deadlock. Subsequently, a Tenants' Defence League was set up to alleviate the evicted.

If Balfour's remedial policies were notable, so, also, was his energetic policy of coercion in response to the Plan of Campaign from 1887 to 1891. It was for this that he would be excoriated as 'Bloody Balfour'. Curtis sees this as a turning point to a more aggressive level of confrontation.[15] A scuffle at Mitchelstown in Cork in 1887 resulted in the deaths of several civilians at the hands of the Royal Irish Constabulary and Balfour's subsequent public defence of the police won him few friends, although privately he admitted to a miscarriage of justice and formulated new regulations for police conduct to ward against future such incidents. His Criminal Law Amendment Act was especially harsh, although one of his supporters claimed that never was a 'good instrument more impartially and effectively deployed'.[16] This is harder to credit when one considers the usage of the battering ram and siege weapons against defenceless tenants which was felt to be an outrage.

The Congested Districts Board

Still, his historical legacy was not all bleak. Along with the land act of 1891 came the establishment of a Congested Districts Board (CDB) which aimed to alleviate poverty in the worst-off rural areas. It would try to give poor people a kick-start into entrepreneurialism and self-improvement. The board would be given a proper administrative function and would be financed from funds still available from Gladstone's disestablishment act. It was a far-reaching and imaginative scheme, inspired by the ideas of radical Liberal Unionist Joseph Chamberlain; it also bore the hallmarks of some common-sense practicality. The idea was to provide subsidies and training so that home industries would flourish. Another priority would be to foster agricultural improvements. It also strove to correct the imbalances in society by resettling tenants on larger holdings for the sake of economic viability.

The CDB was designed to be a long-term solution to some of the most pressing problems of Ireland and, indeed, the scheme – for all its weaknesses – lasted 32 years, no mean feat in itself. Twenty years into it, it encompassed twice as many hectares as it had done initially. The focus on infrastructure was a promising one, as it provided money for roads, bridges and, most notably of all, the light railway system in the west. The encouragement of cottage industry also featured prominently and, although some scholars have criticised the small-scale emphasis of the schemes, it is hard to see how promoting large industry would have worked in these remote areas. There was no shame in starting small.

There were, however, undeniable flaws which became more apparent with the passage of time. Foremost among them is the fact that it did not arrest the haemorrhaging of western Ireland, either economically or demographically. It did, however, go some way towards rectifying the imbalances in Irish society and staving off impoverishment and, had it been better funded, it would undoubtedly have gone further. The original grant of £41,000 did increase to £530,000 by 1912, but schemes of the sort soaked up money and there were always shortfalls which limited the realm of their activities. Comparisons with Gladstone's policies were often made. The same supporter of Balfour previously quoted wrote that '[h]is policy, both repressive and remedial, is chiefly remarkable for the lack of that grandeur which Mr Gladstone sought to infuse into all his Irish schemes'.[17] This is unquestionably true – one of the whole points of constructive Unionism was precisely to de-dramatise Irish issues, to get people talking about profits and poverty rather than politics. It is evidence of Balfour's contribution that he not only introduced change, but he changed the job description, expanding the humdrum role of the chief secretary: by 1900, the office was responsible for 29 government departments. All this indicates a sea change. Yet, it is not a complete shift. A continuum is visible. The Conservatives built on the legacy of Gladstone's earlier acts. The very fact that Gladstone had put Ireland on the political map meant that the Conservatives had to become more involved, whether they wanted to or not.

Initiatives for Improvement from Below

Not all initiatives at regeneration came from the government in this period. Horace Plunkett was a landed Irishman who popularised the co-operative movement to improve produce and create a new sense of morale and community among farmers. In 1894, he founded an umbrella organisation, the Irish Agricultural Organisation Society (IAOS), which, in the space of ten years, sheltered 876 co-ops. Inspired by his experience of ranching in Wyoming, he felt that the Irish could have 'better farming, better business and better living'. Under the aegis of the IAOS, creameries were founded, produce was better marketed, equipment and fertiliser supplied and credit distributed through unions. Irish farmers could keep up to date more easily by reading its journal, the *Irish Homestead*. The movement flourished to such an extent that the Conservative government established a Department of Agriculture in 1899 and appointed Plunkett as vice president. It was not an altogether successful arrangement. Plunkett was an agriculturalist, not a politician, and, in fact, he downgraded the political struggle when he could. He was, as his biographer says, committed to nationality, not nationalism.[18] A. E. (George William Russell) in 1912 proclaimed that it was necessary to reach into the 'deeps below the constitution where national wisdom or national folly are generated among the people'.[19] It was this substratum of national character that was felt to be key to change, reform and social improvement.

The Local Government Act

Yet, it might truly be said that no struggle was apolitical. The Local Government Act of 1898 was no exception. It was truly revolutionary in its significance, although cloaked in the humble guise of local government. But the local was, in its way, decisive. The legislation was brought safely through Parliament by Gerald Balfour, brother of Arthur, who had become chief secretary of Ireland in 1895 under Salisbury's third administration. What the act did was undercut the systemic power of the landed aristocracy through the Grand Jury System. Now, local affairs would be administered by elected councils – rural, urban and counties. Roads, Poor Law, housing and public health would be under a new aegis. The irony of a Conservative government sponsoring this kind of change is notable. The landlord classes were rendered irrelevant at a stroke. They were deprived of a key aspect of their hold over the country. The significance of this is huge – Gailey affirms that it 'profoundly shaped the Irish nation which was to emerge after 1921'.[20]

What was being granted, in effect, was a form of local home rule because the elections permitted the legal entry of a whole new class of people into mainstream *political* life, albeit in a small way. Every occupier was given a vote for council – this was a revolution in of itself. Nationalist candidates (in particular Sinn Féin members) were often elected and there they could acquire invaluable experience in doing politics. George Wyndham followed on from Balfour as chief secretary from 1900–1905. He continued in the same vein, furthering land purchase schemes and fostering social and economic reform.

The Land Purchase Act of 1903 (Wyndham Act) was a most ambitious coup and some see it as his one substantial achievement.[21] This affected an extraordinary sociological shift. Over the next 17 years, 9 million acres would change hands and 2 million more pending. Lyons considers this act to be the apogee of the policy of constructive Unionism both because of the content of the act itself and the way in which it was not conceded from above but 'worked out in collaboration with leading nationalists'.[22] However the promise of a new kind of unity was short lived and the period of Conservative reform came to a rather abrupt end. The following year, the Irish Reform Association drew up a plan for devolution and one of Wyndham's civil servants was associated with it. Wyndham was tarnished by association and resigned in 1905. Unionists felt betrayed. Were the Conservatives trying to introduce Home Rule by stealth?

Evaluation of Conservative Reforms

With the sweeping election victory for the Liberals in 1906, Conservative domination was at an end. Evaluations of late nineteenth-century Conservative policy on Ireland vary greatly. The most robust claim about the effects of all these reforms came from the pen of an observer, Barker, who wrote in 1919 of a 'regenerated Ireland, living a new and prosperous life, with a peasantry helped and aided, largely by its own co-operative effort, beyond the peasantry of any other country. Tomorrow we trust to see a self-governing Ireland, still a part of the British Commonwealth'.[23] No doubt this was somewhat rose tinted, even from the point of view of the time. It certainly falsifies what was happening politically. If Conservative policy had intended to depoliticise Irish issues, it had not succeeded. The most damning conclusion comes from Gailey who claims that the British government sought to change the 'very character of Irish politics, without the means, the method or any great motivation' and only left 'two extremely suspicious and insecure parties to become utterly inflexible'.[24] That said if, in the wider sense, British policy had intended to ward off the threat of socialism, it did succeed in fostering conservatism among the rural classes.[25]

Northern Developments

One of these parties was being forged in the north of the country. We are so used to thinking of Unionism as a primarily northern phenomenon that we forget that, until about 1893, the real initiative came from southern Unionists. They were more culturally diverse and metropolitan, according to Jackson, and the shift to northern-based Unionism was to a much more localised, narrow and hard-line version.[26] Religiously, the north's Presbyterian and Anglican majority were ever more comfortably dominant. In 1885, they constituted 52 per cent of the population and in 1901, 56 per cent. There was a high concentration of Protestants in the most economically successful counties, such as Antrim, Armagh, Down and Londonderry. Yet, majorities were slippery things and it was easy to see that provincial majority became minority when considering the population of the island as a whole. There was therefore a reliance on the Union to keep the status quo. This is what made Home Rule in 1885 so deeply problematic – suddenly, they would be vulnerable to Roman Catholicism, to the potential influence it would have over politics. The declaration of papal infallibility in 1871 only added strength to the animus. Home Rule would be 'Rome Rule', it was feared.

It was not merely the question of religion which gnawed at the newly militant Unionist in the late nineteenth century. Ulster by then had become truly a great city of the Empire, playing an important part in a narrative of extraordinary success, if at some cost. Its association with Britain gave its entrepreneurs access to innovative techniques and gave its markets potentially global reach. This association also came with a certain risk, as Gibbon rightly observes. The Belfast market was so geared towards export that their gains were absolutely dependent on the maintenance of the connection with Britain. It was not a simple narrative of success: Ulster capitalists and industrialists knew that, without Britain, they were in a highly precarious position.[27] Linen and shipbuilding were keys to the power of Ulster, whilst iron, steel and marine engineering also flourished. Power looms had transformed the linen industry in places like Belfast, Lurgan and Ballynane and, by 1900, it was employing up to 60,000 people, many of them women and children. The human price was high as conditions and wages remained substandard, but, nevertheless, it was an industry at the very forefront of Ulster's industrial revolution. The shipbuilding that took place on Queen's Island outside Belfast was another success story. An English Presbyterian, Edward Harland, came together with Hamburg Jewish Lutheran Gustav Wolff and later a charismatic Quebecois, William Pirrie, to manage this initiative and transform it into something competitive. Supplying the White Star Line with transatlantic ocean liners was proof that they had arrived. The magnificent and fated Titanic was built there from 1909–11.

Business was booming, it is true, but along sectarian lines. It is important to realise that those effectuating the Industrial Revolution and the labour aristocrats in skilled jobs in Ulster were mainly Protestant. Catholics were a liminal people 'on the outside looking in'.[28] No piece of evidence is more striking than the fact that they composed an unhealthy 3 per cent of the Belfast Chamber of Commerce. Among the lower end of the working class, among those deemed unskilled, conflict broke out frequently between

Catholics and Protestants, one incident in 1886 causing 31 deaths and several hundred injuries.

The Unionist Alliance with Conservatives

Protestants were more determined than ever to ward off the dangers of Home Rule, convinced that their progressive, godly, sober and thrusting ways of life would be disturbed by a political merger with feckless rural southerners. From 1886 onwards, an alliance between the Conservative Party and the Unionists was cemented. Indeed, Gailey contends that Conservative conciliation policy was aimed not so much at nationalists but at Unionists in the first place.[29] What was the real nature of the connection between Toryism and Unionism? Conventional wisdom is that it is as it seems – a natural fit between two groups with entrenched establishment values and a strong dose of anti-Catholicism. Some scholars, such as Cooke and Vincent, have a problem with the concept of 'Tory Unionism', however, seeing it, instead, as a 'string of miscellaneous and limited Tory alliances for limited and immediate purposes'.[30] This may indeed approach the truth more than a cosy belief in their 'permanent' connection after 1886. It was not such a perfect fit as might be presumed. Randolph Churchill, who proved so willing to play the Orange card in public, privately referred to them as 'those foul Ulster Tories'. The very low-church, middle-class nature of Ulster Unionism was something of a turn-off. Wyndham's biographer puts it well when he speaks of the distaste for the 'evangelical vulgarities, the urban grubbiness, and the commercial banalities of Ulster Unionism'.[31] Accordingly, whilst the Conservative–Unionist connection gave Ulstermen some reassurance, it did not make them complacent. A Conservative Party might not always see eye-to-eye with them or might have other priorities, so the onus was upon them to organise themselves and mobilise for their own cause. They were conscious that one day they 'might have to look to themselves'.[32] In that, of course, they were uncannily right.

Chapter 16

CELTIC RENAISSANCE

Historiography

Ireland witnessed outstanding developments in the late nineteenth and early twentieth centuries in both culture and politics. It is common to refer to the former, at least, as a renaissance; a claim could be made for the latter, as well. Characteristic of both was an articulation of what it meant to be Irish, although there was much variety in the answers proffered. Instead of taking a narrative of Celtic revival for granted, some questions immediately present themselves. In what sense can we talk of a phenomenon of Celticism in a post-colonial environment when the very word is redolent of a particular form of power relations? Secondly, what were the origins of revivalism and how did it relate to other movements in Europe? It is no longer tenable to talk of Gaelic exceptionalism – most historians now put it in a context of several other earlier Gaelic revivals and a pan-Celtic fascination.[1] It is also possible to read the movement as emblematic of the growing interest in the spiritual content of nationhood – those things like myth, value, symbol and memory which go towards the articulation of an identity.[2] A movement of cultural renaissance is not uncommon in a society growing in self-awareness. A further question which may well be debated is to what extent the cultural was also political. In particular, the links with the tradition of independent nationalism must be investigated.

The term Celtic is quite deeply problematic, a 'philological abstraction' invented in the eighteenth century,[3] and its usage has been disparate and imprecise. Although its ethnic and linguistic claims are highly suspicious in themselves, there is no denying the power of this one construction. As Leerssen makes clear in his survey essay on the subject, it owes many of its connotations to the early phase of its development from 1650 to 1850 when ideas of the sublime, of nature and the noble savage happened to be in vogue. As a result, the idea of Celticism came to connote peripherality (both geographic and cultural), pre-modernity (backwardness, quaintness) and spirituality (mysticism, otherworldliness, femininity).[4] These three features remained engrained – and still are, indeed, in the bogus construction of Celticism for the tourist industry. Leerssen is quick to note that the construct carries echoes of a particular 'power relationship'. Those who were deemed to be Celts had 'no power over the fact that they were beginning to be called that name; they underwent, passively, a process of scrutiny, investigation and classification over which they had not control'.[5]

As against a narrative of Irish exceptionalism, it is important to realise that the origins of Celtic revivalism do not occur in Ireland. Properly speaking, it was the Welsh antiquarians who took up the subject, followed by the publication of the extremely popular Ossianic writings in the 1760s in Scotland.[6] Ossian was considered to be the Homer of northwestern Europe and an awakening of interest in Celtic heroic literature meant that, by the mid-1800s, it was something to be studied and appreciated by ethnographers and philologists.[7] The Irish revival takes places against this background, but it should not be seen as the first of its kind in the country. Hutchinson identifies two previous manifestations – the first in the late 1700s, the second in the 1830s. In that sequence the Gaelic revival of 1890–1921 came third and was the most encompassing of the waves, characterised by anti-imperialism and a projection of Ireland as a 'superior rural Gaelic communalist civilization exemplifying to a corrupt power-hungry world a higher synthesis of the spiritual and material.[8] As regards political culture, the Irish direction had an impact. The Scottish Home Rule association was established in 1886, reflecting among other things the dissatisfaction of the crofter class. Such movements figured even more prominently in Wales, Cymru Fydd (Wales of the Future) being a particularly good example. The Irish experience thus informs and is informed by that of Scotland and Wales in its awareness of its alienation from imperial metropolitan culture and its assertion of difference. The Celtic fringe (a phrase which was coming into common currency in the 1890s) was awakening to a great consciousness of its own distinctiveness. However, there are distinctions to be drawn, the chief of which was the more radical profile of the 'Irish Ireland' movement.[9] Irish revivalism must not merely be put into its Celtic context, but also into a global setting. Certainly there were stirrings in many countries of the world aimed at finding their spiritual core. The construction of national identities, especially in those places which were grappling with the notion of statehood, was particularly intense. Germany is a classic example. So also the Hungarians and the Italians. The Indian National Congress was established in 1885; in time it came to endorse a policy of *swadeshi* (our own country), a word closely akin in meaning to 'Sinn Féin'.

With regard to the cultural movement's political content, there is no simple answer. It is possible to argue that all was politically intoned. The emphasis on folklore, for instance, could be seen as an attempt at recreating (inventing?) a unitary, antique identity. A vision of the national self could be reflected through the 'prism of symbols and mythologies of the community's heritage'.[10] In Gellner's more general words, the majority of nations have 'navels invented for them by their own nationalist propaganda'.[11] Maybe this is one instance. The usage of Gaelic could be regarded as an emphatic defiance of the conqueror's tongue. Some would not see the relationship between the cultural and political quite so directly. Thus, Townshend would say that the Gaelic Athletic Association and the Gaelic League were hijacked by extremists, that it was a small minority that pushed them in a more politically radical direction.[12] There was a central paradox to the Anglo-Irish literary revival which although it saw itself at first as 'an alternative to, or even a denial of, politics, helped to foster a new separatist political tradition'.[13] The cultural movement 'became dominated by political considerations'.[14] A question then follows. How important is the cultural movement in determining the shape of the nation? How important is it influencing those people who would go on to resist British rule? For all that it is obviously important, John Hutchinson back in 1987 argued that too little academic attention had been given to cultural nationalism and its role in nation building. This has changed, although it is true to say that literary critics, more than historians, are prominent in the field.[15]

When we go to look at the characteristics of the cultural movement, the matter is rather slippery. Was it a movement of the intelligentsia or the people? Hutchinson, who focuses on the role of the former, distinguishes between two kinds of cultural nationalist – what we may call the 'formulators' (that is to say, the scholars, artists and poets) and the 'presenters' (the media and politicians) who make culture speak politics.[16] But it was not merely a matter of the intelligentsia 'creating' something out of nothing – they depended on their own experience or constructs of the people (often the country dwellers) and drew on native traditions of folklore and language. Another question to ask is whether the cultural movement was imaginative and creative in its assumptions and principles or grounded in historical truth. Although there was considerable scholarship within the movement, there was also ample room for myth-creation. The theses of Ireland's unique history and special destiny were propounded by writers such as Eoin MacNeill and by Yeats himself. 'History, therefore, reserved for Ireland a special destiny, in which the romantic poet, fashioning its reservoir of myths into a coherent vision, would transform the revolt of the elite into a national insurrection of the spirit that would launch a new renaissance of the peoples.'[17]

Matters Anthropological

It may be cogently argued that the Celtic revival took place against a backdrop of competing anthropologies. Anglicisation had been both fact and process in the nineteenth century. The Union had established this politically. The creep of English institutions, the imports of English goods and the very dazzling nature of its imperial might had culturally encroached upon Ireland and left it, in the words of Douglas Hyde, 'despoiled of the bricks of nationality'.[18] Furthermore, consistent anti-Irish prejudice in the British press had taken on a more malevolent and racialist tone over the decades so that, by the 1870s, the image of the 'ape-like' Celt depicted in *Punch* with crude features and a long jaw (a sign of evolutionary primitivism, according to the phrenologists of the day) was common currency.[19] Only recently has an extraordinary photographic collection come to light, the work of Trinity College anthropologist Charles R. Browne. It has been put on display for the first time at the time of writing on 3 May 2012 in the Blasket Centre in Dunquin.[20] Together with a team of head hunters, Browne travelled the western coast from 1891–1900 taking Irish cranial measurements to prove 'nigrescence'. The task was to explain how a primitive (white) race could exist so near to Britain in the height of its imperial glory. Skulls of dead islanders were housed in the Museum of Comparative Anatomy in Trinity College Dublin. No doubt it assuaged the complacency of the imperial elite to read their subordinates as innately inferior and to have the science of the craniometer to back it up. Even the more positive view of Celticism that was propounded first by Ernest Renan in *La Poésie des Races Celtiques* (1854) and later by cultural theorist Matthew Arnold was condescending. In the views of many, the Celt was essentially feminine and irrational and would, inevitably, be assimilated by a superior Saxon (Teutonic) culture.[21]

The Gaelic League

As a result, movements for nativism felt challenged to construct a more favourable and capacious national anthropology. The literary critic Gregory Castle convincingly avers this in his study of *Modernism and the Celtic Revival* (2001) but the point need not just be confined to the Anglo-Irish dramatists.[22] The crucial battleground for reconstructing a national anthropology was language. Gaelic usage had plummeted in the period – 50 per cent spoke it as their primary language in 1841, a mere 14.5 per cent in 1891. English was now the dominant means of interaction. 'My soul frets in the shadow of his language', Stephen Daedalus is made to say in Joyce's *A Portrait of the Artist as a Young Man* (1916). There was a strand of what Laura O'Connor has called 'linguicism' in the movement – an extreme hatred for English as a language that had killed off the native tongue.[23] Ironically, just at the moment when the trend was probably irreversible, a vigorous attempt was made to reassert Irish and Irishness. Thus it was that the Gaelic League was founded in 1893 not merely to preserve the remnant but to restore it to its rightful place in the country. It was a great moment for leagues and associations: across Europe, thousands joined in what may be called 'identity-crusade' organisations. In the context of growingly impersonal urban environments, it became a very fashionable trend indeed. Eoin MacNeill and Douglas Hyde, its founders, conducted an energetic campaign of de-Anglicisation, a sort of linguistic call to arms which was articulated through their weekly newspaper, An Claidheamh Soluis, 'The Sword of Life'.

The key to the movement's success was its apparent ubiquity. Itinerant teachers were critical to its progress as were the summer schools held in the Gaeltacht regions. Six hundred branches had been formed by 1904 with 50,000 members. Ten years later it had 100,000. Even if not all were equally zealous, this was still considerable. The league began to make advances in having Irish taught in schools – to do this, teacher training colleges were established across the country. It also encouraged the establishment of an annual Feis Ceoil in 1897, a festival of music in which young people would compete. This occurred through the patronage of Dr Annie Patterson, an Anglican Ulsterwoman who has the distinction of being the first British (or indeed Irish) woman to achieve a doctorate in music, and Edward Martyn, a well-heeled Catholic patron of the arts. The latter also became president of Na hAisteoirí, an Irish language drama troupe.

That the league was political in some sense seems incontestable – yet, to what extent? It was surely a political statement to choose to revive a language stigmatised by the establishment. Lyons holds it to be a 'major instrument in the search for' a properly Gaelic identity.[24] By creating cross-country networks of affiliation, it also made the whole national community easier to imagine. It could be situated in terms of Anderson's European 'lexicographic revolution', an illustration of the growing conviction that languages were 'the personal property of quite specific groups' and that these groups 'were entitled to their autonomous place in a fraternity of equals.[25] Moreover, it was political in the sense that those who joined it were often separatist in orientation. It was, argues Garvin, 'the central institution in the development of the Irish revolutionary elite'.[26] The Irish Republican Brotherhood (IRB), for example, infiltrated the movement. Most of those who would sign the proclamation of a republic in 1916 were members. Although not overtly political, the league could be said to have fostered an ethos of separatism and a habit of mobilisation of resources and organisation which gave many a Gaelic Leaguer a taste for associational life. It also showed up the Irish Parliamentary Party.

They were from a generation which had adopted English fully; they would now be accused of being West Britons for their failure to speak Irish. Lastly, although not a sectarian movement, its membership was overwhelmingly Catholic and southern. Douglas Hyde, it is true, was a Protestant, but he was a rare breed. In all these ways, the Gaelic League was, intentionally or not, politicising and political.

The Cultivation of National Sport

It is possible to tell a story of Irish exceptionalism with regard to sport – possible, but not advisable. The revival of Irish sports should be firmly placed in a Victorian context, at once as an outgrowth of a growing culture of leisure and as a reaction to the popularity of British games. A notable trend in Victorian England was the formalisation of sports and games and its connections with politics, eugenics, empire building and the construction of masculinities have been studied. Something equivalent occurred in Ireland except that it was endowed with a distinctive nationalistic tone. Apart from the so-called 'garrison games', which kept pace with mainland Britain, popular sports had been quite a haphazard affair up to this. Hurling, football and handball were all played, but rules varied from place to place, referees had no whistle and days were often soured (or enlivened) by faction fighting. Rules started to be drawn up in the late 1860s, but it was felt that more was needed. Michael Cusack, a civil servant and amateur athlete, and P. W. Nally, an athlete and member of the IRB, both met in July 1879 and agreed that something must be done to preserve the physical strength of the Irish race. The Gaelic Athletic Association (GAA) was thus founded in 1884 with the aim of organising Irish sports, drafting coherent and generally acceptable rules and planning recreation, especially for the poor. It was distinctly populist in tone, in contrast to the Irish Amateur Athletic Association and The Dublin Amateur Athletic Club which were for the elites. One Michael Davin was made president; Nally was already in prison.

The choice of patrons was significant – Archbishop Croke of Cashel provided Catholic credibility, Parnell political and Davitt agrarian prestige. Croke was the most important figurehead. One might glean from this some of the prestige which the post-Famine church possessed in non-religious domains. A man of national vision, he hailed the new development as another sign that Ireland was throwing off England's 'stuff and broadcloths, her masher habits and [...] effeminate follies'.[27] According to Cusack, the association spread like a 'prairie fire'. The evidence supports this. Attendance and participation levels were high. It was a channel for youthful male energies and identities. It gave new colour to the countryside on Sundays: the jersey became a badge of county identity. Its most divisive (and political) feature was the so-called ban that forbade its members from playing rugby and cricket and soccer. Furthermore, members of the British Army were not allowed to join the GAA. Was this aggressive or purely defensive? Certainly the construction of a barrier was a definite sign that not even games were apolitical. It inscribed identity on the field. This was perhaps unimaginative and, certainly, Croke and Cusack did not approve, but their instincts were overborne.

Was it political in other ways too? One could argue that politics was inscribed in its very genesis. In an anonymous article entitled 'A word about Irish athletics' in 1884, Cusack wrote the following:

> No movement having for its object the social and political advancement of a nation from the tyranny of imported and enforced customs and manners can be regarded as perfect if it has not made adequate provision for the preservation and cultivation of the National pastimes of the people.[28]

This was a very clear statement of intent. Such a nationalist statement was further borne out by the presence of the IRB within its ranks. They were attracted by the proto-military nature of team sports. But there were tensions in the ranks between the constitutionalists and the physical force men. The GAA supported Parnell after the split, the only significant organisation to do so.

The Anglo-Irish Literary Revival

The Anglo-Irish literary revival was born in the last two decades of the nineteenth century. It is a moment of extraordinary and apparent synthesis between nationality and impressive – in some cases, outstanding – art, which commands the attention of historian and literary critic alike. In some respects the least overtly political, it sits ill with the 'Irish Ireland' movement at times, adamant about its claim to autonomy and transcendence in the cause of art. It began with the Pan-Celtic Society (1888) in London and, from its earliest years, the name of William Butler Yeats was associated with it. He had been inspired by a meeting with an old Fenian, John O'Leary, to plough his talents into a truly Irish cause. It is perhaps ironically fitting that Yeats and many of the revivalists should come from the Protestant Anglo-Irish classes themselves. According to Castle, they were in an 'acutely ambivalent position between colonizer and colonized' and their very alienation provided a fund of creativity. Indeed, Castle goes as far as to say that they, especially Yeats and J. M. Synge, wrote like ethnographers or anthropologists seeking to create a total picture of the Celtic race. [29]

As against any thesis which overemphasises cultural populism, the role of aristocratic patrons was notable – among them, Lady Gregory and Edward Martyn. It was old school in the sense that it was an elite phenomenon. Art could not apparently survive without lavish patronage, fine dinners and country houses wherein to write. The Irish National Literary Society was founded to represent this new wave of poetry, plays and folklore. What is to be made of their fascination with the antique? Was it a romantic posture, an escape from the constraints of modernity? Or was their veneration for the constructed past a sign of their very modernity? It is both. It was also a somewhat political choice. The focus on the *fianna* (warriors) and *filid* (poets/scholars) was meant to signal the reversal of the country's 'inner decay'. [30] As Thomas Bartlett shrewdly notes, their imaginary land of the past possessed 'the inestimable attractions of being free of both Catholics and Protestants (and grubby middle classes)'. [31] It made its political point, often controversially so. In 1898, the Irish Literary Theatre was born to stage the new works, many of which were designed to show the 'deeper thoughts and emotions of Ireland'. Personification of Ireland as a woman had a long literary history and she continued to be represented thus, notably in Yeats's play *The Countess Cathleen* (1892). The efforts of these writers represent a serious attempt to imbue Irish literature in English with meaningful and noble themes in open defiance of the buffoon of an Irishman and the 'shameless shamrockery' habitual on the British stage. [32]

The most notable development was the establishment of the Abbey Theatre in 1904, thanks to a generous subsidy from a philanthropic English woman. One name in particular was associated with its early days, that of John Millington Synge. His *Playboy of the Western World* caused riots on its opening night in 1907 because of its depiction of a crude, vicious peasantry. The Dublin bourgeoisie, including Sinn Féiners like Arthur Griffith, were mightily offended as were the Fenians in the US when it appeared there several years later. Yeats lamented their philistinism and proclaimed subsequently that Romantic Ireland was 'dead and gone'. [33] This was the fissure line – the cosy consensus between art and nationality was no more. Yeats would be associated with the nationalist struggle because of his love for the revolutionary Maud Gonne, but in his heart he was disillusioned. He wanted Ireland to become intellectually free of British materialism and the pieties of a narrow and defensive nationalism. Later, he would come to feel a grudging admiration for the men of 1916 and acknowledge the 'terrible beauty' they brought to bear upon the city and the country. [34] But he spoke a complex language.

Despite the fissures of the cultural revivalist movement, its growing influence on the country was undeniable. It is hard to measure this but it is possible to regard 1899 as a dividing point, as Hutchinson has done. Before that, a very small minority had been enthused by literary and linguistic novelties. By the turn of the century, the cultural movement was 'growing up'. It was attracting the Catholic intelligentsia, including those at University College Dublin. It filled the 'gap' left by the fall of Parnell and the disorganisation of the Irish Party, who seemed aging and ineffective by comparison.[35] Growing numbers of teachers and civil servants spoke Irish. In these ways, the cultural movement acquired greater prominence and gave legitimation and form to ideas about Ireland's nationhood.

Reasons for the Revival of Separatism

As well as a cultural efflorescence, the impetus for full-blown political separatism received a new lease of life after 1898. There were several reasons for this. Firstly, there was no doubt but that separatism fed off the new ways of expressing culture and identity. The centenary of the 1798 rebellion alone would have sent many thoughts in that direction – there were ripples of excitement perceptible throughout republican networks. In 1901, Queen Victoria died. She had visited Ireland for the last time in 1900 and there had been much fuss and fluster surrounding her visit, showing once again a fairly benign attitude towards monarchy that we already have had occasion to note. Her passing marked the end of an era: the winds of change were already sweeping through the British Empire. So much was clear. 1901 also marked the centenary of the Act of Union. People would look back and consider what it had done and failed to do; many of their experiences had been negative.

There was, furthermore, an imperial context informing a new wave of politicisation – the Boer War. Irish soldiers had fought in all British wars in the nineteenth century. Indeed, Horne comes up with the staggering statistic that, in the 1830s, 40 per cent of the British Army was Irish.[36] But there was a new dimension here: the coordination of an Irish brigade fighting with the Boers against the British in South Africa (1899–1902) gave some taste of what militant solidarity could do, a feeling of the oppressed acting in unison. It is no surprise that one of the new personages to emerge onto the Irish political scene had spent 2 years living in South Africa – yet another Irish figure who had had significant experience abroad. Arthur Griffith was a pugnacious Dubliner born in 1871, representing a new political generation. The newness of his programme lay in the particular conjunction of ideas. Between the now comparatively demure parliamentary campaign for Home Rule and the militant Fenian wing, it was possible to find a *via media* and Griffith was just the man to do it. In 1899, he founded a newspaper, the *United Irishman*, to advocate radical separatism, but the more innovative aspect of his political thought was expressed in *The Resurrection of Hungary: A Parallel for Ireland*, published in 1904.

Griffith's Agenda

Griffith's early career is always associated with the idea of abstention from Westminster. Although sometimes credited with originating the idea, this is not, in fact, true because O'Connell had flirted with the idea before him. His achievement lies in bringing the idea forward. Griffith's thinking must be placed in a European context. Political thought in Ireland was often overly introspective. In drawing inspiration from the 1867 secession of Hungary from Austria, Griffith's ideas were a breath of fresh air. The principle was dazzlingly simple: Irish MPs should simply walk out of Westminster and force the establishment to take the resulting arrangement – a Council of Three Hundred – as a *fait accompli*. They would still retain their loyalty to the Queen. Griffith's manner of putting his case was novel and irreverent. If Ireland always had to keep one eye on Britain, she would acquire a 'squint'.[37] The Irish must go their own way, do their own thing – 'Sinn Féin' (we ourselves) would be the name of the movement he founded. It was a homely name full of breezy self-assertion. He had no time for the current parliamentarians under John Redmond. He agreed with a close friend of his, William Rooney, who called them the 'green-liveried henchmen of the British connection'.[38]

Griffith was, in some ways, a loose cannon, remaining his own man despite his connections with a variety of movements. He did become part of the IRB, but he was not really of them. His immediate aims were very often cultural: he wished to foster Irish language and history. Hutchinson sees him as one of the key figures in making cultural nationalism the 'dominant ideological force in Irish society between 1900 and 1906'.[39] If cultural nationalism was sometimes mystical and overly aspirational, this was certainly not the case for Griffith. He robustly advocated the need for national self-respect. His point was that the Irish could do a lot to help themselves and that they should not live off a victim mentality. There was a moral core to his agenda. He also showed an interest in what we could call micro-nationalism, in progress and in modernity, which was not always a concern of more romantic and so-called advanced nationalists. He was keen that the urban middle classes should be productive and industrious. Griffith was a practical man, not an ideologue – the Irish, he insisted, could facilitate their own empowerment, both economically (by buying Irish goods) and culturally (by distinguishing themselves along national lines).

Practically speaking, he began this project of empowerment through his newspaper and, in 1900, through the first amalgamation of patriotic societies with the designation 'Cumann na nGaedheal'. This society was joined in 1903 by a fresh initiative, the National Council. This was designed to be a support group for nationalists in local politics – helping them get elected to the various corporations, for example. At the same time that Griffith was putting vigour into the southern campaign, the Dungannon Clubs in the north of the country sprang into existence under the aegis of a Quaker, Bulmer Hobson, and a Catholic, Denis McCullough. This was the outgrowth of the same sort of phenomenon – the desire to help Irish people by associational life to overcome the psychological state of dependency and narratives of victimhood.

Sinn Féin

The pressure to unify these strands into a coherent whole came from the Irish Americans. They were, as always, the 'voices off', influencing what was happening on the Irish stage. The Irish across the Atlantic were not merely ideological supporters of the radical cause but, by sending money, they made those very causes financially viable. Thus it came about that Sinn Féin was born in 1908. It was Griffith's expression, 'we ourselves', that conjured up the notions of self-reliance which he had sought to foster. Nevertheless, he declined to lead the movement, leaving it instead to one John Sweetman. The self-abnegation was quite deliberate. Griffith was wary about the potential divisiveness of translating a small movement into a genuine political party that would fight elections. Accordingly, he stepped back, but the party itself went ahead. The party's importance, in the long term, would be incalculable, but its later fame would be, in many ways, an accident of history. Its early days were modest in successes, if bold in their claims. That Ireland should be made independent with a parliament of its own (the 1782 arrangement was recalled) was the first plank in Sinn Féin's constitution. Yet, it also allowed for a connection with the monarch, although there were internal tensions on this issue.

In truth, Sinn Féin, in the early years, could be accused of being somewhat vague in its programme. It was never more than a minority movement on the fringes of political activity. It did attract attention, however, and the journalist in Griffith could not but realise that the name caught on widely, so much so that the authorities in the castle were soon nicknaming all separatists as 'Shinners'. Such promiscuity of association would have considerable effects in a later moment of the story. For now, it was merely an interesting misrepresentation. Just as interesting was the infiltration of the

IRB into its ranks. The IRB was a fitter, leaner entity at this time than at any stage previously. Although by the early 1900s they were somewhat dormant, with very little to show for themselves, the arrival of T. J. Clarke from America in 1907 had given the secret movement new energies and focus. His tobacconist's on Parnell Street became a hub of activities, where young zealots rubbed shoulders, producing an inevitable newspaper (*Irish Freedom*) and discussing long-term strategies. The third clause of their constitution declared that the IRB would 'lend its support to every movement calculated to advance the cause of Irish independence'.[40] It was a closed 'core'; Sinn Féin was a convenient 'front'.

Chapter 17

THE STORY OF IRISH SOCIALISM

Historiography

One is sometimes all too tempted to treat the national story as the main narrative of the period. As regards the early twentieth century, this would be particularly unfair because the social question had recently erupted onto the political scene and was clamouring for attention in more ways than one. The nineteenth century had seen the gradual politicisation of social affairs, especially in urban areas. This had begun in Britain in the late 1830s when Thomas Carlyle had announced the urgency of dealing with the so-called 'condition of England' question. The poor and their rights and wrongs, as he had put it, were newly visible. By 1900, it was called the 'social question', indeed at times 'the problem of problems', and it was a great preoccupation of legislators and social reformers, filled with dread, as they were, about the growth of an 'underclass' and the consequent degeneration of a society and an empire.

The social history of Ireland long had to play second fiddle to the political history. D. G. Boyce observes in this regard that '[t]he class struggle in Ireland was a nationalist struggle; therefore the only class which stood in the way of freedom was the peculiar class which stood for the union'.[1] This began to change firstly under the influence of Marxist and neo-Marxist historians such as Rumpf and Hepburn. The history of labour was considered and it was forwarded that, although a late starter, Ireland's experience of socialism in the early twentieth century was somewhat 'explosive', as well as proving attractive to European communist thinkers.[2]

But the field is now much more expansive and not subject to any one theoretical model, although certain themes such as the history of labour, class, gender and religion are commonplace. A measure of historiographical change is provided by Diarmaid Ferriter's *The Transformation of Ireland*

1900–2000 (2004) in which a much more inclusive social history is integrated than in many more traditional works.[3] The major question for us at this point is whether or not Ireland could have had a socialist revolution. Were the conditions ripe? Dublin's misery is often studied, but whether misery of itself translates into a revolutionary impulse is another matter. Traditionally, the 1913 lockout is regarded as a potential catalyst of societal upheaval – a kind of revolution *manqué*. But this story is not quite so simple. The leaders were charismatic, but in the long term, they compromised their initiative by poor tactics, conflating ideologies of socialism and nationalism, and a failure to achieve a truly popular mandate.[4] It could also be said that the Irish Question was simply 'not about who owned the means of production in industry but about who owned the land'.[5] There was not enough popular impetus behind urban socialism. The other question to ask is to what extent was the social question swallowed up by nationalist politics? There were some pure socialists and some syncretic socialists like Connolly who tried to fuse both ideologies. Nationalists, for their part, tended to say that, once independence was granted, society would adjust itself and all would be well. It could be argued that they, with a few notable exceptions, did not have in mind a radical societal shift.

Social Contexts in Dublin, 1900s

The condition of Ireland was historically a very different one than Britain because the society remained more rural, but, nevertheless, despite the lack of industrial revolution in the south, cities were growing and, with them, all the attendant problems of poor hygiene, disease, overcrowding and loss of identity. It is true that cholera epidemics were now a thing of the past – there had been four violent outbreaks in the nineteenth century: 1832–33, 1848–50, 1853–54, and 1866–67. But that did not leave Dublin in a flourishing condition. By 1900, it had a population of over 400,000 people. The inhuman aridity of the modern city and the jungle of market forces had very obvious victims. Evidence for pervasive urban impoverishment is miserably compelling for the late nineteenth and early twentieth century. Although a Public Health Committee set up in 1866 had introduced some improvements in the water supply, the abolition of cellar dwellings, waste disposal and the introduction of water closets and public baths, much remained undone. It was only in 1906 that the drain system to carry city sewage beyond the harbour was established. In 1878, a public health act banned swine living in the same quarters as people and made vaccination compulsory for those under 14. Some semi-philanthropic housing built, for instance, by the Guinness family, provided 4,500 dwellings for Dubliners. There is even intriguing evidence raised by Murray Fraser in his study, *John Bull's Other Homes* (1996), that

Ireland was an experimental ground for Britain in wading into the question of state subsidies for housing.[6] These were all incremental steps of improvement, but still there was a higher urban death rate than for any other large city in Europe or America. Not for nothing does Leopold Bloom, in James Joyce's *Ulysses* (1922), quip, 'The Irishman's house is his coffin.'[7]

Life expectancy, in fact, was 7–10 years lower in Dublin than it was in Connaught. Infant mortality rates stood at 153 per 1,000, compared to London's 89. One in three children under the age of five might be expected to die. The sight of fathers carrying the small coffins to an early morning burial was a habitual sight. The slums of Dublin were particularly notorious. A 'Report into the Housing of the Dublin Working Classes' (1913)[8] found that 26,000 families (at least 87,000 people) lived in 5,000 tenements. This may not have been as bad as New York, but it was bad enough. Thirty-seven per cent of families lived in one room accommodation – compare that with 15 per cent in London and 1 per cent in Belfast.[9] The only visitors – ministering priests, inspectors or rent collectors – saw decaying houses, hoards of ill-clothed and ill-fed children and the whole populace living there ravaged by premature age and illness. Disease was rife – deaths from TB in particular were very high – and alcoholism alarmingly commonplace. The state of the streets was not admirable. The *Lancet* reported in 1899–1900 on its 'barbaric uncleanliness'.[10] In short, Dublin's situation was anything but desirable.

Irish Urban Centres Abroad

The Irish who went abroad and either lived in Britain or stayed there for certain portions of the year tended to inhabit much the same conditions in the cities that they went. This led to the stereotyping of racial inferiority and innate dirtiness from the 1880s onwards when eugenics and hygiene became faddish among the chattering classes. As we have seen from a previous chapter, the connection between exploited and discontented Irish workers and socialism was an obvious one. However, the labour movement may have been slow to take off in Ireland. For this failure, Lyons offers two reasons – firstly, that the political question of Union dwarfed all others and, secondly, that the country outside the northeast did not develop heavy industry.[11] But it was stoked into life by the turn of the century. Fintan Lane considers there to have been a vibrant tradition of socialism in the late nineteenth century with the Dublin branch of the Socialist League founded in 1885 and the Irish Socialist Republican Party (ISRP) in 1896.[12] This reflects wider Western European trends. Moreover, at about this time, new unions – general unions of unskilled workers, gas workers and dockers, for example – began to emerge with the purpose of campaigning for higher wages and better conditions of labour.

A robust sort of solidarity was born through union meetings and May Day demonstrations. That there was a high correlation between urban centres across the British Isles is made apparent by the fact that the two most celebrated Irish labour leaders were born in the slums of Britain.

The Irish Labour Movement

James Connolly was born in an Edinburgh slum; James Larkin in Liverpool.[13] Both were of Irish parentage. Their backgrounds reveal the pattern of migrating across, not upward. There was a sort of slum transnationalism at work. Connolly's father was a manure carter; Larkin's a forge labourer. Connolly, a largely self-educated man, became convinced of the values of socialism very early on. He had had an eclectic career – printer's devil, baker, factory worker, soldier – before being drawn more closely into the labour movement. In 1896, he established the ISRP which advocated public ownership of the land, nationalisation of industries and a range of radical positions like universal suffrage (to include women), a 48-hour work week, a minimum wage and state education. Any radical script of the sort called for a newspaper of its own and, accordingly, the not very successful *Worker's Republic* was founded in 1898.

Connolly was not, however, purely socialist and it is upon his internal ambiguities that most historians focus. Socialism self-proclaimed as an internationalist creed. In its purest form, it cut across national divides and united workers in a collective struggle against the forces of capitalism. But, inevitably, the reality was more complex. As the Second International discovered from 1889–1914, it was 'notoriously difficult to interest the members of the public in international affairs' of the sort they promoted.[14] Instead, socialism brushed up alongside nationalist movements, especially among the Poles living in Russia and Germany, the Czechs living in Austro-Hungary and, of course, the Irish inhabiting the British Empire. Connolly found both ideologies alluring: the generally accepted interpretation is that he moved from socialism to nationalism, but the roots of duality are visible from an earlier period. His nationalism set him at odds with purely ideological socialism. In a sense, he adapted and rephrased Marx's dictum, 'Workers of the world unite, you have nothing to lose but your chains.' It became this: Workers of *Ireland* unite. Their chains linked them not merely to exploitative capitalist masters, but also to an exploitative imperial power. Ireland had both a national and a social question.

Connolly's approach was a clear dilution of Marxist theory and has been critiqued by purists, but the compromise had obvious strengths. Coughlan sees him as an original, linking the 'working-class ideal of socialism with the categories of the citizen and the native, with the republicanism of the former and the nationalism of the latter'.[15] Irish leaders are often criticised for being overly political to the detriment of concern for the social question. Connolly could not fall foul of such criticism. His was a way of knitting together two powerful contemporary agendas under the umbrella of egalitarianism. It was a way of 'socialising' the national question and 'nationalising' the social question. He contended that the demands of the poor would be better met by the nation than by a foreign elite. His influence helped to give Irish socialism a particular greenish tint from its early days and perhaps stalled the creation of a vibrant labour tradition, independent of nationalism. National rather than transnational solidarity was what really mattered.

The question we need to ask of Connolly is which he put first and when – social reform or political change so as to secure it? Until 1913, it could be said Connolly concentrated on the first avenue; afterwards, he turned towards the second. This is what ultimately would make him the principal socialist proponent of the 1916 rising. In what was seemingly becoming a rite of passage for Irish leaders, Connolly spent seven years from 1903 to 1910 in America, founding another newspaper called the *Harp* and cultivating various sectors of socialist and national opinion whilst there. A trade union leader, Daniel de Leon, was a particular influence, but they fell out before too long. Connolly was not an easy man at the best of times, but his talent and his force attracted James Larkin who asked him to be secretary to the Belfast branch of the Irish Transport and General Workers' Union (ITGWU). Connolly, keen to get back to Ireland, agreed.

Larkin, almost a decade his junior, was a combustible force in the labour movement. He joined the Independent Labour Party in 1892 and, becoming a docker, soon rose to the ranks of foreman. As such, he was earning £3 and 10 shillings a week, which put him in the higher tier of the working class. He had come into an awareness of his own talents not through the route of formal education but through his experience of speaking to fellow dock workers. These were heady times for British socialism. Since the late 1880s, unions had become more militant and, just before the end of the century, there had been the first national walkout. Larkin showed his mettle in 1905 in a strike in Liverpool and, although the National Union of Dock Labourers did not achieve victory, his talent at organisation was thought so remarkable that he was asked to work for the union full time. He began organising workers in Scotland. Soon he was preaching the politics of discontent more widely and his labour activities were further enhanced by his move to Dublin in 1907. Never one to shy away from an opening, he established the ITGWU in 1908, which avowed a socialist programme and hoped to unite both skilled and unskilled workers and thus break down the petty divisions between these two groups. Defiantly proclaiming 'each for all and all for each', it was a militant organisation, prepared to use all the means at its disposal to make employers sit up and take notice.[16] By 1913, it boasted 10,000 members.

Such plebeian radicalism touched a chord and his paper, the *Irish Worker* (1911), sold up to 90,000 copies a week. The creed of Larkinism was fiery, engaging and charismatic – its force was not long in making enemies among the employer class. There followed the most infamous showdown between labour and capital in twentieth-century Ireland. Were it not for the 1916 rebellion, indeed, the 1913 lockout could lay claim to being the drama of the decade. It was the largest labour struggle in the whole of the United Kingdom up to that point and thus an event of some significance. It must be seen as the culmination of a wave of strikes from 1910–12 in Britain among seamen, stevedores, bargemen, railworkers, coalminers and dock labourers. Although the end of the lockout was damp and miserable for the trade union movement, it is not inconceivable that it could have brought the country into an insurrectionary state; in which case, it would have been primarily social rather than political.

The 1913 Lockout

The struggle was a titanic one, or so, at least, the historical myth is generally presented. A recent historian, Padraig Yeates, begs to differ. Not only was it shabbier, bloodier and more mundane than often described, but it was an unnecessary dispute, prodded into existence by two inconvenient personalities – Larkin's and William Martin Murphy's.[17] The latter, head of the Dublin Employers' Federation represented the force for order or exploitation (depending on one's point of view). The crude image of William 'Murder' Murphy is not historically tenable. He was, in fact, reputed as a fair employer himself; he was also a nationalist and had been a member of the Irish Political Party (IPP). A fabulously successful capitalist he indubitably was. He had made a large amount of money out of paper and transport, a typical early twentieth-century way of acquiring a fortune and a position. He was a press baron and chairman of the Dublin United Tramway Company, one of the new well-groomed business elite who were afraid that union activity would lead to revolution and the stuttering of economic growth. If he was a villain, he was a very modern one.

Larkin's fieriness antagonised him. In 1913, he decided to take the ITGWU on by persuading 300 employers to agree not to employ any of its members. That was to raise the stakes unbearably. Larkin chose the week of the Dublin Horse Show in August – the week of maximum disruption and publicity – to call workers out on strike. And they came. Employers responded by locking them out – up to 20,000 of them. The six months that followed had more than their share of drama. A 'Bloody Sunday' incident saw scuffles between crowds and policemen, resulting in injuries and deaths on both sides. The leaders, Larkin and Connolly, among others, all found themselves behind bars. For families, the loss of the weekly wage, such as it was, meant misery and the prospect of a very bleak winter. Up to 100,000 men, women and children were affected; in a city of 400,000, this cut very deeply indeed.[18] Charity flourished, but even charity was accused of being political. One attempt to foster Catholic children to English (and therefore presumably Protestant) parents ended in controversy. Lyons undoubtedly exaggerates when he says that the children were 'left to wither in the sanctity of their slums',[19] there was a lot of withering going on, anyway, and, during the winter, most of the workers quietly trooped back to work. A few months away from slum conditions would hardly have made a material difference to the health of most.

The end was a squalid one and Larkin was not without blame. Although to view him as someone with a 'semi-mystical enthusiasm for riot' is dismissive and unfair,[20] he had, it is true, played his cards extremely badly. Despite having received considerable financial aid from the British Trade Union Congress (TUC) (£150,000 in money and food), he denounced his benefactors for not calling out sympathetic strikes in Britain. The TUC had debated his demands in December 1913 and rejected them ten to one. His anger seemed like ingratitude for all that they *had* done and funding quickly dried up. An incident like this seriously detracts from Rumpf's claim that he was a pragmatist.[21] Despite the fact that the episode was regarded with great interest by international socialists (Lenin amongst them), it had no glorious conclusion that could serve as an example for others. Some compromises were made with the unions. The ITGWU was not totally defunct afterwards, but it had lost much of its spirit and many of its members. The hold that employers had over workers was basic – money and food. With a hungry family of four or five or more, the language of justice and rights seemed secondary. Better to go back, as Connolly bitterly remarked, to the 'lash of the slave driver'.[22] However, Lee does point out that, although the employers clearly won the battle, they did lose the war. 'Larkin', he writes, 'had broken the bond of deference and had created a conscious sense of identity among the unskilled workers, the most degraded single sector of Irish society'.[23] He may overstate the positives achieved by the lockout, but there is no doubting that it goaded local government into reviewing the housing situation in the capital and prodded sectors of the middle classes, including some influential Catholics, into taking the doctrine of social action more seriously.

Legacies of the Lockout

The lockout had a number of significant legacies. First, it took the stuffing out of at least one of the labour movement's leaders. Larkin was all fire, but he coped ill with failure and disillusionment. He took matters very personally and left for America where, for a combination of reasons, he stayed until 1923. When he returned, it would not be to his old unquestioned leadership position. He was ever only a marginal figure in Irish political life thereafter and his reputation as 'Big' Jim was very much that of earlier years. Unsurprisingly, when world war broke out in 1914, he declared it to be a capitalist plot and would have nothing to do with it. Of course, this 'cemented his international reputation as a revolutionary socialist'.[24] Unlike Connolly's advocacy of a synthesis between socialism and nationalism, Larkin was more purely the socialist and believed that this imperial war was being foisted on the shoulders of hapless workers who would bear the greatest burden. But Larkin was not in Ireland to make this point loudly. Connolly was left in charge of the movement and it was a Connolly who was turning towards politics for a solution to Ireland's social ills.

The lockout also brought into existence an Irish Citizen Army (ICA). It was created by the leaders to protect demonstrators against Murphy's men and the police with batons. Its volunteers were armed with hurley sticks, showing the obvious connections between native sports and militarism. It was not an effective army and all but collapsed at the end of the lockout. However, it had potential as an idea. In 1914, the socialist playwright Seán O'Casey suggested that a revived ICA might have its role to play in any drama that would ensue. It was more ambitiously political now and the first plank of its constitution (itself a sign of maturity) was to claim ownership of the land of Ireland for the people of Ireland. Anyone with a belief in this doctrine and in equal rights could ask for admittance. It is certain that the context of international war lent a new defiance to the ICA's tones. Over its headquarters and that of the ITGWU in Liberty Hall hung the bold message: 'We serve neither King nor Kaiser but Ireland.'[25]

One of the stalwarts of the ICA was the personification of eccentricity: Countess Constance Marckievicz. An Anglo-Irish Gore-Booth married to a Polish count, she had her hand in everything that was moving in Ireland – the literary renaissance, women's rights, the Irish Boy Scouts (which she founded), charity work and, now, the ICA. She may have seemed like a dilettante, but she was ardently committed. There was something of the self-styled Joan of Arc about Constance – she liked nothing better than to dress in a uniform. This was the woman who would be the first female MP elected to the British Parliament under the terms of the Representation of the People

Act (1918), but who would not take her seat on principle. Indeed, it is worth mentioning at this point that women played what one historian would call a 'formidable part in the winning and the making of the new state'.[26] There was something about the Irish national movement that facilitated the relatively seamless entry of women into politics. Hart notes that the tradition of revolutionary republicanism was probably the 'most female-dependent major movement in modern Irish history'.[27]

Chapter 18

THE HOME RULE CRISIS

Interpretations

The social crisis was overshadowed by a larger political crisis of the years 1910–14 which involved high politics in Westminster and high drama in Ireland. What distinguishes the third Home Rule episode from former controversies was the greater importance of the Ulster question, the threat of violence with which the matter was attended and the debate about whether or not the British state could or would use force to impose a settlement. If they had, there could well have been a civil war, for it seems unlikely that either side would have backed down. But the counter-factual is an alluring distraction. Civil war did not take place. Hart would argue that the situation was not 'even potentially revolutionary'.[1] Instead the Great War broke out and the Home Rule bill was put on hold for the duration with momentous consequences. Conventionally, historians regard the Unionist and Conservative combination as key to the untimely abortion of a full settlement.[2] Whether the means they took to do this (militarisation) were legitimate forms of resistance, as they claimed, is highly doubtful. Conservative involvement made the whole murkier still and potentially destabilising to the entire political system. Darwin regards the episode as an emphatic contradiction of any kind of metropolitan consensus.[3] But it is possible to read further into the matter. Patricia Jalland puts the initial blame squarely on Asquith's shoulders. He was too passive, failed to see how serious the opposition was and lost the initiative in 1912 when he might have made a real difference.[4] O'Day emphasises the flaws of the bill itself which gave its opponents so many 'soft targets' but also the 'unprecedented' opposition of Unionists and the relatively passive role of Irish Home Rulers who were 'consigned to the sidelines' in a British party political struggle.[5]

Late Edwardian Liberalism

British party politics, as ever, conditioned prospects for the Irish Question. This was the era of so-called New Liberalism which boasted a more interventionist agenda than old-style Gladstonianism. Was Edwardian Liberalism interested in Ireland? The general thinking would answer in the negative, although Jackson has qualified this somewhat.[6] The Conservative Party, meanwhile, from the opposition benches, retained their strong association with Unionism. Entrenched principle was involved, so also were personal connections. Up to 25 per cent of their MPs were northern Unionists, southern Irish gentry or married into these families. A sweeping majority in the election of 1906 left the Liberals in a very safe position and happily independent of Irish support. However, the good times would not last. Herbert Henry Asquith's ministry (from 1908) became bemired in controversial legislation. Worried by some of the health and hygiene problems already discussed, the government needed money to fund an extensive project for welfare reforms in Britain. Most controversially, David Lloyd George, as chancellor of the exchequer, introduced the radical People's Budget of 1909, which squeezed the rich through super taxes, death duties, land and petrol tax. The House of Lords rejected it (350 to 75), thus provoking a dramatic constitutional crisis. Later, with a public mandate, Asquith's government took its revenge by abolishing their veto power in the 1911 Parliament Act.

This constitutional crisis was of huge significance to Ireland in two ways. Firstly, the fact that House of Lords had lost its veto made the cause of Home Rule a much more hopeful one as they would no longer be able to reject a measure outright. Secondly, after such disruption and defection, the Liberals would need the support of the Irish MPs once again. The 84 Irish Parliamentary Party (IPP) members were thus occupying a strategic position. John Redmond, a mild-mannered member of the Catholic gentry, was unquestionably the leader of the reunited Irish Party. He had been attached to Parnell but, after his death, he was a conciliatory influence to bring the party back into unity in 1900. Jackson praises his statesman-like ability, saying that he was a 'parliamentary mountaineer' but as Ferriter points out, with some justice, his reunification of the party was more about 'survival' than 'rejuvenation'.[7] He was not another Parnell. Wags said that he had been so long in Westminster that he had forgotten what Ireland was like.[8] He had no interest in the Irish Ireland movement. Although respected, he failed to capture the public imagination. By 1910, he was already old guard, a steady chairman, not a chief. There is an argument that he was unlucky in his context – Asquith was no Gladstone. Like many Irish leaders, his peculiar position forced him into opacity: in America, to raise funds, he spoke of an Irish nation in a way that suggested independence. In Britain, he was prepared to accept a more modest measure of devolution than Gladstonian Home Rule, although when the opportunity came for a wider measure in 1912, he took it. 'Our stake in the Empire is too large for us to be detached from it' he ruminated to a Liberal journalist in 1908 and, in 1910, to the *Daily Express* he gave guarantees of Irish imperial loyalty.[9]

But British opponents of Home Rule – and there were many such – deemed that the reverse would be the case. Home Rule was incompatible with the true nature of empire. Ireland was an intimate part of imperial power: what happened there mattered for the fate of the Empire as a whole. Joseph Chamberlain reputedly remarked in 1893 that, if Ireland were a thousand miles away, it would have been accorded self-government long since. That might well have been true. The Irish Question was problematic because of its very proximity. It was also an even more troubling question now for Britons of a conservative hue because of imperial anxieties, notably the Anglo–German naval race and the popular fears of a German invasion in the near future. For many in the early 1900s, Ireland had become 'the keystone in the arch of Empire and national security, without which collapse and ruin would inevitably follow'.[10] Only in that context can we understand the high emotions surrounding the passage of the Third Home Rule Bill and the extraordinary phenomenon of Conservative politicians conspiring to thwart the government.

The Third Home Rule Bill 1912

The crisis surrounding the Third Home Rule Bill, introduced by Asquith in April 1912, is indicative of the state of political and public emotions surrounding the issue. It would turn out to be, in a very real sense, an imperial crisis. Party opponents, Jackson notes, 'who normally set aside their differences beyond the hustings and the debating chamber, refused to dine with one another'.[11] It was the ultimate divide. But at the start there were signs of hope that the matter could be dealt with efficiently and fairly. Patricia Jalland regards 1912 as a 'unique opportunity' for the Liberals to settle the Irish Question, in which case they fudged it badly.[12] Indeed, she argues that failure here played a huge role in the ultimate decline of the Liberal Party, something which, she claims, has not been properly considered by historians. Not all would accept her thesis.

Asquith deserves some credit for tackling the issue, untouched since Gladstone's time. He made some effort to understand the matter from within: his visit to Dublin in July 1912 as an 'Ambassador of Peace' augured well. In his memoirs, he recalled the enthusiasm of the population.

Only one suffragette threw a hatchet at them and that, fortunately, just grazed Redmond's cheek. The Women's Social and Political Union, incidentally, angry at the IPP for having withdrawn its support from the Conciliation Bill that would have given women the vote, had extended their violent activities to Dublin. Asquith spoke in Burkean language, saying that 'no reluctant tie can be a strong one' and expressing his hope that the Anglo–Irish connection would be remade to be voluntary, spontaneous, affectionate and real.[13] All this was mild, crowd-pleasing, general stuff. Beneath the surface, Jalland sees him as 'paternalistic and élitist', something which may have counted against his chances.[14] He certainly was not an enthusiast for it, nor a visionary in the Gladstonian manner and he left many of the details to David Lloyd George, his chancellor of the exchequer, Winston Churchill, president of the Board of Trade and Augustine Birrell, the chief secretary of Ireland from 1907–16.

Perhaps his biggest failure was that he did not wake up to the problem of Ulster early enough. By 1911, the Unionist movement had become 'to all intents and purposes an Ulster phenomenon'. The southerners who played a role did so within a northern context.[15] When, in February 1912, the more prescient Lloyd George and Churchill mooted a proposal for Ulster exclusion, Asquith rejected it. The bill came before the Commons, therefore, simply as an all-Ireland measure, very like the 1893 antecedent except that representation in Westminster had been reduced from 80 to 42.[16] One significant difference was that the Lord Lieutenant had more powers – to indefinitely postpone legislation. It has been argued that it was a very careful, well-prepared bill, even the best Home Rule measure *qua* measure.[17] There was not much debate about it in the Commons and it passed the third reading with a healthy majority of 110, but was rejected in the House of Lords. As the latter had by now lost their power of veto, they could merely delay its passing for two years and amendments could meanwhile be made in the form of suggestions. That was the rub. Much would intervene in the space of those two years so that, by the time it eventually did receive royal assent on 18 September 1914, the bill 'had ceased to be relevant to the Irish situation'.[18]

From legislative settlement to political irrelevance – how did this happen? It happened through the polarisation of Irish opinion, north and south, and the militaristic way in which this was expressed. The lines of battle emerged in the creation of two bodies, the Ulster Volunteer Force (UVF) to fight against Home Rule and the Irish Volunteer Force in its defence. Eoin MacNeill wrote perceptively in 1913 that it was an obvious truth that 'all Irish people, Unionist as well as Nationalist, are determined to have their way in Ireland'.[19] He had noticed what was, in fact, occurring: not merely a hardening of determination but a greater willingness to act on the basis of that determination, to assert themselves. The 'rigidities' of Irish politics were to make themselves felt anew.[20]

The Ulster Volunteer Force[21]

It was Ulster who first asserted itself with the creation in January 1913 of the UVF under the aegis of Edward Carson. In 1910, Carson, of Scotch-Presbyterian and Anglo-Irish descent, had become *de facto* leader of the twenty or so Unionist Irish in Westminster. Devotion to the Union he claimed to be the 'guiding star of his political life'.[22] Asquith's bill had goaded him into action and these two years are perhaps the culmination of his achievement – he was best seen in opposition.[23] His ultimate end was to have the bill scotched altogether. It was, in his words, the 'most nefarious conspiracy that has ever been hatched against a free people'; his manner of proceeding was to make of Ulster a special case of resistance. This was based on the not unreasonable view that to exempt Ulster from the settlement would fatally undermine the whole. If the government could be convinced of Ulster's implacable opposition, then the chances were that the bill would collapse in its entirety. His leadership and that of another Unionist MP, Captain James Craig, waxed strongly in the north. A. T. Q. Stewart, whose 1967 work on *The Ulster Crisis* is still a classic, claims that Craig's massive strength 'derived from a frontier tradition, from the memories of plantation and a Scot covenanting past'.[24] Craig knew the grassroots of the movement intimately, and was content that the articulate Carson should be front man whilst he worked in the wings. Both complemented each other.

Nowhere was the implacable opposition to Home Rule more emphatically expressed than in the Ulster Volunteer Force. What surprises Townshend is the slowness with which this came into existence, although he acknowledges that, as far as Britons were concerned, it happened with disarming speed, hobbling their poorly conceived optimism.[25] The phenomenon was called 'Ulsteria' by the wags. Progress was rapid; drilling went ahead. These men meant to fight if need be. Even rifles were obtained, under the legal guise of the firearms' licence. British authorities let it be. The Solemn League and Covenant of September 1912 was a marvellously successful dramatic set piece. Almost half a million ordinary Ulster Protestants signed the document, a pledge of loyalty to the monarch and a protest against the disaster that would be Home Rule. It was mass politicisation assuredly – women were involved as well as men – and it was also superb propaganda. Carson signed first with a silver pen. The whole act was processional and historic. But, as Jackson hastens to point out, the Unionist campaign was also 'relentlessly modern', using the camera, moving pictures, the press and distributing millions of flyers, rosettes, medals and even commemorative chinaware.[26]

Had they got right on their side? Were they, as Carson claimed, really being driven out by force or was Unionist opposition as 'irresponsible' as Beckett would have it?[27] Townshend, a fairly neutral observer, thinks that they had fear on their side (he leaves it open as to whether it was reasonable or unreasonable), but not constitutionalism. There had been large constitutional change before, so they could not object on the grounds of lack of precedence. They were not, he argues, acting legitimately by threatening 'to use force to uphold the status quo' – any more than those who opposed the Reform Bill of 1832 or vaccination legislation.[28]

Support from Britain was very forthcoming. Sometimes it came through very establishment channels indeed. Andrew Bonar Law, the Conservative leader, called the Liberal government a 'revolutionary committee which has seized by fraud upon despotic powers'.[29] A very partisan interpretation sees him as 'excessively Tory in the matter of having no political imagination whatsoever'.[30] However that may be, his support of the cause was vital. In June 1913 there was a debacle in Hammersmith, London, when 6,000–7,000 Italian rifles were found in a pub on King Street, care of Captain Budd, brother-in-law of a Tory MP. As well as all the covert collusions, there was overt support for Ulster. In March 1913, the British League for the Support of Ulster and the Union was established. It was supported by 100 peers, 120 MPs and boasted 10,000 members by 1914. Most notable of all was the contribution of Rudyard Kipling, then at the height of his fame and the first Englishman to win the Nobel Prize for Literature (1908). He was violently opposed to the Liberal government and saw the Ulster Question as a battleground on which to fight for a wider and endangered imperial agenda. He gave £30,000 to the cause, made angry anti-government speeches and set up refugee committees. Mincing no words, he captured the implacable spirit behind the covenant in his poem 'Ulster 1912'.[31]

> What answer from the North?
> One Law, one Land, one Throne
> If England drive us forth
> We shall not fall alone!

The hint of malice in the last line was not accidental. The force of Ulster Unionism was more intransigent than legally minded Carson expected and, curiously, although his rhetoric suggested unity and his following suggested loyalty, the cause more than the man was their focus and thus Carson's control was never absolute. He did accept the arming of the UVF in 1914, but with some reluctance. His legal background made him ultimately open to compromise, to coming to terms. But the rank-and-file had set their teeth. Here it may be argued that there is a discernible difference between Unionist and nationalist movements. In the former, it was the rank-and-file who were more adamantly militaristic; in the case of the latter, it would be the hard-line leaders who set themselves on the course of violence.

The Irish Volunteers

Where the north began, the south soon followed, and it was Eoin MacNeill, Celtic scholar and writer, who advocated a pro–Home Rule equivalent to be called the Irish Volunteers. It was purely imitative. They were there to ensure that there would be no compromise at this last stage. Townshend notes how odd it is that the 'Irish Ireland' movement, which was so Catholic in orientation, felt so strongly against the exclusion of Protestants in the settlement.[32] Unlike 'Ulsterism', this was a militia in defence of what the government proposed and it appealed to a group who did not necessarily like their politics murky in backroom smoke and the whisperings of revolution. This seemed like something solid and out in the open. In any case, it caught on, although it did not convert the UVF as MacNeill somewhat naively imagined it would. At an opening meeting in the rotunda, 3,000 joined. Marching bands undoubtedly helped, as did the presence of charismatic speakers like MacNeill himself and Patrick Pearse, whose genius for oratory was only recently discovered. The Act of Union was repudiated; the language of the movement emphatic in its desire to recover the common 'rights and liberties of the Irish'.[33] The Volunteers were a citizen militia – the emphasis on masculine values and discipline was apparent. There were those like Pearse who believed that the possession of arms was itself an 'assertion of a nation's virility', that it would restore to men effective power.[34] The movement made a claim to legitimacy, seeking to deflect accusations of aggression by espousing as its motto 'defence not defiance'.[35]

Of course, there was a very fine line. Some might argue that the formation of a private army was itself a defiance of the state. The secretive Irish Republican Brotherhood (IRB) was very much at work within the movement, although MacNeill himself was not a member. The abstruse role played by the IRB needs to be unravelled – was it involvement or infiltration, co-operation or subversion? Although not quite a Leninesque core of professional revolutionaries – most had day jobs – IRB men did have something of the same sense of professional commitment to a cause. There was also the same presumption, an arrogant one, about the laxity of the masses. This is a fairly typical pattern in the typology of the revolutionary and accounts for the disjunction between their rhetoric (generally reaching out *ad populum*) and their actions (elitist and undemocratic). When it came to it, it was felt that the masses diluted; in the IRB, the message of separatism was drunk neat. But that did not mean that 'mass' movements could not be used as a means to greater ends. Their very constitution stated its support for every movement advancing the cause of independence. So the Volunteers were obviously attractive to them from the first and they clearly relished operating through a popular open movement: it allowed more freedom of action. It is not hard to avoid seeing an element of play acting in this conviction that people could be manipulated from behind the scenes. It was to account for much of the subsequent confusion, however, and indeed may betray a certain naivety of approach. But perhaps we would accuse Lenin of just that had the Bolshevik Revolution through the Soviets failed.

Gunrunning and Curragh Mutiny

The pace of the crisis quickened with two spates of illegal gunrunning which called into question the 'legal' boasts of these civilian armies. The episodes also illustrate the comparative organisation and resources of the two forces and the double standard of the authorities. The UVF gunrunning occurred in Larne, Co. Antrim on 24 April 1914; the other was in Howth, Co. Dublin for the Volunteers on 26 July. The former was much the more successful of the two. It brought in 20,000 rifles and 3.5 million rounds of ammunition – a cavalcade of motor cars was waiting to transfer the weapons in what was an immaculately planned execution. Its effect was not only practical: Jackson's point is that it became a 'focal point' for Unionist 'self-congratulation and pride thereafter'.[36] The July spate in the south brought in a mere 1,500 rifles, most dating from the Franco–Prussian War of 1870–71. Notwithstanding, the relative importance of the one and the relative failure of the other, the reaction of the British authorities heavily weighed against the southerners. There was a scuffle in Bachelors Walk that day in which British troops shot and killed several unarmed citizens. The unequal treatment was especially galling and Redmond was furious. In fact, it is now a very plausible theory that Andrew Bonar Law, the new leader of the Conservative Party (renamed for the time being as the National Unionist Association of Conservative and Liberal Unionist Organisations), had met the Unionist ring leaders and approved of their actions in advance.[37] If true, that was quite an extraordinary move.

The whole emphasised even more the stark contrast between the Ulster force and its southern counterpart. The former contained within its ranks many reserve officers from the British Army, well-trained signalling corps, ambulances, nurses, cooks, transport and commissariat contingents – a truly 'formidable' entity, according to Denman.[38] The Volunteers could not hope to compete. Meanwhile, a troubled John Redmond looked on and, angered by stalling negotiations in Westminster, became convinced that if the UVF meant seriously to exert force to overturn the desired Home Rule settlement, it was high time for him to lend legitimacy to what was happening in the south. Accordingly, he plied control of the Volunteers from MacNeill's hands, negotiating that the IPP should nominate members to the committee. Clearly, he and the rest of the party elite were already grooming themselves as the new rulers of the Ireland that was to come.

By early 1914, the Irish military situation was truly schizoid. There were, in effect, four armies: the Irish Citizen Army, the UVF, the Volunteers and the British Army, not to speak of the constabulary, which was seen by many as an army of occupation. This, says Townshend slyly, was 'certainly too many for comfort or safety'.[39] Recognition that a problem had become a crisis came in March 1914. Sir Arthur Paget, General Officer Commanding in Ireland, was told to prepare to send troops to Ulster in case there should be any resistance to the Home Rule measure soon to be given royal assent. He interpreted the orders with a little more latitude than desirable, so when it filtered down the chain of command, it seemed less like a precaution and more of an order for 'active operations'. At the Curragh camp in Kildare, the commanders of the third and fifth cavalry division were especially irate and 60 of the former resigned as well as many artillery and infantry officers. Mutiny was a bold gesture, showing a preference for resignation rather than coercion of their coreligionists and political affiliates. They were reinstated afterwards, but the episode had shaken the British establishment. To the nationalists, the affair illustrated the inherent Unionist bias of the British armed forces.

The Bill on the Eve of War

The bill was, nonetheless, given royal assent in the spring of 1914 and a suggestion was made to exclude Ulster from the provision of Home Rule. The Buckingham Palace conference in July 1914 was a grand – indeed, a royal – attempt at brokerage, gathering together the British governing elite, the Irish Unionist Alliance and the IPP. It was a first attempt at a formal peace talk and, as such, deserving of praise. It was, nonetheless, an abject failure. The impasse was complete and, as Asquith pointed out in a private aside, dangerous. All the worse that it was a matter 'which to English eyes seems inconceivably small and to Irish eyes immeasurably big'.[40] Such a view seems to have been engrained; as Dangerfield says in his 1935 work with a casual callousness, '[t]he prospects of a little blood-letting in Ireland [...] seem of little importance when one thinks of the terrible slaughter which the world was soon to endure'.[41]

However, we should be alive to the fact that this story was not merely a petty national one but a truly imperial one. John Darwin, in *The Empire Project: The Rise and Fall of the British World System 1830–1970* (2009), regards the whole episode of crisis from 1912–14 as 'astonishing' and believes that it completely undermines the argument that the 'British world-system owed its strength and cohesion to shrewd pragmatism and liberal instincts of the governing elite in London'.[42] The party elites were in a tangle, both wedded to their Irish allies and wanting to secure political advantage at home. His point is here that the 'men in London' were reacting to lobbies and trying to reframe policy on the spot. The Irish situation could well have taken on the aspect of civil war. Yet, there were other and worse tangles in the summer of 1914, although at first British newspapers were full of Irish news and had very little to say about the latest Balkan debacle. European war broke out just weeks after the Buckingham Palace Conference had come to a sorry end and soon nobody could talk of anything else.

Chapter 19

WORLD WAR AND INSURRECTION

Ireland's Experiences of War

Then came the Great War. Every institution, almost, in the world was strained. Great Empires have been overturned. The whole map of Europe has been changed. The position of countries has been violently altered. The modes of thought of men, the whole outlook on affairs, the grouping of parties, all have encountered violent and tremendous changes in the deluge of the world. But as the deluge subsides and the waters fall short we see the dreary steeples of Fermanagh and Tyrone emerging once again. The integrity of their quarrel is one of the few institutions that has been unaltered in the cataclysm which has swept the world.[1]

Thus did Winston Churchill bitterly sum up the dreary parochial 'sameness' of the Irish Question in 1918. The bitterness at the persistence of the utterly parochial, the microcosmic dramas of the Irish was not merely a Churchillian attitude. The same must have struck many in the British establishment – that there still was an Irish Question in 1918 that required dealing with. No doubt there was an element of truth in what he said, but it is also extremely reductive. Ireland had been thoroughly reshaped by the experience of war. Only to the bored and frustrated did the steeples look similar. There are two strands of the story that particularly deserve attention. For convenience, we may label them as the national story and the international story. The former concerns what happened within the nation, the latter the playing out of war. It is the former story that usually dominates in the historiography and yet both are highly interconnected. Without the context of war, the Irish Question might have looked very different. The war provided a superficial and short-lived sense of unity, and evoked Irish loyalism in both north and south. But the longer it went on, the more the cracks began to emerge so that it could even be said that the war 'cemented the notion of "two Irelands"'.[2] Whether indeed this change was due to the war itself or the rising or the reaction to the rising is an open question.

The International Story

The story of the Irishmen's involvement in the Great War has received unequal treatment. The Protestant north has consistently emphasised its military commitment to the British Empire and used the experience to bind themselves even further to the metropolitan power. In the south, the contribution made by Irishmen to the war effort has often been overlooked. This was a blind spot of nationalist historiography post-independence. Denman rightly labels it a 'historical no-man's land'.[3] Participation was deemed almost betrayal and veterans kept quiet about their experience. The public memory of war was all but extinguished in the south except in Protestant communities with a few Catholic exceptions. Whereas the Ulstermen had their memorial, those from the south had none. Since the late 1980s, an effort has been made to recover and reintegrate this story into the mainstream. Kevin Myers, former journalist of the *Irish Times*, was primarily responsible for bringing the issue to the attention of the general public. More recently, there has been a flurry of works on the subject, focusing on a variety of aspects including women, the home front, trade unions, wages, recruitment propaganda and shell shock.[4] As the south has become more comfortable with this dimension of its history, the war has even become something of a historical point of unity for both 'nations' on the island. In 1998 a communal monument was unveiled in the form of a round tower near Ypres, symbolic of the peace process.

The story is rightfully told not merely because it illustrates the loyalism felt by many Irishmen towards the British Empire and, more pragmatically, their need for employment, but also because, as Fitzpatrick points out in purely numeric terms, more Irish people (250,000) enlisted in it than in the nationalist War of Independence. As such, he sees it as having 'overwhelming importance' on people's lives.[5] The population began to hear of the horrors of the trenches where 30,000 of their compatriots died. However much historiography might try to relegate this story to second place, it is obvious that the experience of war must have shaped the lives of the generation. Adrian Gregory and Senia Paseta hold that its outstanding effect was to politicise 'almost every facet of civilian and military involvement'.[6]

Redmond's Leadership

The involvement of the Irish in war is also historically important because of its connection with Redmond's leadership of the Irish Volunteer Force. In supporting the Irish war effort, he earned the opprobrium of nationalists, but his motivations were reasoned through and complex. He did genuinely believe in the justice of the cause. The demand for national liberties had now become a broad quest for liberty. But, as Denman points out, there was 'self-interest' as well as 'idealism' behind his attitude towards Irish involvement.[7] He thought it would be strategic if Ireland showed her loyalty by rallying to the Union Jack. It was logical that showing goodwill towards Britain in a crisis might do them a service when said crisis abated. He also believed that Ireland could prove the point of her nationhood by becoming militarily involved in this struggle. Redmond might have been optimistic (nationalist historiography would portray him as naive), but his logic was faultless. The very same month in which Home Rule was put on the statute books – that is to say, September 1914 – Redmond was in Ireland encouraging his volunteers to go out to war in defence of 'freedom' and 'right'.[8] Home Rule was suspended until the war should be over, but that, it was felt, would be before Christmas and Redmond probably already had his eye on the future settlement and the establishment of a national army on the basis of the Volunteers. It is not difficult to read Redmond's game. He was determined to exploit this opportunity, a potentially unitive one for the whole island, in order to carve out an executive leadership role for himself in the new dispensation. His whole attitude reveals his confidence and optimism, characteristics that would become less and less shared as the war dragged on. There is a further nuance to his views, according to some. He wanted to keep Irish men militarily fit so that, if the Home Rule settlement did come down to a fight, they would be prepared.[9] We are a long way from interpreting Redmond as the toadying West Briton nationalist historiography would have. Still, the paradox remains that he persuaded thousands to join an army that 'just a short time before, had been killing Irishmen on the streets of Dublin'.[10]

For the vast majority, that is to say, for about 150,000–170,000 men, Redmond's recruitment drive proved resonant. The National Volunteers, as they then became, fought alongside the British and their history became mired in the mud and blood of the trenches. Many of them fought in the existing Irish regiments, but as Asquith refused to increase the number, many others served in British regiments and were not allowed distinctive badges which would mark them out as Irish – a small but telling injustice. The Ulster Volunteer Force (UVF) made up a 36th Division, giving it 13 new battalions. Some of these men had the distinction of having been the only group to have achieved their objectives on the infamous first day of the Battle of the Somme. That year, there were no Orange parades in Ulster on 12 July. The Orange bluster had become real. They had sealed their covenant with Britain in blood. How could the British establishment *not* afford them special treatment afterwards?[11] The gauntlet was thrown down.

The National Story

Not all Irish patriots would find themselves able to accept such a leap. As far as the Volunteers were concerned, the remainder was a not negligible minority of 11,000. It included many of the most vocal and assertive types.[12] Truculence or principle? Those who chose to go against the grain, against the wild enthusiasm of war, had their reasons. The fact that they were not won over with blandishments indicates a certain rigidity of outlook – they had distinguished themselves by opposition to the general momentum and would stand by their position. It also indicates a level of nationalist introversion: they saw no reason to become embroiled in a foreign quarrel. At a convention in October 1914, the leftover Volunteers proclaimed resistance to forcing Irishmen into arms until a free national government of Ireland had been established. Although it cannot be said that these men had revolution in mind, there was a certain feeling of alienation from this imperial conflict and a belief that British difficulty might well be Irish opportunity. Tight-lipped, stiff-jawed, they had the run of the country. There were even overtures made to Germany to involve itself in a flank attack on Britain.

Interpreting the Rising

The nationalist story culminates in the week-long Easter Rising, half way through the war in 1916. Interpretations of the rising are many and various.[13] Naturally, the episode forms a central part of traditional nationalist historiography and its characters part of its hagiography. It is the high point of the salvation drama – redemption by bloodletting. It was the supreme response to centuries of unbearable repression and the genuine expression of what the people wanted, even if the people did not yet know that they wanted it. The fact that the rebels were a tiny group does not make supporters of this interpretation blink. The leaders were true heroes, descendants in a long tradition of republicanism from Wolfe Tone, Robert Emmet and the Fenians. The view of the rising as noble and ennobling, the faith and fatherland version, is summed up by Dorothy MacArdle who lyrically declares that '[i]n the character of these men as in the terms of the Proclamation were united the faith and pride in the Irish Nation, the passion for freedom and social justice, and the ideal of a civilisation inherently Irish, which had inspired Ireland's resistance to conquest for centuries'.[14]

Revisionist historians have qualified this story on a number of levels. They have taken an almost malicious delight in dethroning its importance as an event, locating its real importance in the train of events that occurred afterwards. They refuse to see it as a simple affair in its causation or its consequences and eschew the pieties of patriotic hagiography. As against the notion of constantly wearisome oppression, Garvin paraphrases an unpublished Pocock idea that the Irish revolutionary movement 'derived its energies from a series of grievances that were slowly being rectified'.[15] Beckett insists that it did not come about as the result of 'unbearable oppression'.[16] The rising was botched, shambolic, unprofessional, bungled, inconsequential or consequential only in a negative way. More seriously, it was an aberration, a poet's fantasy of violence. Scholars have taken in particular to uncovering the obscure corners of this philosophy of violence. F. S. L. Lyons accuses the rebel leaders of a kind of bloodlust – equivalent, in a more introverted way, to continental ennui at the boredom of bourgeois life. He believes that there existed a quite 'deliberate cult of violence' among the plotters.[17] Townshend disparages the intellectual paucity of republicanism – their 'bare mental furniture' which obsessed over violence. It may even be, with the scholarly Pearse, a kind of pathology.[18] Anderson, in his general study of nationalism, ponders what makes people willingly die for 'such limited imaginings' and the same could be pondered here.[19] Several questions flow from the above. Are revisionists right in presenting the rising as a 'historical aberration, an outbreak of atavistic and even fascistic violence designed to thwart a peaceable and democratic settlement of affairs'?[20] And did the rebel leaders cement a culture of political violence and integrate it into the DNA of the foundation of the Irish state? Ferriter, it must be said, thinks that an extreme revisionist approach is too simplistic and that there was 'much more' to the rebels than mystical wishful thinking and bloodlust.[21]

Other questions concern the democratic nature of the rising and the nature of its achievements, both of which revisionists have been sceptical about. As against a narrative of immediate popular acceptance, historians have emphasised how unpopular the rising was at first and how horrified public opinion was at the destruction of the city. The relationship of the rebels to the will of the people and democracy was 'complicated' to say the least. It may have even sowed anti-democratic seeds which would go on to develop into the intransigence of civil war.[22] To return to public opinion, Townshend is sceptical of the notion of an innate national consciousness latent in the people – it may be that such a consciousness was 'remorselessly constructed by intellectuals'.[23] Did the rising, in and of itself, really change anything, socially?

Practically speaking, the answer is in the negative. It has often been said, for example, that the labour movement went into the General Post Office in 1916 and never came out. Some claim that there was no socialist reason for them to get involved.[24] Others might say that the dynamism of the labour movement was 'captured' by republicans.[25] Intriguingly, Conor Cruise O'Brien maintains that, had they waited until the conscription crisis (which followed in 1918), there might have been a chance that they could have caused mutiny within the armies and then triggered a socialist upheaval.[26] But most of the rebels were far from socialist. What did they realistically hope to achieve and change? Did they realistically plan to change anything? Could it just have been an extravagant and ill-fated 'rhetorical gesture'? asks Townshend.[27] Even if one does not go quite so far as this, there is no doubt but that it did possess importance as a political gesture – an enacted gesture. Foy and Barton place the interpretative emphasis on the 'tremendous imaginative power' the episode and its aftermath exercised over contemporaries.[28] In this curious rising, the rebels were better off dead than alive.

Explaining the Rising

The complexities of 1916 are in large part due to the yoking of secretive and open nationalist movements. All Irish rebel movements in the past had been riddled with informers and agents – thus, strict secrecy was felt to be necessary in what we may describe as the core circles. But secrecy had its problems and, when the time came for clear messages, confusion was inevitable. Who was to be let in the know? Who duped? How were secret movements to infiltrate open movements? How were the backstage men to convince the populace to act? All these problems complicated the revolutionary process and made it chaotic from the start. It is thus a particular challenge for the historian to disentangle all the strands and reconstruct the back story. Yet, it must be attempted.

Three layers may be identified: the Military Committee (later Council), the Supreme Council of the Irish Republican Brotherhood (IRB) and the open movements of the Irish Volunteers and the Irish Citizen Army (ICA). The strongest hand lay with those men who were involved, sooner or later, in all three. These were the men who would sign the Proclamation of the Republic in Easter Week 1916: Thomas Clarke, Sean MacDiarmada, Thomas MacDonough, Patrick Pearse, Éamonn Ceannt, Joseph Mary Plunkett and James Connolly. It is worth considering how they fit into the patterns of classic rebel typology. It is significant that all seven were published writers, whether literary or journalistic. Although most modern revolutions contain writers within their ranks (one thinks back to the German liberals of 1848), to have a full complement is unusually high. It gives the episode a literary and poetic character which would prove important. The rising would bear the hallmarks of those who, as it were, thought through the pen first and sword second.

There is also something paradoxical and condescending in their relationship with the masses. But this is very typical of revolutionary types. Chalmers Johnson, in his study of *Revolution and the Social System* (1964), points outs that conspirators claim to act on behalf of, in the name of and for the sake of the masses but crucially *not* in conjunction with them.[29] This is exactly what will happen here. It is not that the plotters deny that the majority matters, but that they, a tiny minority, will make a huge claim for themselves – that of knowing what lies in the best interests of the majority. Of the seven, three in particular deserve to be singled out because of their particular impact – or perhaps indeed peculiar impact on the political thought and praxis of the revolution. Patrick Pearse, Thomas MacDonough and Joseph Mary Plunkett were a trio of romantic idealists – all of them poets who spoke politics in that very idiom and all of them self-dramatists who couched the struggle in epic terms.

Patrick Pearse

Of the three, Pearse was the most striking. A man of English background on his father's side and of Gaelic sympathies on his mother's, Pearse was an educationalist drawn to the cause of Ireland in an extraordinarily intense way. He is a supremely contradictory figure and interpretations range from the hagiographic to the psychosocial.[30] Several strands of his character bear particular representation. First was the modernity of his ideas on education; he despised the murder machine of the British system. Second was his social concern which could have but never did transmute into socialism. For him, Ireland's social malaise was brought about by foreign domination. Although his analysis was not quite like Connolly's, the two did share a concern for the social question and their collaboration could be seen in the formulation of the Easter Proclamation of 1916. Thirdly, there was a tendency to read the current political situation in mystical terms, weaving Catholic and revolutionary nationalism together.[31] In some respects, this was a very peculiar mix. After all, Pius IX condemned extreme nationalism in the *Syllabus of Errors* of 1864, but there was enough expanse in Catholic thought for Pearse to square the circle.

This brings us to the most important aspect of his political theology: the notion of blood sacrifice. There was a strong strain of messianism in his sense of self. In order to save the country, he genuinely believed that blood sacrifice was necessary. This was not at all atypical of the younger generation pre-1914. There is much evidence to suggest that religiously intoned sacrificial ideas were mapped onto political and military ideas of the day (hence why the outbreak of World War I in 1914 generated such fervid mystical rapture among some). In that sense, Pearse was very much a man of his time. But the form this belief took in him was distinct. This was not about communal bloodletting. Instead, one man must die for the people. In his seminal work on *Political Violence in Ireland* (1983), Townshend sees him as a 'moralist of political violence'.[32] In that, he was uniquely interesting among the revolutionaries. More recently, some have questioned the historical obsession with this reading of Pearse. Ferriter, for example, believes that too much attention has been given to Pearse's writings on blood sacrifice and that his position is much more complex than that.[33]

Now all this seems rather unusual given the fact that Pearse was not a military man but rather an idealist and, in some respects, deeply impractical. But perhaps only an idealist could be wedded to violence with such purist fervour. In any case, he was not merely a theorist about this. He felt increasingly that the time had come for action. As Lyons points out, his was not a 'religion of meekness' but a 'religion of the Apocalypse'.[34] Ruth Dudley Edwards makes the interesting and plausible claim that his lack of military expertise would not have mattered to him so much because his object was simply do better – to hold out longer than Wolfe Tone, Robert Emmet, the Young Irelanders and the Fenians. To fail was inevitable but to fail better was his object.[35]

The Developments of 1915

One of the ironies of the rising is that it was meant to take place in 1915. Early that year, there was a clear acceleration of the pace of radical activity. Poetry was all very well but strategy, too, had to be thought about. Commandants were appointed and, in due course, met to discuss plans; a secret Military Council was established by the IRB in May. A moment of collective emotion was necessary for rallying the various strands of the radical movement and that moment did indeed come, as if on cue, in the funeral of Jeremiah O'Donovan Rossa, that veteran Fenian, on 1 August. The Volunteers, the ICA and the IRB turned out in full regalia and cheered Pearse's rousing oration in which he declared that an unfree Ireland could never be at peace. His words sounded splendidly defiant and militaristic and the volley of shots over the grave seemed to back them up. Connolly now spoke publicly of the need for the ICA to fight for republican values. There was no clearer sign that the socialist had become fully nationalist in his agenda. Yet, for all the solidarity, the envisaged rising in September did not go ahead because of the imprisonment of some of its would-be leaders and the shortage of arms.

Whether anyone fully knew everything that was going on in the months from December 1915 to April 1916 is doubtful. The web of plotting was very dense indeed. Furthermore, aspiring leaders could be accused of a degree of naivety. The five key plotters – Ceannt, MacDonough, Plunkett, Clarke and Pearse – had no military experience and somewhat clumsily co-opted James Connolly into their midst as a means of remedying this. They were all IRB men – Connolly was now brought in – but even elements *within* the IRB were to be kept at arm's length from now on. A front man, Denis McCullough, was appointed as head of its Supreme Council – he had, apparently, no idea that there even was a Military Council. It was all spectacularly devious.

The Plotters and the Volunteers

The plotters were also powers in the Volunteer movement which would be crucial in the event of a rising. However, they were not actually in control of it and they did not reckon sufficiently with the moderate personality and cautious views of Eoin MacNeill, the official chief of staff. MacNeill emphasised the defensive and downplayed the offensive nature of the Volunteers. He knew that there were people at work in the movement who had other ideas, but he was unwilling to provoke a further split by calling them out. He was, it is true, prepared to showcase the Volunteers in the early months of 1916: the rally in March with its thousands of men marching in uniform through the streets of Dublin was an attention-getting affair. Where he differed from the plotters was that he was not prepared to sacrifice men to the slaughter with no hope of practical gain.

The Failure to Secure Arms

The Military Council, meanwhile, had liaised with John Devoy in the United States about the possibility of getting arms. It had been mooted as early as 1914 that Germany should be approached. How realistic was this? Objectively, it seemed like a plausible way of proceeding on the principle that the enemy of one's enemy is one's friend. But Germany had a two-fronted war on its mind and was hardly likely to conduct a flank attack on Britain. Nevertheless, Roger Casement, a former British official of Anglo-Irish descent, went to Germany to talk 'business'. A figure of endless controversy, he had the rather grand idea of persuading the German government to form an Irish brigade in their war effort. His aims were idealistic and his efforts somewhat confused; 'pledges' did emerge from the connection, but no brigade. Practically speaking, his connections with the separatist movement were ambivalent.

The same could not be said for John Devoy. He was a crucial link in persuading the Germans to send 20,000 rifles and ten machine guns to Tralee. Unbeknown to the interested parties, the British Admiralty had actually broken the German code and were able to intercept the weapons and ammunition on the *Aud Norge* on Good Friday, that is to say 21 April, and arrest Casement, who was deposited by a U-boat unceremoniously in Tralee Bay. How much the destroyed weapons would have changed the course of the rising is doubtful, but they almost certainly would have prolonged it. The subsequent trial in London found Casement guilty of high treason; he endured public glare because of reputed homosexuality and was executed in Pentonville prison on 3 August. By then, he was the 16th person to be executed for treason.

Machinations

Meanwhile, in Dublin, things were descending into a state of utter confusion. MacNeill was neither rash nor imprudent and believed that the Volunteers should only act if they were at risk of suppression or if the country were at risk of conscription. Neither of these cases applied, at least, until the emergence or, more correctly, the planting of the so-called Castle Document, a forgery purporting to be an order of the Dublin administration and calling for the suppression of the Volunteers and the military occupation of Dublin. It would, it was hoped, goad MacNeill into committing the Volunteers to action. The whole episode has its moments of almost farcical play acting. MacNeill took the bait and ordered his men to resist suppression. Defensive to the last, he had no more radical plans. Behind his back, Pearse had issued orders preparing for insurrection and MacNeill, hearing this, was at first angry, but then, upon learning of the imminent arrival of the *Aud Norge*, open to the possibility. The charged days of Holy Thursday to Easter Sunday presented many *volte-faces*. The sinking of the *Aud Norge* and the information that the Castle Document was but a forgery imposed upon him by friends, made MacNeill justifiably livid and utterly opposed to a rising on Sunday. An angry exchange between Pearse and MacNeill broke the rapport between the two. It is hard not to feel some sympathy for MacNeill, who had behaved honourably throughout. Pearse, set on his fearful course of action, was above thinking of the constraints of etiquette. MacNeill's swift countermanding order allowed for no doubt that the rising was off:

> Volunteers completely deceived. All orders for special action are hereby cancelled and on no account will action be taken.[36]

Finally, or so it seemed, in the full glare of welcome and unwelcome knowledge, a decision had been reached and it was perfectly in keeping with a prudent judgement of the realities and the counter-productive nature of a struggle. Easter Sunday thus brought no rising.

Yet MacNeill was once again hoodwinked. On the Sunday evening, Pearse sent out couriers to the chosen Volunteer officers with the hardly cryptic message that operations would start at noon that day, Monday. Delivered in the early hours of Monday morning, and with all the dithering of the last few days, even a simple message could confuse. Two consequences followed. One was that the rising would not be countrywide. Many received the order too late; local outbreaks in Galway and Wexford were just that, localised and inconsiderable. The second consequence was that the message did not reach even all Dublin units of the Volunteers in time; 1,600 Volunteers and members of the Citizen Army were fielded: this was but a token number of the potential strength that they could have called upon, had circumstances been ideal.

The Rising

The rising began on Easter Monday, 24 April 1916.[37] The beginnings were inauspicious. 'Just look at that awful crowd', commented one Lieutenant Chalmers from his station at the General Post Office (GPO) on Sackville Street. Approaching the building were about 150 men with rifles and sledgehammers and behind them two dray horses and a cab loaded with guns, pikes and explosives. It was an unlikely procession to threaten the might of the British Empire. Within a very short time, Chalmers had been bound and put in a telephone booth, all men and women of peace asked to leave the GPO and preparations had begun to barricade the building. Just before 3 PM, a new flag was raised on high – that of the Irish Republic. 'Isn't it grand?'[38] said James Connolly, in command of the motley group of insurgents. The wireless flashed across that Ireland had proclaimed a republic and ships relayed the message throughout the night. By Tuesday morning, the 'news' was sprawling on the front of the American papers. What did it mean? And what would it come to mean to the curious Dubliners who happened to be in the city centre that April day and to the people as a whole? The narrative above gives us two intimations about the nature of the rising. First, it was not a mass uprising and, second, its words, symbols and performance were just as important – more important indeed – than its deeds.

Was the rising that followed 'doomed to disaster before it had even begun'?[39] It is possible to aver that it was. There was an almost risible lack of clarity in its planning and coordination. Confusion was in the lifeblood of the rising – planned, systemic confusion, not merely surface chaos. Moreover, the leadership was in no way homogenous, rather the reverse. There was a poor chain of command and communication. Deceit and subterfuge had left even willing recruits greatly confused. Rebels had acted more childishly than professionally in the lead-up. There was no transformative moment to kick-start the rebellion, no 'fall of the Bastille' episode to bring the population on side. Furthermore, it was all about playing in the backroom. The revolutionaries constituted no more than a fringe movement in Irish society. Yet, for all the inevitable failure, the episode would prove to be a crucial fulcrum of modern Irish history. So how did this come about?

At first blush, the facts of the matter do not betoken anything more than a heroically shabby attempt at resistance, crushed by the overwhelming power of artillery. Some key buildings in Dublin were seized and held for a week. These are the central and relatively unremarkable facts. The General Post Office became the centre of rebel power, the bastion of new authority and legitimacy for the week-long Irish Republic. The post office, so much part of the Victorian communications revolution, was an obvious location, but, in reality, a poor strategic choice for headquarters. College Green would have been somewhat better, not that any choice of headquarter could have saved the fate of the botched affair.

The insurgents were undoubtedly brave and fought clean. But they were an unrepresentative minority. The Irish media was, in general, horrified at the destruction visited on the city as a result. Dubliners were ill-at-ease, although there was some plain curiosity and some looting activity. British manpower was brought in to make the crucial difference. On Easter Monday, the rebels were outnumbered 3 to 1. That increased to 20 to 1 in subsequent days. It was a very squalid defeat. A British gunboat, the *Helga*, unleashed its force from the River Liffey. Gracious Sackville Street was destroyed. Within the week, the insurgents had surrendered unconditionally. In absolute terms the casualties were not massive. Still, 450 lay dead, 2,614 were wounded and nine were missing. The capital was shaken, but quickly, once again, the Union Jack was raised over the GPO and the flag of the Irish Republic torn down.

Legacies

So much for the narrative of squalid defeat. There is another strand, announced by Pearse from the GPO on the first day, which meant very little to anyone at the time but would come to be seen as a definitive moment in the creation of Irish statehood. This was the Proclamation of the Irish Republic, the foundation document of statehood.

> Irishmen and Irishwomen, in the name of God and of the dead generations from which she receives her old tradition of nationhood,

Ireland, through us, summons her children to her flag and strikes for her freedom.[40]

As revolutionary political rhetoric, it was lyrical and grandiose, the very poetry of political thought. In its terseness and some of its expressions, it recalled the American Declaration of Independence of 1776; indeed the 'exiled children' of America did receive a specific mention. He denounced the foreign usurpations which had done so much to foster social divisiveness. He depicted a whole genealogy of struggles for freedom. Now, he proclaimed, was the time to strike 'in full confidence of victory'.[41] They must have seemed peculiar words indeed for an event so comparatively small and so shabbily concluded. Yet, all this does not in the least negate the document's importance for subsequent Irish history. For Lyons, it constitutes the insurrection's 'principal achievement', a courageous declaration of a new political reality.[42] This document was not merely an articulation of a republic; there was a socialist element visible, too, which recalls an earlier moment in the story. James Connolly's influence was patent in the proclamation's guarantee of 'religious and civil liberty, equal rights and equal opportunities to all its citizens'.[43] This was sweepingly liberal language, indeed, in the context of the times. They were never called to put any of this fine agenda into practice and there may be some truth in the cliché that the labour movement went into the GPO on Easter Monday and never came out.

That the proclamation became a fount of a new political dispensation is not so much because of the rising but because of what occurred in its aftermath. Ironically, the success of the rising may be more due to British policy than anything else and, in particular, the actions of one man, General John Maxwell. Under powers given him by the Defence of the Realm Act (DORA) 1914, which allowed the government to act with extra powers in a wartime emergency, Maxwell had immediately been sent over as military governor with plenary powers, the very caricature of 'gung-ho military machismo'.[44] He arrived on 28 April with the intention of implementing martial law to the full. He arrested over three thousand people – many of whom had nothing to do with the rising and were released on Asquith's orders in mid-May. Fifteen men, including all the signatories of the proclamation, were executed beginning on 3 May at 3.30 AM and ending on 12 May. Although the viceroy, Redmond and others sought to dissuade the pursuit of full-on reprisals on the grounds that it would do more harm than good, Maxwell was entirely unmoved. After he had dealt with the 15 key plotters, he had planned on executing 97 more, but Asquith finally intervened and prevented a bloodbath. Historians are divided as to whether this reaction was a 'mild' or provocatively severe one.[45] It is generally accepted that the British government made a mistake in executing the leaders, as it made them appear as the real enemies of civil liberty.[46] Maxwell cannot be held altogether responsible for the savage reaction, however. Something must be attributed to his political superiors and indeed the context of total war. But he certainly played the key role.[47]

The executions are said to have transformed public opinion and made the men into myths. Ireland has a long tradition of hailing martyrs in song and verse into which the new seamlessly fit. The fact that the already dying Plunkett was allowed to marry his sweetheart the night before his execution added the element of heart-wrenching romantic tragedy. The two brothers, Patrick and William Pearse, were shot – the former's poignant poem from the viewpoint of his mother was written in his final hours. Connolly's execution in a wheelchair added even more to the sense of outrage. However unconventional their faith journeys, all were confessed at the end (with the possible exception of Thomas Clarke) and their posthumous status as devout Catholics, fortified, as they would have said, by the rites of Holy Church, was important in making the public revere them even more. It was thus a moment of synthesis between Catholicism and the national struggle – all was swept up in an outpouring of national grief. Even the traditional and conservative hierarchy, although not approving the rebellion itself, began to draw closer to the nationalist position.[48] The failure of the episode had become a 'moral force in its own right'.[49] The British government did an almost spectacularly good job at alienating moderate Irish people. John Maxwell was promoted to full generalship in 1919 – salt rubbed into wounds.

The rising episode and its aftermath constituted a national sensation. Although the traditional narrative has long been punctured, the event remains a crucial turning point in Irish history in more ways than one. In the introduction, we established the sensational content of Irish history and this is a striking instance of the same, where nationalism and storytelling fed off each other – 'an astonishingly effective piece of street theatre' in a 'drama-mad' city.[50] The leaders seem to have had an instinct for it; the population's imagination was fired. Politics are too often considered to be in the realm of the rational; here the politics of emotion became so much more important. The rising had been distasteful to many, but the government reaction even more so. Royal Irish Constabulary inspectors charted the shift in opinion – masses said for the dead, sales of photographs, publications, popularity of commemorative songs and increasing arm thefts.[51] This sense of outrage was combined with a growing distrust of Redmond's apathetic political party, which was then having no luck in persuading Asquith, and

later Lloyd George, that Home Rule should be extended to all 32 counties at
the end of the war. Trust in old methods and old men had been undermined
in 1916, some might say fatally. The rising, failed though it was, had woken
the population up to new ways of political thinking and action. Would the
country be the same again? The answer lay firmly in the negative.

Chapter 20

THE RISE OF SINN FÉIN

Debates

The rise of Sinn Féin poses several puzzles. The first is the puzzle of its sudden re-emergence after years of being in the political doldrums. The fact that its rise is based on a misunderstanding is one of the choicest ironies of the era. Not all would see the resurrection of the party as a mystery. Hart believes that it replicates the flowering of the nationalist movement in 1879–82.[1] The second question concerns the revolutionary status of the Sinn Féin experiment. Fitzpatrick upholds the revolutionary status of those years 1916–20 and more widely to 1923. One could argue that, just by existing in the form it did, it was revolutionary. Abstaining from Westminster and establishing a new political tradition puts the episode in a category of its own. It is easy, however, to overlook the traditionalism of the experiment and be completely taken in by the narrative of revolution. In no way did the new men make a *tabula rasa* of existing systems and start over – much was drawn from British parliamentary and civic tradition and procedure. Augusteijn has it that the whole nation-building process was 'profoundly influenced' by British political culture. Hart points out that their 'sophisticated political machine' was inspired by the Irish Parliamentary Party (IPP).[2] In relying on familiar systems, Mitchell argues that they showed much prudence.[3] Furthermore, the absence of any social component to this revolution is notable. Labour, famously, stood aside in the general election of 1918, thus writing themselves out of the major historical traditions. For Townshend, the lack of a social transformation makes it look old-fashioned.[4] The absence of revolutionary character is also remarkable in some of the chief architects of the new dispensation. Some of these were 'men of words' by preference rather than 'men of violence'. The traditional narrative sees everyone as part of the seamless whole; this model is clearly inadequate – tensions and conflicts were rife between segments of the party. Which had the upper hand at any one time is a question *bien posée*.

Contingencies

The rise of Sinn Féin was contingent on a misunderstanding. After the events of spring, when looking for an open movement to blame or to praise for the uprising, Sinn Féin was the only obvious candidate. A Sinn Féin rebellion it certainly was not, but a Sinn Féin rebellion it came to be called and Arthur Griffith's lacklustre party thus stood to gain when the tide of public opinion turned in favour of the heroic dead. The momentum started when Lloyd George, prime minister of a wartime coalition ministry since 7 December 1916, released the 600 or so Irish prisoners in British gaols, among them the unfortunate Griffith himself, who had been indiscriminately punished along with the physical-force revolutionaries. The public rejoiced at the general amnesty and began to attach itself to Sinn Féin as the spiritual inheritors of the rising, although this process was more gradual than traditionally believed. Several by-elections showed the shift of opinion amongst the electorate. Joseph Mary Plunkett's father, supported by Sinn Féin, was elected in Roscommon on 4 February 1917 and in June that year, the newly released Éamon de Valera, who alone of all the senior commandants had not been executed (probably because of his American citizenship), was elected for east Clare. Dressed in his Volunteer uniform to hear the result, he represented a visible link to the past. The vote displaced the IPP candidate and, although Farrell says that there was nothing inevitable about the decline of the IPP at this point, this is surely a little hard to credit.[5] In any case, the 'Shinners', as they were called, pointedly refused to take their seats in Westminster as Griffith had long advised. As de Valera declared in his campaign speech, they stood for the 'tricolour' not the 'Union Jack'.[6]

The Emergence of Éamon de Valera

De Valera already stood out as a natural leader. Born in 1882 in New York of Spanish and Irish parentage, he had spent much of his childhood with relatives in Limerick. An education at Blackrock College and the Royal University fitted him as a maths teacher. He is argument without end to historians – a hero in the formation of modern Ireland in some accounts, a Machiavellian who turned Ireland down a conservative path in others. So what was the man like when he first made his presence felt on an Ireland he would dominate for decades? In his thirties, he already had a formidable sense of authority and gravitas. People may have felt that he was a 'Parnell redivivus'[7] – certainly with his cool temperament, discipline and detachment he was in a different league to some of his more hot-tempered contemporaries for whom the fire of romanticism burned a little too brightly for political prudence. De Valera also had Catholic credibility – something that would be not a little important in Sinn Féin's rise to power, for the church, which had been wary of the republican movement up to this, began to be open to its possibilities. That de Valera was an intransigent thinker allows for little doubt.[8]

It may seem a little forced to comment once again on elusiveness and ambivalence, but the typology of modern Irish leaders has often led us to the conclusion that they were, in fact, game players – if not always by temperament, at least by context. De Valera was a genuinely clever man, clever in a bookish and mathematical way that no other Irish leader had been before him. It was therefore inevitable that he would delight in complexities which would seem coy or even facetious to less able men. For now, however, he was unambiguously a plausible chief to emerge from a period of chaos. Perhaps his very niceness as to distinctions made him stand out in a context where there was no idea of what was going to happen next.

He was also rapidly acquiring an authoritative peace-time voice, declaring that Easter week had 'achieved its object' and that another week of the sort would be a 'superfluity'.[9] This was to put the past firmly in its place – inspiration but not a model for further action. In fact, though his later attitude would help to exacerbate the lines of the Civil War, he was not essentially a man of violence, being more scholastic by temperament. Boyce has emphasised how traditional, how Parnellite, his rhetoric was at this point,[10] how anxious he was to express continuity not merely with the rising but with the old IPP. This was a deliberate ploy to woo the petty bourgeoisie, the respectable farmers, shopkeepers, priests and clerks who were used to such language. It clearly worked. Already one may see this as a second phase of revolution – a much more considered, less impulsive form designed not just to make sensational headlines but to make material change in the Irish political situation. He was helping to chart a new course.

In October 1917, at the Sinn Féin Ard Fheis, he was duly made president, Griffith ceding his place with magnanimous grace to the younger man. The language of constitutionalism was a feature throughout. Farrell makes the acute observation that the 'mention of another armed insurrection was greeted with laughter'.[11] At this gathering, too, it was decided that Ireland should seek international recognition as an independent republic. Already they were thinking ahead to the peace talks after the war. Several months later in January 1918, they would be given further confidence by reading the American Democratic president Woodrow Wilson's celebrated Fourteen Points, especially the clause advocating self-determination.

These points were the first articulation of America's global moral pitch in the twentieth century and they struck many aspirational national groups with great forcefulness. It is an antidote to the usual narrow nationalist story to realise just how central the acquisition of international recognition was to these fledgling politicians. It was a way of trying to appeal over the heads of the men in London to the wider community. The Irish were not alone in pinning their hopes on a Wilsonian new world – they were to be sadly deceived, as it turned out. At the same Ard Fheis, it was decided that a new assembly, a *dáil*, should be set up. The usage of Gaelic nomenclature was significant. This was to be no rerun of a 1782 compromise. These men wanted a new departure.

Reconstruction of the IRB and the Volunteers under Michael Collins

Parallel to the reconstruction of Sinn Féin was the revival of both the IRB and the Irish Volunteers. The main force here was the 27-year-old Michael Collins – a 'guerilla supremo in the making', as Foster describes him.[12] The Collins–de Valera dichotomy has been drawn constantly in the literature and perhaps overdrawn at times. There was, it is true, much to distinguish and divide. Physically, it was the distinction between the 'Long Fella' and the 'Big Fella' – the gaunt face of the academic *versus* the open face of the cabellero. De Valera was self-consciously intelligentsia, an 'adept at splitting hairs';[13] Collins, a man of action. Their relations were at first cordial, although not close: both of them respected but never warmed to each other. Yet, both had similar ideas about Ireland[14] and a considerable streak of pragmatism. Collins' pragmatism had led him to deplore the way the rising was conducted in the manner of a 'Greek tragedy'[15] – plenty of heroics with very little substance. He scorned the poetic bungling of military jobs – his 'war' would be conducted along very different lines. And, indeed, he proved to be an inspiration for twentieth-century guerrilla warfare – Mao Tse-Tung and Yitzhak Shamir admired him. Intriguingly, de Valera showed his pragmatism in admitting in private that he would not have had time for Pearse if he had known his real object was martyrdom.[16] For the rest, his pragmatism took the form, for now, of being a force for reconciliation between the various strands of the nationalist movement. Ironically, neither de Valera nor Collins were ultimately extremists, although both would be pushed into more extreme positions than either would have liked. They would both be 'painted into a corner', in Foster's words, although that was still to come.[17] In 1917, all one could say was that the two of them had emerged as leaders of the various nationalist movements.

British Policy Blunders 1918

Lloyd George's gracious release of internees was not followed by a policy of continued conciliation. Frankly, the popularity of the revived Sinn Féin worried government, as did the intransigent rhetoric of its leaders. To coerce was obviously nothing new – accordingly, in 1917, the wearing of military uniforms, public meetings and drilling were all banned. Thomas Ashe, a leading light in the Volunteer movement, was arrested with 30 *confrères* and went on hunger strike whilst in prison. A botched attempt to force feed him resulted in his untimely death and the result was another massive political funeral with 30,000 in attendance. A volley of shots was fired over his grave – another martyr for the cause.

There were yet other more significant reasons alienating even Irish moderates from the reactionary direction of British policy. A Britain that was haemorrhaging badly on the Western Front had long pondered the advantages to be accrued by extending conscription to Ireland. The resulting Military Service Act of April 1918 was met with a nationwide anti-conscription campaign. The IPP under John Dillon (Redmond had died a disappointed man a month previously) noisily withdrew from Westminster in protest and, with Sinn Féin, the Catholic hierarchy and the Trade Union Congress all insisting on the same point, the government was forced to withdraw. It was a rare (and important) moment of national unity.

Revenge was swift. On 11 May, Field Marshal Viscount French was made viceroy – a man with no time for parley with rebels. He was determined to break sedition in Ireland and he saw sedition everywhere. Previously, 25,000 troops had been garrisoned there; by November 1918, that number was 87,500. This was extraordinary given that these were the last few months of World War I. French set the tone for the British campaign in Ireland till 1921. The government invented a German plot and, claiming that the Irish were once again in league with the all-but-defeated Germans to stage a revolt, the leaders of the various movements were arrested almost immediately. Sinn Féin and the Volunteers were suppressed and martial law was proclaimed in the most 'disturbed' areas of the country. Michael Collins' success in avoiding capture would be of crucial significance: physical force men remained, whilst many of the more moderate figures like de Valera, Griffith and William Cosgrave (the representative for Carlow-Kilkenny) were out of action.

Democratisation

November 1918 brought to an end the war and an end to the vapid dream of the IPP for Home Rule. A firm Lloyd George, already concentrating on the larger issues of postwar reconstruction, declared the measure withheld until 'the condition of Ireland makes it possible'.[18] And those who would inform him of that condition would be a hostile Dublin Castle administration, determined on seeing trouble everywhere. But the winds of change were already sweeping through the postwar world. The following month was to bring a general election – one that would be fought on the basis of a new franchise. Democratisation had been one corollary of the global four-year struggle. The ordinary men who had fought so courageously and the people on the home front who had sacrificed themselves nobly had all earned their citizenship laurels and ought to be entitled to vote. This privilege would even be extended to women over the age of 30. The Representation of the People Act (1918) had raised the Irish electorate from 700,000 to 2 million at a stroke. Farrell calls the subsequent election the 'most critical contest in twentieth-century Ireland'.[19] How were these old and first-time voters going to cast their vote? The fact that two-thirds of them were voting for the first time had an important consequence – 'old partisan loyalties' were less likely to figure the pressing concerns of the day.[20] There had been a sea change. Sinn Féin won 73 seats, 45 of them obtained whilst their representatives were still in prison. Unionist candidates won 26 seats and the IPP a paltry six. Crushingly, Dillon was beaten by de Valera in May by 5,243 votes.

Interpretations of the 1918 Election

The traditional view of this is to say that it was Sinn Féin's 'electoral landslide'.[21] Farrell qualifies this somewhat, but still acknowledges that it was a moment of transition.[22] How had they achieved such clear dominance in the south? They had won the election not merely through garnering the laurels of 1916 (the 'nostalgia' vote) but through downright hard work and energetic campaigning. Its local clubs had been very active in preparation for the event and its platform was unambiguous – abstention from Westminster and the commitment to using 'any and every means' for resisting Britain. Foster sees in this a Parnellite ambiguity, especially as regards violence.[23] Still, the Shinner candidates did not do anything so rash as to espouse the language of blood sacrifice. This meant that the ordinary respectable middle classes would be more likely to vote for them. Boyce, in particular, emphasises how the battle was fought in traditional language, about who had kept true to the 'essential nature of the Irish demand'.[24] Garvin, however, casts a whole other light on 1918, claiming that there was much intimidation, impersonation and stuffing of ballot boxes and that it, therefore, was not a fair democratic contest.[25]

The results of this dramatic election meant many things. It spelt the end for the IPP who had conclusively lost the battle for hearts and minds.

Dillon retired from politics. Home Rule had been a great tradition working within the framework of constitutionalism, but it had had its day. It is hard to avoid Jackson's judgement that it had been a 'history of failure, of high ideals and ambitions together with crushing humiliation and disappointment'.[26] A new era was emerging. The election meant, also, that the appropriation of 1916 by Sinn Féin was complete. The public had recognised the 'oneness' of the nationalist agenda. This was no hole-in-the-corner event, this was a national election which they had conclusively won. They responded to this confidence by doing exactly what Griffith had urged since the early 1900s – they abstained from Westminster and founded their own *dáil*. The IPP and the Unionists naturally declined to join them. It would be a one-party government laying claim to the governance of the island.

The First Dáil

The First Dáil had a very shadowy existence, enjoying what can only be called the pantomime of power. In 1919, it met 14 times, in 1920, three times and, in 1921, four times. Its comparative regularity in 1919 indicated that the British authorities did not at first know quite what to do about it. It was indeed a conundrum for the authorities (much as the by-election of 1828 had been). The MPs had been elected legally, so much was clear – to crush the chosen representatives of the people would mean war. War did follow. But the first meeting of the Dáil, attended by a mere 27 representatives on 21 January 1919, happened without drama except the very drama of its occurrence. That was drama enough for the present. Most of the key Sinn Féiners of 1918 were essentially 'political animals' not 'bold Fenian men'.[27] The intransigent Teachta Dála (TD) for Waterford, Cathal Brúgha, was made temporary leader in the absence of those who were in prison. Ministries were duly formed.

The most striking feature is the very unsensational banality of all this. There was no declaration of war, but rather the business of the day. There were formal proceedings – the Dáil Constitution, the Declaration of Independence and the Easter Proclamation of 1916, a Message to the Free Nations of the World and a Democratic Programme were all read aloud and approved. What Farrell notes is its moderation, 'surprising in a country on the edge of a war of liberation'.[28] This was to obey the traditional script of government, although the whole episode had its element of unreality.

Seeking International Recognition

The new 'government' knew that whatever they might feel or declare, the world would judge it on the basis of *de jure*, not *de facto*, solutions.

Accordingly, attempts were made to present Ireland's case for independence at the postwar Peace Conference, just then beginning in Paris. It was not unreasonable to think that this approach might work. The Irish-American lobby was strong and Wilson's avowal of the principle of self-determination appeared very much in their favour. Had not the Irish people democratically spoken? But fine principles did not always translate into action where action would have been impractical and distasteful – Ireland was Britain's internal business and Wilson had no intention of diverting talks into channels that would discomfit his ally. Wilson, besides, had no personal commitment to the Irish cause and had been angered by the pro-German tone of activists in the war years. So Sean T. O'Kelly was spurned in Paris and the international solution to Ireland's legal status was thus scotched. According to Michael Kennedy, the Irish Question was seen as an utterly 'irrelevant distraction'.[29] Although few historians mention it, it could well have been an opportunity missed, although whether Unionists would be content with international arbitration in favour of the majority is distinctly implausible. What Ireland needed in 1919, claims Boyce, was a Gladstone, someone with vision and a belief in international arbitration as a means to regulate injustices.[30] Instead there was the grudging Churchill who said, as cabinet minister, that 'nothing would annoy the Irish more than the conviction that they were not absorbing the minds of the people of Great Britain'.[31]

Business as Usual?

The new 'government', although hampered by fundamental legal ambiguities, nevertheless, began to get on with the business of the day in a somewhat haphazard fashion. By the spring, 52 members had shown up. It was a fairly young group – 75 per cent of them were under the age of 45 and largely Roman Catholic. Interestingly, for such an agricultural country, farmers were poorly represented – most were middling professionals (journalists, teachers and civil servants). The years 1916–20 were largely their story. De Valera had now been elected president and, in another bid to seek international recognition as well as funds, went to America very soon afterwards. His strength was always drawn from America.[32] Owen Dudley Edwards, musing on the controversy of such an embarkation at such a time, is still mystified: did he seriously think to pull off a coup or was he just escaping from a situation which he felt to be escalating beyond his control?[33] It is hard to say. It will be the first of several controversial decisions to absent himself.

The British government's formal suppression of the Dáil in September 1919 banished all 'normal' government activity. It was a body on the move and hunted from then on, improvising and thrusting forward somewhat wildly. Of course, no offices could be established – transient 'safe' houses served the purpose. What is remarkable, claims Lyons, is that anything was achieved at all in such uncertain circumstances.[34] Modest success stories include Collins' raising of a National Loan of £358,000 and Robert Childers Barton's establishment of a land bank to assist farmers in land purchase schemes. Attempts were made to replace the British legal system with Dáil courts. Defiance was taking very elaborate forms indeed. This brings out the theme of continuity even in a movement which the British read as revolutionary. *Plus ça change, plus que reste le même.* The machine and proceedings of government derived from a Westminster and Whitehall model. Farrell, in particular, is emphatic in bringing out that, in the new state, political values were articulated in a modern and British way.[35] It was not particularly politically, economically or socially radical. Mitchell refers to the regime as 'mildly reformist within the parameters of liberal capitalism'.[36] We should not focus so exclusively on a narrative of change as to lose sight of underlying but very obvious continuities.

Blame for the Anglo–Irish War

Still, there were now two claims to legitimacy and they were clearly incompatible. War was inevitable in such circumstances. Perhaps it is invidious to ask which side was most responsible. One could advance the argument that Sinn Féin were legal representatives of the people and that the British government should have met them as such *before* the outbreak of hostilities. One could add, as Townshend does, that the government had 'undermined constitutionalism since 1916 by repeatedly deferring Home Rule' and that the primary and more serious blame thus lay with them.[37]

One could also argue that, in abstaining from Westminster, Sinn Féin had no constitutional mandate and that they put themselves outside the framework of the laws of the land. The war began with a skirmish in Co. Tipperary in which two Royal Irish Constabulary (RIC) officers were killed by some Volunteers. This could be received as an act of terror against the legitimate authorities. There are plausible cases to be made for both sides of the argument and it is well to leave the matter open to debate. The three years that followed brought all the sources of conflict to a rather bloody *dénouement*. Although the Irish Republican Army (IRA) have waged, on and off, their own style of war against Britain ever since, the period 1919–21 represents the last full-blown Anglo–Irish war. It deserves consideration accordingly.

Chapter 21

THE ANGLO–IRISH WAR

Interpretations

The Irish War of Independence is traditionally told as a heroic David-and-Goliath struggle, a sort of victory achieved through skirmishes, ambushes, sophisticated spying and all the localised drama of guerrilla warfare. A certain romanticism clings to the popular account, enhanced by veterans' biographies (such as Dan Breen's My *Fight for Irish Freedom* [1924]) and the 1997 film, *Michael Collins*. Even Lyons is not immune – he comments on the 'stoic' endurance by the population of a long war that proves that the Irish did not want a quiet life but possessed the 'impulse to fight, to hold on, to contend with almost insuperable difficulties and almost impossible odds'. He makes the claim that, out of the ashes of war, rose 'the deathless phoenix of independent nationality'.[1] This claim seems rather inflated.

It is hard to get at some of the real stories for the simple reason that both the British and the Irish governments have been remarkably slow to release documents, presumably because of their great sensitivity.[2] Yet, despite a slow start, inroads have been made to the popular account on several levels. Firstly, the question of whether or not it was actually a war has been articulated. The Irish War of Independence has been so labelled by generations of Irish people enjoying the fruits of free statehood and, from 1949 onwards, republicanism. It was regarded as a necessary step in embarking on the road to full national autonomy. It must be said, however, that the British government did not consider it to be a genuine war at all. Lloyd George, who would remain prime minister until 1922, disdainfully declared that 'you do not declare war on rebels'.[3] Was this mere imperial posturing? Was British policy put on a war footing or not? According to Beckett, it is more tenable to speak of 'troubles' because it was less about governments and the peoples and more about two 'largely irresponsible armed forces'.[4] Townshend tellingly entitles his chapter on the conflict 'guerrilla struggle'. He does not regard the British government as attempting a reconquest of Ireland.[5] Still, it was not without blame for the outbreak of hostilities because it had undermined its own legitimacy by the repeated deferral of Home Rule.[6]

Questions have also been raised about the nature of violence. The Black and Tans are traditionally depicted as the ruthless villains of the piece and the Irish Republican Army (IRA) the innocent freedom fighters. In this reading it is very much a 'Tan War'. But one man's freedom fighter is another's terrorist. Hart notes how random the violence often was and how, by 1921, both Crown forces and the IRA were shooting more civilians than each other.[7] Ferriter observes that the IRA's killing of civilians seems to have been 'unusually high' and some of it came from motivations of revenge and spite rather than politics.[8] Another question worth probing is the relationship between the IRA and the people. It was once supposed to be entirely favourable and uniform. Now, the picture seems more complex. Hopkinson argues that there were strong elements of a civil as well as a colonial conflict.[9] IRA support is now envisaged as more localised and even limited. Finally, as against the narrative that the war was a necessary step in the progress towards a genuine settlement, questions have been raised as to how necessary the conflict was in achieving what they were going to be given, that is, dominion status. Here there is a definite cleavage of opinion. Foster questions its necessity but Fanning disagrees with him.[10]

The Outbreak of War

Let us return to its origins. The first shots of a conflict nearly always obtain a special symbolism for all that they may have been random and uncoordinated. This is the case for the incident at Soloheadbeg on 21 January 1919. Eight Volunteers shot dead two Royal Irish Constabulary (RIC) members and stole arms and gelignite for hand grenades. Ironically, the two men shot were Irish, but their membership of the RIC left them in an ambiguous position, as it was considered by many to be a genuine army of occupation. The RIC was especially vulnerable in 1919. It consisted of 10,000 men scattered in often lonely outposts in the country. Because they were a military police, armed with rifles, revolvers and bayonets, attacking them was a prime way of getting arms. This is just what happened. Hostility also came from the Dáil. De Valera said that they must be made to feel how 'vile is the position they occupy'.[11]

Ranged against them was a force which had begun to call itself the Irish Republican Army, or IRA for short. Many of them had been Volunteers. In absolute terms, they were a curious kind of army, but they had some crucial advantages. Fundamentally, they were well adapted to a war of the weak versus the strong. The 'war', indeed, was a very unconventional one as any conflict had to be between two such unevenly matched powers. The IRA fought guerrilla-style with pistols, shotguns and rifles aided by a sophisticated spy system. They were localist, dispersed and capable of guarding their movement's secret. The anonymity of fighters without uniforms was supremely advantageous. The Crown forces were, by contrast, very obvious and easier targets; there was nothing to distinguish an IRA man from an ordinary citizen.

Their lack of discipline in some respects was, for now, another of their strengths. They were a law unto themselves, dashing from engagement to engagement with a sort of cavalier freedom of action, then disappearing into the crowd. They blazed a trail of violence and the Dáil often had to try to pick up the pieces. Above all they were mobile. Dubbed 'flying columns', they went around in groups of around 30–35 men, engaged in an action or an ambush and then disappeared. As guerrillas, they had to give an impression of ubiquity, of being unpredictable. The IRA did a good job in this improvised war – the British rarely knew where the next strike would be. Their relative 'success' will emerge clearly by contrast with the figures of 1916. No noble heroics for these new men – what mattered was surviving an encounter and living to fight another day. Who were they? Peter Hart has examined their profile in some depth and concluded that they were disproportionately drawn from the skilled urban worker class and typically unmarried. As he wryly says, they were 'unusually unwed even by Irish standards'.[12] They were 'the boys', favoured by many of the public. Only 5 per cent were 40 or older. This was a generation that had spent its formative years imbibing the programmatic ideology of the 'Irish Irelanders' and cultural revivalists. They were especially active in Munster, most notably Cork.[13] Bandon was the 'Gaza strip of the Irish intifada'.[14]

Leadership

The question of leadership was a particularly vexed one. Cathal Brúgha was chief of staff and later minister for defence, but Michael Collins, as adjutant-general of the Volunteers and director of organisation and director of intelligence, had effective power. Neither liked the other. In part, this was personal. Brúgha was jealous of Collins' undoubted charisma and his legendary status as military hero. In part, it was because of the complicated nature of their respective positions. As minister of defence, Brúgha was supposed to have authority over what occurred on the ground. But normal dispensations were suspended in such an atypical and irregular conflict – the upper hand lay with he who could command the interest and thus the loyalty of the population.

De Valera, meanwhile, left the country in the middle of 1919 and went on a six month tour of the United States. He wanted to do this in his capacity as president of the Dáil, of the Irish Republic and of Sinn Féin and he succeeded in securing $10 million for the Irish national loan. The wisdom of his going at all in such circumstances is, however, debatable. The initiative now lay with Collins and his blend of ruthlessness and carelessness. He was careless, almost cavalier, about his own personal safely, cycling around Dublin on a daily basis, undisguised, whilst the price on his head was £10,000. At the same time, he was utterly ruthless in coordinating a network of assassins, the Squad, as it was called, who did his bidding when needed. He commanded huge loyalty from a core of devoted followers and the population as a whole. He was especially adept at maintaining connections – maids, barmen, porters, bootblacks, dockers and telephone operators all spied for him. The Anglo–Irish War was, in a very real sense, 'his' operation.

Notable Incidents

As befits the nature of guerrilla war, it was one of sporadic incident rather than protracted fighting. Some incidents deserve particular mention. On 13 May 1919, a daring rescue of a rebel youth in Limerick led to the death of another two unfortunate constables. It was an incident made significant because of what happened afterwards. The jury cleared the 'killers' of murder. The British authorities were outraged at this perversion of justice as they saw it and banned Sinn Féin organisations, the Irish Volunteers and Cumann na mBan. A second jury decision further raised the temperature. On 7 September 1919, there was an attack in Fermoy, Co. Cork, where the IRA seized rifles and killed one soldier in so doing. The jury, deciding on the case, declared that this was an act of war, not of murder. The response of the soldier corps was to wreck the jury's homes, which was response enough. But of course this begs the question. Was it a war or wasn't it? Lloyd George, as we have seen, did not see it so, or was, at any rate, unwilling to admit it in public. He wanted to put the Irish troubles firmly in their place and not give them official 'status'.

He also had strategic reasons for refusing to magnify what was taking place. Ideally, he wanted it to remain a 'police problem'. Once it was labelled war that meant garrisoning more troops and risking the consequences that might ensue. It would also mean a greater outlay of money which the postwar government could ill afford. Yet, the limitations of his circumspect policy were soon evident. The harried police were resigning in large numbers or were begging for transfers from remote areas. It was the least popular job option in 1919. De Valera had urged their social ostracisation and the Irish, no strangers to the practice of boycott, obeyed. If the 'Irish job is a policeman's job',[15] as the government insisted, then it was clear that the policeman's lot was not a happy one.

The Arrival of Ex-servicemen

At last the government found a way of squaring the circle. They decided to supplement the police force with thousands of ex-servicemen. This brings us to the most reputedly notorious aspect of the conflict. Whose idea this was remains a moot point – some say General Henry Hugh Tudor, police advisor to Dublin Castle from 1920 onwards, others Churchill – but it must have seemed like a very sensible solution at the time. It would achieve many desirable effects. First, it would alleviate demobilisation problems in Britain by providing new jobs for jaded veterans. Second, although it would make this an 'army' not just a police job, it would still not seem like an all-out war effort. Lastly, of course, it was expected that it would save the Irish situation from descending into further chaos. Strong action from strong men was the order of the day. Even to speak conservatively, it is safe to say that these ex-servicemen were not by any means the *crème de la crème* of the armed forces. Some were brutalised by their experiences on the front. The traditional stereotype is that many were almost psychotically violent. Curran maintains that, although there were criminals and psychotics in their midst, most were not. But they were problematic, nonetheless, as administrators of justice and the force of law. These self-indulgent, undisciplined military enthusiasts hated the Irish – they were veterans who 'wanted the excitement of military life without its discipline or boredom'.[16] It was a most unfortunate mix. The first group that came were quickly labelled the Black and Tans, after the name of a local Limerick hunt, and they soon made a name for themselves for drunken rampaging and callous brutality. They got 50p a day for their pains. Their name, along with Oliver Cromwell's, is still remembered as a byword for infamy in Ireland to this day. There were about 7,000 of them in the country for the duration. Auxiliaries (6,000 of them) were also drafted in – being ex-officers, they were paid twice as much. Certainly, these men did not win 'hearts and minds' by fighting nasty, sometimes taking their anger out on a whole village or town. They only served to push the population further into the open arms of the rebels. The Palme d'Or–winning 2006 film *The Wind That Shakes the Barley* makes this abundantly clear.

Some events, in particular, caused outrage. The murder of the Lord Mayor of Cork by the RIC was just such an example. His successor, Terence MacSwiney, was arrested in 1920, went on hunger strike and died. A young

Kevin Barry was caught during an arms raid and was executed. Folk memory had another young man to mourn. The worst incident came to be known as Bloody Sunday. On the morning of 21 November 1921, Collins' Squad shot dead 11 British intelligence officers in their homes and hotels. It was done with an almost awful professionalism. That afternoon, Auxiliaries made their way to the national sporting ground, Croke Park, as part of a search operation. It is said that the IRA let off some warning shots. In any case, the Auxiliaries proceeded to shoot into the crowd, killing 12 and wounding 16. This was seen as being a direct reprisal on innocent citizens for the morning's killings, although, as we have seen, the matter is more complex.

Not only did the ex-servicemen alienate moderate Irish people from Lloyd George's government, they also outraged British liberal opinion. The prime minister was, in any case, having a difficult time convincing staunch liberals that he was one of them – although his reputation was high in 1918 for winning the war, many were increasingly disenchanted with his peacetime record. The reports that filtered back from Ireland were received with great anger. In many ways, there was nothing particularly new about Lloyd George's policy of coercion. British authorities throughout the nineteenth century had made full use of the policy. Sometimes there had been an outcry, often there had not. The Irish needed keeping in check. But this was an age in which the media possessed a much greater power to question and critique government policy. There was not quite such confidence as there had been in the prewar days about the innate superiority of the Anglo-Saxon race. Furthermore, there was growing moral discomfort among certain sectors of the public with the abuses of imperialism and the Black and Tans, with their crude reprisals, seemed to be emblematic of the worst usages of their power. Clearly, as Lee says, the British 'lost the propaganda war with a spectacular series of own goals'.[17]

The Government of Ireland Act 1920

Where would all this end? Clearly not with the Government of Ireland Act of 1920, Lloyd George's half-hearted attempt at concession. Having waited so long and prevaricated so much, to impose a settlement suitable only to the north and seemingly oblivious to the sea change in the south has to be one of the most peculiar episodes of all. It was an extraordinary moment to choose. Lloyd George was still prime minister, but precariously so, with a cabinet heavily Conservative. The framing of the act was indeed unequivocally traditionalist, confirming, as it did, 'unaffected and undiminished', the authority that the UK Parliament had over 'all persons, matters and things in Ireland'.[18] It just was not so simple anymore. Sinn Féin was in the ascendant in all the by-elections. In the general election in the south in May 1921, Sinn Féin won a staggering 124 seats. War had enhanced its popular mandate.

Towards Peace

The situation appeared to be in deadlock. Yet the conflict could not last and at least two people were determined that it should not. One was King George V, who had reigned since 1910 and was watching with disgust the downward spiral of Anglo–Irish relations. The other was de Valera. He had quietly sought to remove Collins from the temptations of violence for a little by sending him to America, but the firebrand refused. Still, de Valera was determined. How to control the gunmen? It was a real dilemma. As Owen Dudley Edwards notes, 'time and again, before and after the Treaty and Civil War, he was swept aside by the gunmen's logic, he had to go through motions that the repudiation had been no repudiation'.[19] He proposed in 1921 that 'murderous' activity should be rejected – in this, nobody supported him. He could not call into question (overtly) the gunman's tradition, however much he may have wished to – it was as much as his position was worth. After all, he owed everything to 1916. Just then, he was seen as something of a crank. Collins, for example, regarded the chief as a 'fine, symbolic figure, scholarly and somewhat out of touch with reality'.[20] Ironically, he was the more realistic of the two at this point. It was clear that the IRA could not hold out for ever.

There were other factors that were coming into play which promised peace. The British realised that they were clearly not winning the war. Victory on either side was impossible.[21] Moreover, it was proving tremendously costly and a PR disaster. Months of violence had left hundreds dead and public opinion outraged. Rumours of Black and Tan viciousness, in particular, had horrified a respectable British public. A gracious and powerful speech given by George V at the opening of the Northern Irish parliament in June 1921 urged both sides to stretch out the hand of 'forbearance and conciliation, to forgive and forget'.[22] It was probably the most important Irish speech made by a British monarch in centuries. Lloyd George was keen to meet de Valera and the day they met for the first time, 11 July 1921, a peace truce was signed. It was immaculately obeyed. The war, if war it was, was now over.

Evaluations of the Anglo–Irish War

There was a uniqueness about this conflict that deserves some consideration. Unlike other uprisings from 1798 to 1916, which were unambiguously unsuccessful, this one could lay claim to much more concrete successes. Two in particular spring to mind – the constant aggravation of the enemy and the achievement of a popularity that no previous episode had known. Townshend is unambiguous about acknowledging this. In fact, he gives as the primary reason why Britain initiated proceedings for a truce, the fact that the republican campaign proved 'too determined, too resilient, and too resourceful to be put down'.[23]

But granting the plausibility of this interpretation, this still leaves us with a puzzle. How did such inconsiderable forces with little training hold at bay troops so vastly experienced and backed by the resources of what was still the greatest imperial power in the world? The key was less military and more psychological. The publicity given to daring and heroic episodes on the part of the rebels and to wanton cruelty on the part of official forces could not but stir up minds and hearts in the national cause. In a sense, the fighters, the 'hillside men', could call on *all* traditions of conflict in the last century: agrarian, Fenian, and Parnellite. In that way, they strode the land with great confidence. Later, the IRA would like to claim the war as their victory and, whilst this would be to exaggerate, it would be just as false to say that they had lost.

But in the arrogant appropriation of 'victory' lay the seeds of future problems. According to Boyce, these men had given political violence a 'new lease of life in Ireland'.[24] There was a sense in which their 'war' did not just end neatly in 1921 and has not ended since. The general public, sick of violence, was overjoyed at the end of hostilities. But the hillside men had become intoxicated by the language and the logic of the gun. They would come to look upon the episode of war as four glorious years and nostalgia would drive them into continuing the struggle in other contexts.

In the course of the war, their very freedom of action was presented as a strength. After the war, it would prove to be deeply concerning for a state trying to monopolise the exercise of legitimate force. The IRA were their own men. They made their own rules and they did not march to the beat of the one drum. They would have difficulty 'settling down' to a bourgeois life. It would be a challenge for them to acquire new terms of reference, to accept the inevitable compromises of settlement. A die-hard faction under Liam Lynch and Rory O'Connor was already clearly visible.

In short, the War of Independence hardened the lines of militant republicanism. Previously, republicanism had been one of several avenues. Let the Irish decide what form of government they would enjoy once they had secured independence. But now, the extreme militant wing had dyed themselves completely in republican green. 'The Republic of Ireland *is* and *will be*' their newspaper, *An t'Óglach* (The Volunteer), declared.[25]

There was an implacability there which foretold an uneasy future. Ronan Fanning points out the paradoxical question facing them in 1921 – does the 'mere fact of negotiation with a foreign power whose authority has already been cast off in theory constitute a betrayal of the revolution'?[26] Some answered in the affirmative and the result would be civil war.

Chapter 22

NORTH AND SOUTH SETTLEMENTS

Interpretations

These were the settlements that did not truly settle the Irish Question. Two pieces of legislation were effected in this period, the Government of Ireland Act and the Anglo–Irish Treaty. As a result of the terms of the latter, a civil war broke out. The divisions mark the origin of the party system in southern Ireland; not the least of ironies was that Britain's political legacy in 1920–22 was to create the lines of political division thereafter. The chief questions surround the nature of these divisive acts and the attribution of responsibility. The Government of Ireland Act has its admirers and critics – whilst some see it as a democratic solution, other historians are keen to point up the flaws, especially in the light of contemporaneous European developments towards self-determination.[1] Austen Chamberlain himself regarded it as an 'illogical and indefensible' compromise.[2] The merits of the Anglo–Irish Treaty are also highly contested, a contest heightened by the legacy of political division in Ireland between pro- and anti-Treaty forces. Arthur Mitchell sees the Treaty as a 'giant step forward in the struggle' for freedom.[3] It is also possible to see it as the fount of unacceptable division and the start of an invidious 'process by which two individuals, de Valera and Collins [...] became the prism through which much of the history of this period was assessed'.[4] Many historians have sought to apportion blame. Was it de Valera's fault for not attending the London Conference in the first place or his fault for allowing the anti-Treaty side to become politically respectable?[5] Was the deputation a weak one, browbeaten by an able cabinet team? Lyons has critiqued this common view.[6] Was Lloyd George to blame? Even O'Day, who believes he deserves some credit, regards him as a trickster.[7] It could be argued that the government was at fault for not attending to de Valera's clever constitutional solution, that there was an element of myopia which blocked off the possibility of a settlement which might have been acceptable to all but the most entrenched and militaristic.[8]

If we grant that the Treaty indeed was a reasonable settlement fitting for both sides, does the fault remain with the hard-liners at home who refused to accept a generous compromise and brought the country into schism? Civil War historiography in Ireland is still relatively immature and concentrates principally on personalities, assuming that there would have been no Civil War but for Collins' and de Valera's enmity.[9] Recently, however, there is much more emphasis on whether or not the issue was about democracy. Garvin sees the year 1922 (not 1916 or 1918) as the birth of Irish democracy, a formative episode in its twentieth-century history brought into existence by the activities of the pro-Treaty protagonists.[10] Kissane has argued that ideology in the Civil War may be less important than we think and that existing personal, factional and local rivalries may be key in the conflict. Afterwards ideology was mapped onto the conflict.[11] In short, there is no consensus on the causation and the consequences of the Civil War except to acknowledge its pivotal role in the creation of the new state and in its political polarisations.

Partition

As mentioned previously, the Government of Ireland Act of 1920 cut right across the War of Independence. Although its provisions for the south were null and void, it is still a vitally important act because it legislated for partition. It was thus an act heavy with significance for the future of Anglo–Irish relations. The partition separated the six counties of the north from those of the south. Henceforth the house would be divided. Already this was to modify an entity of historic tradition – for Ulster had always boasted nine counties, not six. The act called for two parliaments, one in Dublin, the other in Belfast; each would possess the powers of local self-government. They were heavily circumscribed (but no more so, indeed, than that proposed in previous Home Rule bills). Such matters as defence, foreign policy and finance would remain under the control of Westminster.

Why divide the six counties from the rest? Simply put, it was hoped that this would solve the Ulster problem. Nobody wanted to see militant Ulsterism revived and it has been argued that the rising and the War of Independence in the south were a godsend to Unionists who had more reason than ever to protest against throwing their lot in with 'rebels'.[12] Apart from fear and pragmatism, the decision of partition could be said to reflect an enlightened attitude of the British government, a desire to keep like with like. It has even been suggested that it was a reasonably egalitarian solution to an intractable issue. The desires of nationalists and Unionists were incompatible and the act did no more than recognise that. This case has been argued by F. W. Boal and J. Neville H. Douglas who call it the 'only possible democratic solution'.[13]

However, one is entitled to be a little sceptical about this last point of view. It was not a truly democratic solution even by the standards of the day. This was an era in which the democratic plebiscite became a respectable option, as endorsed by the newly born League of Nations. In 1920, there were plebiscites, for example, in East Prussia and Schleswig. Majorities were being allowed to decide where they wanted to be. This principle of choice was flouted in the counties of northern Ireland. There were Catholic majorities in Tyrone and Fermanagh and yet these counties were considered part of the northern settlement. There were, in turn, substantial Protestant communities in border constituencies who were left outside. Surely if self-determination and democracy had been the government's policy, the map would have looked rather differently. At least, there would have been a proper public debate and a vote which would have made the process more transparent.

This leads to a further question. Supposing a plebiscite had reduced the north to a mere four counties, would this have been politically viable? Recent historiography suggests that it could have been. Nothing, claims Michael Laffan, would have been 'inherently absurd' in just the Protestant areas having their own institutions. After all, Luxembourg was a state smaller than the county of Antrim and with a population only two-thirds that of Belfast.[14] It is a compelling point. So why were alternative solutions not proposed? Two reasons can be postulated. First, the British government lacked commitment to a Wilsonian new world vision. Britain was a core member of the League of Nations and supported its agenda of peace and open diplomacy up to a point, but it was also an autonomous empire used to doing things its own way. It had no intention of subjecting its own internal dilemmas to new-fangled international rules of the game like democratic voting. On that basis, a plebiscite was never going to be offered.

Second is the point that Joseph Lee makes to the effect that the settlement was a partisan one, designed with the maximum Protestant convenience in mind. He writes that the 'border was chosen explicitly to provide unionists with as much territory as they could safely control'.[15] This makes sense. Lloyd George's cabinet was disproportionately Conservative and thus favourable to the Unionist agenda. In this analysis, the aim of the British government appears in a new light. It was not its aim to keep divided and fractious communities away from each other but rather to 'ensure Protestant supremacy over Catholics even in predominantly Catholic areas'.[16] This interpretation seems to fit the facts more readily.

Sometimes known as the Fourth Home Rule Bill, the resultant Government of Ireland Act, passed on 23 December 1920, was an inglorious and ironic end to the saga of Home Rule. It was inglorious because its erstwhile proponents in the south had all but melted away and it was ironic because its opponents in the north professed themselves content with self-government insofar as it applied to their province alone. The anti–Home Rulers had become Home Rulers and the provisions of the act lasted in the north until the Troubles in 1972. James Craig, the stalwart of the 1912 Unionist campaign, was made the first prime minister. His task, a demanding one, would be to stabilise the new state, to defend it from encroachments, to temper the overenthusiastic zealots of the Unionist cause and to keep a watchful eye on what the British would do next. It had become a habit with such as he. The northern parliament opened in July 1921 and it was at its inauguration in Belfast City Hall that George V had made his celebrated plea for peace between the two halves of the country.

Invitation to Treat

In regard to the southern 26 counties, the settlement of 1920 was worthless. What would the negotiations of 1921 bring? The truce of July was followed by an invitation to London for a conference. The aims of the conference were to ascertain 'how the British empire may be reconciled with Irish national aspirations'.[17] This was moderately conciliatory but still essentially conservative language. Lee notes the importance of the 'how' and the absence of 'whether'.[18] Whatever else the conference would bring, no negotiation would bring a republic. The Irish connection with Britain might be redefined to a greater or lesser extent; there was no question of it being removed. Already the language in which the invitation was framed was one of practical politics, of compromise, a crucial point that Collins in particular would insist upon in the fierce debates surrounding the Treaty's acceptance. To agree to go at all was to agree to the horse trading that would ensue, to leave the protective shrine of doctrinaire republicanism and make a deal with the enemy, risking the consequences. A bare awareness of the legal mandate of the conference sufficed to show that. Any negotiators would have to retract, to a greater or lesser extent, on principle so as to make practical gains. The scent of compromise thus hung around the mission from the start.

Lloyd George and de Valera

The negotiations took five months in total, the Treaty being eventually signed on 6 December. First came the four preliminary meetings between

Lloyd George and de Valera. Brought together for the first time, they both sized each other up. This is the last of the great duologues between a British and Irish leader that we shall have occasion to consider. There was more riding on it than on any other meeting in the past. The prime minister was forced to deal with a man whose career to date had been one of defiance to the government, who had witnessed his associates executed and had himself been imprisoned by the British justice system on more than one occasion. The very encounter was a dramatic one.

Both were slippery by nature. Lloyd George was known as 'the Welsh Wizard' and was adept in subtleties and verbal machinations. Even he found de Valera almost impossible, claiming that talking to him was like picking up 'mercury with a fork'. 'Why doesn't he try a spoon'? de Valera had said on hearing of this afterwards.[19] The prime minister, anxious to get on with the actual business of a settlement, fumed against de Valera's obsession with history. The latter insisted on giving him a long lesson on the wrongs Britain had done Ireland starting with Cromwell. His interlocutor's patience wore thin. But de Valera was a subtle creature and was probably buying time. At first, the positions of both were intransigent – de Valera insisted on independence and Lloyd George offered no more than dominion status. But then, the former shifted ground and began to show some flexibility. He mooted the question of foreign arbitration, a reasonable and progressive solution, but Lloyd George refused, presumably, as Laffan says, because he knew deep down that his Ulster policy was indefensible.[20] Then de Valera proceeded to outline a new way out of the impasse: external association. It was his brainchild and he flourished it at every opportunity to general incomprehension. Essentially, it meant that Ireland would have her own sovereignty (an important legal status) but retain her connection 'externally' with the Commonwealth (a necessary compromise with tradition). Ever the mathematician, he drew a Venn diagram for his colleagues in which the British Commonwealth was represented by a large circle within which were five smaller circles, each representing one of the self-governing countries of that group of nations. The president sketched in Ireland as a circle outside the large circle but touching it. Was this to be deliberately abstruse? Most historians have argued that his was an imaginative and indeed an inspired constitutional solution and, as constitutional lawyers have pointed out, rather ahead of its time.[21] It is to be doubted whether Lloyd George took the trouble of grasping it, or for that matter whether Irish die-hards would have found any association acceptable. The answer is probably not, although de Valera's personal sway would have counted for something with many of them. The summit talks ended with nothing decided.

The Conference

In October, Lloyd George called a conference to London – a sort of legitimation of the *de facto* government. Times had changed. He was now ready to do business with rebels. The question of who would act as the delegates was immediately and inevitably a controversial one, although historians divide on the question of how much it mattered for the actual terms of the Treaty or the subsequent outbreak of civil war. Cathal Brúgha and Austin Stack, implacable and truculent, refused at once. Their brand of republicanism did not admit parley with the men in London. Collins was highly reluctant but ultimately amenable. Gavan Duffy and Eamon Duggan were both lawyers and thus obvious choices. Robert Barton came with a background in economic matters. Arthur Griffith was the chairman of the delegation. So much has been said of the inherent weakness of the delegation that not enough has been made of its strengths. Lyons sees it as a 'very strong' delegation in the range and ability of its talents.[22]

Some weakness must be outlined, however. First, the brunt of the debates fell heavily on Griffiths and Collins. Secondly, the self-imposed absence of the extreme republican wing on the delegation meant that their voices were unheard in London but heard loudly at home. Most importantly of all, the chief was notably absent. He was, after all, their leader since 1917 and, in the ways of debate and subtlety of mind, head and shoulders above the others. Second, he was at one remove from military operations during the war in strong contrast to Collins and would perhaps have had a stronger hand at the negotiating table. Thirdly, he had already met Lloyd George and they now knew how each other worked. Experience could be an advantage on such a stressful occasion.

Interpreting de Valera's Absence

Why did he not go? Interpretations vary. Machiavellianism has been mooted by his critics. This reading would suggest that he wanted to keep clear of blame when things went wrong, as he knew they would. This is probably the most unfair reading; that said, he would not be human if he did not take some wry pleasure in commanding military supremo Collins to go to the negotiating table and suffer. Lee absolves de Valera from the imputation of Machiavellianism and attributes to him a real desire to maintain unity. His position of aloofness at such a time would be enough, he felt, to 'wean the doctrinaires into accepting' an inevitable compromise.[23] This interpretation is, however, complicated by the fact that de Valera himself did not accept the compromise but we must not read too far ahead at this point.

There are other possible interpretations. His own given reason was that, as president, he was a symbolic creature and therefore should not go. This is more plausible than it sounds on two counts. First, Owen Dudley Edwards has identified a strand in his political make-up in which he very much styled himself as the 'priest-king'.[24] It was quite typical for him to see himself in somewhat esoteric fashion as mystical head of the ancient Gaelic nation. Symbols do not negotiate. He had developed a political theology of his own to replace the monarchic system. If this sounds too abstract, more mundane factors may have preyed upon his mind. He may have been thinking about a recent American example. President Wilson had gone to Paris for six months to negotiate the postwar settlement at Versailles. Afterwards, it was felt by many that the American delegation would have been in a stronger position had the president *not* gone. Summit diplomacy had its limitations. By remaining at home, there would have been a larger layer of authority and pressure. By going, one went all in.

The British Delegation

The six Irish plenipotentiaries were confronted with a politically mature and outrageously experienced delegate from Britain. Clearly, they *had* gone all in. This formidable team, which included Lloyd George, Churchill (secretary of state for the colonies), Austen Chamberlain (Lord Chancellor) and Lord Birkenhead (Lord Privy Seal), were playing their own game on home ground. The Irish, who had built their careers since 1917 on abstention from Westminster, had now to do business in the very context they had spurned. Not that the Irish were naïve by any means or let the awesomeness of the occasion blind them as to the realities. Still, it is a fact that they did not feel comfortable there, for all Collins' popularity among society women. Griffith, Collins, Duffy and Barton, badgered and confused, all thought of resigning and coming home at some stage or other. That they remained is testament to their fortitude and their deep desire not to split ranks.

Negotiations and the Treaty

At the debates in London, the Irish prioritised a whole-country solution, whereas the British sought firstly to clarify Ireland's constitutional status. Aware that James Craig had flatly refused to come to the talks, the government had no intention of reneging on the 1920 settlement behind his back, instead proposing a Boundary Commission to determine the appropriate north/south boundary. This may have sounded promising to harried Irish delegates – it appeared to be the most there was on offer and diplomacy, like politics, is the art of the possible. In a sense, Craig, for all his implacable non-involvement, was exercising remote control over the proceedings because Lloyd George had promised him news by 6 December and so even the Treaty deadline was established according to the convenience of Ulster. Working towards such a deadline was unfair – it put enormous pressure on the delegation and was compounded by the ultimatum that, if they did not sign, there would be war within three days. Was this bluff? It is most probable. It was very undiplomatic, to say the least, and at 2.10 AM, the weary men signed and the British counter-signed. The deed was done. Collins believed that he had signed his death warrant.

By the terms of the Treaty, Ireland was granted dominion status. A dominion was somewhere in between a colony and a state. It was much more generous than Home Rule. Canada had been given this under Gladstone back in 1867; in 1907, she was joined by Australia, New Zealand and Newfoundland. In 1910, it was the turn of the Union of South Africa. Ireland was a late arrival. It simplified things considerably – henceforth she would manage her own policies on finance, the economy, the judiciary, police and the army. British forces, so long a focus of hatred, would withdraw. They would, however, maintain three naval ports in Ireland – entirely understandable, given that British imperial power was supremely naval. The British representative in Ireland would be known as the governor general. To safeguard loyalty, all Dáil members would take an Oath of Allegiance to the king 'in virtue of the common citizenship'.[25]

What are we to make of these concessions? At one level they are considerable. In terms of status, Ireland had caught up on other 'white' territories of the British Empire. It thus finally benefitted from the Liberal wave of self-government which had occurred on and off since the 1860s. Secondly, it did away with much of the baggage of the past – the symbols that had been increasingly regarded as illegitimate since 1801 – most of all the garrisoning and armed policing. Thirdly, there was the *promise* of further change within the very fact of the Treaty. This was born out in the future. In 1926, the Balfour Declaration would lay out that all dominions were 'autonomous communities' within the Empire, thus equalising their status. The Anglo–Irish Treaty, even if wrung out of a browbeaten Britain, did nonetheless reveal that the men in London could reconsider the future of their territories. Collins' well-chosen words, in regard to the Treaty, are often cited – it was 'not the ultimate freedom that all nations desire [...] but the freedom to achieve it'.[26]

Opposition

Not all members of the Dáil agreed. Disagreement soon became savage. The oath, in particular, was hard to stomach. The debates raged for several weeks, de Valera confounding everybody with his 'Document No. 2', outlining his 'external association' alternative. Such scholasticism, needless to say, did not have wide appeal. The result of the vote went in favour of the Treaty, albeit by a fairly narrow margin – 64 to 57. There is no doubting the real sense of betrayal felt by the 57, especially the six women MPs, although whether more could have been realistically achieved is a moot point.[27] Once one had agreed to do business with the establishment, then it was always going to be on the establishment's terms. On 10 January, de Valera led his followers from the chamber in protest against using the Dáil as a means to establish a provisional government as the Treaty had required.

Whilst the Dáil was riven, the only winners were the Ulster Unionists. They formally withdrew from the terms of the Treaty and their situation was thus left intact. As their settlement was already a *fait accompli*, it was unlikely to be dislodged by a boundary commission. That commission, indeed, when it finally emerged in 1924–25 was headed by Richard Feetham, a known imperialist with experience in South Africa and, unsurprisingly, the border was left as it was. The Unionists were, in Laffan's words, remarkably 'ungracious in victory'.[28] Sectarianism was the order of the day when treating the region's Catholic inhabitants. The Ulster Volunteer Force (UVF) was revived in the summer of 1920. Five thousand Catholics were ejected from their jobs and there were lootings and burnings of Catholic places. Over the next two years the conflict would kill 428 and wound 1,766. Therein lay the seed of the future Troubles. The north was not truly solved – it still is not.

Provisional Government in the South

It was unfortunate for the authority of the new government that it should have been made provisional. The plan was that, within 12 months, the British would have dismantled their rule and that the Irish Free State would be officially established. But this arrangement was, to say the least, a very confusing one. It was also unhelpful in the sense that anti-Treaty forces were on the look out for vulnerabilities and this ambiguous situation was a prime example. The Irish Republican Army (IRA) had split definitively. General Richard Mulcahy guaranteed their loyalty to the fledgling state but he could not prevent the defection of some of its leading officers, notably Rory O'Connor, Liam Mellows and Liam Lynch, and some of its members, especially in Munster. There were now regulars and irregulars, free-staters and republicans. The appalling shape of civil war dichotomies had emerged. The latter were intransigent in their rejection of all the Treaty stood for and again we see the logic of a very resolute minority at work. As in 1916, the minority laid claim to a greater moral mandate than the majority, that of being adamantly *right* and that of knowing what was best for the people as a whole. This seems to be the most plausible interpretation of their stance. Was this legitimate? Their ambiguous relationship with the will of the people has often been remarked upon.[29] However, Hart absolves them somewhat from this charge, claiming that there was no 'fascist or communist-style dismissal of electoral democracy' and pointing out that republicans did not rig or suppress an election or contemplate a *coup d'état*.[30]

Matters took a darker turn when, on 9 April 1922, the irregulars appointed a seven-man army council and, within days, had occupied the Four Courts and other buildings in Dublin. The bitter irony is not lost on us. Another April had found Dublin besieged, but here the enemy was not the British so much as former comrades-in-arms. In the general confusion surrounding the British abandonment of barracks and Royal Irish Constabulary (RIC) outposts, strategic advantage could be gained. Limerick was a particularly contested spot, but pro-Treaty forces managed to dissipate the trouble.

All hope for peace was not yet lost and, before the election, Collins and de Valera made a pact to fight it on a national coalition platform. Collins later withdrew from this, probably under pressure from Lloyd George. Divides disfigured the result. Pro-Treaty candidates won 58 seats; anti-Treaty 36 seats. The nation had spoken – the majority favoured the Treaty. Garvin says that the result was an 'insecure and inexperienced elite' presiding over a 'population that wanted unheroic things'.[31] He nonetheless sees this as the first open democratic contest in Ireland and claims, revealingly, that the supporters of the Treaty were more 'modern in mentality' and better at 'running things' whilst those opposed to it were better at 'romantic indignation' and the refusal to face reality head-on.[32] The question was whether or not the latter would respect this democratic outcome. As we have seen, the extremists were never democrats, except when it suited them. The assassination of Sir Henry Wilson, field marshal and Unionist MP, in London the following day made British authorities ever more adamant that the new government should prove their colours by taking action against anti-Treaty rebels in the Four Courts. It was an intolerable situation, with Churchill significantly hinting that if no action were taken, Britain would go about protecting its own interests. Interestingly, Wilson was the only British politician to be assassinated in the course of the conflict.[33] From now on, it would be an all-Irish bloodbath.

Civil War

Coercion – so long an instrument in British hands, used so frequently in the course of the century – was finally to be used by the Irish against their own compatriots in the very dawn of this new political era. It was a biting irony indeed. Even without British hints, Collins was coming to the conclusion that action must be taken at once before the situation escalated. An ultimatum was duly issued to the republicans. No answer was received by the required deadline of 4 AM on 28 June and thus the Civil War began – of all wars, the most tragic. Two days later, the 200 men occupying the Four Courts were forced to surrender. Fighting continued in Dublin city into early July – 64 died, 300 were wounded. Then, the conflict spread to the rest of the country. It was a painful but predictable outcome. The hills held a lot of discontents used to skirmishing.

Munster was the key republican stronghold. The irregulars held sway in what could be called a 'Munster Republic' for an ostensibly impressive 10 months despite losing the key cities of Limerick, Cork and Waterford early on. How Munster held out is largely attributable to tactics learned in the War of Independence, now put to even deadlier use in the struggle against former comrades-in-arms. There was also an element of reverse stereotyping. Collins' troops – there were now about 50,000 in arms, aided by British ammunition and guns – were sometimes known as the 'Green and Tans'. There is no doubt that the irregulars were fighting a 'replica' struggle.

De Valera's position was, as usual, subtle. One could say that he was fighting his own little war on behalf of a doctrine that nobody understood. In fact, he was not involved in actual fighting at all. He did try to call a halt to conflict, but there was an intransigent core of leaders who would have none of it. Liam Lynch was the most notable at this point. He commanded the first southern division of the irregulars. What was in his mind? Perhaps he thought that if it went on long enough, it would destabilise the settlement. If so, it was negative rather than positive fighting – one cannot imagine the British government being at all ready to come to terms with the irregulars had they been victorious.

The months of sporadic fighting brought deaths, most notably that of Collins. An ambush at Béal na mBláth in Cork turned into an exchange of fire and Collins was left dead with a bullet through his head. Why had they stopped to exchange fire? His chauffeur had wanted to 'drive like hell' and get clear of the gunmen but Collins had overruled him. This was the impulse of soldier rather than statesman.[34] The guerrilla supremo could not resist a fight. His death was a loss indeed and his funeral the occasion for a national outpouring of grief. He was much loved in life; he was worshipped in death. There is a significant strand of thought which venerates him to this day: Tim Pat Coogan's biography is a notable example.[35] The popular Neil Jordan film *Michael Collins* (1996) cemented his reputation still further. But worship is not the correct attitude for a historian. Perhaps, like Hamlet, he was 'likely, had he been put on, to have proved most royally'. He was a towering figure and an unambiguously charismatic one. But there is also a possibility that Collins' leadership would have been overly executive and, with the general shift to the right in the 1930s, this could have led to greater extremes of militaristic control. After all, his 'Squad' of hitmen looked rather like the proto-military groups that sprung up over Europe after World War I. His most effective moments showed him at his most brutal. No doubt, however, it is idle to speculate on how Collins would have proved in the long term. We shall never know.

Griffith's death from a brain haemorrhage only days earlier had deprived Ireland of another leader. A replacement was found in William Cosgrave. A chairman, not a chief, he was regarded by Churchill as a leader 'of higher quality than any who had yet appeared'.[36] And indeed, perhaps what Ireland did need was not personality but probity, not heroics but hard work. It was under his aegis that the free state was official declared on 6 December 1922. It was also under his rule that the harshest punitive treatment for rebels was issued. He was hard in the rather surprising way that only a mild man can be. Military courts were set up and the penalty was summary execution. These were emergency powers with a vengeance. Almost 80 republicans were executed in such a manner, including Rory O'Connor who had been best man at the wedding of the minister for home affairs, Kevin O'Higgins. Not even personal friends were spared. To that, add another 13,000 who were gaoled. Ironically, the ruthlessness of the new government was greater than many British administrations in the past. Maybe, to take up Townshend's point, that is why it worked.[37] Britain had a habit of being too ruthless to win people over and not ruthless enough to actually crush the problems. This new free state, cutting its teeth in national conflict, was certainly getting the monopoly of legitimate violence.

April 1923 saw the death of hard-liner Liam Lynch and the declaration of a cease-fire. By 24 May, it was officially over. Men of action and men of words – there had been so many of both over the years of struggle and conflict. Finally, it was left to a man of words, de Valera, to tell the 'Legion of the Rearguard' as he liked to call them, that 'further sacrifice of life would now be in vain'.[38] O'Connell had once said that Ireland was not worth the shedding of one drop of blood. But subsequent decades had disfigured that view, ennobling blood sacrifice in the national cause. But now, even that idea was wearing thin. 'Too long a sacrifice / Can make a stone of the heart', wrote Yeats in his poem 'Easter 1916'.[39] Ireland needed nothing so much as peace to reconstruct itself in its new state of partial freedom.

Chapter 23

CONCLUSION

The overarching narrative from 1800 to 1922 begins with Union and ends with partition and disunion. Another and cruder way of saying this is that it began with Anglo–Irish conflict (1798–1800) and ended with an all-Irish war. In between, there is more than a fair share of conflict too. Almost omnipresent was, as Lyons observed in the conclusion of his 1979 Clarendon Lectures in Oxford, an 'anarchy in the mind and in the heart which forbade not just unity of territories but also "unity of being"'.[1] The consciousness of this state of disturbance and disequilibrium is a constant finding for the historian of modern Ireland. Ireland is, for Thomas Bartlett, a 'theatre of disorder'.[2] The story of the malignancies of Irish history is almost too familiar. To understand her history means engaging with the ideology and practice of official coercion, the occurrence of rebellion and war, of hunger and exodus, and, throughout, of endemic levels of violence in the shape of ambushes and evictions, boycotting and assault. It was not a society which could be said to have achieved long-term stability in this period – turbulence was the rule rather than the exception. It was a place which, for example, in 1870, spent £1 million on maintaining its police forces, £668,202 relieving its paupers and a mere £373,950 on educating its children. Every other day from 1921, the *Times* ran a story about the Irish Republican Army (IRA). Told in this way, Ireland's history is an especially unhappy one. It is profoundly disfigured, shot through with violence.

This story, at times, seemed to obscure the less overtly sensational stories of the period. This is probably inevitable, but still unfairly ahistorical. The other narratives deserve their place alongside. Primary among them was the success story of the industrialisation of the north. Also notable was the achievement of Catholic emancipation, the rise of a Catholic middle class and a devotional revolution where popular piety found varied modes of expression and a new identity. Furthermore, trade, transport, communications and leisure activities were all revolutionised, as we have established, and the Irish did indeed share in some of the fruits of a mid-Victorian boom. There was a growing underlying stability despite the outbreaks of violence. The tide was raising many boats. Prosperity for many inched upwards. Moreover, in three ways Ireland was most certainly ahead of Britain. First, this was as regards the national educational system where it was in advance by 40 years. Second, it was ahead in harnessing the power of the masses and public opinion to bring pressure to bear on the charmed circles of power. The fact that Ireland was the first country organising mass campaigns and monster meetings is significant in historical terms. Thirdly, Irish politicians under Parnell inspired the development of tighter modes of party organisation than had hitherto been the case and thus made a significant contribution to British party politics.

Towards the end of the 1800s, we have descried the quiet but huge transformation of Irish society by the disestablishment and land acts which facilitated rural *embourgeoisement* and the growth of a farmer class. The mechanics and administration of independent Ireland were already being forged. Finally, there is the matter of culture. Lyons may well deplore the divisive nature of cultures in the era, but divisions there will always be. It does not detract from the extraordinary revivalism in the 1890s and 1900s which put Ireland very definitely on the international literary map. Culture gave the Irish a new sense of themselves which enabled them to throw off the stereotypes that viewed them as a lesser race.

The light and shadow – the *chiaroscuro* – of Irish history is thus incontestable. Faced with these contrasts and ambiguities, we once again are driven to ask: What was the Irish Question? At any one stage, there were multiple questions. Who defined it varied. It was, first and foremost, political and, if political, agrarian, since land was the basis of power. The Irish Question laid out at Westminster, dissected, dealt with, temporarily 'solved' and ignored was one articulation. Intimately connected, there was the Irish Question as defined by the vested landed interests – the 'Horse-Protestants', as playwright Brendan Behan slyly called them.[3] In this period, they were already in the twilight of their power and very soon would be *déclassé*. Did they sense it? Were they aware of their terminal decline? They certainly tried to hold on to what they had, but, by 1900, their position was anomalous. Ironically, it was a Conservative government who had undercut the substance of their power with its land acts.

The Irish Question was also, increasingly, a sectarian one. As defined by Presbyterian Ulstermen, closely associated with British mores and industrial success, the question could only be answered by maintaining the Union and they became steadily more intransigent with every attempt to dilute the connection. Theirs was the logic of the pound and Protestantism – the much vaunted orange card. By contrast, the emerging and aspiring Irish Catholic middle classes, whether clerical or lay, were articulating demands about national rights and status. At first these were eminently compatible with Union – but by the end of the period, that had changed radically. Dominion status, at the very least, was the aim.

The Irish Question was also adopted, with a logic all their own and an agenda which struck fear into the heart of the establishment, by those whom we may call, roughly speaking, 'the men on the hills' – the men to whom violence would never be objectionable. The harnessing of their energies in agrarian – and later political – causes would be crucial in determining the ultimate nature of the struggle and its *dénouement* in bloody civil war. But it was the Irish Question as articulated by the romantics and intellectuals that, in terms of political thought, came to matter most. Incipient in the Young Ireland movement of the 1840s, this boasted a line of descendants in the cultural nationalist movement and in the language and ideology of the rebels of 1916. When an Irish republic was finally declared to sceptical spectators, it was in a poet's voice, that of Patrick Pearse. The republic would only be made official in 1949, but there was nothing new then that had not been said before. There is a compellingly paradoxical quality to modern Irish history in all its various facets. At its most extreme, this paradox approaches, in the words of W. B. Yeats, a 'terrible beauty'.[4] Its history is fearful in its implacable divisions, epically indulgent in its fiercest tragedies and strangely quiet about its achievements. Great advances as well as great hatred – very little room.

CHRONOLOGY

1798	United Irishmen Rebellion
1800	Act of Union passed
1801	Union of Great Britain and Ireland takes effect (1 January)
1803	Rising of Robert Emmet
1820	Accession of George IV
1823	Catholic Association established
1829	Catholic emancipation
1830	Accession of William IV
1831	Tithe War begins
1832	Great Reform Act (Ireland)
1835	Lichfield House Compact
1837	Accession of Queen Victoria
1840	Municipal Corporations Act
1840	National Association for Full Justice or Repeal Association established
1842	Founding of the *Nation* newspaper
1843	Year of monster meetings for repeal
1845	Maynooth crisis
1845–51	An Gorta Mór – The Great Famine
1846	Repeal of the Corn Laws
1848	Young Ireland Rebellion
1849	Queen Victoria's first visit
1850	Representation of the People Act for Ireland
1853	Queen Victoria's second visit
1853	Dublin Great Exhibition
1858	Foundation of what would become the Irish Republican Brotherhood (IRB)
1858	First transatlantic cable communication

1859	Foundation of the Fenian Brotherhood
1859	The *Irish Times* newspaper founded
1859	Birthdate of the British Liberal Party
1861	Queen Victoria's third visit
1866	Public Health Committee established
1867	Failed Fenian rising; terrorist incidents in Britain
1868	Gladstone becomes prime minister
1869	Disestablishment of the Church of Ireland
1870	First Land Act – the Landlord and Tenant Act
1873	Founding of the Home Rule League
1875	Election of Charles Stewart Parnell for Meath
1879	Irish National Land League founded
1879–82	Land War
1880	Parnell's leadership of the Irish Parliamentary Party
1881	Second Land Act – the Land Law Act
1882	Kilmainham Treaty
1885	Gaelic Athletic Association (GAA) founded
1885	Ashbourne Land Act – the Purchase of Land Act
1885	Irish Loyal and Patriotic Union established
1886	First Home Rule Bill
1887	Plan of Campaign
1888	Pan-Celtic Society
1891	Solar eclipse and death of Parnell
1892	Irish National Literary Society
1893	Second Home Rule Bill
1893	Establishment of the Gaelic League
1894	Irish Agricultural Organisation Society
1896	Irish Socialist Republican Party
1898	Local Government Act
1899	The *United Irishman* newspaper founded
1900	Queen Victoria's fourth visit
1901	Accession of Edward VII
1903	Wyndham's Land Act – the Land Purchase Act
1904	Abbey Theatre established
1905	Birth date of Sinn Féin
1906	Liberal government in power
1907	*Playboy of the Western World* riots
1910	Accession of George V
1910	Two general elections – Irish party holds balance
1910	Edward Carson, leader of the Ulster Unionist Council
1911	Parliament Act

1912	Third Home Rule Bill
1912	Ulster Solemn League and Covenant
1913	Formation of Volunteer forces, north and south
1913	Dublin Lockout
1914	Curragh Mutiny and gun running
1914	Buckingham Palace Conference
1914	World War I; Home Rule on statute book but suspended
1916	Easter Rising; execution of leaders
1917	Release of political prisoners
1918	Conscription crisis
1918	End of World War I; Representation of the People Act
1918	Sinn Féin win general election
1919	First Dáil Eireann
1919–21	Anglo–Irish War
1920	Government of Ireland Act
1921	George V opens Northern Ireland parliament
1921	Anglo–Irish Treaty
1922	Civil war in southern Ireland
1922	Irish Free State (Saorstát Éireann) established
1922	Six northern counties opt out of the free state
1923	End of the Civil War

NOTES

Introduction

1 Townshend has a useful classification of violence. See Charles Townshend, *Political Violence in Ireland: Government and Resistance since 1848* (Oxford: Clarendon Press, 1983), 407–8.

2 Alvin Jackson, 'Unionist History', in *Interpreting Irish History: The Debate on Historical Revisionism*, ed. Ciaran Brady (Dublin: Irish Academic Press, 1994), 253.

3 A. B. Cooke and John Vincent, *The Governing Passion: Cabinet Government and Party Politics in Britain, 1885–86* (Brighton: Harvester Press, 1974); Patricia Jalland, *Liberals and Ireland: The Ulster Question in British Politics to 1914* (Brighton: Harvester Press, 1980).

4 Townshend, *Political Violence in Ireland*; David Miller, *Queen's Rebels: Ulster Loyalism in Historical Perspective* (Dublin: University College Dublin Press, 2007).

5 Dorothy MacArdle, *The Irish Republic* (Dublin: Irish Press, 1937).

6 P. S. O'Hegarty, *A History of Ireland under the Union, 1801–1922* (London: Methuen, 1952), 3.

7 The best introduction to these debates and their proponents is in Ciaran Brady's *Interpreting Irish History: The Debate on Historical Revisionism* (Dublin: Irish Academic Press, 1994).

8 F. S. L. Lyons, 'The Burden of Our History', in *Interpreting Irish History*, ed. Brady, 91.

9 Jackson, 'Unionist History', 253.

10 Roy Foster, *Modern Ireland 1600–1972* (London: Penguin, 1988).

11 Desmond Fennell, 'Against Revisionism', in *Interpreting Irish History*, ed. Brady, 189.

12 Brendan Bradshaw, 'Nationalism and Historical Scholarship in Modern Ireland', in *Interpreting Irish History*, ed. Brady, 201.

13 Brady, 'Constructive and Instrumental: The Dilemma of Ireland's First "New Historians"', in *Interpreting Irish History*, ed. Brady, 10.

14 Townshend, *Political Violence in Ireland*; David P. Nally, *Human Encumbrances: Political Violence and the Great Irish Famine* (Notre Dame, IN: University of Notre Dame Press, 2011); Peter Gray, *Famine, Land and Politics: British Government and Irish Society, 1843–1850* (Dublin: Irish Academic Press, 1999).

15 See Mary Daly, 'Recent Writings on Modern Irish History: The Interaction between Past and Present', *Journal of Modern History* 69, no. 3 (1997): 512–33 for an excellent, short review on the historiographical debates.

16 T. C. Barnard's *A New Anatomy of Ireland: The Irish Protestants, 1649–1770* (New Haven: Yale University Press, 2003) provides a detailed description of each strand of Protestant society in Ireland from 1649 to 1770. For a shorter treatment of the Protestant nation see J. C. Beckett, *A Short History of Ireland* (London: Hutchinson, 1966), 96–129.

17 Foster, *Modern Ireland 1600–1972*, 173.

18 Thomas Bartlett's *The Fall and Rise of the Irish Nation: The Catholic Question, 1690–1830* (Dublin: Gill & Macmillan, 1992) is a valuable introduction to the fall and rise of the Catholic nation, 1690–1830.

19 For example, see Bartlett, *Fall and Rise*, 45–65.

20 For example, see Bartlett, *Fall and Rise*.

21 D. G. Boyce and Alan O'Day, eds, *Parnell in Perspective* (London: Routledge, 1991), 9.

22 Foster, *Modern Ireland 1600–1972*, 215.

23 Solid histories of Ulster, loyalism and Unionism include Peter Gibbon, *The Origins of Ulster Unionism: The Formation of Popular Protestant Politics and Ideology in Nineteenth-Century Ireland* (Manchester: Manchester University Press, 1975); Patrick Buckland, *Ulster Unionism*, 2 vols (Dublin: Gill & Macmillan, 1972–73); Miller, *Queen's Rebels*; Allan Blackstock, *Loyalism in Ireland, 1789–1829* (Woodbridge: Boydell Press, 2007); and Boyce and O'Day, eds, *Parnell in Perspective*.

24 A. T. Q. Stewart, *The Ulster Crisis* (London: Faber & Faber, 1967), 18.

25 The Poynings' Law of 1494 and the Declaratory Act of 1719 made Ireland subject to Westminster. Irish legislation was conditional on British approval. The executive was controlled from Britain not Ireland. The Irish parliament met only intermittently when convened by the Crown.

26 For treatment of the British relationship to events in France see H. T. Dickinson, *British Radicalism and the French Revolution* (Oxford: Blackwell, 1985); and Dickinson, ed., *Britain and the French Revolution, 1789–1815* (Basingstoke: Macmillan, 1989).

27 R. B. McDowell, *Ireland in the Age of Imperialism and Revolution, 1760–1800* (Oxford: Clarendon Press, 1979), 351; for a discussion of the French Revolution and Ireland, see chapter 9.

28 For its links with France see Marianne Elliott, *Partners in Revolution: The United Irishmen and France* (New Haven: Yale University Press, 1982) and David Dickson and Hugh Gough, eds, *Ireland and the French Revolution* (Dublin: Irish Academic Press, 1990).

29 Gibbon, *The Origins of Ulster Unionism*, 22–43 discusses the origins of Orangeism.

30 The rebellion of 1798 has received very comprehensive treatment in literature. See, for example, McDowell, *Ireland in the Age of Imperialism and Revolution*, 594–651; see also Thomas Bartlett et al., eds, *1798: A Bicentenary Perspective* (Dublin: Four Courts Press, 2003).

Chapter 1. Forging the Union

1 Quoted in William Hague, *William Pitt the Younger: A Biography* (London: HarperCollins, 2005), 45

2 Arthur Griffith, *The Resurrection of Hungary: A Parallel for Ireland*, 3rd ed. (Dublin: Whelan & Son, 1918).

3 For full treatment of the history of Ulster Unionism see Allan Blackstock, *Loyalism in Ireland, 1789–1829* (Woodbridge: Boydell Press, 2007); D. G. Boyce and

Alan O'Day, eds, *Parnell in Perspective* (London: Routledge, 1991); Patrick Buckland, *Ulster Unionism*, 2 vols (Dublin: Gill & Macmillan, 1972–73); and Peter Gibbon, *The Origins of Ulster Unionism: The Formation of Popular Protestant Politics and Ideology in Nineteenth-Century Ireland* (Manchester: Manchester University Press, 1975).

4 Oliver MacDonagh , *Ireland: The Union and its Aftermath* (Dublin: University College Dublin Press, 1997), 10.

5 Liam Kennedy and D. S. Johnson. 'The Union of Ireland and Britain, 1800–1921', in *The Making of Modern Irish History: Revisionism and the Revisionist Controversy*, ed. D. G. Boyce and Alan O'Day (London: Routledge, 1996), 59.

6 J. G. A. Pocock, 'The Union in British History', in *Transactions of the Royal Historical Society*, vol. 10, 6th series (2000), 181–96.

7 See Chapter 2.

8 G. C. Bolton, *The Passing of the Irish Act of Union* (Oxford: Oxford University Press, 1966), 184.

9 Patrick M. Geoghegan, *The Irish Act of Union: A Study in High Politics, 1798–1801* (Dublin: Gill & Macmillan, 1999).

10 Dáire Keogh and Kevin Whelan, eds, *Acts of Union: The Causes, Contexts and Consequences of the Act of Union* (Dublin: Four Courts Press, 2001).

11 Roy Foster, *Modern Ireland 1600–1972* (London: Penguin, 1988); D. C. Boyce, *Nineteenth-Century Ireland: The Search for Stability* (Dublin: Gill & Macmillan, 1990); Keogh and Whelan, *Acts of Union*.

12 Geoghegan, *The Irish Act of Union*, 2.

13 Ronald Hyam, *Britain's Imperial Century 1815–1914* (Palgrave Macmillan, 1976); William Roger Louis, Andrew Porter and Alaine Lowe, *The Oxford History of the British Empire. Volume III: The Nineteenth Century* (Oxford: Oxford University Press, 1990).

14 H. T. Dickinson's *British Radicalism and the French Revolution* (Oxford: Blackwell, 1985) and *Britain and the French Revolution, 1789–1815* (Basingstoke: Macmillan, 1989) offer a good overview of the subject of Britain in its interactions with the French Revolution.

15 For more on Pitt's empire-building see Hague, *William Pitt the Younger*, 349, 384.

16 David Dickson and Hugh Gough, eds, *Ireland and the French Revolution* (Dublin: Irish Academic Press, 1990), David Dickson, Dáire Keogh and Kevin Whelan, *The United Kingdom: Republicanism, Radicalism and Rebellion* (Dublin: Lilliput Press, 1993) and Marianne Elliott, *Partners in Revolution: The United Irishmen and France* (New Haven: Yale University Press, 1982) are good places when considering the influence of French radicalism on Ireland in the 1790s. Thomas Bartlett et al. (eds, *1798: A Bicentenary Perspective* [Dublin: Four Courts Press, 2003]) consider the 1798 rebellion from the perspective of the bicentennial.

17 The classic account of the period 1760–1800 is that of R. B. McDowell, *Ireland in the Age of Imperialism and Revolution, 1760–1800* (Oxford: Clarendon Press, 1979).

18 Boyce, *Nineteenth-Century Ireland*, 19.

19 William Pitt, *The Speeches of the Right Honourable William Pitt in the House of Commons*, vol. 3, ed. William Hathaway (London: Longman, Hurst, Rees and Orme, 1808), 255.

20 Geoghegan, *The Irish Act of Union*, 71.

21 Pitt, *Speeches*, 254–5. See also 270–71.

22 Ibid., 268, 258.

23 Ibid., 258–9.

24 Ibid., 266.

25 Boyce, *Nineteenth-Century Ireland*, 19.

26 Pitt, *Speeches*, 266.

27 Ibid., 264.

28 Pitt to Rutland, 6 January 1785, 'Correspondence between the Right Honble. William Pitt and Charles, duke of Rutland, lord lieutenant of Ireland, 1781–1787', London   1892.   Online: http://www.archive.org/stream/correspondencebe00pitt/correspondencebe00pitt_djvu.txt (accessed 27 August 2013).

29 See Chapter 2.

30 Pitt, *Speeches*, 261.

31 Thomas Bartlett, *The Fall and Rise of the Irish Nation: The Catholic Question, 1690–1830* (Dublin: Gill & Macmillan, 1992).

32 McDowell, *Ireland in the Age of Imperialism and Revolution*, 687.

33 Richard Brinsley Sheridan, *Speech of Richard Brinsley Sheridan in the House of Commons* (31 January 1799) (Dublin: Printed for James Moore, 1799), 9.

34 The Act of Union Virtual Library project is supported by the Belfast Public Libraries, the Centre for Data Digitisation and Analysis at Queen's University, Belfast, the Linen Hall Library, the Public Record Office of Northern Ireland (PRONI), Information Services at Queen's University, the Ulster Folk and Transport Museum and the Ulster Museum. It can be accessed at http://www.actofunion.ac.uk/.

35 J. C. D. Clark, *The Language of Liberty, 1660–1832: Political Discourse and Social Dynamics in the Anglo-American World* (Cambridge: Cambridge University Press, 1993) charts the evolution of the discourse of liberty in the Anglo-American world.

36 Benedict Anderson, *Imagined Communities: Reflections on the Origins and Spread of Nationalism* (London: Verso, 1983); Ernest Gellner, *Nations and Nationalism* (Oxford: Blackwell, 1983); Eric Hobsbawm, *Nations and Nationalism since 1780* (Cambridge: Cambridge University Press, 1990).

37 See, for example, Anthony D. Smith, *The Ethnic Origins of Nations* (Oxford: Basil Blackwell, 1986) and Adrian Hastings, *The Construction of Nationhood: Ethnicity Religion and Nationalism* (Cambridge: Cambridge University Press, 1997). The spectrum of views is rather wider than this brief sketch has been able to show.

38 John Foster, *Speech of the Right Honourable John Foster Speaker of the House of Commons of Ireland, delivered in Committee* (17 February 1800) (Dublin: Printed for James Moore, 1800), 2–3; in a speech made 17 February 1800.

39 Ibid., 1

40 Ibid., 2–3.

41 John Collis, *An Address to the People of Ireland on the Projected Union* (Dublin: Printed for James Moore, 1799), 6.

42 Quoted in Geoghegan, *The Irish Act of Union*, 99.

43 J. Foster, *Speech* (17 February 1800), 17.

44 Ibid., 4–5.

45 Ibid., 17.

46 Ibid., 2–3.

47 J. Foster, *Speech of the Right Honourable John Foster Speaker of the House of Commons of Ireland, delivered in Committee* (19 March 1800) (Dublin: Printed for James Moore, 1800), 2, 37.

48 R. Foster, *Modern Ireland 1600–1972*, 167–8.

49 Collis, *An Address to the People*, 3.

Chapter 2. Dawn of A New Century

1 G. C. Bolton, *The Passing of the Irish Act of Union* (Oxford: Oxford University Press, 1966); David Wilkinson, 'How Did They Pass the Union? Secret Service Expenditure'. *History* 82, no. 266 (1997): 223–51.

2 Quoted in John Ehrman, *The Younger Pitt: The Consuming Struggle*, 187.

3 Richard Brinsley Sheridan, *Speech of Richard Brinsley Sheridan in the House of Commons* (31 January 1799) (Dublin: Printed for James Moore, 1799), 5.

4 W. E. H. Lecky, *A History of Ireland in the Eighteenth Century* (London: Longmans, Green & Co., 1892).

5 Boyd Hilton, *A Mad, Bad, and Dangerous People? England 1783–1846* (Oxford: Oxford University Press, 2008), 43.

6 Wilkinson, 'How Did They Pass the Union?', 223–251.

7 Hilton, *A Mad, Bad, and Dangerous People?*, 65.

8 His findings are generally supported. See Patrick M. Geoghegan, *The Irish Act of Union: A Study in High Politics, 1798–1801* (Dublin: Gill & Macmillan, 1999), 87 and William Hague, *William Pitt the Younger: A Biography* (London: HarperCollins, 2005), 454.

9 Paul Bew, *Ireland: The Politics of Enmity, 1789–2006* (Oxford: Oxford University Press, 2007), 61.

10 Oliver MacDonagh, *The Hereditary Bondsman: Daniel O'Connell, 1775–1829* (London: Weidenfeld & Nicolson, 1988), 94.

11 Geoghegan, *The Irish Act of Union*, ix.

12 Roy Foster, *Modern Ireland 1600–1972* (London: Penguin, 1988), 289.

13 Quoted in R. B. McDowell, *Ireland in the Age of Imperialism and Revolution, 1760–1800* (Oxford: Clarendon Press, 1979), 704.

14 J. C. Beckett, *Confrontations: Studies in Irish History* (London: Faber, 1972), 137.

15 Quoted in Hague, *William Pitt the Younger*, 454.

16 George III, 'Letter to William Pitt', February 1801, Public Records Office, *Chatham Papers*, C.IV.

17 Geoghegan, *The Irish Act of Union*, 226

18 Hilton, *A Mad, Bad, and Dangerous People?*, 97.

19 Beckett, *A Short History of Ireland* (London: Hutchinson, 1966), 132.

20 Liam Kennedy and D. S. Johnson, 'The Union of Ireland and Britain, 1800–1921', in *The Making of Modern Irish History: Revisionism and the Revisionist Controversy*, ed. D. G. Boyce and Alan O'Day (London: Routledge, 1996), 35.

21 Daniel O'Connell, *Correspondence of Daniel O'Connell* (London: John Murray, 1888), I: 426.

22 Beckett, *A Short History of Ireland*, 132.

23 Kennedy and Johnson, 'The Union of Ireland and Britain', 61–2.

24 Joel Mokyr, *Why Ireland Starved: A Quantitative and Analytical History of the Economy of Ireland, 1800 to 1850* (London: George Allen & Unwin, 1983).

25 Kennedy and Johnson, 'The Union of Ireland and Britain', 61.

26 Beckett, *Confrontations*, 138.

27 Patrick M. Geoghegan, 'Emmet, Robert', in *Dictionary of Irish Biography*, ed. James McGuire and James Quinn (Cambridge: Cambridge University Press, 2009).

28 J. G. A. Pocock, 'The Union in British History', in *Transactions of the Royal Historical Society*, vol. 10, 6th series (2000), 196.

29 Geoghegan, *The Irish Act of Union*, vii.

30 Beckett, A Short History of Ireland, 130.
31 See Chapters 4, 12, 15.

Chapter 3. Catholic Mobilisations

1 Thomas Bartlett, The Fall and Rise of the Irish Nation: The Catholic Question, 1690–1830 (Dublin: Gill & Macmillan, 1992), 317.

2 Patrick O'Farrell, 'The Irish in Australia and New Zealand, 1791–1870', in Ireland under the Union I: 1801–1870, vol. 5 of A New History of Ireland, ed. W. E. Vaughan and T. W. Moody (Oxford: Oxford University Press, 1989), 660–61.

3 Donal McCartney, 'The Changing Image of O'Connell', in Daniel O'Connell: Portrait of a Radical, ed. Kevin B. Nowlan and Maurice O'Connell (Belfast: Appletree Press, 1984), 29.

4 Paul Smith, Disraeli: A Brief Life (Cambridge: Cambridge University Press, 1996), 7.

5 McCartney, 'The Changing Image of O'Connell', 19.

6 Quoted in ibid., 19–20.

7 Oliver MacDonagh, The Emancipist: Daniel O'Connell, 1830–47 (London: Weidenfeld & Nicolson, 1989), 47; Robert Dudley Edwards, Daniel O'Connell and His World (London: Thames & Hudson, 1975).

8 Thomas Duddy, A History of Irish Thought (London and New York: Routledge), 214–17.

9 Fergus O'Ferrall, Catholic Emancipation: Daniel O'Connell and the Birth of Irish Democracy, 1820–1830 (Dublin: Gill & Macmillan, 1985).

10 R. V. Comerford, 'O'Connell, Daniel (1775–1847)', in Oxford Dictionary of National Biography (Oxford: Oxford University Press, 2004). Online edition October 2009: http://www.oxforddnb.com/index/20/101020501/ (accessed 2 September 2013).

11 Quoted in MacDonagh, The Hereditary Bondsman: Daniel O'Connell, 1775–1829 (London: Weidenfeld & Nicolson, 1988), 53.

12 McCartney, 'The Changing Image of O'Connell', 28.

13 MacDonagh, The Hereditary Bondsman, 57.

14 32 George III c.21.

15 See, for example, O'Connell's speech to House of Commons, 19 April 1831. Hansard. Online: http://hansard.millbanksystems.com/commons/1831/apr/19/parliamentary-reform-bill-committee#S3V0003P0_18310419_HOC_39 (accessed 2 September 2013).

16 MacDonagh, The Hereditary Bondsman, 104.

17 Quoted in MacDonagh, States of Mind: A Study of Anglo–Irish Conflict, 1780–1980 (London: Allen & Unwin, 1983), 24.

18 Northern Whig, 21 January 1841, quoted in Paul Bew, Ireland: The Politics of Enmity, 1789–2006 (Oxford: Oxford University Press, 2007), 152.

19 James Murphy, 'Fashioning the Famine Queen', in Victoria's Ireland? Irishness and Britishness, 1837–1901, ed. Peter Gray (Dublin: Four Courts Press, 2004), 15.

20 Bew, Ireland, 146.

21 O'Ferrall, Catholic Emancipation.

22 William Conyngham Plunket, speech to Parliament 'On Catholic Relief', 21 February 1821. Online: http://bartleby.com/268/6/13.html (accessed 28 August 2013).

23 O'Connell to the Catholics of Ireland, 1 January 1821, quoted in Patrick John Kenedy, The Life of Daniel O'Connell, the Liberator (New York: P. J. Kenedy, 1904), 458.

24 D. C. Boyce, *Nineteenth-Century Ireland: The Search for Stability* (Dublin: Gill & Macmillan, 1990), 39.

25 Quoted in MacDonagh, *The Hereditary Bondsman*, 206.

26 Boyce, *Nineteenth-Century Ireland*, 43.

27 Ibid., 38.

28 J. A. Reynolds, *The Catholic Emancipation Crisis in Ireland, 1823–29* (New Haven: Yale University Press, 1954), 43; O'Ferrall, *Catholic Emancipation*, xiv.

29 Quoted in Roy Foster, *Modern Ireland 1600–1972* (London: Penguin, 1988), 298.

30 MacDonagh, *The Hereditary Bondsman*, 210.

31 Reynolds, *The Catholic Emancipation Crisis*, 43.

32 O'Ferrall, *Catholic Emancipation*, 39.

Chapter 4. The Achievement of Emancipation

1 R. V. Comerford, 'O'Connell, Daniel (1775–1847)', in *Oxford Dictionary of National Biography* (Oxford: Oxford University Press, 2004). Online edition October 2009: http://www.oxforddnb.com/index/20/101020501/ (accessed 2 September 2013).

2 G. I. T. Machin, 'British Catholics', in *The Emancipation of Catholics, Jews and Protestants: Minorities and the Nation-State in Nineteenth Century Europe*, ed. Rainer Liedtke and Stephan Wendehorst (Manchester: Manchester University Press, 1999), 11.

3 See for example Fergus O'Ferrall, *Catholic Emancipation: Daniel O'Connell and the Birth of Irish Democracy, 1820–1830* (Dublin: Gill & Macmillan, 1985), xiv.

4 Scott Bennett, 'Catholic Emancipation, the "Quarterly Review", and Britain's Constitutional Revolution', *Victorian Studies* 12, no. 3 (1969): 285n4.

5 Wendy Hinde, *Catholic Emancipation: A Shake to Men's Minds* (Oxford: Blackwell, 1992).

6 Ibid., 187.

7 Richard W. Davis, 'Wellington and the "Open Question": The Issue of Catholic Emancipation, 1821–1829'. *Albion* 29, no. 1 (1997): 53.

8 Hinde, *Catholic Emancipation*, 187.

9 Rainer Liedtke and Stephan Wendehorst, eds, *The Emancipation of Catholics, Jews and Protestants: Minorities and the Nation-State in Nineteenth-Century Europe* (Manchester: Manchester University Press, 1999).

10 Ibid., 190–95.

11 O'Ferrall, *Catholic Emancipation*, xiii.

12 Thomas Bartlett, *The Fall and Rise of the Irish Nation: The Catholic Question, 1690–1830* (Dublin: Gill & Macmillan, 1992), 269.

13 J. A. Reynolds, *The Catholic Emancipation Crisis in Ireland, 1823–29* (New Haven: Yale University Press, 1954), 31.

14 O'Ferrall, *Catholic Emancipation*, 145–6, 170–74, 225, 269–77, 279–80.

15 See Boyd Hilton, *A Mad, Bad, and Dangerous People? England 1783–1846* (Oxford: Oxford University Press, 2008), 314–28 for a discussion of the divisions between so-called High and Liberal Toryism.

16 Daniel O'Connell, letter to the Knight of Kerry, 12 September 1829, in O'Connell, *Correspondence of Daniel O'Connell* (London: John Murray, 1888), I: 194.

17 See Hilton, *A Mad, Bad, and Dangerous People?*, 379–83.

18 Quoted in ibid., 383.

19 P. V. Fitzpatrick persuaded him. The idea of a Catholic running as a parliamentary candidate had first been raised by John Keogh.

20 O'Connell, 'Letter to Charles Sugrue', 14 May 1829, in O'Connell, *Correspondence*, I: 188.

21 Reynolds, *The Catholic Emancipation Crisis*, 51.

22 Comerford, 'O'Connell, Daniel (1775–1847)'.

23 O'Connell, 'O'Connell's Election Address' (1828). University College Cork, Multitext Project in Irish History. http://multitext.ucc.ie/d/OConnells_Election_Address_1828 (accessed 27 August 2013).

24 Ibid.

25 O'Connell, *The Memoirs, Private and Political of Daniel O'Connell, Esq., from the Year 1776 to the Close of the Proceedings in Parliament for the Repeal*, compiled from official documents by Robert Huish (London, 1836), 439.

26 In S. J. Connolly, 'Mass Politicisation and Sectarian Conflict, 1823–1830', in *Ireland under the Union I: 1801–1870*, vol. 5 of *A New History of Ireland*, ed. W. E. Vaughan and T. W. Moody (Oxford: Oxford University Press, 1989), 103.

27 Quoted in MacDonagh, *The Hereditary Bondsman: Daniel O'Connell, 1775–1829* (London: Weidenfeld & Nicolson, 1988), 255.

28 Robert Peel, 11 August 1828, cabinet memorandum to Wellington, quoted in Peel, *Sir Robert Peel: From his Private Papers*, vol. 2, ed. Charles Stuart Parker (London: John Murray, 1899), 55.

29 Roy Foster, *Modern Ireland 1600–1972* (London: Penguin, 1988), 301.

30 Peel, 11 August 1828, cabinet memorandum to Wellington, quoted in Peel, *Private Papers*, 55.

31 Peel, 5 March 1829, 'Speech on the Measure for the Removal of the Roman Catholic Disabilities', in Peel, *The Speeches of the Late Right Honourable Sir Robert Peel, Bart, Delivered in the House of Commons*, vol. 1, 1810–1829 (London: Routledge, 1853), 699.

32 Hinde, *Catholic Emancipation*, 92–3, 113–15.

33 10 Geo IV, c. 7 (13 April 1829).

34 Quoted in Eric J. Evans, *The Forging of the Modern State: Early Industrial Britain, 1783–1870*, 3rd ed. (Essex: Pearson Education, 2001), 258.

35 Christopher Hibbert, 'George IV (1762–1830)', *Oxford Dictionary of National Biography* (Oxford: Oxford University Press, 2004). Online edition January 2008: http://www.oxforddnb.com/index/10/101010541/ (accessed 2 September 2013).

36 Davis, 'Wellington and the "Open Question"', 54.

37 O'Connell, 'Letter to Charles Sugrue', 6 March 1829, in O'Connell, *Correspondence*, I: 174.

38 Liedtke and Wendehorst, eds, *The Emancipation of Catholics, Jews and Protestants*, 5.

39 Roy Foster, *Modern Ireland 1600–1972*, 302.

40 Evans, *The Forging of the Modern State*, 258.

41 O'Connell, 'Letter to James Sugrue', 12 March 1829, in O'Connell, *Correspondence*, I: 178. Emphasis in original. See also 6 March letter.

42 O'Connell, *Observations on the Corn Laws, on Political Pravity and Ingratitude* (Dublin: Samuel J. Machen, 1842), 11.

43 O'Ferrall, *Catholic Emancipation*, 38.

44 Hinde, *Catholic Emancipation*, 184.

45 Ibid., 185.

46 O'Ferrall, *Catholic Emancipation*, xiii.

47 Hinde, *Catholic Emancipation*, 185–6.

48 D. C. Boyce, *Nineteenth-Century Ireland: The Search for Stability* (Dublin: Gill & Macmillan, 1990), 54–5.

49 Hilton, *A Mad, Bad, and Dangerous People?*, 392–4.

50 In Evans, *The Forging of the Modern State*, 259.

51 Quoted in Hinde, *Catholic Emancipation*, 187.

52 Machin, 'British Catholics', 10.

53 O'Connell, 'Letter to James Sugrue', 14 May 1829, in O'Connell, *Correspondence*, I: 186. Emphasis in original.

Chapter 5. Ireland Under Whig Government

1 Oliver MacDonagh , 'The Age of O'Connell: 1830–45', in *Ireland under the Union I: 1801–1870*, vol. 5 of *A New History of Ireland*, ed. W. E. Vaughan and T. W. Moody (Oxford: Oxford University Press, 1989), 158.

2 Angus Macintyre, *The Liberator: Daniel O'Connell and the Irish Party, 1830–1847* (New York: Macmillan, 1965), xiv.

3 Ibid., xiv–vi; Robert Dudley Edwards, *Daniel O'Connell and His World* (London: Thames & Hudson, 1975), 44–5.

4 For example, see Dudley Edwards, *Daniel O'Connell and His World*, 69–88.

5 Dudley Edwards, *Daniel O'Connell and His World*, 55.

6 Daniel O'Connell, 'Letter to Thomas Davis', 30 October 1844, in O'Connell, *Correspondence of Daniel O'Connell* (London: John Murray, 1888), II: 339.

7 Dudley Edwards, *Daniel O'Connell and His World*, 47; Roy Foster, *Modern Ireland 1600–1972* (London: Penguin, 1988), 306.

8 Boyd Hilton, *A Mad, Bad, and Dangerous People? England 1783–1846* (Oxford: Oxford University Press, 2008), 430.

9 Macintyre, *The Liberator*, 20.

10 Ian Newbould, *Whiggery and Reform, 1830–41: The Politics of Government* (Stanford: Stanford University Press, 1990).

11 Peter Mandler, *Aristocratic Government in the Age of Reform: Whigs and Liberals, 1830–1852* (Oxford: Clarendon Press, 1990), 2.

12 O'Connell, 'Letter to Lord Dunham', 21 October 1834, in O'Connell, *Correspondence*, I: 498. 'Letter to Lord Dunham', 21 October 1834.

13 Wendy Hinde, *Catholic Emancipation: A Shake to Men's Minds* (Oxford: Blackwell, 1992), 185.

14 Newbould, *Whiggery and Reform*, 297, also 293–8.

15 Hilton, *A Mad, Bad, and Dangerous People?*, 540.

16 Macintyre, *The Liberator*, 28.

17 Quoted in Hilton, *A Mad, Bad, and Dangerous People?*, 495.

18 Ibid., 495.

19 MacDonagh, *The Hereditary Bondsman: Daniel O'Connell, 1775–1829* (London: Weidenfeld & Nicolson, 1988), 273.

20 Patrick M. Geoghegan, *King Dan: The Rise of Daniel O'Connell 1775–1829* (Dublin: Gill & Macmillan), 28.

21 Paul Bew, *Ireland: The Politics of Enmity, 1789–2006* (Oxford: Oxford University Press, 2007), 125.

22 Hilton, *A Mad, Bad, and Dangerous People?*, 384.

23 Paul Adelman and Robert Pearce, *Great Britain and the Irish Question, 1798–1922*, 3rd ed. (London: Hodder & Stoughton, 2008), 38.

24 Dudley Edwards, *Daniel O'Connell and His World*, 44.

25 Cited in Bew, *Ireland*, 127.

26 Hilton, *A Mad, Bad, and Dangerous People?*, 538, for example, talks of the rise of a Catholic middle class in this decade.

27 Mandler, *Aristocratic Government*.

28 O'Connell, 'Letter to the King of Kerry', 6 February 1829, in O'Connell, *Correspondence*, IV: 7.

29 Eric J. Evans, *The Forging of the Modern State: Early Industrial Britain, 1783–1870*, 3rd ed. (Essex: Pearson Education, 2001), 483.

30 He would later become fourth Earl of Derby and prime minister three times.

31 Macintyre, *The Liberator*, 29.

32 Gearóid Ó Tuathaigh, *Ireland before the Famine, 1798–1848* (Dublin: Gill & Macmillan, 1972), 172.

33 Hilton, *A Mad, Bad, and Dangerous People?*, 496.

34 Ibid., 496–7.

35 Dudley Edwards, *Daniel O'Connell and His World*, 44.

36 See entry on 'Coercion Acts', in S. J. Connolly, ed., *Oxford Companion to Irish History* (Oxford: Oxford University Press, 2002), 101–2.

37 Charles Townshend's *Political Violence in Ireland: Government and Resistance since 1848* (Oxford: Clarendon Press, 1983) is the classic study of political violence in Ireland after 1848. See also David P. Nally, *Human Encumbrances: Political Violence and the Great Irish Famine* (Notre Dame, IN: University of Notre Dame Press, 2011).

38 Max Weber, 'Politics as a Vocation', in *Max Weber: Essays in Sociology* (New York: Oxford University Press, 1946).

39 Thomas More, quoted in Fergus O'Ferrall, *Catholic Emancipation: Daniel O'Connell and the Birth of Irish Democracy, 1820–1830* (Dublin: Gill & Macmillan, 1985), xiv.

40 O'Connell, *The Memoirs, Private and Political of Daniel O'Connell, Esq., from the Year 1776 to the Close of the Proceedings in Parliament for the Repeal*, compiled from official documents by Robert Huish (London, 1836), 508.

41 Newbould, *Whiggery and Reform*, 296–7.

42 Quoted in Roy Foster, *Modern Ireland 1600–1972* (London: Penguin, 1988), 294.

43 L. P. Curtis, *Anglo-Saxons and Celts: A Study of Anti-Irish Prejudice in Victorian England* (New York: New York University Press, 1968), 47, 3.

44 MacDonagh, *States of Mind: A Study of Anglo–Irish Conflict, 1780–1980* (London: Allen & Unwin, 1983), 42.

45 Christopher Clark, *Iron Kingdom: The Rise and Downfall of Prussia, 1600–1947* (London: Allen Lane, 2006), 465–6.

46 Foster, *Modern Ireland 1600–1972*, 292.

47 Mary Daly, *The Famine in Ireland* (Dundalk: Dublin Historical Association, 1986), 28–9.

48 Quoted in Nally, *Human Encumbrances*, 99.

49 Quoted in W. E. H. Lecky, *Leaders of Public Opinion in Ireland* (New York: Appleton & Company, 1876), 264.

50 Dudley Edwards, *Daniel O'Connell and His World*, 70.

51 MacDonagh, *The Emancipist: Daniel O'Connell, 1830–47* (London: Weidenfeld & Nicolson, 1989), 119.

52 See page 54.

53 See Eric J. Evans, *Sir Robert Peel: Statesmanship, Power and Party* (London: Routledge, 1991), 39–47.

54 Bew, *Ireland*, 143.

55 John Russell, *Selections from Speeches of Earl Russell 1817 to 1841* (London: Longmans, Green & Co., 1870), 17.

56 For comments on his role, see, for example, Dudley Edwards, *Daniel O'Connell and His World*, 56–7.

57 Bew, *Ireland*, 150.

58 Peter Gibbon, *The Origins of Ulster Unionism: The Formation of Popular Protestant Politics and Ideology in Nineteenth-Century Ireland* (Manchester: Manchester University Press, 1975), 66.

59 Hilton, *A Mad, Bad, and Dangerous People?*, 539.

60 MacDonagh, *The Emancipist: Daniel O'Connell, 1830–47* (London: Weidenfeld & Nicolson, 1989), 163–8 discusses O'Connell's dealings with the Dublin Protestant artisans.

61 Dudley Edwards, *Daniel O'Connell and His World*, 53.

62 Foster, *Modern Ireland 1600–1972*, 306.

63 Donal McCartney, 'The Changing Image of O'Connell', in *Daniel O'Connell: Portrait of a Radical*, ed. Kevin B. Nowlan and Maurice O'Connell (Belfast: Appletree Press, 1984), 29.

64 Liam Kennedy and D. S. Johnson, 'The Union of Ireland and Britain, 1800–1921', in *The Making of Modern Irish History: Revisionism and the Revisionist Controversy*, ed. D. G. Boyce and Alan O'Day (London: Routledge, 1996), 36.

Chapter 6. The Campaign for Repealing Union

1 Oliver MacDonagh, *The Emancipist: Daniel O'Connell, 1830–47* (London: Weidenfeld & Nicolson, 1989), x.

2 See pages 79–86.

3 Robert Dudley Edwards, *Daniel O'Connell and His World* (London: Thames & Hudson, 1975), 72, reprints an image taken from the edition of *Punch* in question.

4 L. P. Curtis, *Anglo-Saxons and Celts: A Study of Anti-Irish Prejudice in Victorian England* (New York: New York University Press, 1968), 52–3.

5 MacDonagh, *The Emancipist*, 224.

6 Dudley Edwards, *Daniel O'Connell and His World*, 70.

7 MacDonagh, *States of Mind: A Study of Anglo–Irish Conflict, 1780–1980* (London: Allen & Unwin, 1983), 59.

8 Dudley Edwards, *Daniel O'Connell and His World*, 83.

9 Boyd Hilton, *A Mad, Bad, and Dangerous People? England 1783–1846* (Oxford: Oxford University Press, 2008), 539.

10 O'Connell on 14 May 1843, quoted in Paul Adelman and Robert Pearce, *Great Britain and the Irish Question, 1798–1922*, 3rd ed. (London: Hodder & Stoughton, 2008), 43.

11 D. C. Boyce, *Nineteenth-Century Ireland: The Search for Stability* (Dublin: Gill & Macmillan, 1990), 74.

12 Quoted in Adelman and Pearce, *Great Britain*, 42.

13 O'Connell, speech in Galway, 17 September 1843, quoted in John Flanedy, ed., *A Special Report of the Proceedings in the Case of the Queen against Daniel O'Connell [...] on an indictment for Conspiracy and Misdemeanour* (Dublin: James Duffy, 1844), 145.

14 MacDonagh, *The Hereditary Bondsman: Daniel O'Connell, 1775–1829* (London: Weidenfeld & Nicolson, 1988), 104.

15 Quoted in MacDonagh, *States of Mind*, 57.

16 Roy Foster, *Modern Ireland 1600–1972* (London: Penguin, 1988), 308.

17 Kevin B. Nowlan and Maurice O'Connell, eds, *Daniel O'Connell: Portrait of a Radical* (Belfast: Appletree Press, 1984), 3.

18 Adelman and Pearce, *Great Britain*, 43; MacDonagh, *States of Mind*, 58.

19 MacDonagh, *States of Mind*, 57; MacDonagh, *The Emancipist*, 226–43 deals with the mass meetings.

20 MacDonagh, 'Review', *Victorian Studies* 27, no. 4 (1984): 526.

21 Foster, *Modern Ireland 1600–1972*, 313.

22 Nowlan and O'Connell, eds, *Daniel O'Connell*, 18.

23 See pages 75–86.

24 Fergus O'Ferrall, *Catholic Emancipation: Daniel O'Connell and the Birth of Irish Democracy, 1820–1830* (Dublin: Gill & Macmillan, 1985), xiv.

25 Quoted in Wendy Hinde, *Catholic Emancipation: A Shake to Men's Minds* (Oxford: Blackwell, 1992), 184.

26 Gearóid Ó Tuathaigh, 'O'Connell, Daniel', in *Dictionary of Irish Biography*, ed. James McGuire and James Quinn (Cambridge: Cambridge University Press, 2009).

27 Dudley Edwards, *Daniel O'Connell and His World*, 76.

28 Quoted in J. A. Reynolds, *The Catholic Emancipation Crisis in Ireland, 1823–29* (New Haven: Yale University Press, 1954), 37.

29 John Mitchel, *Jail Journal* (Dublin: M. H. Gill & Son, 1913).

30 For instance, see the revisionist viewpoint in Dudley Edwards, *Daniel O'Connell and His World*, 86.

31 O'Connell to the House of Commons ,1832, quoted in MacDonagh, *The Emancipist*, 136.

32 Quoted in Nowlan and O'Connell, eds, *Daniel O'Connell*, 27.

33 MacDonagh, *The Hereditary Bondsman*, 3.

34 Ó Tuathaigh, 'O'Connell, Daniel'.

35 Richard P. Davis, *The Young Ireland Movement* (Dublin: Gill & Macmillan, 1988), 235–6 undermines the traditional view somewhat and quotes a speech where O'Connell is urging people in Skibereen to use 'your proper language' rather than the 'vulgar Saxon tongue'.

36 Reynolds, *The Catholic Emancipation Crisis*, 47.

37 O'Ferrall, *Catholic Emancipation*, 289.

38 Dudley Edwards, *Daniel O'Connell and His World*, 81–3; Ó Tuathaigh, 'O'Connell, Daniel'.

39 See page 65.

40 Thomas Duddy, *A History of Irish Thought* (London and New York: Routledge), 215–18.

41 Ó Tuathaigh, 'O'Connell, Daniel'.

42 K. Theodore Hoppen, 'Review of Books', *Albion: A Quarterly Journal Concerned with British Studies* 19, no. 1 (1987): 153.

43 Ibid., 153.

44 MacDonagh, *The Emancipist*, x.

45 Reynolds, *The Catholic Emancipation Crisis*, 32.

46 Quoted in Ó Tuathaigh, 'O'Connell, Daniel'.

47 Dudley Edwards, *Daniel O'Connell and His World*, 75.

48 Paul Bew, *Ireland: The Politics of Enmity, 1789–2006* (Oxford: Oxford University Press, 2007), 126.

49 Conor Cruise O'Brien, 'Foreword', in Maurice O'Connell, *Daniel O'Connell: The Man and His Politics* (Dublin: Irish Academic Press, 1990).

Chapter 7. The Age of Peel

1 Roy Foster, *Modern Ireland 1600–1972* (London: Penguin, 1988), 310.
2 Robert Dudley Edwards, *Daniel O'Connell and His World* (London: Thames & Hudson, 1975), 62.
3 Richard P. Davis, *The Young Ireland Movement* (Dublin: Gill & Macmillan, 1988), 1.
4 Boyd Hilton, *A Mad, Bad, and Dangerous People? England 1783–1846* (Oxford: Oxford University Press, 2008), 541.
5 Oliver MacDonagh, *States of Mind: A Study of Anglo–Irish Conflict, 1780–1980* (London: Allen & Unwin, 1983), 161.
6 Foster, *Modern Ireland 1600–1972*, 311.
7 Davis, *The Young Ireland Movement*, 232.
8 F. S. L. Lyons, *Ireland since the Famine* (London: HarperCollins, 1973), 108–9.
9 James Quinn, 'Mitchel, John', in *Dictionary of Irish Biography*, ed. James McGuire and James Quinn (Cambridge: Cambridge University Press, 2009).
10 Christine Kinealy, *Repeal and Revolution: 1848 in Ireland* (Manchester and New York: Manchester University Press, 2009); Robert Sloan, *William Smith O'Brien and the Young Ireland Rebellion of 1848* (Dublin: Four Courts Press, 2000).
11 Kinealy, *Repeal and Revolution*, 292.
12 Lyons, *Ireland since the Famine*, 105, 112.
13 Ibid., 111.
14 John Molony, 'Davis, Thomas Osborne', in *Dictionary of Irish Biography*, ed. James McGuire and James Quinn (Cambridge: Cambridge University Press, 2009).
15 John Mitchel, *Jail Journal* (Dublin: M. H. Gill & Son, 1913).
16 James Quinn, 'Mitchel, John'.
17 MacDonagh, 'Ideas and Institutions, 1830–1845', in *Ireland under the Union I: 1801–1870*, vol. 5 of *A New History of Ireland*, ed. W. E. Vaughan and T. W. Moody (Oxford: Oxford University Press, 1989), 199.
18 Norman Gash, *Politics in the Age of Peel: A Study of the Technique of Parliamentary Representation, 1830–1850* (London: Longmans, Green & Co., 1953); *Mr Secretary Peel: The Life of Sir Peel to 1830* (London: Longmans, 1961); *Sir Robert Peel: The Life of Sir Robert Peel after 1830* (Harlow: Longman, 1972).
19 Gash, *Mr Secretary Peel*, 13–14.
20 Hilton, 'Peel: A Reappraisal', *Historical Journal* 22, no. 3 (1979): 589.
21 Hilton, *A Mad, Bad, and Dangerous People?*, 392–4.
22 Quoted in Eric J. Evans, *The Forging of the Modern State: Early Industrial Britain, 1783–1870*, 3rd ed. (Essex: Pearson Education, 2001), 307.
23 Robert Peel 'Speech to the Commons', 9 May 1843. *Hansard*. Online: http://hansard.millbanksystems.com/commons/1843/may/09/union-with-ireland#S3V0069P0_18430509_HOC_7 (accessed 29 August 2013). See also a much earlier speech, dated 15 April 1834, in which he declared that repeal 'must make Great Britain a fourth-rate power of Europe, and Ireland a savage wilderness'. *Hansard*. Online: http://hansard.millbanksystems.com/commons/1834/apr/25/repeal-of-the-union-adjourned-debate#S3V0023P0_18340425_HOC_35. (accessed 29 August 2013).

24 Evans, *The Forging of the Modern State*, 315.

25 Quoted in Hilton, *A Mad, Bad, and Dangerous People?*, 541.

26 Quoted in Donal Kerr, *Peel, Priests and Politics: Sir Robert Peel's Administration and the Roman Catholic Church in Ireland, 1841–46* (Oxford: Clarendon Press, 1982), 121.

27 Hilton, *A Mad, Bad, and Dangerous People?*, 542–3.

28 MacDonagh, *The Emancipist: Daniel O'Connell, 1830–47* (London: Weidenfeld & Nicolson, 1989), 263; Hilton, *A Mad, Bad, and Dangerous People?*, 542.

29 Hilton, *A Mad, Bad, and Dangerous People?*, 541; Peter Gray, *Famine, Land and Politics: British Government and Irish Society, 1843–1850* (Dublin: Irish Academic Press, 1999), 55–94.

30 Quoted in Thomas Bartlett, *Ireland: A History* (Cambridge: Cambridge University Press, 2010), 279.

31 Lyons, *Ireland since the Famine*, 94.

32 Colin Barr's, *Paul Cullen, John Henry Newman and the Catholic University of Ireland, 1845–1865* (Notre Dame, IN: University of Notre Dame Press, 2003) is the most recent full-length history of the Catholic University of Ireland and the reasons why the Newman–Cullen project failed.

33 Peel, cabinet memorandum, 17 February 1844, quoted in Hilton, *A Mad, Bad, and Dangerous People?*, 541.

34 Hilton, *A Mad, Bad, and Dangerous People?*, 532.

35 Quoted in Evans, *Sir Robert Peel: Statesmanship, Power and Party*, 2nd ed. (Abingdon: Routledge, 2006), 315.

36 Hilton, *A Mad, Bad, and Dangerous People?*, 542.

37 Foster, *Modern Ireland 1600–1972*, 315.

38 Hilton, 'Peel: A Reappraisal', 614.

39 Hilton, *A Mad, Bad, and Dangerous People?*, 554.

40 Evans, *Sir Robert Peel* (2006), 72.

41 Peel, speech to Commons 15 May 1846. *Hansard*. Online: http://hansard. millbanksystems.com/commons/1846/may/15/com-importation-bill-adjourned-debate#S3V0086P0_18460515_HOC_31 (accessed 29 August 2013).

42 R. V. Comerford, 'O'Connell, Daniel (1775–1847)', in *Oxford Dictionary of National Biography* (Oxford: Oxford University Press, 2004). Online edition October 2009: http://www.oxforddnb.com/index/20/101020501/ (accessed 2 September 2013).

43 MacDonagh, 'Review', *Victorian Studies* 27, no. 4 (1984): 526.

44 Kerr, *Peel, Priests and Politics*, 356.

45 Ibid., 306.

Chapter 8. Explaining the Famine

1 Pierre Nora, ed., *Les Lieux de Mémoire*, vol. 1: *La République* (Paris: Gallimard, 1984), vii–xlii.

2 Cormac Ó Gráda, 'Making History in Ireland in the 1940s and 1950s: The Sage of *The Grand Famine*', in *Interpreting Irish History: The Debate on historical Revisionism*, ed. Ciaran Brady (Dublin: Irish Academic Press, 1994), 284.

3 Cecil Woodham-Smith, *The Great Hunger: Ireland 1845–1849* (London: Hamish Hamilton, 1962), 407.

4 J. S. Donnelly, 'The Administration of Relief, 1847–51', in *Ireland under the Union I: 1801–1870*, vol. 5 of *A New History of Ireland*, ed. W. E. Vaughan and T. W. Moody (Oxford: Oxford University Press, 1989), 330.

5 State of New Jersey Education Department, 'New Jersey Commission on Holocaust Education'. Online: http://www.state.nj.us/education/holocaust/curriculum/ (accessed 29 August 2013).

6 This incident is quoted in Ó Gráda, *Ireland Before and After the Famine* (Manchester: Manchester University Press, 1988), 80.

7 Roy Foster, *Modern Ireland 1600–1972* (London: Penguin, 1988), 320.

8 L. M. Cullen, *An Economic History of Ireland since 1660* (London: Batsford, 1972).

9 Robert Dudley Edwards and T. Desmond Williams, eds, *The Great Famine: Studies in Irish History 1845–52* (Dublin: Browne and Nolan, 1956), vii.

10 Robert Dudley Edwards' academic diary, 11 September 1952, quoted in Ó Gráda, 'Making History in Ireland', 286; Dudley Edwards and Williams, *The Great Famine*.

11 Brendan Bradshaw, 'Nationalism and Historical Scholarship in Modern Ireland', in *Interpreting Irish History: The Debate on Historical Revisionism*, ed. Ciaran Brady (Dublin: Irish Academic Press, 1994). This was first published in an article in *Irish Historical Studies* in 1988–89 and later republished as an essay in Brady's collected volume investigating revisionism.

12 Bradshaw, 'Nationalism and Historical Scholarship', 204.

13 Ibid., 205.

14 Ó Gráda, 'Making History in Ireland', 278.

15 Ó Gráda, *Ireland Before and After the Famine*, 80.

16 Amartya Sen, *Poverty and Famines: An Essay on Entitlement and Deprivation* (Oxford: Clarendon Press, 1981), 1. Emphasis in original.

17 Gearóid Ó Tuathaigh, *Ireland before the Famine, 1798–1848* (Dublin: Gill & Macmillan, 1972), 127.

18 Cullen, *An Economic History*, 101.

19 Mary Daly, *The Famine in Ireland* (Dundalk: Dublin Historical Association, 1986), 21.

20 K. H. Connell, *The Population of Ireland, 1750–1845* (Oxford: Clarendon Press, 1950).

21 Daly, *The Famine in Ireland*, 4.

22 Ibid., 2.

23 Ibid., 5.

24 Ó Gráda, *Ireland Before and After the Famine: Explorations in Economic History, 1800–1925*, 2nd ed. (Manchester: Manchester University Press, 1993), 18.

25 Foster, *Modern Ireland 1600–1972*, 319.

26 Ó Gráda, *Ireland Before and After the Famine*, 17.

27 Potatoes in the morning, potatoes at noon, and if we wake in the middle of the night, we'll get potatoes again.

Chapter 9. Response to Famine

1 Christine Kinealy, *The Great Empire: Impact, Ideology and Rebellion* (Basingstoke: Palgrave, 2002), 33.

2 Peter Gray, *Famine, Land and Politics: British Government and Irish Society, 1843–1850* (Dublin: Irish Academic Press, 1999); David P. Nally, *Human Encumbrances: Political Violence and the Great Irish Famine* (Indiana: University of Notre Dame Press, 2011).

3 Russell announcing his programme for Ireland in 1846, quoted in Kinealy, *The Great Empire*, 36.

4 Nally, *Human Encumbrances*, viii. See also Gray, *Famine, Land and Politics* for an intellectual history of responses to the famine.

5 Amartya Sen, *Poverty and Famines: An Essay on Entitlement and Deprivation* (Oxford: Clarendon Press, 1981).

6 Nally, *Human Encumbrances*, 134.

7 Gearóid Ó Tuathaigh, *Ireland before the Famine, 1798–1848* (Dublin: Gill & Macmillan, 1972), 219.

8 G. C. Boase, 'Trevelyan, Sir Charles Edward, first baronet (1807–1886)', rev. David Washbrook, in *Oxford Dictionary of National Biography* (Oxford: Oxford University Press, 2004). Online edition January 2010: http://www.oxforddnb.com/view/printable/27716 (accessed 2 September 2013).

9 Quoted in David Steele, 'Villiers, George William Frederick, fourth earl of Clarendon (1800–1870)', in *Oxford Dictionary of National Biography* (Oxford: Oxford University Press, 2004); online edition May 2009: http://www.oxforddnb.com/index/28/101028297/ (accessed 29 August 2013).

10 Ibid.

11 Quoted in J. S. Donnelly, 'The Administration of Relief 1846–47', in *Ireland under the Union I: 1801–1870*, vol. 5 of *A New History of Ireland*, ed. W. E. Vaughan and T. W. Moody (Oxford: Oxford University Press, 1989), 297. Emphasis in original.

12 Ibid., 299.

13 Ibid., 296–7.

14 Donal Kerr, *The Catholic Church and the Famine* (Blackrock: Columba Press, 1996) discusses this phenomenon, 83–9.

15 Quoted in Justin Huntly McCarthy, *Ireland since the Union: Sketches of Irish History from 1798 to 1886* (London: Chatto & Windus, 1887), 141.

16 Joel Mokyr, *Why Ireland Starved: A Quantitative and Analytical History of the Economy of Ireland, 1800 to 1850* (London: George Allen & Unwin, 1983), 263–8.

17 For his proposal about railways, see Lord G. Bentinck, speech to the House of Commons , 4 February 1847, *Hansard*. Online: http://hansard.millbanksystems.com/commons/1847/feb/04/railways-ireland (accessed 20 January 2013).

18 Lord John Russell, speech to the House of Commons, 4 February 1847, *Hansard*. Online: http://hansard.millbanksystems.com/commons/1847/feb/04/railways-ireland (accessed 20 January 2013). See also the 11 February debate.

19 Gray, *Famine, Land and Politics*, viii.

20 Hilton, *The Age of Atonement: The Influence of Evangelicalism on Social and Economic Thought, 1785–1865* (Oxford: Clarendon Press, 1992).

21 Trevelyan, 15 January 1848, quoted in J. Hart, 'Sir Charles Trevelyan at the Treasury', *English Historical Review* 85 (1960): 99.

22 Quoted in Kinealy, *The Great Empire*, 4.

23 Quoted in Cormac Ó Gráda, *Ireland Before and After the Famine: Explorations in Economic History, 1800–1925*, 2nd ed. (Manchester: Manchester University Press, 1993), 127.

24 Anthony Trollope, *Castle Richmond* (New York: Harper & Brothers, 1860), 471–2.

25 Ó Gráda, *Ireland Before and After the Famine* (Manchester: Manchester University Press, 1988), 113.

26 Gray, *Famine, Land and Politics*, 331.

Chapter 10. Post-Famine Ireland

1 F. S. L. Lyons, *Ireland since the Famine* (London: HarperCollins, 1973), 16.

2 R. V. Comerford, 'Churchmen, Tenants and Independent Opposition, 1850–56', in *Ireland under the Union I: 1801–1870*, vol. 5 of *A New History of Ireland*, edited by W. E. Vaughan and T. W. Moody (Oxford: Oxford University Press, 1989); Joseph Lee, *The Modernisation of Irish Society, 1848–1918* (Dublin: Gill & Macmillan, 1973).

3 D. H. Akenson, *The Irish Diaspora: A Primer* (Belfast: The Institute of Irish Studies, Queen's University, 1993); Comerford, *The Fenians in Context: Irish Politics and Society, 1848–82* (Dublin: Wolfhound Press, 1985); T. W. Moody, ed., *The Fenian Movement* (Dublin: Mercier Press, 1968).

4 Akenson, *The Irish Diaspora*, 142. This whole chapter deals with Ireland and the Empire, 141–51.

5 Comerford, 'Ireland 1850–70: Post-Famine and Mid-Victorian', in *Ireland under the Union I*, ed. Vaughan and Moody; Peter Gray, ed., *Victoria's Ireland Irishness and Britishness, 1837–1901* (Dublin: Four Courts Press, 2004).

6 Lee, *The Modernisation of Irish Society*.

7 Tom Garvin, *Nationalist Revolutionaries in Ireland 1858–1928* (Oxford: Clarendon Press, 1987), 3.

8 James Murphy, 'Fashioning the Famine Queen', in *Victoria's Ireland?*, ed. Gray, 18.

9 L. M. Cullen, *An Economic History of Ireland since 1660* (London: Batsford, 1972).

10 Ibid.

11 Quoted in Lyons, *Ireland since the Famine*, 44.

12 Terence Brown, *Ireland: A Social and Cultural History, 1922–2002* (London: Harper Perennial, 2004), 18.

13 Lyons, *Ireland since the Famine*, 45.

14 David Fitzpatrick, '"A Peculiar Tramping People": The Irish in Britain, 1801–70', in *Ireland under the Union I*, ed. Vaughan and Moody (Oxford: Oxford University Press, 1989), 627.

15 Eric J. Evans, *The Forging of the Modern State: Early Industrial Britain, 1783–1870*, 3rd ed. (Essex: Pearson Education, 2001), 454.

16 Fitzpatrick, '"A Peculiar Tramping People"', 626.

17 Akenson, *The Irish Diaspora*, 272, 157–87.

18 Patrick O'Farrell, 'The Irish in Australia and New Zealand, 1791–1870', in *Ireland under the Union I*, ed. Vaughan and Moody, 672.

19 R. Ford, ed. *Popular Irish Readings in Prose and Verse* (Paisley and London: Alexander Gardener, 1897), 121.

20 L. P. Curtis, *Anglo-Saxons and Celts: A Study of Anti-Irish Prejudice in Victorian England* (New York: New York University Press, 1968).

21 Evans, *The Forging of the Modern State*, 455.

22 Ibid., 456.

23 David Noel Doyle, 'The Irish in North America, 1776–1845', in *Ireland under the Union I*, ed. Vaughan and Moody (Oxford: Oxford University Press, 1989), 684.

24 Roy Foster, *Modern Ireland 1600–1972* (London: Penguin, 1988), 341.

25 Brown, *Ireland*, 19.

26 Lyons, *Ireland since the Famine*, 52.

27 Comerford, 'Ireland 1850–70', 381.

28 Howard died in 1864; Palmerston continued as prime minister until his death in 1865.

29 Quoted in Paul Bew, *Ireland: The Politics of Enmity, 1789–2006* (Oxford: Oxford University Press, 2007), 241.

30 Comerford, 'Churchmen, Tenants and Independent Opposition'.

31 Quoted in Foster, *Modern Ireland 1600–1972*, 298.

32 J. C. Beckett, *A Short History of Ireland* (London: Hutchinson, 1966), 147.

33 Bew, *Ireland*, 242.

34 Emmet Larkin, *The Consolidation of the Roman Catholic Church in Ireland, 1860–1870* (Dublin: Gill & Macmillan, 1987).

35 Donal Kerr, *The Catholic Church and the Famine* (Blackrock: Columba Press, 1996), 56.

36 Comerford, 'Ireland 1850–70', 387.

37 Larkin, *Consolidation of the Roman Catholic Church*, xv–vii.

38 Brown, *Ireland*, 25.

39 Lyons, *Ireland since the Famine*, 43.

40 Akenson, *The Irish Diaspora*, 9.

Chapter 11. Mid-Victorian Ireland

1 A German traveller, Johann Georg Kohl's, comments on visiting Ireland in 1842, quoted in Richard P. Davis, *The Young Ireland Movement* (Dublin: Gill & Macmillan, 1988), 9.

2 R. V. Comerford, 'Ireland 1850–70: Post-Famine and Mid-Victorian', in *Ireland under the Union I: 1801–1870*, vol. 5 of *A New History of Ireland*, ed. W. E. Vaughan and T. W. Moody (Oxford: Oxford University Press, 1989); Peter Gray, ed., *Victoria's Ireland Irishness and Britishness, 1837–1901* (Dublin: Four Courts Press, 2004).

3 As against that, note Arthur Balfour's cynical comment about her 1900 visit. 'No one can suppose she goes to Ireland for pleasure', Balfour to Lord Salisbury, 7 March 1900, quoted in L. P. Curtis, *Coercion and Conciliation in Ireland, 1880–1892: A Study in Conservative Unionism* (Princeton: Princeton University Press, 1963), 419.

4 Christine Casey, *The Buildings of Ireland: Dublin* (New Haven: Yale University Press, 2005), 64.

5 Alvin Jackson, 'Irish Unionism, 1870–1922', in *Defenders of the Union: A Survey of British and Irish Unionism since 1801*, ed. D. G. Boyce and Alan O'Day (London: Routledge, 2001), 116.

6 Thomas Flanagan, 'Literature in English, 1801–91', in *Ireland under the Union I: 1801–1870*, vol. 5 of *A New History of Ireland*, ed. W. E. Vaughan and T. W. Moody (Oxford: Oxford University Press, 1989), 499.

7 Benedict Anderson, *Imagined Communities: Reflections on the Origins and Spread of Nationalism* (London: Verso, 1983), 115.

8 See pages 179–82.

9 D. H. Akenson, 'Pre-University Education, 1782–1870', in *Ireland under the Union I*, ed. Vaughan and Moody, 536.

10 Comerford, 'Ireland 1850–70', 375.

11 Asa Briggs, *Victorian Things* (London: Batsford, 1988).

12 Comerford, 'Ireland 1850–70', 378.

13 Casey, *The Buildings of Ireland*, 71.

14 Michael Billig, *Banal Nationalism* (London: Sage, 1995).

15 Jackson, 'Irish Unionism, 1870–1922', 121.

16 *Nation*, 3 June 1865, 11, quoted in University College Dublin School of Archeology, 'Heritage Council Report on St. Stephen's Green Dublin South Inner City'. Online: http://www.ucd.ie/archaeology/documentstore/hc_reports/lod/st_stephens_green_final.pdf (accessed 28 July 2013).

17 Comerford, 'Ireland 1850–70', 390.

18 W. E. Vaughan, 'Ireland c.1870', in *Ireland under the Union I*, ed. Vaughan and Moody, 763.

19 Tom Garvin, *Nationalist Revolutionaries in Ireland 1858–1928* (Oxford: Clarendon Press, 1987), 1.

20 Comerford, *The Fenians in Context: Irish Politics and Society, 1848–82* (Dublin: Wolfhound Press, 1985), 8; ibid., 2.

21 Charles Townshend, *Political Violence in Ireland: Government and Resistance since 1848* (Oxford: Clarendon Press, 1983), 27.

22 Garvin, *Nationalist Revolutionaries*, 34.

23 Paul Bew, *Ireland: The Politics of Enmity, 1789–2006* (Oxford: Oxford University Press, 2007), 245.

24 Garvin, *Nationalist Revolutionaries*, 35.

25 Sean Cronin, *Marx and the Irish Question* (Dublin: Repsol Publications, 1977), 3. Marx was the *Tribune*'s English correspondent 1851–61.

26 Anthony Coughlan, 'Ireland's Marxist Historians', in *Interpreting Irish History: The Debate on Historical Revisionism*, ed. Ciaran Brady (Dublin: Irish Academic Press, 1994), 291.

27 Marx's speech to the German Workers' Educational Society in London, 16 December 1867. Online: http://www.marxists.org/history/international/iwma/documents/1867/irish-speech.htm (accessed 29 October 2013).

28 See, for instance, comments on this in Garvin, *Nationalist Revolutionaries*, 127.

29 Quoted in Cronin, *Marx and the Irish Question*, 28.

30 For more coverage of the 1867 rising see T. W. Moody, ed., *The Fenian Movement* (Dublin: Mercier Press, 1968) and Comerford, *Fenians in Context* .

31 Quoted in Leon Ó Broin, *Fenian Fever: An Anglo-American Dilemma* (London: Chatto & Windus, 1971), 133.

32 Robert Kee, *The Bold Fenian Men* (London: Quartet Books, 1972), 48.

33 A copy of the whole song may be found in Patrick John Kenedy, *The Universal Irish Song Book: A Complete Collection of the Songs and Ballads of Ireland* (New York: P. J. Kenedy, 1884), 53.

34 Garvin, *Nationalist Revolutionaries*, 33.

Chapter 12. Gladstone's First Mission

1 John Morley, *The Life of William Ewart Gladstone* (London: Macmillan, 1903); J. L. Hammond, 'Preface', *Gladstone and the Irish Nation* (London: Frank Cass & Co., 1964).

2 John Vincent, 'Gladstone and Ireland', *Proceedings of the British Academy* 63 (1977): 228.

3 Michael Winstanley, *Gladstone and the Liberal Party* (London: Routledge, 1990), 17–18.

4 Richard Shannon, *Gladstone*, 2 vols (London: Penguin, 1999), II: xv.

5 Shannon, *Gladstone: God and Politics* (London: Hambledon Continuum, 2008), 378.

6 D. G. Boyce, 'Introduction: Tract for the Times? The Enduring Appeal of Gladstone and Ireland', in *Gladstone and Ireland: Politics, Religion, and Nationality in the Victorian Age*, ed. D. G. Boyce and Alan O'Day (Basingstoke: Palgrave Macmillan, 2010), 1 notes this general view.

7 Ibid., 5.

8 Shannon, *Gladstone*, II: 57.

9 Winstanley, *Gladstone and the Liberal Party*, 29.

10 Eugenio Biagini, *Gladstone* (Basingstoke: Macmillan, 2000), 90.

11 Quoted in Morley, *The Life of William Ewart Gladstone*, 383.

12 Hammond, *Gladstone and the Irish Nation*, 721.

13 Shannon, *Gladstone*, I: 453.

14 Shannon, *Gladstone: God and Politics*, xi.

15 W. C. Sellar and R. J. Yeatman, *1066 and All That* (York: Methuen, 1999), 116.

16 See Bernard Porter, 'Gladstone and Imperialism', in *Gladstone: Ireland and Beyond*, ed. Mary E. Daly and K. Theodore Hoppen (Dublin: Four Courts Press, 2011), 169–78 for an interesting exposé of his views surrounding imperialism.

17 Edmund Burke, *Second Speech on Conciliation with America* (London, 1775).

18 Winstanley, *Gladstone and the Liberal Party*, 19–36.

19 Ibid., 29.

20 R. V. Comerford, 'Gladstone's First Irish Enterprise', in *Ireland under the Union I: 1801–1870*, vol. 5 of *A New History of Ireland*, ed. W. E. Vaughan and T. W. Moody (Oxford: Clarendon Press, 1989), 441–2.

21 W. E. Vaughan, 'Ireland c.1870', in *Ireland under the Union I*, ed. Vaughan and Moody, 726.

22 Hammond, *Gladstone and the Irish Nation*, 88.

23 Ibid., 86–7.

24 Vaughan, 'Ireland c.1870', 728.

25 Boyce, 'Introduction: Tract for the Times?', 8.

26 Alvin Jackson, 'Irish Unionism, 1870–1922', in *Defenders of the Union: A Survey of British and Irish Unionism since 1801*, ed. D. G. Boyce and Alan O'Day (London: Routledge, 2001), 118.

27 Shannon, *Crisis of Imperialism* (London: Hart Davis, MacGibbon, 1974), 79; Comerford, 'Ireland 1850–70: Post-Famine and Mid-Victorian', in *Ireland under the Union I: 1801–1870*, vol. 5 of *A New History of Ireland*, ed. W. E. Vaughan and T. W. Moody (Oxford: Oxford University Press, 1989), 383.

28 Hammond, *Gladstone and the Irish Nation*, 98–9.

29 Gladstone to Archbishop H. E. Manning, 16 February 1870, in W. E. Gladstone and H. E. Manning, *The Correspondence of Henry Edward Manning and William Ewart Gladstone*, ed. Peter Erb (Oxford: Oxford University Press, 2013), 189.

30 Biagini, *Gladstone*, 48–9.

31 Winstanley, *Gladstone and the Liberal Party*, 13.

32 Shannon, *Crisis of Imperialism*, 79.

33 Comerford, 'Ireland 1850–70', 383

34 Biagini, *Gladstone*, 90.

35 Benjamin Disraeli, 'Speech of B. Disraeli at the Free Trade Hall', Manchester, 3 April 1872, 25. Bristol Selected Pamphlets. Online: http://www.jstor.org/stable/60249422 (accessed 4 March 2010).

36 Philip Bull, 'Butt, Isaac', in *Dictionary of Irish Biography*, ed. James McGuire and James Quinn (Cambridge: Cambridge University Press, 2009).

37 See the minimal entries in Robert Blake, *Disraeli* (London: Prion, 1998).

38 Ibid., 496.

39 C. S. Parnell, *Words of the Dead Chief: Being Extracts from the Public Speeches and Other Pronouncements of Charles Steward Parnell* (Dublin: Sealy, Bryers and Walker, 1892), 6 (17 September 1876).

Chapter 13. Parnell and The Land League

1 Michael Davitt, *The Fall of Feudalism in Ireland: Or the Story of the Land League Revolution* (London: Harper & Brothers, 1904).
2 Paul Bew, *Charles Stewart Parnell* (Dublin: Gill & Macmillan, 1980), 136.
3 For his background see Roy Foster, *Charles Stewart Parnell: The Man and His Family* (Hassocks: Harvester Press, 1979).
4 Conor Cruise O'Brien, *Parnell and His Party* (Oxford: Clarendon Press, 1957), 6.
5 R. Barry O'Brien, *The Life of Charles Stewart Parnell, 1846–1891*, 2 vols (Dublin, 1898), II: 352.
6 D. G. Boyce and Alan O'Day, eds, *Parnell in Perspective* (London: Routledge, 1991), 1.
7 The effect of his fall on the literati was notably emphasised by Joyce and Yeats. For example, see O'Brien, *Parnell and His Party*, 355.
8 See Philip Bull, 'The Fall of Parnell: The Political Context of His Intransigence', in *Parnell in Perspective*, ed. D. George Boyce and Alan O'Day (London: Routledge, 1991), 144. See 129–47 for discussion of the political context of Parnell's final intransigence.
9 R. V. Comerford, 'The Parnell Era, 1883–91', in *Ireland under the Union II: 1870–1921*, vol. 6 of *A New History of Ireland*, ed. W. E. Vaughan (Oxford: Clarendon Press, 1996), 80.
10 Ibid.
11 Bew, *Charles Stewart Parnell*, 144–5.
12 R. B. O'Brien, *The Life of Charles Stewart Parnell*, I: 104.
13 C. C. O'Brien, *Parnell and His Party*, 9.
14 Parnell, speech at Wexford, 26 October 1879, in C. S. Parnell, *Words of the Dead Chief: Being Extracts from the Public Speeches and Other Pronouncements of Charles Steward Parnell* (Dublin: Sealy, Bryers and Walker, 1892), 7.
15 T. P. O'Connor, *The Parnell Movement: Being the History of the Irish Question from the Death of O'Connell to the Present Time* (New York: Caskell Publishing Company, 1891), 150.
16 F. S. L. Lyons, *Charles Stewart Parnell* (London: Fontana, 1978), 611–13.
17 Foster, *Modern Ireland 1600–1972* (London: Penguin, 1988), 403.
18 See Comerford, 'The Politics of Distress, 1877–82', in *Ireland under the Union II*, ed. Vaughan, for discussion of the land war.
19 Bew, 'Parnell and Dayitt', in *Parnell in Perspective*, ed. Boyce and O'Day, 38.
20 Parnell, *Words of the Dead Chief*, 25.
21 Devoy, 25 October, cable to the president of the Supreme Council of the IRB, quoted in Lyons, *Parnell* (London: Collins, 1977), 80–81.
22 Parnell, *Words of the Dead Chief*, 21–2.
23 Comerford, 'The Politics of Distress, 1877–82', 28.
24 C. J. Woods, 'Parnell and the Catholic Church', in *Parnell in Perspective*, ed. Boyce and O'Day, 12–13.
25 Speech of 31 January 1880, in Parnell, *Words of the Dead Chief*, 31.
26 Foster, *Modern Ireland 1600–1972*, 411.
27 Comerford, 'The Politics of Distress, 1877–82', 42.
28 Ibid., 40.

29 Parnell, speech at Ennis, 19 September 1880, in Parnell, *Words of the Dead Chief*, 42.

30 Parnell, 'Debate on the Milltown Meeting', 26 June 1879, in ibid., 18.

31 Parnell, interview with James Redpath, 19 September 1880, in ibid., 43.

32 O'Brien, *Parnell and His Party*, 9.

33 Comerford, 'The Politics of Distress, 1877–82', 47.

34 Ibid., 51.

35 Lyons, *Ireland since the Famine* (London: HarperCollins, 1973), 173.

36 Quoted in John Morley, *The Life of William Ewart Gladstone* (London: Macmillan, 1903), 61.

37 Parnell, speech at Wexford, 9 October 1881, in Parnell, *Words of the Dead Chief*, 57.

38 Speech of 9 October 1881, in ibid., 57.

39 Comerford, 'The Politics of Distress, 1877–82', 49.

40 Lyons, *Ireland since the Famine*, 173–4.

41 Comerford, 'The Politics of Distress, 1877–82', 51.

42 J. L. Hammond, *Gladstone and the Irish Nation* (London: Frank Cass & Co., 1964), 723.

43 Eugenio Biagini, *Gladstone* (Basingstoke: Macmillan, 2000), 93.

Chapter 14. The Irish Liberals: A Union of Hearts?

1 Gladstone bears down on the present debate surrounding the future of Britain, D. G. Boyce, 'Introduction: Tract for the Times? The Enduring Appeal of Gladstone and Ireland', in *Gladstone and Ireland: Politics, Religion, and Nationality in the Victorian Age*, ed. D. G. Boyce and Alan O'Day (Basingstoke: Palgrave Macmillan, 2010), 4–6. Jackson has compared Gladstone and Tony Blair, Alvin Jackson, *Home Rule: An Irish History 1800–2000* (London: Weidenfeld & Nicolson, 2004), 5–6.

2 Boyce, 'Introduction: Tract for the Times?', 10.

3 Eugenio Biagini, *British Democracy and Irish Nationalism, 1876–1906* (Cambridge: Cambridge University Press, 2007), 4.

4 Alan O'Day, *Irish Home Rule, 1867–1921* (Manchester: Manchester University Press, 1998), 309.

5 Jackson, *Home Rule*, 2–3.

6 N. C. Fleming, 'Gladstone and the Ulster Question', in *Gladstone and Ireland: Politics, Religion, and Nationality in the Victorian Age*, ed. D. G. Boyce and Alan O'Day (Basingstoke: Palgrave Macmillan, 2010), 140–41.

7 Biagini, *British Democracy and Irish Nationalism*, 4.

8 A. B. Cooke and John Vincent, *The Governing Passion: Cabinet Government and Party Politics in Britain, 1885–86* (Brighton: Harvester Press, 1974).

9 Jackson, *Home Rule*, 75.

10 Jackson, 'Irish Unionism, 1870–1922', in *Defenders of the Union: A Survey of British and Irish Unionism since 1801*, ed. D. G. Boyce and Alan O'Day (London: Routledge, 2001), 115.

11 Ibid., 115.

12 Charles Townshend, *Political Violence in Ireland: Government and Resistance since 1848* (Oxford: Clarendon Press, 1983), 188.

13 Boyce, 'Weary Patriots: Ireland the Making of Unionism', in *Defenders of the Union*, ed. Boyce and O'Day, 26–7.

14 O'Day, *Irish Home Rule*, 97–101.

15 Cooke and Vincent, *The Governing Passion*, 24, 50–52, 55–6.

16 Ibid., 53.

17 R. V. Comerford, 'The Politics of Distress, 1877–82', in *Ireland under the Union II: 1870–1921*, vol. 6 of *A New History of Ireland*, ed. W. E. Vaughan (Oxford: Clarendon Press, 1996), 28.

18 Gladstone, letter to W. E. Foster, Irish secretary, 12 April 1882, in W. E. Gladstone, *The Gladstone Diaries: With Cabinet Minutes and Prime Ministerial Correspondence*, vol. 10: January 1881–June 1883, ed. H. G. C. Matthew (Oxford: Oxford University Press, 1990), 238.

19 Boyce, *Nineteenth-Century Ireland: The Search for Stability* (Dublin: Gill & Macmillan, 1990), 176.

20 Quoted in O'Day, *Irish Home Rule*, 103.

21 Boyce, *Nineteenth-Century Ireland*, 175.

22 O'Day, *Irish Home Rule*, 107.

23 J. C. Beckett, *A Short History of Ireland* (London: Hutchinson, 1966), 154–5.

24 Quoted in Graham Goodlad, 'British Liberals and the Irish Home Rule Crisis: The Dynamics of Division', in *Gladstone and Ireland*, ed. Boyce and O'Day, 105.

25 O'Day, *Irish Home Rule*, 108.

26 Quoted in James Loughlin, *Gladstone, Home Rule and the Ulster Question* (Dublin: Gill & Macmillan, 1986), 112.

27 Fleming, 'Gladstone and the Ulster Question', 140.

28 Quoted in O'Day, *Irish Home Rule*, 113.

29 These were the words of William Johnson, MP for South Belfast quoted in ibid., 114.

30 Quoted in ibid., 108.

31 Ibid., 116.

32 Gladstone, speech to the House of Commons on Government of Ireland Bill, second reading, adjourned debate, 7 June 1886. *Hansard*. Online: http://hansard.millbanksystems.com/commons/1886/jun/07/second-reading-adjourned-debate (accessed 30 August 2013).

33 J. L. Hammond, *Gladstone and the Irish Nation* (London: Frank Cass & Co., 1964), 489.

34 Jackson, *Home Rule*, 75.

35 O'Day, *Irish Home Rule*, 155.

36 H. C. G. Matthew, 'Gladstone, William Ewart (1809–1898)', in *Oxford Dictionary of National Biography* (Oxford: Oxford University Press, 2004). Online edition May 2011: http://www.oxforddnb.com/index/10/101010787/ (accessed 30 August 2013).

37 Michael Winstanley, *Gladstone and the Liberal Party* (London: Routledge, 1990), 62.

38 Jackson, *Home Rule*, 94.

39 Quoted in Richard Shannon, *Gladstone*, 2 vols (London: Penguin, 1999), II: 544.

40 O'Day, *Irish Home Rule*, 92.

41 Hammond, *Gladstone and the Irish Nation*, 721.

42 Gladstone, speech to the House of Commons on Government of Ireland Bill, second reading, adjourned debate, 7 June 1886. *Hansard*. Online: http://hansard.millbanksystems.com/commons/1886/jun/07/second-reading-adjourned-debate (accessed 30 August 2013).

43 Boyce, 'Introduction: Tract for the Times?', 1.

44 For further details of the Plan of Campaign, see pages 171–2.

45 F. S. L. Lyons, *The Fall of Parnell 1890–91* (London: Routledge & Kegan Paul, 1960), 23–9.

46 Paul Bew, *Charles Stewart Parnell* (Dublin: Gill & Macmillan, 1980), 145.

47 Quoted in Lyons, *Parnell* (London: Collins, 1977), 614.

48 Comerford, 'The Parnell Era, 1883–91', in *Ireland under the Union II*, ed. Vaughan, 76.
49 Lyons, *Ireland since the Famine* (London: HarperCollins, 1973), 199–200.
50 Lyons, *Charles Stewart Parnell* (London: Fontana, 1978), 201.
51 Lyons, *Ireland since the Famine*, 201.

Chapter 15. Constructive Unionism, 1886–1906

1 Eunan O'Halpin, *The Decline of the Union: British Government in Ireland, 1892–1920* (Dublin: Gill & Macmillan, 1987), 2.
2 F. S. L. Lyons, 'The Aftermath of Parnell, 1891–1903', in *Ireland under the Union II: 1870–1921*, vol. 6 of *A New History of Ireland*, ed. W. E. Vaughan (Oxford: Clarendon Press, 1996), 99.
3 Andrew Gailey, *Ireland and the Death of Kindness* (Cork: Cork University Press, 1987), 40.
4 L. P. Curtis, *Coercion and Conciliation in Ireland, 1880–1892: A Study in Conservative Unionism* (Princeton: Princeton University Press, 1963), viii.
5 Lyons, *Ireland since the Famine* (London: HarperCollins, 1973), 31.
6 A. B. Cooke and John Vincent, *The Governing Passion: Cabinet Government and Party Politics in Britain, 1885–86* (Brighton: Harvester Press, 1974), 71.
7 Gailey, *Ireland and the Death of Kindness*, 4–5.
8 Andrew Roberts, *Salisbury: Victorian Titan* (London: Weidenfeld & Nicolson, 1999), 52.
9 Ibid., 53.
10 Quoted in Roberts, *Salisbury*, 53.
11 Robert Cecil Salisbury, *The Government of Ireland: Lord Salisbury's Alternative Policy* (London: National Press Agency, 1886), 1.
12 Quoted in Roberts, *Salisbury*, 53.
13 Quoted in Gailey, *Ireland and the Death of Kindness*, 1.
14 R. V. Comerford, 'The Parnell Era, 1883–91', in *Ireland under the Union II*, ed. Vaughan, 69.
15 Curtis, *Coercion and Conciliation*, 174.
16 Michael J. F. McCarthy, *Mr. Balfour's Rule in Ireland* (Dublin: Hodges, Figgis, and Co., 1891), 29.
17 Ibid., 37. For fuller treatment on Balfour's role in Ireland, see C. B. Shannon, *Arthur J. Balfour and Ireland, 1874–1922* (Washington: Catholic University of America Press, 1988).
18 Philip Bull, 'Plunkett, Sir Horace Curzon (1854–1932)', in *Oxford Dictionary of National Biography* (Oxford: Oxford University Press, 2004). Online edition January 2008: http://www.oxforddnb.com/index/35/101035549/ (accessed 30 August 2013).
19 A. E. [George William] Russell, *Cooperation and Nationality: A Guide for Rural Reformers from This to the Next Generation* (Dublin: Maunsel, 1912), 80–81.
20 Gailey, *Ireland and the Death of Kindness*, 40.
21 Patrick Maume, 'Wyndham, George', in *Dictionary of Irish Biography*, ed. James McGuire and James Quinn (Cambridge: Cambridge University Press, 2009).
22 Lyons, 'The Aftermath of Parnell, 1891–1903', 97.
23 Ernest Barker, *Ireland in the Last Fifty Years, 1866–1918*, 2nd ed. (Oxford: Clarendon Press, 1919), 147.
24 Gailey, *Ireland and the Death of Kindness*, 322.
25 Ibid., 314.

26 Alvin Jackson, 'Irish Unionism, 1870–1922', in *Defenders of the Union: A Survey of British and Irish Unionism since 1801*, ed. D. G. Boyce and Alan O'Day (London: Routledge, 2001), 123–4.

27 Peter Gibbon, *The Origins of Ulster Unionism: The Formation of Popular Protestant Politics and Ideology in Nineteenth-Century Ireland* (Manchester: Manchester University Press, 1975), 142.

28 D. C. Boyce, *Nineteenth-Century Ireland: The Search for Stability* (Dublin: Gill & Macmillan, 1990), 204.

29 Gailey, *Ireland and the Death of Kindness*, 311.

30 Cooke and Vincent, *The Governing Passion*, 67.

31 Patrick Maume, 'Wyndham, George'.

32 Boyce, *Nineteenth-Century Ireland*, 205.

Chapter 16. Celtic Renaissance

1 John Hutchinson, *The Dynamics of Cultural Nationalism* (London: Allen & Unwin, 1987), 48–113; Terence Brown, ed., *Celticism* (Amsterdam: Rodopi, 1996).

2 Anthony D. Smith, *The Ethnic Origins of Nations* (Oxford: Basil Blackwell, 1986), 2–3. Smith's approach to studying nationhood is symbolic.

3 Laura O'Connor, *Haunted English: The Celtic Fringe, the British Empire and De-Anglicization* (Baltimore: Johns Hopkins University Press, 2006), xii.

4 Joep Leerssen, 'Celticism', in *Celticism*, ed. Terence Brown (Atlanta: Rodopi, 1996), 3–20.

5 Ibid., 6.

6 Ibid., 11.

7 Robert Dudley Edwards, *Daniel O'Connell and His World* (London: Thames & Hudson, 1975), 84–5.

8 Hutchinson, *The Dynamics of Cultural Nationalism*, 48–113, 115.

9 Leerssen, 'Celticism', 12.

10 Smith, *The Ethnic Origins of Nations*, 11–14.

11 Ernest Gellner, *Nationalism* (London: Weidenfeld & Nicolson, 1997), 96.

12 Charles Townshend, *Easter 1916* (London: Allen Lane, 2005), 17.

13 Vivien Mercier, 'Literature in English, 1891–1921', in *Ireland under the Union II: 1870–1921*, vol. 6 of *A New History of Ireland*, ed. W. E. Vaughan (Oxford: Clarendon Press, 1996), 357.

14 Dudley Edwards, *Daniel O'Connell and His World*, 88.

15 Hutchinson, *The Dynamics of Cultural Nationalism*, 2.

16 Ibid., 3; O'Connor, *Haunted English*; Chris Morash, 'Celticism: Between Race and Nation', in *Ideology and Ireland in the Nineteenth Century*, ed. Tadhg Foley and Seán Ryder (Dublin: Four Courts Press, 1998).

17 Hutchinson, *The Dynamics of Cultural Nationalism*, 133.

18 Douglas Hyde, *The Necessity for De-Anglicising Ireland* (Leiden: Academic Press, 1994), xii.

19 L. P. Curtis, *Anglo-Saxons and Celts: A Study of Anti-Irish Prejudice in Victorian England* (New York: New York University Press, 1968).

20 National Museum of Ireland, 'The Irish Headhunter'. Online: http://www.museum.ie/en/exhibition/the-irish-headhunter.aspx (accessed 16 December 2013).

21 Ernest Renan, *La Poésie des Races Celtiques*, trans. William G. Hutchison (London: Walter Scott, 1854, reprinted 1896); Matthew Arnold, *On the Study of Celtic Literature*

(London: Smith, Elder & Co., 1867). For discussion of anti-Irish prejudice and stereotyping see Curtis, *Anglo-Saxons and Celts* and *Apes and Angels: The Irishman in Victorian Caricature* (Newton Abbot: David & Charles, 1971).

22 Gregory Castle, *Modernism and the Celtic Revival* (Cambridge: Cambridge University Press, 2001).

23 O'Connor, *Haunted English*, xiii.

24 F. S. L. Lyons, 'The Aftermath of Parnell, 1891–1903', in *Ireland under the Union II*, ed. Vaughan, 105.

25 Benedict Anderson, *Imagined Communities: Reflections on the Origins and Spread of Nationalism* (London: Verso, 1983), 84.

26 Tom Garvin, *Nationalist Revolutionaries in Ireland 1858–1928* (Oxford: Clarendon Press, 1987), 78, emphasis added by author. See 78–106 for a chapter on the politics of language and literature.

27 Thomas William Croke, 'A Letter from Archbishop Thomas William Croke to Michael Cusack, Indicating His Acceptance of the Role of Patron of the Gaelic Athletic Association', from 'The Gaelic Athletic Association', *Freeman's Journal* (24 December 1884). University College Cork, Multitext Project in Irish History. Online: http://multitext.ucc.ie/d/Archbishop_Croke__the_GAA_November_1884 (accessed 31 October 2013). 'Masher' means somebody who forces himself on another.

28 Michael Cusack, 'Origins of the Gaelic Athletic Association' (1884). University College Cork, Multitext Project in Irish History. Online: http://multitext.ucc.ie/d/Origins_of_the_Gaelic_Athletic_Association_1884 (accessed 30 August 2013).

29 Castle, *Modernism and the Celtic Revival*, 3, 9.

30 Smith, *The Ethnic Origins of Nations*, 195.

31 Thomas Bartlett, *Ireland: A History* (Cambridge: Cambridge University Press, 2010), 348.

32 Ibid., 347.

33 W. B. Yeats, 'September 1913', in *The Collected Works of W. B. Yeats Volume I: The Poems*, rev. 2nd edition, ed. Richard J. Finneran (New York: Scribner, 2010), 108.

34 Yeats, 'Easter 1916', in ibid., 180.

35 Hutchinson, *The Dynamics of Cultural Nationalism*, 166–8.

36 John Horne, ed., *Our War: Ireland and the Great War* (Dublin: Royal Irish Academy, 2008), 78.

37 Quoted in Ulick O'Connor, *Michael Collins and the Troubles* (New York: Norton & Company, 1996), 30.

38 Quoted in Lyons, *Ireland since the Famine* (London: HarperCollins, 1973), 249.

39 Hutchinson, *The Dynamics of Cultural Nationalism*, 168.

40 Quoted in Alvin Jackson, *Ireland 1798–1998: War, Peace and Beyond* (Sussex: Wiley Blackwell, 2010), 106.

Chapter 17. The Story of Irish Socialism

1 D. G. Boyce, *Nationalism in Ireland* (London: Croom Helm, 1982), 327.

2 E. Rumpf and A. C. Hepburn, *Nationalism and Socialism in Twentieth-Century Ireland* (Liverpool: Liverpool University Press, 1977), 10; Anthony Coughlan, 'Ireland's Marxist Historians', in *Interpreting Irish History: The Debate on Historical Revisionism*, ed. Ciaran Brady (Dublin: Irish Academic Press, 1994), 288–305 provides an excellent overview of the contribution of Ireland's Marxist historians. See also Desmond

Greaves, *The Life and Times of James Connolly* (London: Lawrence & Wishart, 1961) for a classic Marxist biography of James Connolly.

3 Diarmaid Ferriter, *The Transformation of Ireland 1900–2000* (London: Profile Books, 2004), 44–80.

4 Padraig Yeates, *Lockout: Dublin 1913* (Dublin: Gill & Macmillan, 2001).

5 Sean Cronin, *Marx and the Irish Question* (Dublin: Repsol Publications, 1977), 15.

6 Murray Fraser, *John Bull's Other Homes: State Housing and British Policy in Ireland, 1883–1922* (Liverpool: Liverpool University Press, 1996). The Dublin Town Plan Competition 1914 introduced the garden suburb principle.

7 James Joyce, *Ulysses* (New York: Random House, 1986), 90.

8 'Report of the Departmental Committee into the Housing Conditions of the Working Classes in the City of Dublin', Dublin 1913. Online: http://multitext.ucc.ie/d/Housing_Report_Dublin_1913 (accessed 30 August 2013).

9 See F. S. L. Lyons, *Ireland since the Famine* (London: HarperCollins, 1973), 277–8. Also Ferriter, *The Transformation of Ireland*, 50–54.

10 Quoted in Joseph O'Brien, *Dear, Dirty Dublin: A City in Distress 1899–1916* (Berkeley: University of California Press, 1982), 103.

11 Lyons, 'The Aftermath of Parnell, 1891–1903', in *Ireland under the Union II: 1870–1921*, vol. 6 of *A New History of Ireland*, ed. W. E. Vaughan (Oxford: Clarendon Press, 1996), 108–9.

12 Fintan Lane, *Origins of Modern Irish Socialism, 1881–1896* (Cork: Cork University Press, 1997), 2.

13 See Ferriter, *The Transformation of Ireland*, 166–9 for a comparative introduction.

14 James Joll, *The Second International, 1881–1915* (London: Weidenfeld & Nicolson, 1955), 116.

15 Anthony Coughlan, 'Ireland's Marxist Historians', in *Interpreting Irish History: The Debate on Historical Revisionism*, ed. Ciaran Brady (Dublin: Irish Academic Press, 1994), 294.

16 Jim Larkin, speech outside Mountjoy Prison, 28 October 1913. Quoted in http://www.thejournal.ie/clare-daly-jim-larkin-559888-Aug2012/ (accessed 5 December 2013).

17 Yeates, *Lockout*, xi.

18 Lyons, *Ireland since the Famine*, 283.

19 Ibid.

20 George Dangerfield, *The Strange Death of Liberal England* (London: Serif, 1997), 116.

21 Rumpf and A. C. Hepburn, *Nationalism and Socialism*, 11.

22 Quoted in Lyons, *Ireland since the Famine*, 284.

23 Joseph Lee, *The Modernisation of Irish Society, 1848–1918* (Dublin: Gill & Macmillan, 1973), 150.

24 Emmet Larkin, 'Larkin, James (1874–1947)', in *Oxford Dictionary of National Biography* (Oxford: Oxford University Press, 2004). Online edition May 2007: http://www.oxforddnb.com/index/37/101037656/ (accessed 2 September 2013).

25 Quoted in Austen Morgan, *James Connolly: A Political Biography* (Manchester: Manchester University Press, 1988), 150.

26 Owen Dudley Edwards, *Éamon de Valera* (Cardiff: University of Wales, 1987), 31; see also Sinéad McCoole, *No Ordinary Women: Irish Female Activists in the Revolutionary Years, 1900–1923* (Dublin: O'Brien Press, 2003) and Ferriter, *The Transformation of Ireland*, 174–6.

27 Peter Hart, 'Defining the Irish Revolution', in *The Irish Revolution, 1913–1923*, ed. Joost Augusteijn (Basingstoke: Palgrave Macmillan, 2002), 22.

Chapter 18. The Home Rule Crisis

1　Peter Hart, 'Defining the Irish Revolution', in *The Irish Revolution, 1913–1923*, ed. Joost Augusteijn (Basingstoke: Palgrave Macmillan, 2002), 19.

2　George Dangerfield, *The Strange Death of Liberal England* (London: Serif, 1997), 72–120.

3　John Darwin, *The Empire Project: The Rise and Fall of the British World-System, 1830–1970* (Cambridge: Cambridge University Press, 2009), 300.

4　Patricia Jalland, *Liberals and Ireland: The Ulster Question in British Politics to 1914* (Brighton: Harvester Press, 1980), 13.

5　Alan O'Day, *Irish Home Rule, 1867–1921* (Manchester: Manchester University Press, 1998), 241.

6　Alvin Jackson, *Home Rule: An Irish History 1800–2000* (London: Weidenfeld & Nicolson, 2004), 106.

7　Ibid., 123, Diarmaid Ferriter, *The Transformation of Ireland 1900–2000* (London: Profile Books, 2004), 130.

8　Dangerfield, *The Strange Death*, 72.

9　Quoted in Darwin, *The Empire Project*, 298.

10　David Powell, *The Edwardian Crisis: Britain, 1901–1914* (Basingstoke: Macmillan, 1996), 141.

11　Jackson, *Home Rule*, 5.

12　Jalland, *Liberals and Ireland*, 13.

13　H. H. Asquith, *Memories and Reflections, 1852–1927*, vol. 2 (London: Cassell, 1928), 36–9.

14　Jalland, *Liberals and Ireland*, 15.

15　Jackson, 'Irish Unionism, 1870–1922', in *Defenders of the Union: A Survey of British and Irish Unionism since 1801*, ed. D. G. Boyce and Alan O'Day (London: Routledge, 2001), 125.

16　O'Day, *Irish Home Rule*, 240 considers that the similarities with previous Home Rule bills was superficial.

17　Ibid., 297.

18　A. T. Q. Stewart, *The Ulster Crisis* (London: Faber & Faber, 1967), 18.

19　MacNeill. 'The North Began', *An Claidheamh Soluis*, 1 November 1913, quoted in Russell Rees and Anthony C. Hepburn, *Ireland 1905–1925*, Documents and Analysis, vol. 2 (Newtownards: Colourpoint Books, 1998), 133.

20　Darwin, *The Empire Project*, 299.

21　For full treatment of the UVF, see Stewart, *The Ulster Crisis*, also Charles Townshend, *Political Violence in Ireland: Government and Resistance since 1848* (Oxford: Clarendon Press, 1983), 245–61.

22　D. G. Boyce, 'Carson, Edward Henry, Baron Carson (1854–1935)', in *Oxford Dictionary of National Biography* (Oxford: Oxford University Press, 2004). Online edition January 2011: http://www.oxforddnb.com/templates/article.jsp?articleid=32310&back= (accessed 2 September 2013).

23　Jackson, 'Carson, Edward Henry Baron Carson of Duncairn', in *Dictionary of Irish Biography*, ed. James McGuire and James Quinn (Cambridge: Cambridge University Press, 2010). Online: http://dib.cambridge.org/viewReadPage.do?articleId=a1514 (accessed 1 August 2013 [subscription required]).

24　Stewart, *The Ulster Crisis*, 43.

25　Townshend, *Political Violence in Ireland*, 245.

26 Jackson, *Home Rule*, 137.

27 J. C. Beckett, *A Short History of Ireland* (London: Hutchinson, 1966), 156.

28 Townshend, *Political Violence in Ireland*, 248.

29 Quoted in Powell, *The Edwardian Crisis*, 146.

30 Dangerfield, *The Strange Death*, 77.

31 Rudyard Kipling, *The Works of Rudyard Kipling* (Hertfordshire: Wordsworth Editions, 2001), 244.

32 Townshend, *Political Violence in Ireland*, 256. Townshend notes how odd it is that the 'Irish Ireland' movement, which was so Catholic in orientation, felt so strongly against the exclusion of Protestants.

33 Quoted in Francis P. Jones, *History of the Sinn Fein Movement and the Irish Rebellion of 1916* (New York: P. J. Kenedy & Sons, 1917), 211.

34 Ruth Dudley Edwards, *Patrick Pearse: The Triumph of Failure* (London: Gollancz, 1977), 179.

35 Quoted in John Ranelagh, *A Short History of Ireland*, 3rd ed. (Cambridge: Cambridge University Press, 2012), 191.

36 Jackson, 'Unionist History', in *Interpreting Irish History: The Debate on Historical Revisionism*, ed. Ciaran Brady (Dublin: Irish Academic Press, 1994), 260.

37 Jackson, *Home Rule*, 4.

38 Terence Denman, *Ireland's Unknown Soldiers* (Dublin: Irish Academic Press, 2008), 19.

39 Townshend, *Political Violence in Ireland*, 261.

40 Asquith, *Letters to Venetia Stanley* (Oxford: Oxford University Press, 1982), 109.

41 Dangerfield, *The Strange Death*, 280.

42 Darwin, *The Empire Project*, 300.

Chapter 19. World War and Insurrection

1 Winston Churchill, speech to the House of Commons on the Irish Free State (Agreement) Bill, 16 February 1922. *Hansard*. Online: http://hansard.millbanksystems.com/commons/1922/feb/16/irish-free-state-agreement-bill (accessed 3 September 2013).

2 Adrian Gregory and Senia Paseta, eds, *Ireland and the Great War: 'A War to Unite Us All'?* (Manchester: Manchester University Press, 2002), 4.

3 Terence Denman, *Ireland's Unknown Soldiers* (Dublin: Irish Academic Press, 2008), 16.

4 David Fitzpatrick, ed., *Ireland and the First World War* (Dublin: Trinity History Workshop, 1986); Gregory and Paseta, *Ireland and the Great War*; Stephen Walker, *Forgotten Soldiers: The Irishmen Shot at Dawn* (Dublin: Gill & Macmillan, 2008); John Horne, ed., *Our War: Ireland and the Great War* (Dublin: Royal Irish Academy, 2008).

5 Fitzpatrick, *Ireland and the First World War*, viii.

6 Gregory and Paseta, *Ireland and the Great War*, 2.

7 Denman, *Ireland's Unknown Soldiers*, 28.

8 Quoted in Joseph P. Finnan, *John Redmond and Irish Unity 1912–1918* (New York: Syracuse University Press, 2004), 89.

9 Denman, *Ireland's Unknown Soldiers*, 28.

10 Ibid., 37.

11 A. T. Q. Stewart, *The Ulster Crisis* (London: Faber & Faber, 1967), 242. It is important to note, *en passant*, that most of the recruits were from neither the UVF nor the Irish Volunteers. Denman, *Ireland's Unknown Soldiers*, 36.

12 Denman, *Ireland's Unknown Soldiers*, 33.

13 The most useful historiographical summation is to be found in Charles Townshend, *Easter 1916* (London: Allen Lane, 2005), 344–59.

14 Dorothy MacArdle, *The Irish Republic* (Dublin: Irish Press, 1937), 157.

15 Tom Garvin, *Nationalist Revolutionaries in Ireland 1858–1928* (Oxford: Clarendon Press, 1987), 1.

16 J. C. Beckett, *A Short History of Ireland* (London: Hutchinson, 1966), 160.

17 F. S. L. Lyons, 'The Revolution in Train, 1914–1916', in *Ireland under the Union II: 1870–1921*, vol. 6 of *A New History of Ireland*, ed. W. E. Vaughan (Oxford: Clarendon Press, 1996), 192.

18 Townshend, *Political Violence in Ireland: Government and Resistance since 1848* (Oxford: Clarendon Press, 1983), 258, 283.

19 Benedict Anderson, *Imagined Communities: Reflections on the Origins and Spread of Nationalism* (London: Verso, 1983), 7.

20 Gregory and Paseta, *Ireland and the Great War*, 3.

21 Diarmaid Ferriter, *The Transformation of Ireland 1900–2000* (London: Profile Books, 2004), 142.

22 Richard English, *Ernie O'Malley: IRA Intellectual* (Oxford: Clarendon Press, 1998), 84.

23 Townshend, *Political Violence in Ireland*, 26.

24 Ibid., 284.

25 E. Rumpf and A. C. Hepburn, *Nationalism and Socialism in Twentieth-Century Ireland* (Liverpool: Liverpool University Press, 1977), 12.

26 Conor Cruise O'Brien, 'Epilogue. The Embers of Easter 1916–66', in *1916: The Easter Rising*, ed. Owen Dudley Edwards and Fergus Pyle (London: MacGibbon & Kee, 1968), 225–7.

27 Townshend, *Political Violence in Ireland*, 286.

28 Michael Foy and Brian Barton, *The Easter Rising* (Stroud: The History Press, 2011), 327.

29 Chalmers Johnson, *Revolution and the Social System* (Stanford: Stanford University Press, 1964), 51.

30 MacArdle, *The Irish Republic*; Ruth Dudley Edwards, *Patrick Pearse: The Triumph of Failure* (London: Gollancz, 1977).

31 Ruth Dudley Edwards, *Patrick Pearse: The Triumph of Failure* (Dublin: Poolbeg, 1990), 161.

32 Townshend, *Political Violence in Ireland*, 410.

33 Ferriter, *The Transformation of Ireland*, 142, 148.

34 Lyons, *Ireland since the Famine* (London: HarperCollins, 1973), 335.

35 Dudley Edwards, *Patrick Pearse* (1990), 244.

36 Quoted in Townshend, *Easter 1916*, 137.

37 See Foy and Barton *The Easter Rising* for a full survey account.

38 Connolly to his secretary, Winifred Carney, quoted in Max Caulfield, *The Easter Rebellion* (Westport: Greenwood Press, 1963), 95.

39 Lyons, *Ireland since the Famine*, 365.

40 Proclamation of the Republic of Ireland 1916, quoted in Michael Hopkinson, ed., *The Irish War of Independence* (Dublin: Gill & Macmillan, 2004), 204.

41 Ibid.

42 Lyons, *Ireland since the Famine*, 369.

43 Proclamation of the Republic of Ireland 1916, quoted in Hopkinson, *The Irish War of Independence*, 204.

44 Townshend, *Easter 1916*, 271.

45 Michael Laffan, *The Resurrection of Ireland: The Sinn Féin Party, 1916–1923* (Cambridge: Cambridge University Press, 1999), 50–51; Townshend, *Political Violence in Ireland*, 311–12.

46 See, for example, Beckett, *A Short History of Ireland*, 160; Lyons, *Ireland since the Famine*, 376–9.

47 Townshend, *Easter 1916*, 300.

48 Ibid., 310.

49 Townshend, *Political Violence in Ireland*, 410.

50 Townshend, *Easter 1916*, 355.

51 Foy and Barton, *The Easter Rising*, 326.

Chapter 20. The Rise of Sinn Féin

1 Peter Hart, 'Defining the Irish Revolution', in *The Irish Revolution, 1913–1923*, ed. Joost Augusteijn (Basingstoke: Palgrave Macmillan, 2002), 22.

2 Joost Augusteijn, *The Irish Revolution, 1913–1923* (Basingstoke: Palgrave Macmillan, 2002), 12; ibid., 21.

3 Arthur Mitchell, 'Alternative Government: "Exit Britannia" – the Formation of the Irish National State, 1918–21', in *The Irish War of Independence*, ed. Michael Hopkinson (Dublin: Gill & Macmillan, 2004), 74.

4 David Fitzpatrick, ed., *Revolution: Ireland 1917–1923* (Dublin: Trinity History Workshop, 1990), 8; Townshend, 'Historiography: Telling the Irish Revolution', in *The Irish Revolution*, ed. Augusteijn, 1–17.

5 Brian Farrell, *The Founding of Dáil Eireann and Nation Building* (Dublin: Gill & Macmillan, 1971), 45.

6 Éamon de Valera, by-election speech at Ennis, June 1917, in de Valera, *Speeches and Statements by Eamon de Valera, 1917–73*, ed. Maurice Moynihan (Dublin: Gill & Macmillan, 1980), 1.

7 Roy Foster, *Modern Ireland 1600–1972* (London: Penguin, 1988), 489.

8 D. G. Boyce, *Nationalism in Ireland* (London: Croom Helm, 1982), 317.

9 Quoted in Boyce, *Nationalism in Ireland*, 315–16.

10 Ibid., 316.

11 Farrell, *The Founding of Dáil Eireann*, 20.

12 Foster, *Modern Ireland 1600–1972*, 489.

13 Owen Dudley Edwards, *Éamon de Valera* (Cardiff: University of Wales, 1987), 24.

14 Diarmaid Ferriter, *The Transformation of Ireland 1900–2000* (London: Profile Books, 2004), 261.

15 Quoted in Foster, *Modern Ireland 1600–1972*, 482–3.

16 Dudley Edwards, *Éamon de Valera*, 95.

17 Foster, *Modern Ireland 1600–1972*, 510.

18 Letter from Lloyd George to Bonar Law, 2 November 1918, published in *The Times*, 18 November 1918; quoted in *Englishmen and Irish Troubles: British Public Opinion and the Making of Irish Policy 1918–22* (London: Jonathan Cape, 1972), 44.

19 Farrell, *The Founding of Dáil Eireann*, 26.

20 Ibid., 47.

21 Tom Garvin, *The Evolution of Irish Nationalist Politics* (Dublin: Gill & Macmillan, 1981), 117.

22 Farrell, *The Founding of Dáil Eireann*, 45.
23 Foster, *Modern Ireland 1600–1972*, 491.
24 Boyce, *Nationalism in Ireland*, 318.
25 Garvin, *1922: The Birth of Irish Democracy*, 39.
26 Alvin Jackson, *Home Rule: An Irish History 1800–2000* (London: Weidenfeld & Nicolson, 2004), 2.
27 Boyce, *Nationalism in Ireland*, 324.
28 Farrell, *The Founding of Dáil Eireann*, 51.
29 Michael Kennedy, *Ireland and the League of Nations, 1919–1946: International Relations, Diplomacy and Politics* (Dublin: Irish Academic Press, 1996), 19.
30 Boyce, *Nationalism in Ireland*, 321.
31 Quoted ibid., 321.
32 Tim Pat Coogan, *De Valera: Long Fellow, Long Shadow* (London: Hutchinson, 1993), 1.
33 Dudley Edwards, *Éamon de Valera*, 81–2.
34 F. S. L. Lyons, *Ireland since the Famine* (London: HarperCollins, 1973), 407.
35 Farrell, *The Founding of Dáil Eireann*, xvii.
36 Mitchell, 'Alternative Government', 74.
37 Townshend, *Political Violence in Ireland: Government and Resistance since 1848* (Oxford: Clarendon Press, 1983), 323.

Chapter 21. The Anglo–Irish War

1 F. S. L. Lyons, *Ireland since the Famine* (London: HarperCollins, 1973), 33.
2 Michael Hopkinson, ed., *The Irish War of Independence* (Dublin: Gill & Macmillan, 2004), xvii.
3 Lloyd George, 'Note of Conversation', 30 April 1920, the National Archives (UK), quoted in Maurice Walsh, *The News from Ireland: Foreign Correspondents and the Irish Revolution* (London: I.B. Tauris, 2011), 70.
4 J. C. Beckett, *A Short History of Ireland* (London: Hutchinson, 1966), 162.
5 Charles Townshend, *Political Violence in Ireland: Government and Resistance since 1848* (Oxford: Clarendon Press, 1983), 322, 344.
6 Ibid., 323.
7 Peter Hart, 'Defining the Irish Revolution', in *The Irish Revolution, 1913–1923*, ed. Joost Augusteijn (Basingstoke: Palgrave Macmillan, 2002), 24–5.
8 Diarmaid Ferriter, *The Transformation of Ireland 1900–2000* (London: Profile Books, 2004), 227–8.
9 Hopkinson, *The Irish War of Independence*, xx.
10 Roy Foster, *Modern Ireland 1600–1972* (London: Penguin, 1988), 506; Ronan Fanning, 'Michael Collins – an Overview', in *Michael Collins and the Making of the Irish State*, ed. Gabriel Doherty and Dermot Keogh (Cork: Cork University Press, 1998), 204.
11 Quoted in Robert Kee, *Ourselves Alone* (Penguin, 1989), 75.
12 Hart, *The IRA at War, 1916–1923* (Oxford: Oxford University Press, 2003), 121.
13 Ibid. includes useful maps locating violent incidents 65, 34–41.
14 Ibid., 30.
15 Quoted in Tom Jones, *Whitehall Diary Volume 3: Ireland 1918–1925* (Oxford: Oxford University Press, 1971), 73.

16 J. M. Curran, *The Birth of the Irish Free State* (Alabama: University of Alabama Press, 1980), 37.

17 Joseph Lee, *Ireland, 1912–1985: Politics and Society* (Cambridge: Cambridge University Press, 1989), 43.

18 Article 75 from the Government of Ireland Act 1920 (10 & 11 Geo. V c. 67). Online: http://www.legislation .gov.uk/ukpga/1920/67/pdfs/ukpga_19200067_enpdf (accessed 2 September 2013).

19 Owen Dudley Edwards, *Éamon de Valera* (Cardiff: University of Wales, 1987), 95–6.

20 Ibid., 97.

21 Beckett, *A Short History of Ireland*, 163.

22 Quoted in Alvin Jackson, *Ireland 1798–1998: War, Peace and Beyond* (Sussex: Wiley Blackwell, 2010), 336. The entrance of the king was captured on film and is held by the British Film Institute in Belfast. Online: http://www.digitalfilmarchive.net/dfa/browseDisplay.asp?id=48 (accessed 31 October 2013).

23 Townshend, *The British Campaign in Ireland, 1919–21: The Development of Political and Military Policies* (Oxford: Oxford University Press, 1975), 200–202.

24 D. G. Boyce, *Nationalism in Ireland* (London: Croom Helm, 1982), 324.

25 Quoted in ibid., 325. Emphasis in original.

26 Fanning, *Independent Ireland* (Dublin: Helicon, 1983), 2.

Chapter 22. North and South Settlements

1 F. W. Boal and J. Neville H. Douglas, *Integration and Division: Geographical Perspectives on the Northern Ireland Problem* (London: Academic Press, 1985), 336; Joseph Lee, *Ireland, 1912–1985: Politics and Society* (Cambridge: Cambridge University Press, 1989), 45; Michael Laffan, *The Partition of Ireland* (Dublin: Dublin Historical Association, 1983), 67–8.

2 Quoted in Diarmaid Ferriter, *The Transformation of Ireland 1900–2000* (London: Profile Books, 2004), 240.

3 Arthur Mitchell, 'Alternative Government: "Exit Britannia" – the Formation of the Irish National State, 1918–21', in *The Irish War of Independence*, ed. Michael Hopkinson (Dublin: Gill & Macmillan, 2004), 84.

4 Ferriter, *The Transformation of Ireland*, 239.

5 For example, Tim Pat Coogan, *De Valera: Long Fellow, Long Shadow* (London: Hutchinson, 1993), 309.

6 F. S. L. Lyons, *Ireland since the Famine* (London: HarperCollins, 1973), 430.

7 Alan O'Day, *Irish Home Rule, 1867–1921* (Manchester: Manchester University Press, 1998), 308.

8 Lee, *Ireland, 1912–1985*, 48.

9 For a critique of this view, see Bill Kissane, *The Politics of the Irish Civil War* (Oxford: Oxford University Press, 2005), 238.

10 Tom Garvin, *1922: The Birth of Irish Democracy* (Dublin: Gill & Macmillan, 1996).

11 Kissane, *The Politics of the Irish Civil War*, 5. See chapter 9 for a masterly discussion of the historiography of the Civil War.

12 Charles Townshend, *Political Violence in Ireland: Government and Resistance since 1848* (Oxford: Clarendon Press, 1983), 303.

13 Boal and Douglas, *Integration and Division*, 336.

14 Laffan, *The Partition of Ireland*, 67–8.

15 Lee, *Ireland, 1912–1985*, 45.
16 Ibid., 45–6.
17 Quoted in Lee, *Ireland, 1912–1985*, 47.
18 Lee, *Ireland, 1912–1985*, 47–8.
19 Quoted in Michael Joseph Sullivan, *Ireland and the Global Question* (Cork: Cork University Press, 2006), 130.
20 Laffan, *The Partition of Ireland*, 78.
21 Owen Dudley Edwards, *Éamon de Valera* (Cardiff: University of Wales, 1987), 100; Lee, *Ireland, 1912–1985*, 48.
22 Lyons, *Ireland since the Famine*, 430.
23 Lee, *Ireland, 1912–1985*, 49.
24 Dudley Edwards, *Éamon de Valera*, 11.
25 Documents on Irish Foreign Policy Series, excerpts from the Anglo–Irish Treaty, 6 December 1921. Online: http://www.nationalarchives.ie/topics/anglo_irish/dfaexhib2.html (accessed 8 September 2012).
26 Quoted in Dennis Dworkin, *Ireland and Britain, 1798–1922: An Anthology of Sources* (Indianapolis: Hackett Publishing, 2012), 232.
27 Women were more likely to be anti-Treaty. They played a vital role in the Civil War period. For commentary on this see Garvin, *1922: The Birth of Irish Democracy*, 96.
28 Laffan, *The Partition of Ireland*, 109.
29 Richard English, *Ernie O'Malley: IRA Intellectual* (Oxford: Clarendon Press, 1998), 84.
30 Peter Hart, 'Defining the Irish Revolution', in *The Irish Revolution, 1913–1923*, ed. Joost Augusteijn (Basingstoke: Palgrave Macmillan, 2002), 29.
31 Garvin, *1922: The Birth of Irish Democracy*, 62.
32 Ibid., 92. Elsewhere he regards those opposed to the treaty as part of a tradition of 'fundamentalist republicanism'. Garvin, *Nationalist Revolutionaries in Ireland 1858–1928* (Oxford: Clarendon Press, 1987), 33.
33 Hart, *The IRA at War, 1916–1923* (Oxford: Oxford University Press, 2003), 194–220 examines the incident and concludes that there is no solid evidence for the Collins' conspiracy theory, as is sometimes suggested.
34 Lee, *Ireland, 1912–1985*, 66.
35 Coogan, *Michael Collins: A Biography* (London: Arrow, 1991).
36 Quoted in Stephen Collins, *The Cosgrave Legacy* (Dublin: Blackwater Press, 1996), 34.
37 Townshend, *Political Violence in Ireland*, 409–10.
38 Quoted in Coogan, *De Valera*, 354.
39 W. B. Yeats, *The Collected Works of W. B. Yeats Volume I: The Poems*, rev. 2nd edition, ed. Richard J. Finneran (New York: Scribner, 2010), 180.

Chapter 23. Conclusion

1 F. S. L. Lyons, *Culture and Anarchy, 1890–1939* (Oxford: Clarendon Press, 1979), 177.
2 Thomas Bartlett, *Ireland: A History* (Cambridge: Cambridge University Press, 2010), 246.
3 Brendan Behan, letter to Sinbad Val, October 1952, in Brendan Behan, *Letters of Brendan Behan*, ed. E. H. Mikhail (Quebec: McGill-Queen's University Press, 1952), 54.
4 W. B. Yeats, 'Easter 1916', in *The Collected Works of W. B. Yeats Volume I: The Poems*, rev. 2nd edition, ed. Richard J. Finneran (New York: Scribner, 2010), 180.

BIBLIOGRAPHY

Reference Works

McGuire, James and James Quinn, eds. *Dictionary of Irish Biography*. Cambridge: Cambridge University Press, 2009.
Oxford Dictionary of National Biography. Oxford: Oxford University Press, 2004. Online (January 2010): http://www.oxforddnb.com.

Primary Bibliography

Arnold, Matthew. *On the Study of Celtic Literature*. London: Smith, Elder & Co., 1867.
Asquith, H. H. *Memories and Reflections, 1852–1927*, vol. 2. London: Cassell, 1928.
_____. *Letters to Venetia Stanley*. Oxford: Oxford University Press, 1982.
Barker, Ernest. *Ireland in the Last Fifty Years, 1866–1918*. 2nd edition. Oxford: Clarendon Press, 1919.
Behan, Brendan. *Letters of Brendan Behan*, edited by E. H. Mikhail, Quebec: McGill-Queen's University Press, 1952.
Burke, Edmund. *Second Speech on Conciliation with America*. London, 1775.
Churchill, Winston. *The World Crisis 1911–1918*. London: Penguin, 2007.
Collis, John. *An Address to the People of Ireland on the Projected Union*. Dublin: Printed for James Moore, 1799.
Croke, Thomas William. 'A Letter from Archbishop Thomas William Croke to Michael Cusack, Indicating His Acceptance of the Role of Patron of the Gaelic Athletic Association'. From 'The Gaelic Athletic Association', *Freeman's Journal* (24 December 1884). University College Cork, Multitext Project in Irish History. Online: http://multitext.ucc.ie/d/Archbishop_Croke__the_GAA_November_1884 (accessed 31 October 2013).
Davitt, Michael. *The Fall of Feudalism in Ireland: Or the Story of the Land League Revolution*. London: Harper & Brothers, 1904.
de Valera, Éamon. *Speeches and Statements by Eamon de Valera, 1917–73*, edited by Maurice Moynihan. Dublin: Gill & Macmillan, 1980.
Digital Film Archive. Online: www.digitalfilmarchive.net.
Disraeli, Benjamin. 'Speech of B. Disraeli at the Free Trade Hall', Manchester, 3 April 1872. Bristol Selected Pamphlets. Online: http://www.jstor.org/stable/60249422 (accessed 4 March 2010).

Dworkin, Dennis. *Ireland and Britain, 1798–1922: An Anthology of Sources*. Indianapolis: Hackett Publishing, 2012.

Ford, R., ed. *Popular Irish Readings in Prose and Verse*. Paisley and London: Alexander Gardener, 1897.

Foster, John. *Speech of the Right Honourable John Foster Speaker of the House of Commons of Ireland, delivered in Committee* (17 February 1800). Dublin: Printed for James Moore, 1800.

_____. *Speech of the Right Honourable John Foster Speaker of the House of Commons of Ireland, delivered in Committee* (19 March 1800). Dublin: Printed for James Moore, 1800.

Gladstone, W. E. *The Gladstone Diaries: With Cabinet Minutes and Prime Ministerial Correspondence*, vol. 10: January 1881–June 1883, edited by H. G. C. Matthew. Oxford: Oxford University Press, 1990.

Gladstone, W. E. and H. E. Manning *The Correspondence of Henry Edward Manning and William Ewart Gladstone*, edited by Peter Erb. Oxford: Oxford University Press, 2013.

Griffith, Arthur. *The Resurrection of Hungary: A Parallel for Ireland*. 3rd edition. Dublin: Whelan & Son, 1918.

Hansard Parliamentary Debates. Online: http://hansard.millbanksystem.com.

Her Majesty's Stationery Office. Legislation of the Government of the United Kingdom. Online: www.legislation.gov.uk.

Hyde, Douglas. *The Necessity for De-Anglicising Ireland*. Leiden: Academic Press, 1994.

Jones, Francis P. *History of the Sinn Fein Movement and the Irish Rebellion of 1916*. New York: P. J. Kenedy & Sons, 1917.

Joyce, James. *Ulysses*. New York: Random House, 1986.

Kipling, Rudyard. *The Works of Rudyard Kipling*. Hertfordshire: Wordsworth Editions, 2001.

Marx, Karl and Friedrich Engels. *Ireland and the Irish Question*. Moscow: Progress Publishers, 1971.

Mitchel, John. *Jail Journal*. Dublin: M. H. Gill & Son, 1913.

_____. *The Last Conquest of Ireland (Perhaps)*. Dublin: University College Dublin Press, 2005.

National Archives of Ireland. Online: www.nationalarchives.ie.

O'Brien, R. Barry. *The Life of Charles Stewart Parnell, 1846–1891*. 2 vols. Dublin, 1898.

O'Connell, Daniel. 'O'Connell's Election Address' (1828). University College Cork, Multitext Project in Irish History. http://multitext.ucc.ie/d/OConnells_Election_Address_1828 (accessed 27 August 2013).

_____. *The Memoirs, Private and Political of Daniel O'Connell, Esq., from the Year 1776 to the Close of the Proceedings in Parliament for the Repeal*, compiled from official documents by Robert Huish. London, 1836.

_____. *Observations on the Corn Laws, on Political Pravity and Ingratitude*. Dublin: Samuel J. Machen, 1842.

_____. *Correspondence of Daniel O'Connell*. 2 vols. London: John Murray, 1888.

_____. *Correspondence of Daniel O'Connell*, edited by Maurice R. O'Connell. 8 vols. Shannon and Dublin: Irish University Press, 1972–80.

O'Connor, T. P. *The Parnell Movement: Being the History of the Irish Question from the Death of O'Connell to the Present Time*. New York: Caskell Publishing Company, 1891.

Parnell, C. S. *Words of the Dead Chief: Being Extracts from the Public Speeches and Other Pronouncements of Charles Steward Parnell*. Dublin: Sealy, Bryers and Walker, 1892.

Peel, Robert. *The Speeches of the Late Right Honourable Sir Robert Peel, Bart, Delivered in the House of Commons*, vol. 1, 1810–1829. London: Routledge, 1853.

_____. *Sir Robert Peel: From his Private Papers*, vol. 2, edited by Charles Stuart Parker. London: John Murray, 1899.

Pitt, William. *The Speeches of the Right Honourable William Pitt in the House of Commons*, vol. 3, edited by William Hathaway. London: Longman, Hurst, Rees and Orme, 1808.

Public Records Office, *Chatham Papers*, C.IV.

Plunket, William Conyngham. Speech to Parliament 'On Catholic Relief', 21 February 1821. Online: http://bartleby.com/268/6/13.html (accessed 28 August 2013).

Renan, Ernest. *La Poésie des Races Celtiques*, translated by William G. Hutchison. London: Walter Scott, 1854, reprinted 1896.

Russell, A. E. [George William]. *Cooperation and Nationality: A Guide for Rural Reformers from This to the Next Generation*. Dublin: Maunsel, 1912.

Russell, John. *Selections from Speeches of Earl Russell 1817 to 1841*. London: Longmans, Green & Co., 1870.

Salisbury, Robert Cecil. *The Government of Ireland: Lord Salisbury's Alternative Policy*. London: National Press Agency, 1886.

Trollope, Anthony. *Castle Richmond*. New York: Harper & Brothers, 1860.

Weber, Max. 'Politics as a Vocation'. In *Max Weber: Essays in Sociology*, 77–128. New York: Oxford University Press, 1946.

Yeats, W. B. *The Collected Works of W. B. Yeats Volume I: The Poems*, revised 2nd edition, edited by Richard J. Finneran. New York: Scribner, 2010.

Secondary Works

Adelman, Paul and Robert Pearce. *Great Britain and the Irish Question, 1798–1922*, 3rd edition. London: Hodder & Stoughton, 2008.Akenson, D. H. 'Pre-University Education, 1782–1870'. In *Ireland under the Union I: 1801–1870*, vol. 5 of *A New History of Ireland*, edited by W. E. Vaughan and T. W. Moody, 523–37. Oxford: Oxford University Press, 1989.

_____. *The Irish Diaspora: A Primer*. Belfast: The Institute of Irish Studies, Queen's University, 1993.

Anderson, Benedict. *Imagined Communities: Reflections on the Origins and Spread of Nationalism*. London: Verso, 1983.

Augusteijn, Joost. *The Irish Revolution, 1913–1923*. Basingstoke: Palgrave Macmillan, 2002.

Barnard, T. C. *A New Anatomy of Ireland: The Irish Protestants, 1649–1770*. New Haven: Yale University Press, 2003.

Barr, Colin. *Paul Cullen, John Henry Newman and the Catholic University of Ireland, 1845–1865*. Notre Dame, IN: University of Notre Dame Press, 2003.

Bartlett, Thomas. 'An End to Moral Economy: The Irish Militia Disturbances of 1793'. *Past and Present*, no. 199 (1983): 41–64.

_____. *The Fall and Rise of the Irish Nation: The Catholic Question, 1690–1830*. Dublin: Gill & Macmillan, 1992.

_____. *Ireland: A History*. Cambridge: Cambridge University Press, 2010.

Bartlett, Thomas, Dáire Keogh, David Dickson and Kevin Whelan, eds. *1798: A Bicentenary Perspective*. Dublin: Four Courts Press, 2003.

Beckett, J. C. *A Short History of Ireland*. London: Hutchinson, 1966.

_____. *Confrontations: Studies in Irish History*. London: Faber & Faber, 1972.

Bennett, Scott. 'Catholic Emancipation, the "Quarterly Review", and Britain's Constitutional Revolution'. *Victorian Studies* 12, no. 3 (1969): 283–304.

Bew, Paul. *Charles Stewart Parnell*. Dublin: Gill & Macmillan, 1980.

_____. 'Parnell and Dayitt'. In *Parnell in Perspective*, edited by D. G. Boyce and Alan O'Day, 38–51. London: Routledge, 1991.

_____. *Ireland: The Politics of Enmity, 1789–2006*. Oxford: Oxford University Press, 2007.

Biagini, Eugenio. *Gladstone*. Basingstoke: Macmillan, 2000.

_____. *British Democracy and Irish Nationalism, 1876–1906*. Cambridge: Cambridge University Press, 2007.

Billig, Michael. *Banal Nationalism*. London: Sage, 1995.

Blackstock, Allan. *Loyalism in Ireland, 1789–1829*. Woodbridge: Boydell Press, 2007.

Blake, Robert. *Disraeli*. London: Prion, 1998.

Boal, F. W. and J. Neville H. Douglas. *Integration and Division: Geographical Perspectives on the Northern Ireland Problem*. London: Academic Press, 1985.

Bolton, G. C. *The Passing of the Irish Act of Union*. Oxford: Oxford University Press, 1966.

Boyce, D. G. *Englishmen and Irish Troubles: British Public Opinion and the Making of Irish Policy 1918–22*. London: Jonathan Cape, 1972.

_____. *Nationalism in Ireland*. London: Croom Helm, 1982.

_____. *The Irish Question and British Politics, 1868–1986*. Basingstoke: Macmillan, 1988.

_____. *Nineteenth-Century Ireland: The Search for Stability*. Dublin: Gill & Macmillan, 1990.

_____. 'Weary Patriots: Ireland the Making of Unionism'. In *Defenders of the Union: A Survey of British and Irish Unionism since 1801*, edited by D. G. Boyce and Alan O'Day, 15–38. London: Routledge, 2001.

_____. 'Introduction: Tract for the Times? The Enduring Appeal of Gladstone and Ireland'. In *Gladstone and Ireland: Politics, Religion, and Nationality in the Victorian Age*, edited by D. G. Boyce and Alan O'Day, 1–15. Basingstoke: Palgrave Macmillan, 2010.

Boyce, D. G. and Alan O'Day, eds. *Parnell in Perspective*. London: Routledge, 1991.

_____. *The Making of Modern Irish History: Revisionism and the Revisionist Controversy*. London: Routledge, 1996.

_____, eds. *Defenders of the Union. A Survey of British and Irish Unionism since 1801*. London: Routledge, 2001.

_____, eds. *Gladstone and Ireland: Politics, Religion, and Nationality in the Victorian Age*. Basingstoke: Palgrave Macmillan, 2010.

Bradshaw, Brendan. 'Nationalism and Historical Scholarship in Modern Ireland'. In *Interpreting Irish History: The Debate on Historical Revisionism*, edited by Ciaran Brady, 191–216. Dublin: Irish Academic Press, 1994.

Brady, Ciaran. 'Constructive and Instrumental: The Dilemma of Ireland's First "New Historians"'. In *Interpreting Irish History: The Debate on Historical Revisionism*, edited by Ciaran Brady, 3–31. Dublin: Irish Academic Press, 1994.

Brent, Richard. *Liberal Anglican Politics: Whiggery, Religion and Reform, 1830–1841*. Oxford: Clarendon Press, 1987.

Briggs, Asa. *Victorian Things*. London: Batsford, 1988.

Brown, Terence, ed. *Celticism*. Amsterdam: Rodopi, 1996.

_____. *Ireland: A Social and Cultural History, 1922–2002*. London: Harper Perennial, 2004.

Buckland, Patrick. *Ulster Unionism*. 2 vols. Dublin: Gill & Macmillan, 1972–73.

Bull, Philip. 'The Fall of Parnell: The Political Context of His Intransigence'. In *Parnell in Perspective*, edited by D. George Boyce and Alan O'Day, 129–47. London: Routledge, 1991.

Casey, Christine. *The Buildings of Ireland: Dublin*. New Haven: Yale University Press, 2005.

Castle, Gregory. *Modernism and the Celtic Revival*. Cambridge: Cambridge University Press, 2001.

Caulfield, Max. *The Easter Rebellion*. Westport: Greenwood Press, 1963.

Clark, Christopher. *Iron Kingdom: The Rise and Downfall of Prussia, 1600–1947*. London: Allen Lane, 2006.

Clark, J. C. D. *The Language of Liberty, 1660–1832: Political Discourse and Social Dynamics in the Anglo-American World*. Cambridge: Cambridge University Press, 1993.

Collins, Stephen. *The Cosgrave Legacy*. Dublin: Blackwater Press, 1996.

Comerford, R. V. *The Fenians in Context: Irish Politics and Society, 1848–82*. Dublin: Wolfhound Press, 1985.

_____. 'Ireland 1850–70: Post-Famine and Mid-Victorian'. In *Ireland under the Union I: 1801–1870*, vol. 5 of *A New History of Ireland*, edited by W. E. Vaughan and T. W. Moody, 372–95. Oxford: Oxford University Press, 1989.

_____. 'Churchmen, Tenants and Independent Opposition, 1850–56'. In *Ireland under the Union I: 1801–1870*, vol. 5 of *A New History of Ireland*, edited by W. E. Vaughan and T. W. Moody, 396–414. Oxford: Oxford University Press, 1989.

_____. 'Gladstone's First Irish Enterprise'. In *Ireland under the Union I: 1801–1870*, vol. 5 of *A New History of Ireland*, edited by W. E. Vaughan and T. W. Moody, 431–50. Oxford: Clarendon Press, 1989.

_____. 'The Politics of Distress, 1877–82'. In *Ireland under the Union II: 1870–1921*, vol. 6 of *A New History of Ireland*, edited by W. E. Vaughan, 26–52. Oxford: Clarendon Press, 1996.

_____. 'The Parnell Era, 1883–91'. In *Ireland under the Union II: 1870–1921*, vol. 6 of *A New History of Ireland*, edited by W. E. Vaughan, 53–80. Oxford: Clarendon Press, 1996.

Connell, K. H. *The Population of Ireland, 1750–1845*. Oxford: Clarendon Press, 1950.

Connolly, S. J. 'Mass Politicisation and Sectarian Conflict, 1823–1830'. In *Ireland under the Union I: 1801–1870*, vol. 5 of *A New History of Ireland*, edited by W. E. Vaughan and T. W. Moody, 74–107. Oxford: Oxford University Press, 1989.

_____, ed. *Oxford Companion to Irish History*. Oxford: Oxford University Press, 2002.

Coogan, Tim Pat. *Michael Collins: A Biography*. London: Arrow, 1991.

_____. *De Valera: Long Fellow, Long Shadow*. London: Hutchinson, 1993.

Cooke, A. B. and John Vincent. *The Governing Passion: Cabinet Government and Party Politics in Britain, 1885–86*. Brighton: Harvester Press, 1974.

Coughlan, Anthony. 'Ireland's Marxist Historians'. In *Interpreting Irish History: The Debate on Historical Revisionism*, edited by Ciaran Brady, 288–305. Dublin: Irish Academic Press, 1994.

Cronin, Sean. *Marx and the Irish Question*. Dublin: Repsol Publications, 1977.

Crotty, Raymond. *Irish Agricultural Production: Its Volume and Structure*. Cork: Cork University Press, 1996.

Cullen, L. M. *An Economic History of Ireland since 1660*. London: Batsford, 1972.

Curran, J. M. *The Birth of the Irish Free State*. Alabama: University of Alabama Press, 1980.

Cusack, Michael. 'Origins of the Gaelic Athletic Association' (1884). University College Cork, Multitext Project in Irish History. Online: http://multitext.ucc.ie/d/Origins_of_the_Gaelic_Athletic_Association_1884 (accessed 30 August 2013).

Curtis, L. P. *Coercion and Conciliation in Ireland, 1880–1892: A Study in Conservative Unionism*. Princeton: Princeton University Press, 1963.

_____. *Anglo-Saxons and Celts: A Study of Anti-Irish Prejudice in Victorian England*. New York: New York University Press, 1968.

_____. *Apes and Angels: The Irishman in Victorian Caricature*. Newton Abbot: David & Charles, 1971.

Daly, Mary. *The Famine in Ireland*. Dundalk: Dublin Historical Association, 1986.

_____. 'Revisionism and Irish History: The Great Famine'. In *The Making of Modern Irish History: Revisionism and the Revisionist Controversy*, edited by D. G. Boyce and Alan O'Day, 71–89. London: Routledge, 1996.

_____. 'Recent Writings on Modern Irish History: The Interaction between Past and Present'. *Journal of Modern History* 69, no. 3 (1997): 512–33.

Daly, Mary and K. T. Hoppen, eds. *Gladstone: Ireland and Beyond*. Dublin: Four Courts Press, 2011.

Dangerfield, George. *The Strange Death of Liberal England*. London: Serif, 1997.

Darwin, John. *The Empire Project: The Rise and Fall of the British World-System, 1830–1970*. Cambridge: Cambridge University Press, 2009.

Davis, Richard P. *The Young Ireland Movement*. Dublin: Gill & Macmillan, 1988.

Davis, Richard W. 'Wellington and the "Open Question": The Issue of Catholic Emancipation, 1821–1829'. *Albion* 29, no. 1 (1997): 39–55.

Denman, Terence. *Ireland's Unknown Soldiers*. Dublin: Irish Academic Press, 2008.

Derry, John W. *Politics in the Age of Fox, Pitt and Liverpool*. Hampshire: Palgrave, 2001.

Dickinson, H. T. *British Radicalism and the French Revolution*. Oxford: Blackwell, 1985.

_____, ed. *Britain and the French Revolution, 1789–1815*. Basingstoke: Macmillan, 1989.

Dickson, David and Hugh Gough, eds. *Ireland and the French Revolution*. Dublin: Irish Academic Press, 1990.

Dickson, David, Dáire Keogh and Kevin Whelan. *The United Kingdom: Republicanism, Radicalism and Rebellion*. Dublin: Lilliput Press, 1993.

Donnelly, J. S. 'Famine and Government Response, 1845–6'. In *Ireland under the Union I: 1801–1870*, vol. 5 of *A New History of Ireland*, edited by W. E. Vaughan and T. W. Moody, 272–85. Oxford: Oxford University Press, 1989.

_____. 'Production, Prices and Exports, 1846–51'. In *Ireland under the Union I: 1801–1870*, vol. 5 of *A New History of Ireland*, edited by W. E. Vaughan and T. W. Moody, 286–92. Oxford: Oxford University Press, 1989.

_____. 'The Administration of Relief 1846–47'. In *Ireland under the Union I: 1801–1870*, vol. 5 of *A New History of Ireland*, edited by W. E. Vaughan and T. W. Moody, 294–306. Oxford: Oxford University Press, 1989.

_____. 'The Soup Kitchens'. In *Ireland under the Union I: 1801–1870*, vol. 5 of *A New History of Ireland*, edited by W. E. Vaughan and T. W. Moody, 307–15. Oxford: Oxford University Press, 1989.

_____. 'The Administration of Relief, 1847–51'. In *Ireland under the Union I: 1801–1870*, vol. 5 of *A New History of Ireland*, edited by W. E. Vaughan and T. W. Moody, 316–31. Oxford: Oxford University Press, 1989.

Doyle, David Noel. 'The Irish in North America, 1776–1845'. In *Ireland under the Union I: 1801–1870*, vol. 5 of *A New History of Ireland*, edited by W. E. Vaughan and T. W. Moody, 682–725. Oxford: Oxford University Press, 1989.

Duddy, Thomas. *A History of Irish Thought*. London and New York: Routledge, 2002.

Dudley Edwards, Owen. *Éamon de Valera*. Cardiff: University of Wales, 1987.

Dudley Edwards, Robert. *Daniel O'Connell and His World*. London: Thames & Hudson, 1975.

Dudley Edwards, Robert and T. Desmond Williams, eds. *The Great Famine: Studies in Irish History 1845–52*. Dublin: Browne and Nolan, 1956.

Dudley Edwards, Ruth. *Patrick Pearse: The Triumph of Failure*. London: Gollancz, 1977.

_____. *Patrick Pearse: The Triumph of Failure*. Dublin: Poolbeg, 1990.

Ehrman, John. *The Younger Pitt: The Consuming Struggle*. Stanford: Stanford University Press, 1996.

Elliott, Marianne. *Partners in Revolution: The United Irishmen and France*. New Haven: Yale University Press, 1982.

English, Richard. *Ernie O'Malley: IRA Intellectual*. Oxford: Clarendon Press, 1998.

Evans, Eric J. *Sir Robert Peel: Statesmanship, Power and Party*. London: Routledge, 1991.

_____. *The Forging of the Modern State: Early Industrial Britain, 1783–1870*. 3rd edition. Essex: Pearson Education, 2001.

_____. *Sir Robert Peel: Statesmanship, Power and Party*. 2nd edition. Abingdon: Routledge, 2006.

Fanning, Ronan. *Independent Ireland*. Dublin: Helicon, 1983.

_____. '"The Great Enchantment": Uses and Abuses of Modern Irish History'. In *Interpreting Irish History: The Debate on Historical Revisionism*, edited by Ciaran Brady, 146–60. Dublin: Irish Academic Press, 1994.

_____. 'Michael Collins – an Overview'. In *Michael Collins and the Making of the Irish State*, edited by Gabriel Doherty and Dermot Keogh, 202–10. Cork: Cork University Press, 1998.

Farrell, Brian. *The Founding of Dáil Eireann and Nation Building*. Dublin: Gill & Macmillan, 1971.

Fennell, Desmond. 'Against Revisionism'. In *Interpreting Irish History: The Debate on Historical Revisionism*, edited by in Ciaran Brady, 183–90. Dublin: Irish Academic Press, 1994.

Ferriter, Diarmaid. *The Transformation of Ireland 1900–2000*. London: Profile Books, 2004.

Finnan, Joseph P. *John Redmond and Irish Unity 1912–1918*. New York: Syracuse University Press, 2004.

Fitzpatrick, David, ed. *Ireland and the First World War*. Dublin: Trinity History Workshop, 1986.

_____. '"A Peculiar Tramping People": The Irish in Britain, 1801–70'. In *Ireland under the Union I: 1801–1870*, vol. 5 of *A New History of Ireland*, edited by W. E. Vaughan and T. W. Moody, 623–60. Oxford: Oxford University Press, 1989.

_____, ed. *Revolution: Ireland 1917–1923*. Dublin: Trinity History Workshop, 1990.

Flanagan, Thomas. 'Literature in English, 1801–91'. In *Ireland under the Union I: 1801–1870*, vol. 5 of *A New History of Ireland*, edited by W. E. Vaughan and T. W. Moody, 482–522. Oxford: Oxford University Press, 1989.

Flanedy, John, ed. *A Special Report of the Proceedings in the Case of the Queen against Daniel O'Connell [...] on an indictment for Conspiracy and Misdemeanour*. Dublin: James Duffy, 1844.

Fleming, N. C. 'Gladstone and the Ulster Question'. In *Gladstone and Ireland: Politics, Religion, and Nationality in the Victorian Age*, edited by D. G. Boyce and Alan O'Day, 140–61. Basingstoke: Palgrave Macmillan, 2010.

Foster, Roy. *Charles Stewart Parnell: The Man and His Family*. Hassocks: Harvester Press, 1979.

_____. *Modern Ireland 1600–1972*. London: Penguin, 1988.

Foy, Michael and Brian Barton. *The Easter Rising*. Stroud: The History Press, 2011.

Fraser, Murray. *John Bull's Other Homes: State Housing and British Policy in Ireland, 1883–1922*. Liverpool: Liverpool University Press, 1996.

Gailey, Andrew. *Ireland and the Death of Kindness*. Cork: Cork University Press, 1987.

Garvin, Tom. *The Evolution of Irish Nationalist Politics*. Dublin: Gill & Macmillan, 1981.

_____. *Nationalist Revolutionaries in Ireland 1858–1928*. Oxford: Clarendon Press, 1987.

_____. *1922: The Birth of Irish Democracy*. Dublin: Gill & Macmillan, 1996.

Gash, Norman. *Politics in the Age of Peel: A Study of the Technique of Parliamentary Representation, 1830–1850*. London: Longmans, Green & Co., 1953.

_____. *Mr Secretary Peel: The Life of Sir Peel to 1830*. London: Longmans, 1961.

_____. *Sir Robert Peel: The Life of Sir Robert Peel after 1830*. Harlow: Longman, 1972.

Gellner, Ernest. *Nations and Nationalism*. Oxford: Blackwell, 1983.

_____. *Nationalism*. London: Weidenfeld & Nicolson, 1997.

Geoghegan, Patrick M. *The Irish Act of Union: A Study in High Politics, 1798–1801*. Dublin: Gill & Macmillan, 1999.

_____. *King Dan: The Rise of Daniel O'Connell 1775–1829*. Dublin: Gill & Macmillan, 2008.

Gibbon, Peter. *The Origins of Ulster Unionism: The Formation of Popular Protestant Politics and Ideology in Nineteenth-Century Ireland*. Manchester: Manchester University Press, 1975.

Goodlad, Graham. 'British Liberals and the Irish Home Rule Crisis: The Dynamics of Division'. In *Gladstone and Ireland: Politics, Religion, and Nationality in the Victorian Age*, edited by D. G. Boyce and Alan O'Day, 86–105. Basingstoke: Palgrave Macmillan, 2010.

Gray, Peter. *Famine, Land and Politics: British Government and Irish Society, 1843–1850*. Dublin: Irish Academic Press, 1999.

_____, ed. *Victoria's Ireland Irishness and Britishness, 1837–1901*. Dublin: Four Courts Press, 2004.

Greaves, Desmond. *The Life and Times of James Connolly*. London: Lawrence & Wishart, 1961.

Gregory, Adrian and Senia Paseta, eds. *Ireland and the Great War: 'A War to Unite Us All'?* Manchester: Manchester University Press, 2002.

Hague, William. *William Pitt the Younger: A Biography*. London: HarperCollins, 2005.

Hammond, J. L. *Gladstone and the Irish Nation*. London: Frank Cass & Co., 1964.

Harkness, David. *The Restless Dominion: The Irish Free State and the British Commonwealth of Nations, 1921–1931*. London: Macmillan, 1969.

Hart, J. 'Sir Charles Trevelyan at the Treasury'. *English Historical Review* 85 (1960): 92–110.

Hart, Peter. 'Defining the Irish Revolution'. In *The Irish Revolution, 1913–1923*, edited by Joost Augusteijn, 17–33. Basingstoke: Palgrave Macmillan, 2002.

Hastings, Adrian. *The Construction of Nationhood: Ethnicity Religion and Nationalism*. Cambridge: Cambridge University Press, 1997.

_____. *The IRA at War, 1916–1923*. Oxford: Oxford University Press, 2003.

Hilton, Boyd. 'Peel: A Reappraisal'. *Historical Journal* 22, no. 3 (1979): 585–614.

_____. *The Age of Atonement: The Influence of Evangelicalism on Social and Economic Thought, 1785–1865*. Oxford: Clarendon Press, 1992.

_____. *A Mad, Bad, and Dangerous People? England 1783–1846*. Oxford: Oxford University Press, 2008.

Hinde, Wendy. *Catholic Emancipation: A Shake to Men's Minds*. Oxford: Blackwell, 1992.

Hobsbawm, Eric. *Nations and Nationalism since 1780*. Cambridge: Cambridge University Press, 1990.

Hopkinson, Michael, ed. *The Irish War of Independence*. Dublin: Gill & Macmillan, 2004.

Hoppen, K. Theodore. *Elections, Politics and Society in Ireland, 1832–1885*. Oxford: Clarendon Press, 1984.

_____. 'Review of Books'. *Albion: A Quarterly Journal Concerned with British Studies* 19, no. 1 (1987): 152–255.

Horne, John, ed. *Our War: Ireland and the Great War*. Dublin: Royal Irish Academy, 2008.

Hutchinson, John. *The Dynamics of Cultural Nationalism*. London: Allen & Unwin, 1987.

Hyam, Ronald. *Britain's Imperial Century 1815–1914*. Basingstoke: Palgrave Macmillan, 1976.

Jackson, Alvin. 'Unionist History'. In *Interpreting Irish History: The Debate on Historical Revisionism*, edited by Ciaran Brady, 253–68. Dublin: Irish Academic Press, 1994.

_____. 'Irish Unionism, 1870–1922'. In *Defenders of the Union: A Survey of British and Irish Unionism since 1801*, edited by D. G. Boyce and Alan O'Day, 115–36. London: Routledge, 2001.

_____. *Home Rule: An Irish History 1800–2000*. London: Weidenfeld & Nicolson, 2004.

_____. *Ireland 1798–1998: War, Peace and Beyond*. Sussex: Wiley Blackwell, 2010.

Jalland, Patricia. *Liberals and Ireland: The Ulster Question in British Politics to 1914*. Brighton: Harvester Press, 1980.

Johnson, Chalmers. *Revolution and the Social System*. Stanford: Stanford University Press, 1964.

Joll, James. *The Second International, 1881–1915*. London: Weidenfeld & Nicolson, 1955.

Jones, Tom. *Whitehall Diary Volume 3: Ireland 1918–1925*. Oxford: Oxford University Press, 1971.

Kee, Robert. *The Bold Fenian Men*. London: Quartet Books, 1972.

_____. *Ourselves Alone*. London: Penguin, 1989.

Kenedy, Patrick John. *The Universal Irish Song Book: A Complete Collection of the Songs and Ballads of Ireland*. New York: P. J. Kenedy, 1884.

_____. *The Life of Daniel O'Connell, the Liberator*. New York: P. J. Kenedy, 1904.

Kennedy, Liam and D. S. Johnson. 'The Union of Ireland and Britain, 1800–1921'. In *The Making of Modern Irish History: Revisionism and the Revisionist Controversy*, edited by D. G. Boyce and Alan O'Day. London: Routledge, 1996.

Kennedy, Michael. *Ireland and the League of Nations, 1919–1946: International Relations, Diplomacy and Politics*. Dublin: Irish Academic Press, 1996.

Keogh, Dáire and Kevin Whelan, eds. *Acts of Union: The Causes, Contexts and Consequences of the Act of Union*. Dublin: Four Courts Press, 2001.

Kerr, Donal. *Peel, Priests and Politics: Sir Robert Peel's Administration and the Roman Catholic Church in Ireland, 1841–46*. Oxford: Clarendon Press, 1982.

_____. *The Catholic Church and the Famine*. Blackrock: Columba Press, 1996.

Kinealy, Christine. *The Great Empire: Impact, Ideology and Rebellion*. Basingstoke: Palgrave, 2002.

_____. *Repeal and Revolution: 1848 in Ireland*. Manchester and New York: Manchester University Press, 2009.

Kissane, Bill. *The Politics of the Irish Civil War*. Oxford: Oxford University Press, 2005.

Laffan, Michael. *The Partition of Ireland*. Dublin: Dublin Historical Association, 1983.

_____. *The Resurrection of Ireland: The Sinn Féin Party, 1916–1923*. Cambridge: Cambridge University Press, 1999.

Lane, Fintan. *Origins of Modern Irish Socialism, 1881–1896*. Cork: Cork University Press, 1997.

Larkin, Emmet. *The Consolidation of the Roman Catholic Church in Ireland, 1860–1870*. Dublin: Gill & Macmillan, 1987.

Lecky, W. E. H. *Leaders of Public Opinion in Ireland*. New York: Appleton & Company, 1876.

_____. *A History of Ireland in the Eighteenth Century*. 5 vols. London: Longmans, Green & Co., 1892.

Lee, Joseph. *The Modernisation of Irish Society, 1848–1918*. Dublin: Gill & Macmillan, 1973.

_____. *Ireland, 1912–1985: Politics and Society*. Cambridge: Cambridge University Press, 1989.

Leerssen, Joep. 'Celticism'. In *Celticism*, edited by Terence Brown, 1–20. Atlanta: Rodopi, 1996.

Liedtke, Rainer and Stephan Wendehorst, eds. *The Emancipation of Catholics, Jews and Protestants: Minorities and the Nation-State in Nineteenth-Century Europe*. Manchester: Manchester University Press, 1999.

Loughlin, James. *Gladstone, Home Rule and the Ulster Question*. Dublin: Gill & Macmillan, 1986.

Louis, William Roger, Andrew Porter and Alaine Lowe. *The Oxford History of the British Empire. Volume III: The Nineteenth Century*. Oxford: Oxford University Press, 1990.

Lyons, F. S. L. *The Fall of Parnell 1890–91*. London: Routledge & Kegan Paul, 1960.

_____. *Ireland since the Famine*. London: HarperCollins, 1973.

_____. *Parnell*. London: Collins, 1977.

_____. *Charles Stewart Parnell*. London: Fontana, 1978.

_____. *Culture and Anarchy, 1890–1939*. Oxford: Clarendon Press, 1979.

_____. 'The Burden of Our History'. In *Interpreting Irish History: The Debate on Historical Revisionism*, edited by Ciaran Brady, 87–104. Dublin: Irish Academic Press, 1994.

_____. 'The Aftermath of Parnell, 1891–1903'. In *Ireland under the Union II: 1870–1921*, vol. 6 of *A New History of Ireland*, edited by W. E. Vaughan, 81–110. Oxford: Clarendon Press, 1996.

_____. 'The Revolution in Train, 1914–1916'. In *Ireland under the Union II: 1870–1921*, vol. 6 of *A New History of Ireland*, edited by W. E. Vaughan, 189–206. Oxford: Clarendon Press, 1996.

Machin, G. I. T. *The Catholic Question in English Politics 1820 to 1830*. Oxford: Clarendon Press, 1964.

_____. 'British Catholics'. In *The Emancipation of Catholics, Jews and Protestants: Minorities and the Nation-State in Nineteenth Century Europe*, edited by Rainer Liedtke and Stephan Wendehorst, 11–32. Manchester: Manchester University Press, 1999.

MacDonagh, Oliver. *States of Mind: A Study of Anglo–Irish Conflict, 1780–1980*. London: Allen & Unwin, 1983.

_____. 'Review'. *Victorian Studies* 27, no. 4 (1984): 526–7.

_____. *The Hereditary Bondsman: Daniel O'Connell, 1775–1829*. London: Weidenfeld & Nicolson, 1988.

_____. 'The Age of O'Connell: 1830–45'. In *Ireland under the Union I: 1801–1870*, vol. 5 of *A New History of Ireland*, edited by W. E. Vaughan and T. W. Moody, 158–68. Oxford: Oxford University Press, 1989.

_____. 'Ideas and Institutions, 1830–1845'. In *Ireland under the Union I: 1801–1870*, vol. 5 of *A New History of Ireland*, edited by W. E. Vaughan and T. W. Moody, 193–241. Oxford: Oxford University Press, 1989.

_____. *The Emancipist: Daniel O'Connell, 1830–47*. London: Weidenfeld & Nicolson, 1989.

_____. *Ireland: The Union and its Aftermath*. Dublin: University College Dublin Press, 1997.

MacArdle, Dorothy. *The Irish Republic*. Dublin: Irish Press, 1937.

_____. *The Irish Republic*. Dublin: Wolfhound Press, 1999.

Macintyre, Angus. *The Liberator: Daniel O'Connell and the Irish Party, 1830–1847*. New York: Macmillan, 1965.

Mandler, Peter. *Aristocratic Government in the Age of Reform: Whigs and Liberals, 1830–1852*. Oxford: Clarendon Press, 1990.

McCarthy, Justin Huntly. *Ireland since the Union: Sketches of Irish History from 1798 to 1886*. London: Chatto & Windus, 1887.

McCarthy, Michael J. F. *Mr. Balfour's Rule in Ireland*. Dublin: Hodges, Figgis, and Co., 1891. Online: http://www.jstor.org/stable/60244562 (accessed 29 September 2011).

McCartney, Donal. 'The Changing Image of O'Connell'. In *Daniel O'Connell: Portrait of a Radical*, edited by Kevin B. Nowlan and Maurice O'Connell, 19–31. Belfast: Appletree Press, 1984.

McCoole, Sinéad. *No Ordinary Women: Irish Female Activists in the Revolutionary Years, 1900–1923*. Dublin: O'Brien Press, 2003.

McDowell, R. B. *Ireland in the Age of Imperialism and Revolution, 1760–1800*. Oxford: Clarendon Press, 1979.

Mercier, Vivien. 'Literature in English, 1891–1921'. In *Ireland under the Union II: 1870–1921*, vol. 6 of *A New History of Ireland*, edited by W. E. Vaughan, 357–84. Oxford: Clarendon Press, 1996.

Miller, David. *Queen's Rebels: Ulster Loyalism in Historical Perspective*. Dublin: University College Dublin Press, 2007.

Mitchell, Arthur. 'Alternative Government: "Exit Britannia" – the Formation of the Irish National State, 1918–21'. In *The Irish War of Independence*, edited by Michael Hopkinson, 70–86. Dublin: Gill & Macmillan, 2004.

Mokyer, Joel. *Why Ireland Starved: A Quantitative and Analytical History of the Economy of Ireland, 1800 to 1850*. London: George Allen & Unwin, 1983.

Moody, T. W., ed. *The Fenian Movement*. Dublin: Mercier Press, 1968.

Moody, T. W. and R. Dudley Edwards. 'Preface to Irish Historical Studies'. In *Interpreting Irish History: The Debate on Historical Revisionism*, edited by Ciaran Brady, 35–7. Dublin: Irish Academic Press, 1994.

Morash, Chris. 'Celticism: Between Race and Nation'. In *Ideology and Ireland in the Nineteenth Century*, edited by Tadhg Foley and Seán Ryder, 206–13. Dublin: Four Courts Press, 1998.

Morgan, Austen. *James Connolly: A Political Biography*. Manchester: Manchester University Press, 1988.

Morley, John. *The Life of William Ewart Gladstone*. London: Macmillan, 1903.

Murphy, B. P. *Patrick Pearse and the Lost Republican Ideal*. Dublin: James Duffy, 1991.

Murphy, James. 'Fashioning the Famine Queen'. In *Victoria's Ireland? Irishness and Britishness, 1837–1901*, edited by Peter Gray, 15–26. Dublin: Four Courts Press, 2004.

Nally, David P. *Human Encumbrances: Political Violence and the Great Irish Famine*. Notre Dame, IN: University of Notre Dame Press, 2011.

Newbould, Ian. *Whiggery and Reform, 1830–41: The Politics of Government*. Stanford: Stanford University Press, 1990.

Nora, Pierre, ed. *Les Lieux de Mémoire*, vol. 1: *La République*. Paris: Gallimard, 1984.

Nowlan, Kevin B. and Maurice O'Connell, eds. *Daniel O'Connell: Portrait of a Radical*. Belfast: Appletree Press, 1984.

O'Brien, Conor Cruise. *Parnell and His Party*. Oxford: Clarendon Press, 1957.

———. 'Epilogue. The Embers of Easter 1916–66'. In *1916: The Easter Rising*, edited by Owen Dudley Edwards and Fergus Pyle, 223–40. London: MacGibbon & Kee, 1968.

———. *States of Ireland*. London: Hutchinson, 1972.

———. 'Foreword'. In Maurice O'Connell, *Daniel O'Connell: The Man and His Politics*. Dublin: Irish Academic Press, 1990.

O'Brien, Joseph. *Dear, Dirty Dublin: A City in Distress 1899–1916.* Berkeley: University of California Press, 1982.

O'Brien, R. Barry. *The Life of Charles Stewart Parnell, 1846–1891,* 3rd edition. London: Smith, Elder & Co., 1899.

Ó Broin, Leon. *Fenian Fever: An Anglo-American Dilemma.* London: Chatto & Windus, 1971.

_____. *Revolutionary Underground: The Story of the Irish Republican Brotherhood, 1858–1924.* Dublin: Gill & Macmillan, 1976.

O'Connell, Maurice. *Daniel O'Connell: The Man and His Politics.* Dublin: Irish Academic Press, 1990.

O'Connor, Laura. *Haunted English: The Celtic Fringe, the British Empire and De-Anglicization.* Baltimore: Johns Hopkins University Press, 2006.

O'Connor, Ulick. *Michael Collins and the Troubles.* New York: Norton & Company, 1996.

O'Day, Alan. *Irish Home Rule, 1867–1921.* Manchester: Manchester University Press, 1998.

O'Ferrall, Fergus. *Catholic Emancipation: Daniel O'Connell and the Birth of Irish Democracy, 1820–1830.* Dublin: Gill & Macmillan, 1985.

O'Farrell, Patrick. 'The Irish in Australia and New Zealand, 1791–1870'. In *Ireland under the Union I: 1801–1870,* vol. 5 of *A New History of Ireland,* edited by W. E. Vaughan and T. W. Moody, 661–81. Oxford: Oxford University Press, 1989.

Ó Gráda, Cormac. *Ireland Before and After the Famine.* Manchester: Manchester University Press, 1988.

_____. *Ireland Before and After the Famine: Explorations in Economic History, 1800–1925,* 2nd edition. Manchester: Manchester University Press, 1993.

_____. 'Making History in Ireland in the 1940s and 1950s: The Sage of *The Grand Famine*'. In *Interpreting Irish History: The Debate on Historical Revisionism,* edited by Ciaran Brady, 269–87. Dublin: Irish Academic Press, 1994.

_____. *Black '47 and Beyond: The Great Irish Famine in History, Economy and Memory.* Princeton: Princeton University Press, 1999.

O'Halpin, Eunan. *The Decline of the Union: British Government in Ireland, 1892–1920.* Dublin: Gill & Macmillan, 1987.

O'Hegarty, P. S. *A History of Ireland under the Union, 1801–1922.* London: Methuen, 1952.

Ó Tuathaigh, Gearóid. *Ireland before the Famine, 1798–1848.* Dublin: Gill & Macmillan, 1972.

Patterson, Henry. *Ireland since 1939: The Persistence of Conflict.* Dublin: Penguin Ireland, 2006.

Pocock, J. G. A. 'The Union in British History'. In *Transactions of the Royal Historical Society,* vol. 10, 6th series (2000). 181–96.

_____. 'The Union in British History'. In *The Discovery of Islands: Essays in British History,* 164–78. Cambridge: Cambridge University Press, 2005.

Porter, Bernard. 'Gladstone and Imperialism'. In *Gladstone: Ireland and Beyond,* edited by Mary E. Daly and K. Theodore Hoppen, 169–78. Dublin: Four Courts Press, 2011.

Powell, David. *The Edwardian Crisis: Britain, 1901–1914.* Basingstoke: Macmillan, 1996.

Ranelagh, John. *A Short History of Ireland,* 3rd edition. Cambridge: Cambridge University Press, 2012.

Rees, Russell and Anthony C. Hepburn. *Ireland 1905–1925.* Documents and Analysis, vol. 2. Newtownards: Colourpoint Books, 1998.

Reynolds, J. A. *The Catholic Emancipation Crisis in Ireland, 1823–29.* New Haven: Yale University Press, 1954.

Roberts, Andrew. *Salisbury: Victorian Titan*. London: Weidenfeld & Nicolson, 1999.

Rumpf, E. and A. C. Hepburn. *Nationalism and Socialism in Twentieth-Century Ireland*. Liverpool: Liverpool University Press, 1977.

Ryan, Desmond. *The Rising: The Complete Story of Easter Week*. Dublin: Golden Eagle Books, 1949.

Sellar, W. C. and R. J. Yeatman. *1066 and All That*. York: Methuen, 1999.

Sen, Amartya. *Poverty and Famines: An Essay on Entitlement and Deprivation*. Oxford: Clarendon Press, 1981.

Shannon, C. B. *Arthur J. Balfour and Ireland, 1874–1922*. Washington: Catholic University of America Press, 1988.

Shannon, Richard. *Crisis of Imperialism*. London: Hart Davis, MacGibbon, 1974.

_____. *Gladstone*. 2 vols. London: Penguin, 1999.

_____. *Gladstone: God and Politics*. London: Hambledon Continuum, 2008.

Sheridan, Richard Brinsley. *Speech of Richard Brinsley Sheridan in the House of Commons* (31 January 1799). Dublin: Printed for James Moore, 1799.

Sloan, Robert. *William Smith O'Brien and the Young Ireland Rebellion of 1848*. Dublin: Four Courts Press, 2000.

Smith, Anthony D. *The Ethnic Origins of Nations*. Oxford: Basil Blackwell, 1986.

Smith, Paul. *Disraeli: A Brief Life*. Cambridge: Cambridge University Press, 1996.

State of New Jersey Education Department. 'New Jersey Commission on Holocaust Education'. Online: http://www.state.nj.us/education/holocaust/curriculum/ (accessed 29 August 2013).

Stewart, A. T. Q. *The Ulster Crisis*. London: Faber & Faber, 1967.

Sullivan, Michael Joseph. *Ireland and the Global Question*. Cork: Cork University Press, 2006.

Townshend, Charles. *The British Campaign in Ireland, 1919–21: The Development of Political and Military Policies*. Oxford: Oxford University Press, 1975.

_____. *Political Violence in Ireland: Government and Resistance since 1848*. Oxford: Clarendon Press, 1983.

_____. 'Historiography: Telling the Irish Revolution'. In *The Irish Revolution, 1913–1923,*, edited by Joost Augusteijn, 1–17. Basingstoke: Palgrave Macmillan, 2002.

_____. *Easter 1916*. London: Allen Lane, 2005.

University College Dublin School of Archaeology. 'Heritage Council Report on St. Stephen's Green Dublin South Inner City'. Online: http://www.ucd.ie/archaeology/documentstore/hc_reports/lod/st_stephens_green_final.pdf (accessed 28 July 2013).

Vaughan, W. E. 'Ireland c.1870'. In *Ireland under the Union I: 1801–1870*, vol. 5 of *A New History of Ireland*, edited by W. E. Vaughan and T. W. Moody, 726–800. Oxford: Oxford University Press, 1989.

Vaughan, W. E., ed. *Ireland under the Union II: 1870–1921*, vol. 6 of *A New History of Ireland*. Oxford: Clarendon Press, 1996.

Vaughan, W. E. and T. W. Moody, eds. *Ireland under the Union I: 1801–1870*, vol. 5 of *A New History of Ireland*. Oxford: Oxford University Press, 1989.

Vincent, John. 'Gladstone and Ireland'. *Proceedings of the British Academy* 63 (1977): 193–238.

Walker, Stephen. *Forgotten Soldiers: The Irishmen Shot at Dawn*. Dublin: Gill & Macmillan, 2008.

Walsh, Maurice. *The News from Ireland: Foreign Correspondents and the Irish Revolution*. London: I.B. Tauris, 2011.

Wilkinson, David. 'How Did They Pass the Union? Secret Service Expenditure'. *History* 82, no. 266 (1997): 223–51.

Winstanley, Michael. *Gladstone and the Liberal Party*. London: Routledge, 1990.

Winston, Brian. *Media, Technology and Society: A History: From the Telegraph to the Internet*. London: Routledge, 1998.

Woodham-Smith, Cecil. *The Great Hunger: Ireland 1845–1849*. London: Hamish Hamilton, 1962.

Woods, C. J. 'Parnell and the Catholic Church'. In *Parnell in Perspective*, edited by D. G. Boyce and Alan O'Day, 9–37. London: Routledge, 1991.

Yeates, Padraig. *Lockout: Dublin 1913*. Dublin: Gill & Macmillan, 2001.

GLOSSARY

The Ascendancy – This is shorthand for the Protestant landed class who
dominated politics and society. The story of the nineteenth century
is one of their slow decline. There was also an important Protestant
middle class which is not properly covered by the term Ascendancy.

Board of Works – This body of state was established in 1831 to reduce poverty
by improving the economy. It contained salaried personnel and took
on increasingly extensive powers over the years of the nineteenth
century.

Chief secretary – The chief secretary was the personal assistant to the Lord
Lieutenant. In fact, he had much more political weight than his
technical superior. He was the mouthpiece of government policy
in the House of Commons. He ran the secretarial office. His
responsibilities increased throughout the century. By 1900, he was
responsible for 29 government departments. It was a very demanding
job.

Church of Ireland – The Protestant church founded in the aftermath of the
Henrician Reformation. Since the mid-1500s, it was the established
church but never attracted the allegiance of the majority. Its privileges
and status were immense and, by the 1800s, increasingly questioned.
Gladstone's Disestablishment Act (1869) was a profound systemic
change.

Coercion Acts – A series of laws starting in 1833. These laws empower the
Lord Lieutenant to proclaim a district as disturbed and introduce
martial law and curfews. Legislation such as this is regularly renewed
especially in fraught contexts.

Cottier – The cottier was a labourer who was paid in land. He generally
received a cabin and a very small plot of land to grow potatoes for
his family. Sometimes, he was given turf-cutting rights. His rent was

set against days he worked for farmers at an agreed wage. His services before the Great Famine were particularly useful in the labour-intensive sector of tillage. This class was decimated by 1845–51 and by the swing to livestock farming.

Dublin Castle – The institutional hub of British government in Ireland.

Dublin Corporation – The Dublin Corporation was a civic authority charged with administrative responsibilities in the capital. It was restructured in 1840. The Lord Mayor presided over it.

Embourgeoisement – Refers to the fact of becoming middle class and an indicator of levels of social mobility in a society.

Grand Jury System – This was a system dating back to the Anglo-Normans. It was a form of local government whereby the high sheriff nominated 12–23 jurymen from among the property owners of the country. It was very much a constituent part of Ascendancy power. In 1898, it was deprived of its administrative function.

Laissez-faire – The dominant thinking in political economy for much of the nineteenth century. The belief that the market should be left to its own devices with the minimum of state interference.

Land Agent – This was the landlord's local representative, especially important if the landlord was an absentee. It involved everyday management of land. He had increasing importance in the nineteenth century – collecting rents, establishing leases, valuing property, enforcing property rights. The notorious reputations they acquired are perhaps not altogether deserved, but they were in the firing line during the land agitations of the 1870s and 1880s.

Lord Lieutenant – The Lord Lieutenant (also known as viceroy) was the chief governor of Ireland. He was generally of English or Anglo-Irish Ascendancy stock. It was a position that boasted a very fine salary (£30,000). Its political importance declined in the course of the nineteenth century but its symbolic importance was enhanced. The viceregal court became a hub of the sociocultural elite.

Presbyterianism – A branch of Protestantism, associated primarily with Scotland and later Northern Ireland and America under the influence of Scottish settlers. The hallmarks are a profound belief in the sovereignty of God, the importance of the Sabbath and scriptures, and a confessional and covenant tradition.

Orange Order – The Orange Order was founded in 1796. Its name is a tribute to the Protestant William of Orange who defeated James II at the Battle of the Boyne in 1690. William of Orange was regarded as the saviour of Protestantism in Britain and Ireland. It becomes increasingly political in the course of the nineteenth century and militant after the first suspicion of a Home Rule bill. Its Unionist stance is unambiguous. Its loyalism is a curious phenomenon – they have been, on many occasions, paradoxically 'Queen's rebels'.

Poor Law – A series of laws accumulating since Elizabethan times designed to alleviate some of the problems of poverty and indigence. It was reformed in England in 1834 so as to mark out more clearly the distinction between outdoor and indoor relief. The former consisted of hand-outs; the latter meant the workhouse. Ireland followed suit in 1838.

Roman Catholic Hierarchy – The hierarchy consists of three degrees; the ones of most concern here are the presbyterate (the priests) and the episcopate (the bishops). The priests (both secular and religious) ran the parishes and provided sacraments to their parishioners. Their role in the localities in Ireland was immense. The bishops were responsible for the government of the churches in their diocese and teaching the faithful. They often made their voices heard more widely. In the nineteenth century, there were 36 dioceses.[1]

Tenant Right, also called the Ulster Custom – Its meaning was often summed up by the Three Fs – fair rent, free sale, fixity of tenure. These became increasingly demanded during and after the Great Famine. It was the main agenda of the Tenant League (1850) and the Land League (1879).

Tithe – The tithe was the grant of one-tenth of one's goods to the support of the church. Originally, it functioned as a kind of social welfare tax because the church was the main sponsor of what healthcare there was and education. Tithe was only paid to the Church of Ireland and this was a huge bone of contention.

Ulster Custom – See Tenant Right.

Viceroy – See Lord Lieutenant.

---

1 This website shows the diocesan boundaries: http://www.rootsweb.ancestry.com/~irlkik/ihm/diocese.htm (accessed 31 October 2013).

QUESTIONS

Introduction

1 Assess the features, merits and demerits of the main strands of Irish historiography.
2 The root of all Irish conflict was cultural. Discuss.

Forging the Union

3 In what sense can the Act of Union be seen as the fulcrum of modern Irish history?
4 The Union was, above anything else, an imperial measure. Discuss.

Dawn of a New Century

1 Assess the effects of Union on Ireland and on Britain.
2 The Union – key to Ireland's economic woes in the nineteenth century? Discuss.

Catholic Mobilisations

1 In what sense is O'Connell 'argument without end' to historians?
2 The 1820s saw the development of popular constitutionalism and a proto-democratic mass movement. Discuss.

Achievement of Emancipation

1 Does emancipation in 1829 show that the Union was a flexible instrument for reform?
2 The legislation of 1829 undermined the Union more than it strengthened it. Discuss.

Ireland under Whig Government

1 Was O'Connell a force for good after 1830?
2 Which better sums up the Whigs' rule in Ireland, reform or repression?

The Campaign for Repealing Union

1 What was the nature and impact of the repeal movement?
2 Assess O'Connell's contribution to constitutional nationalism in Ireland.

The Age of Peel

1 The Young Irelanders were responsible for a new trend in Irish nationalism: romanticism. Discuss.
2 How far would you agree that Peel's Irish reforms failed?

Explaining the Famine

1 What historiographical models exist for the Great Famine?
2 The Great Famine came out of a deadly cocktail of growing population, improvident agriculture and over-reliance on a single crop. Discuss the balance of these factors.

Response to Famine

1 Discuss the role of the political parties, the Treasury and charities in responding to the Great Famine. Did the Famine represent a crisis or an opportunity in the project of imperialism?
2 To what extent do you agree with Peter Gray that 'liberal moralities' were behind an inadequate response to the Great Famine?

Post-Famine Ireland

1 What long-term effects did the growth of an *émigré* community have on the country of origin?
2 Discuss the implications of the social, ideological and agricultural changes after the Famine.

Mid-Victorian Ireland

1 How viable is it to talk about Victorian Ireland?
2 To what extent did the Fenian threat represent a renewal of the violent strand in Irish politics?

Gladstone's First Mission

1   Why did Gladstone make it his mission to pacify Ireland?
2   How successful were Gladstone's reforms in satisfying Irish demands?

Parnell and the Land League

1   Was the New Departure new?
2   Gladstone and Parnell's relationship was born out of political necessity more than principle. Discuss.

The Irish Liberals: A Union of Hearts?

1   How far do you agree that the main reason for Gladstone's conversion to Home Rule in 1885 was a desire to regain control of his party?
2   How far was Gladstone to blame for the failure of his own Home Rule reform bill in 1893?
3   What was the nature of Parnell's contribution to the Irish Question, both in life and in death?

Constructive Unionism

1   Is the phrase 'killing Home Rule with kindness' a fair statement of Conservative aims and policy in the 1880s and '90s?
2   How significant were developments in the north of Ireland in the late nineteenth century? How significant were Ulster Unionist links with the Conservative Party?

Celtic Renaissance

1   Is it fair to say that cultural nationalism was more often than not political?
2   Why and how was the separatist strand in Irish politics revived in the early 1900s?

The Story of Irish Socialism

1   To what extent were socialism and nationalism conjoined in the Irish case?
2   What was the significance of the 1913 Dublin Lockout?

The Home Rule Crisis

1   To what extent did the Liberals in 1912 introduce a Home Rule bill because of Irish pressure?
2   Was Ulster opposition to Home Rule more religious and historical or economic and imperial?

World War and Insurrection

1   What divisions among Irish people did World War I expose?
2   How did the Easter Rising contribute to the cause of Irish nationalism?

The Rise of Sinn Féin

1   Account for the timing and nature of the rise of Sinn Féin.
2   The 1918 election represents the birth of Irish democracy. Discuss.

The Anglo–Irish War

1   Was the Anglo–Irish War truly a war?
2   The Government of Ireland Act of 1920 – a redundant attempt at settlement after years of waiting?

North and South Settlements

1   Why partition?
2   To what extent was the Anglo–Irish Treaty the fairest compromise available to signatories and British politicians?
3   Do you agree with the view that the main reason for the Anglo–Irish Treaty of 1921 was the actions of the Irish Republican Army?

Conclusions

1   To what extent is Irish history 1800–1922 best interpreted, in Thomas Bartlett's phrase, as a 'theatre of disorder'?

INDEX